Janez Bogataj

Handicrafts
OF SLOVENIA

Encounters with Contemporary Slovene Craftsmen

JANEZ BOGATAJ

Handicrafts
OF SLOVENIA

Encounters with Contemporary Slovene Craftsmen

ROKUS

Janez Bogataj

Handicrafts
OF SLOVENIA
Encounters with Contemporary Slovene Craftsmen

Text
PROF. DR. JANEZ BOGATAJ
•
Photography
JANEZ PUKŠIČ
•
Design
ŽARE KERIN, KOMPAS DESIGN, D. D.
•
Editor
TADEJA KVATERNIK
•
Translation
ŠPELA BURNIK
•
Language editing
ALAN MCCONNELL-DUFF
IAN HARVEY
JOEL SMITH
•
Introductions
MILAN KUČAN,
PRESIDENT OF THE REPUBLIC OF SLOVENIA

PROF. FRANCE BERNIK, ACADEMICIAN
PRESIDENT OF THE SLOVENE ACADEMY OF SCIENCES AND ARTS
•
Typeset
INTER MARKETING, D. O. O.
•
Litography
BETI JAZBEC, STUDIO ROKUS
•
Paper Supplier
EUROPAPIER, D. O. O. - MEDIAPRINT STORA 150 G/M²

•
Printed by
GORENJSKI TISK, D. D.
•
First Edition
1200 COPIES, LJUBLJANA, MARCH 1999
•
General Sponsor
MINISTRY OF SMALL BUSINESS AND TOURISM OF THE REPUBLIC OF SLOVENIA
•
Published with the help of the Scientific Institute at the Faculty of Arts in Ljubljana
•
© Rokus Publishing House Ltd., Ljubljana 1999
For: Rok Kvaternik
•
All rights reserved. No part of this book may be reproduced or transmitted in any shape or form or by any means, including photocopying, recording or by any information storage and retrieval system, without the written permission of the Publisher.

CIP - Cataloging-in-Publication Data
National University Library, Ljubljana

745/749(497.4)"19"
929:745/749(497.4)

BOGATAJ, Janez
Handicrafts of Slovenia : Encounters with Contemporary Slovene Craftsmen / Janez Bogataj ; [photography Janez Pukšič ; introductions Milan Kučan, France Bernik ; translation Špela Burnik]. - 1st ed., Ljubljana : Rokus, 1999

ISBN 961-209-083-1
97792512

According to the decree n. 415-263/99 of the Ministry of Culture of the Republic of Slovenia, ratified on February 24, 1999, this publication is subject to a 5 per cent sales tax, payable in accordance with the 3rd tariff rate.

UNESCO
Slovene National Commission for UNESCO

8
Rich Diversity
16
Many Types of Wood, Many Lives
52
Cut by the Brook, Split Across the Knee
80
Straw is Woven, the Grain Turns into Bread
94
Corn Husks or Husking – Both are Corn
102
Hand Traces in Clay
134
Thread Over Thread is Woven into a Lovely, Colorful Pattern
158
Honey, Wax and Dough
170
Images of Fertility
180
The Manuscript of the Millennia
192
Between Hammer and Anvil …
206
The Harmony of Form and Content
226
Masterpieces from the Paper Mill
236
The Skin that Remains
248
Replicas of the National Heritage
270
The Encounters Continue …
287
From Words to People

This monograph, Handicrafts of Slovenia, is entering a time and a place marked in significant ways by the transition to the new millennium. This transition encourages us to contemplate the path which mankind has taken so far, the developmental contradictions which have not yet been resolved, those areas where dehumanisation and self-destruction prevail, and also the prospects and hopes for a better and more fulfilling life for all people and all nations - indeed for the whole of mankind. In view of these circumstances, individual and common self-confidence (which is based on the power of the creativity of one's work) and an authentic national image (which can and will be recognisable and interesting for its uniqueness and excellence in the wider and most demanding environments) are more than necessary.

This is precisely the subject of this book: it is the story of the creativity of people living in Slovenia, a country which helps create both the self-confidence based on the creative work of its people and a distinctive cultural image of itself.

Masterpieces of domestic crafts and craftsmanship can most certainly be included among the most exquisite manifestations of man's creativity, and are reflections of the cultural image of the Slovene people; this was the case in the past and is still the case today. They are part of a tradition, and an expression of that tradition and of a rich cultural heritage. They are vivid testimonies to the presence of a creative spirit in the territory covered by Slovenia - the meeting place of the Alpine, Mediterranean and Pannonian regions - and its expressions made material. They are undoubtedly worthy of the respect of present and future generations.

These masterpieces are created in an environment in which the rich heritage of the craft tradition is bound up with contemporary creativity, the demands of daily life, creative and artistic inspiration, the creativity of skilled hands, and high technology. In their own particular ways, they all bear witness to the spiritual image of the Slovenes, to the qualities which enable the existence and development of the Slovene people and their land (and, of course, of all others as well), and ensure a recognisable and enduring identity in the globalised world, with its often contradictory interconnectedness, competition and collaboration.

I believe this monograph will substantiate and expand our knowledge of the exceptionally rich and extensive creativity of craft activities in Slovenia, and will communicate the messages given us by the masterpieces themselves. Many people will, of course, be new to these things. More importantly, I believe it will encourage new work. This monograph is a unique contribution to the Europe we understand as providing a common cultural home, under whose roof many differences and idiosyncrasies can also find a place.

The fact that traditional crafts and their superb masterpieces are presented by such fine masters of their craft is a firm assurance that Handicrafts of Slovenia will fulfil such expectations.

MILAN KUČAN,
PRESIDENT OF THE REPUBLIC OF SLOVENIA

The project addressed by this foreword is a national project and certainly one of the most significant ones for the Slovene nation as it moves into the new century and the new millennium. This monograph represents a first presentation of the project, and is the most reliable and general material available on the craftsmen of contemporary Slovenia.

But what do we understand by the term 'craftsmen' and, in particular, 'contemporary craftsmen'? An explicit answer to this question is given in this monograph, where it is expressed in image and description, while for a definition of the term itself we can use a comparison, a parallel, with similar (though not identical) design activities. Therefore, on the one hand we have domestic, 'folk' crafts; these are crafts, within the traditional meaning of the word, which are dying out since their products can be used only by a small range of consumers and are not always beautiful or attractive in terms of 'design'. The antithesis to domestic crafts is contemporary industrial design and batch production, alluring to the eye but entirely uncharacteristic, neutral and unrecognisable from any national perspective. The contemporary craftsmanship presented in this monograph occupies an area somewhere between the two. It is an intermediate activity - one which relates to both but which displays original and idiosyncratic characteristics.

Contemporary craftsmanship is related to traditional domestic crafts above all in the design process: manual design, which is expressed in the original Slovene term rokodelstvo, meaning 'manual labour'. It shares the materials of traditional craftsmanship, such as wood, paper, glass, stone, precious stones, leather, metals (including precious metals), linen and so on. The functionality and practical value of products of contemporary craftsmanship are also similar to those of traditional craftsmanship to a greater or lesser extent. However, its various characteristics bring contemporary craftsmanship closer to industrial design, with a stress on modern design and its decorative value, which means that the products should be useful, beautiful and designed according to the taste of contemporary man, his way of life and his taste in decoration. We should not forget to mention here the new production technology which is common to both craftsmanship and mass industrial design.

But after all these connections to the past and present have been made, is there anything unique and specific left to contemporary craftsmanship?

Its first special feature is undoubtedly its emphasis on creativity. The products of our contemporary craftsmen are the achievement of their creative efforts, their search for the aesthetic, and their ingenuity. In addition to the creative forces of individuals, which we can no longer trace in either domestic craftsmanship or industrial design to the same extent, its second characteristic, which is connected to the first, should be noted here: the quality of the products. Quality is the most profound motive of all contemporary craftsmen presented in this monograph, and a characteristic which gives greater material value to their products and distinguishes them from traditional craftsmen or industrial designers more than anything else. The third characteristic concerns inspiration. The national distinctiveness of products of contemporary craftsmanship is expressed either directly or indirectly, but certainly in a more contemporary manner than in products of traditional craftsmanship. If there is one characteristic of our craftsmen that follows the trends of the modern world, it is this one.

PROF. FRANCE BERNIK, ACADEMICIAN
PRESIDENT OF THE SLOVENE ACADEMY OF SCIENCES AND ARTS

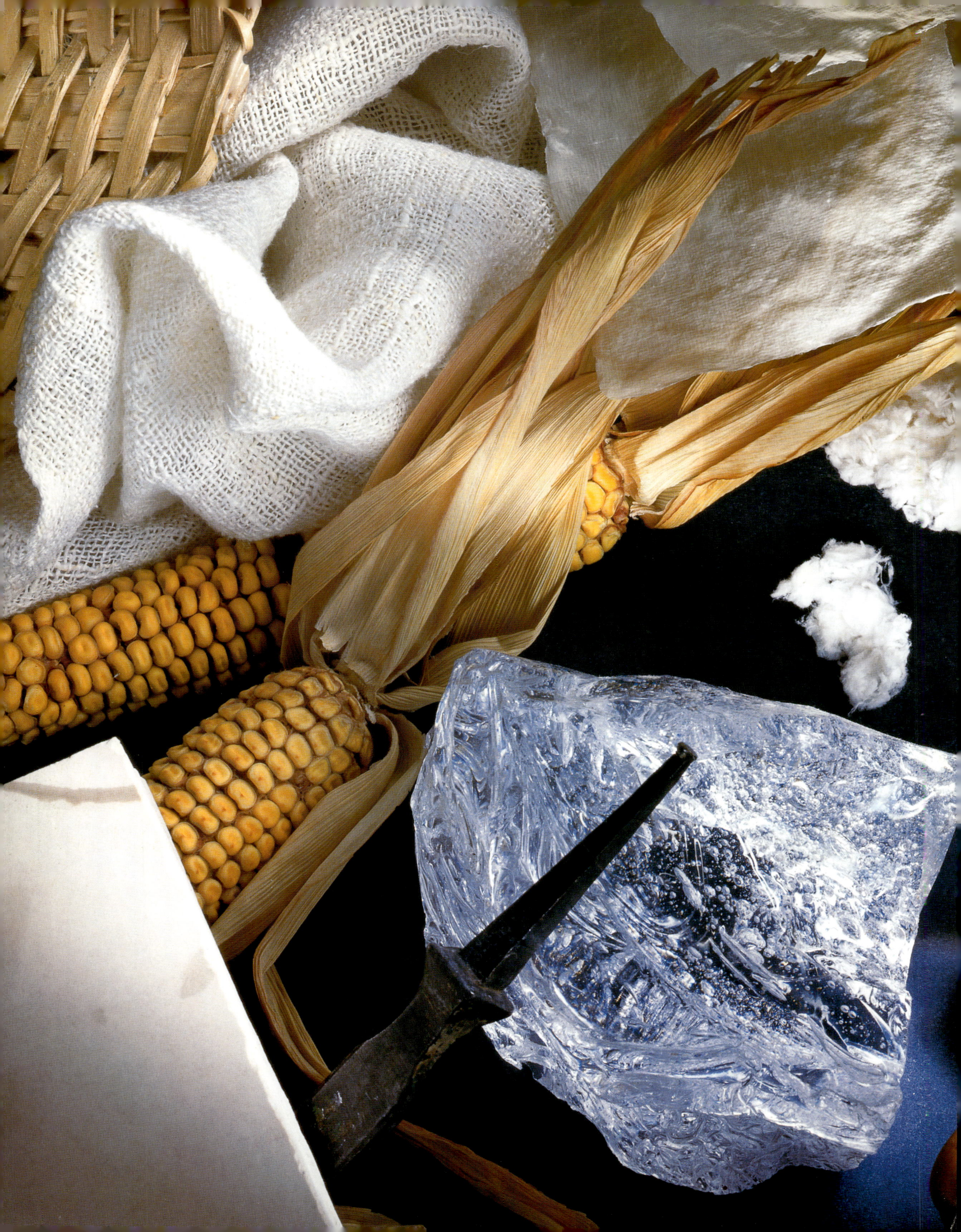

Rich Diversity

Introduction

Rich diversity

With the passing of the 20th century, it is no great discovery that the world is increasingly becoming more developed, not only technically but also generally. This has become general knowledge and one to which the time dimension of our daily life, our holidays, our lifestyle as a whole has succumbed. Although inherently positive in meaning, the term "progress" is now more and more often used with a negative connotation. Perhaps it is true in most cases that the tip of any progress is useful and positive but the furrow, often spreading in a fan on its cutting edge, brings along many negative phenomena, actions, influences and events. Consequently, the triangular symbiosis of man, culture and the environment is frequently destroyed, biased in favor of man at the expense of nature and the cultural environment, although the differentiation of these two elements is, in fact, absurd and pointless.

Simultaneously with this dominant development of the world, a parallel type of progress can be increasingly observed that is gaining significance: one in which man and nature cooperate. In this way, new masterpieces are born that can be linked with historical memory, with our heritage but which can also be completely new creations. In such new masterpieces, however, we cannot ignore the links with our heritage. These links show in the newly-considered forms and meanings, and in the development of expertise in original materials, technique, and work rhythms that the so called "past" has confirmed countless times. Before us are challenging examples of technology, content and function, an inexhaustible basis on which to build and above all to search for new paths and solutions. We are speaking of modern creativity but with a historical dimension. This union is one of the fundamental factors in the preservation of the identity of a country, a place, an environment. This symbiosis not only preserves but also enables the creation of elements that, in the collaboration of functionality and esthetics, produce typicality, character, specialness and distinction. It is this single fundamental message of modern endeavors in numerous creative fields in Slovenia that this book is intended to present. Individual regions, and indeed the world as a whole, are drawing ever closer. The spheres of culture and lifestyle are becoming ever more uniformly similar, we find certain languages becoming dominant, and so forth. As we enter the new millennium, it is essential for the preservation of European and world culture that we preserve the rich diversity of national and local (i.e. individual) identities.

Rich diversity

One of the means of preserving this diversity is undoubtedly to encourage the wide variety of masterpieces, signified by different terms in different languages. In Slovenia, we still refer to them as **HOME AND APPLIED ARTS,** while in other countries activities involving handiwork are divided into three creative fields, related in content and development. First, there is **HANDICRAFT** or **CRAFT** (Handwerk, Heimatwerk, artisanal, artesant, artigianato). The special field of **APPLIED ART** (Kunsthandwerk, Agewandte kunst) follows. Finally, there is **DESIGN** (Gestaltung, Formgebung). The terms applied to each of them developed independently, and reflect the role and importance of individual crafts in different periods. While we attempt to round up this wide scope of creativity in Slovenia in terminological terms, the term **DESIGN-LED CRAFTS,** as a way of desribing all handicraft products, is beginning to establish itself in the English-speaking world. However, it is only used to describe handicrafts in which the knowledge of traditional craft techniques, as well as modern design approaches, are considered. The term ought to signify the symbiosis between the messages from the craft heritage and modern creativity. There is a need in other languages to clearly define the difference between two basic types of handicraft: traditional local handicrafts, which only reproduce objects of historical memory (tradition, lore); and those which unify and observe craft heritage and design principles to make new products. In Slovenia, the term **HANDICRAFTS**, used in the good old meaning of the word, has once again become trendy in modern times. It emphasizes the **ARTISAN, THE CRAFTSMAN** rather than the product, and underlines the importance of **HANDS**, those indispensable tools of creation. For even according to an old Slovene proverb, it is the hand that makes the bread and not the flour! After World War II, the term handicraft was used derogatorily in Slovenia to signify and define everything non-progressive and backward.

Thus, the hand became an alternative to the modern machines and robots which mass-produce products. It is not merely a means by which we strive to preserve the oldest and the most basic contact with materials but also enables us to create new masterpieces, which enrich all aspects of our daily lives.

Rich diversity

These are a few of the reasons which have inspired the creation of this book. Its mission and purpose are not only to introduce the rich versatility of modern Slovene handicrafts in Slovenia and abroad, but it is also a contribution of Slovene crafting knowledge and ideas to the handicrafts of Europe and the world. The questions that present themselves here do not only relate to various fields of artistic creation or design, or to enthusiastic efforts to preserve the craft heritage and the continuation of traditional handicrafts. Nostalgic flirting with this concept of handicrafts is a matter of history today. The question of modern handicrafts is increasingly becoming a social and economic one, as it was centuries ago. In the past, woodcrafts in some parts of Slovenia contributed signifreantly to solving the basic employment and survival problems of the local populace. That might be the reason why the applicability of woodcrafts has been recognized and accounted for by political establishments in various historical periods. Even today, modern handicrafts, with all the positive implications, can contribute significantly to solving the unemployment problem in Europe and the world. An increasing number of countries worldwide strive to preserve their traditional handicrafts. On the one hand, they attend to the preservation of the craft heritage with all related components of historical memory (the use and research of traditional materials, the organization of various courses and workshops, opening schools for prospective craftsmen); on the other, they also develop numerous new forms of creativity based on traditional models. It needs be emphasized again that in the modern, globalized world the question of handicrafts is not only symbolic, but a part of the overall planning our lifestyles and our efforts to attain a better life. At the turn of the century, handicrafts helped preserve one of the world's finest resources - local cultural and creative diversity. This book is a Slovene contribution to the preservation of diverse handicrafts. It is not simply a presentation of the creativity of Slovene handicrafts but mainly a presentation of the many crafts that have evolved over centuries of historic development in this part of Europe. Modern Slovene craftsmen contribute signifrcantly to the creation of recognizable Slovene products, and simultaneously enrich everyone's daily lives and add color to festive occasions in any part of the world.

Rich diversity

The versatility and diversity of contemporary Slovene handicrafts are a consequence of several factors. The most important are the country's specific historical development and its unique geographical position, as well as day-to-day modern influences. A complete historical development, handicrafts included, took place at the crossroads of Europe – the junction of the European Alpine, Mediterranean and Pannonian worlds. This contributed decisively to the development of unique cultures and lifestyles, from economic activities to specific social relations, and the wide scope of spiritual creativity. In handicrafts, this versatility is exemplified in the use of specific craft materials in different regions, which in turn triggered the creation, development and continuation of specific handicrafts in different parts of the country. Wood has thus been the predominant craft material in the Alpine world for centuries, while stone was used in the Mediterranean region and Primorska, especially the Karst. This is the region from which the terminology for natural phenomena first observed there was adopted by languages all over the world. The Pannonian territory is characterized by the use of natural resources such as wheat straw, corn husks and raw materials produced from plants (for example, linen). Prekmurje pottery workshops continue a centuries-old regional tradition, supported by high-quality clay, extracted locally. Other materials available in Slovenia offer an immense number of creative possibilities in working with reeds, osiers, various metals, glass, hand-made paper, tanned leather, and a number of others. The book presents modern craftsmen who shape various masterpieces from individual materials or groups of materials. Most of them present the continuation of the long tradition of crafting skills, and are predominantly traditional. Some of them go back to pre-historic times, while others developed as the consequences of mercantile efforts within the former Habsburg Empire. This book was not planned as a detailed description and rendition of the versatile historical development of individual handicrafts of Slovenia in general, because these have already been presented in two books (*Domestic Crafts in Slovenia*, DZS, LJ 1989, and *Traditional Arts and Crafts in Slovenia*, Domus, Unesco, LJ, 1993).

The book published in 1993 is the contribution by Slovenia, to the Unesco decade of global cultural development, with an emphasis on the safeguarding of traditional culture and folklore as set by the Recommendation on the Safeguarding of Traditional Culture and Folklore endorsed in 1989 at the Unesco General Conference. The new book is a continuation of Slovene endeavours in yet another field of contempopary handicraft creativity.

RICH DIVERSITY

My selection process was helped signifrcantly by the excellent documentation available at the Obrtna Zbornica Slovenije (Chamber of Trades of Slovenia), which has for many years organized the expert evaluation of handicrafts and handcrafted products. More about this area of state support for the development of modern handicrafts in Slovenia (and abroad) will be said in the concluding chapter. The craftsmen and their products were also chosen in reference to my personal documentation, which is the fruit of years of research into handicrafts. The criteria and the evaluation system for the choice of quality items crafted by Slovene artisans have been developed over several years. Today, they also represent a suitable foundation for future work in this field as well. In selecting the craftsmen and products that would eventually appear in this book, their creative opuses also proved helpful. Established artisans with years of craft experience, or those with at least one line of accomplished products, are predominantly mentioned here. Personal style and originality were decisive in choosing of artisans producing traditional handicraft products. The same criteria were naturally not applied in choosing the makers of replicas. In their case, I considered their technical expertise in specialized procedures related to the production of replicas. I would also like to say that only artisans offering ready-finished products were considered, while those who occasionally exhibit or send in prototypes or concepts to various exhibitions and contests were omitted.

When talking about modern handicrafts, the importance of **EXPERIENCE FROM THE CRAFT HERITAGE** cannot be over-emphasized because handicrafts point to man's relationship with his cultural and natural environment. This should never be neglected in emphasizing the importance of modern handicrafts. It is a question of ecology, or better yet, a question of creative symbiosis, which is displayed in the choice of materials as well as in the craft techniques and, last but not least, is evident from the waste material which, in most cases, ultimately returns to its natural environment.

Pottery is a fine example of this. A potter found suitable clay in a local quarry, dug it up and shaped it into earthenware. When the latter was broken and could no longer serve its purpose, the owner disposed of the shards on a dirt path or some other area in the vicinity of his home which needed to be stabilized. This waste clay was later covered by sand or soil, and thus effectively returned to its original environment. The model is taken from history, of course. Broken earthenware is not disposed of in this manner today because laying clay shards onto asphalt roads would make little sense. However, returning the large quantities of plastic waste, which are accumulating at rubbish-heaps all over the world, remains a burning, still unanswered question.

RICH DIVERSITY

The return to the heritage and modernity of handicrafts represents man's attempts to restore the relationship with his cultural and natural environment. This should not be restricted merely to various national parks and open-air ecological museums but encouraged in all spheres of our daily lives. This book was written on the shore of an artificial lake, a water accumulation typical of the period since World War II. Many such lakes were made in the 1950s, when ecology was not of primary importance, and they were not properly tended in subsequent years. Today, the lakeshore is full of tall trees, rooted into an unsuitable terrain, causing various erosions and land slips. Up until World War II, this area was adjacent to the Sava river and overgrown with trees and bushes. Shoreline stability was regularly maintained by cutting individual trees and shrubs. The locals used these for firewood and wickerwork material, as well as for making different wooden tools. But times have changed, and our lives with it. Someone might remark that there is no need for home-crafted wickerwork turnip or potato baskets today, given the variety of more suitable, readily available plastic containers. However, we are overlooking the fact that traditional products can be given new meanings and functions. In other words: a wicker basket for storing potatoes, an indispensable item in every farming household until some decades ago, has become a useful decorative item in many country and city houses today...

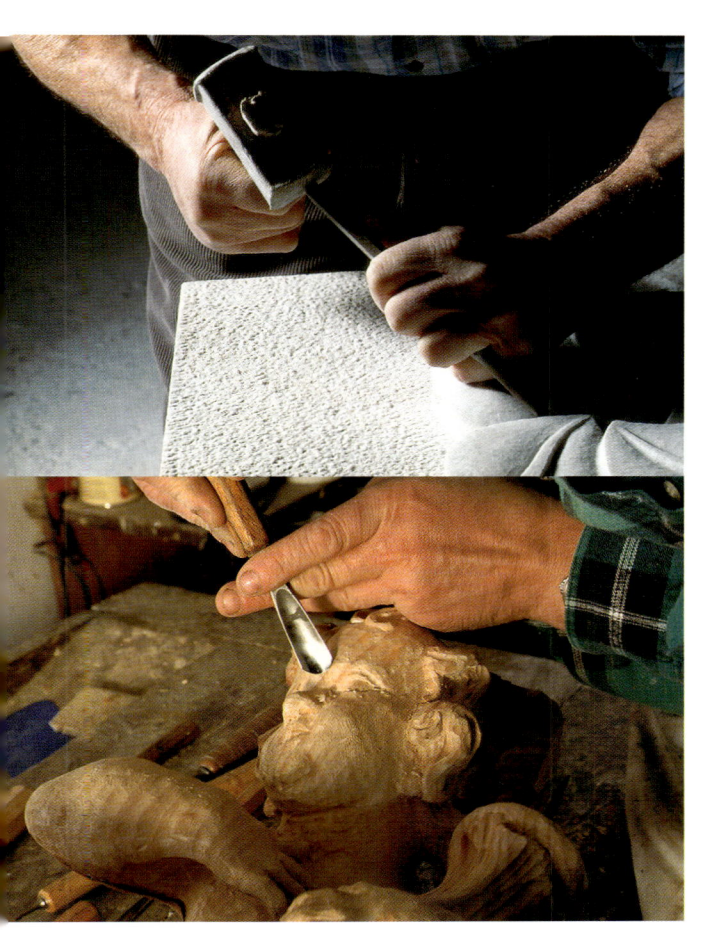

I will not continue with this story. Let these lines be a reminder and a warning. The modernity of the handicraft heritage reminds us, with its alternative and provocative nature, of the traditional values we so easily overlook today, even though they are at arm's length. We often turn a blind eye towards them, let alone take time to notice and learn about them and to recognize that they can enlighten us and improve our lifestyles in many ways, be it in Slovenia or anywhere else in the world.

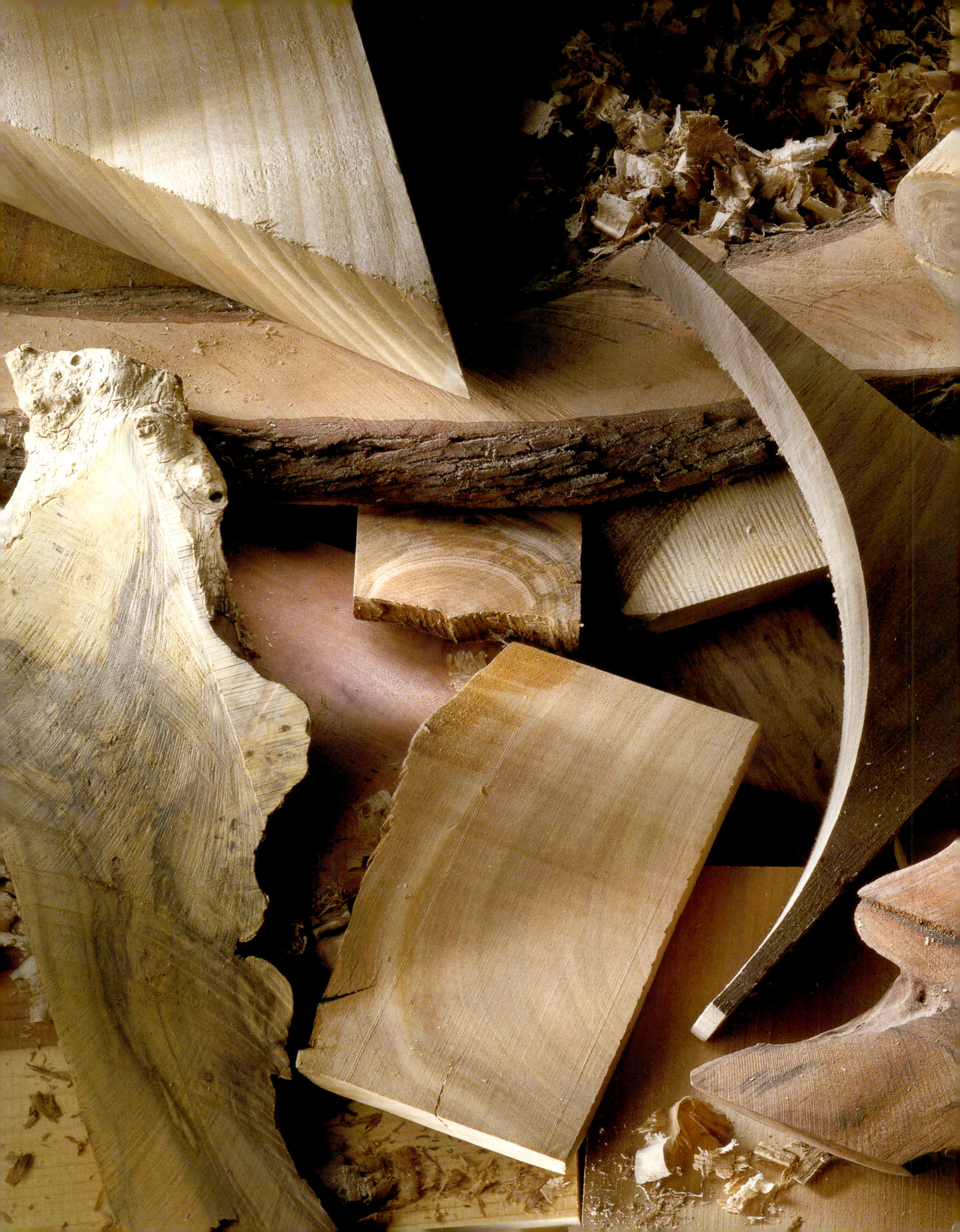

Many Types of Wood, Many Lives

Every type of wood has a special story to tell, a story written in its annual rings. But the message of this old Slovene saying should not be understood only literally. In addition to living a life of its own, wood has always been man's companion, and has helped shape his life as well. Wood and man seem well suited to each other...

Many types of wood, many lives

Althought Slovene handicrafts are exceptionally varied and versatile, the story of wood comes first. Different materials are prevalent in different Slovene regions. So, diverse materials occur in the Mediterranean, pre-Alpine, Alpine and Pannonian regions of Slovenia, but wood is present in all of them. Work with some varieties of wood will be described here; various types of rods, the basic material of the weaver, are presented in the next chapter. Slovenia is a fairly wooded country. You can still come across individual landowners who claim to have planted their forests for their grandchildren's children. Such a relationship towards wood is a common trait of the Slovene people, who understand and value it. Their understanding of wood goes beyond the modern-day striving for quick profit. For centuries it has been their steady companion. They were born and raised with it, grew up with it, which means they also learned from and about it. They translated all the knowledge gained through time into handicrafts, some of which are still strong and thriving today.

MATIJA KOBOLA

In this manner, wood and wood products have shaped the economic life of individual regions, and have left a permanent mark on them. The Ribnica valley, with the Kočevje region and some parts of the Notranjska region, are fine examples of this. The locals from these areas were granted written permission by the Emperor for the free production and trade of home-crafted wood products as early as 1492. The Slovene term commonly used for wood products is *suha roba*-literally, "dry goods". The term is used for a variety of products employed in everyday life. The most typical *suha roba* products of all times are wooden spoons and mixing spoons. As life and economy have changed throughout history, *suha roba* products have changed accordingly. Craftsmen followed the laws of supply and demand, as they still do today. Making wooden goods is predominantly restricted to rural areas now, and is referred to as the home production of wooden goods. Naturally, the range of products changes much faster and more intensively today than in past centuries, because the rhythm of our lifestyles changes much quicker as well. But modern *suha roba* makers craft more and more products on specific commissions rather than pursuing their own original creative ideas. This is understandable, since one needs proper training, and above all personal talent, to obtain the status of a master craftsman. That is why I see a great possibility in establishing specialized workshops that develop original design concepts, i.e. trademarks. In addition to this trend, it still remains indispensable to encourage the replication of heritage objects. Despite the fact that this memory is not particularly rich, there are plenty of heritage objects which are fascinating not only because of their artistic and esthetic value, tested by time, but also because of their possible new functions, even outside of the environment for which they were predominantly intended.

MATIJA KOBOLA, who comes from the village of Šalka vas in the Kočevje region continues to make *suha roba* articles, thus greatly contributing to the preservation and experience of historical memory. He makes (or rather, he hews) beech wood ladles, mixing spoons and specially shaped vessels called *nečke* or *kadunje*. These are shallow, basin-like, oval or round vessels, locally known as *mauterle*. In the past, they were used for separating grain from husks, for transporting and storing various crops (such as beans) and objects. *Nečke* were often bathtubs for bathing babies, or even cribs. The larger ones were used for kneading bread. Their exterior was adorned by combinations of geometric and stylized floral motifs. Because of their central role in bread preparation and infant care, *nečke* were also marked by the initials of Christ. Together with wooden spoons, *nečke* of various sizes and characteristic forms were always in demand as prime *suha roba* items, and Matija Kobola preserves the historical memory of them.

A well-sharpened knife still remains the best tool for working wood. We could also say it is the easiest tool to guide, since it appears to do whatever the craftsman wants it to. The hand pursues the thought, which evaluates the characteristics of the wood and translates them into a well-formed shape. The shape of any product is not only an outward exercise in esthetics, but needs to be functional, and adapted to people's demands.

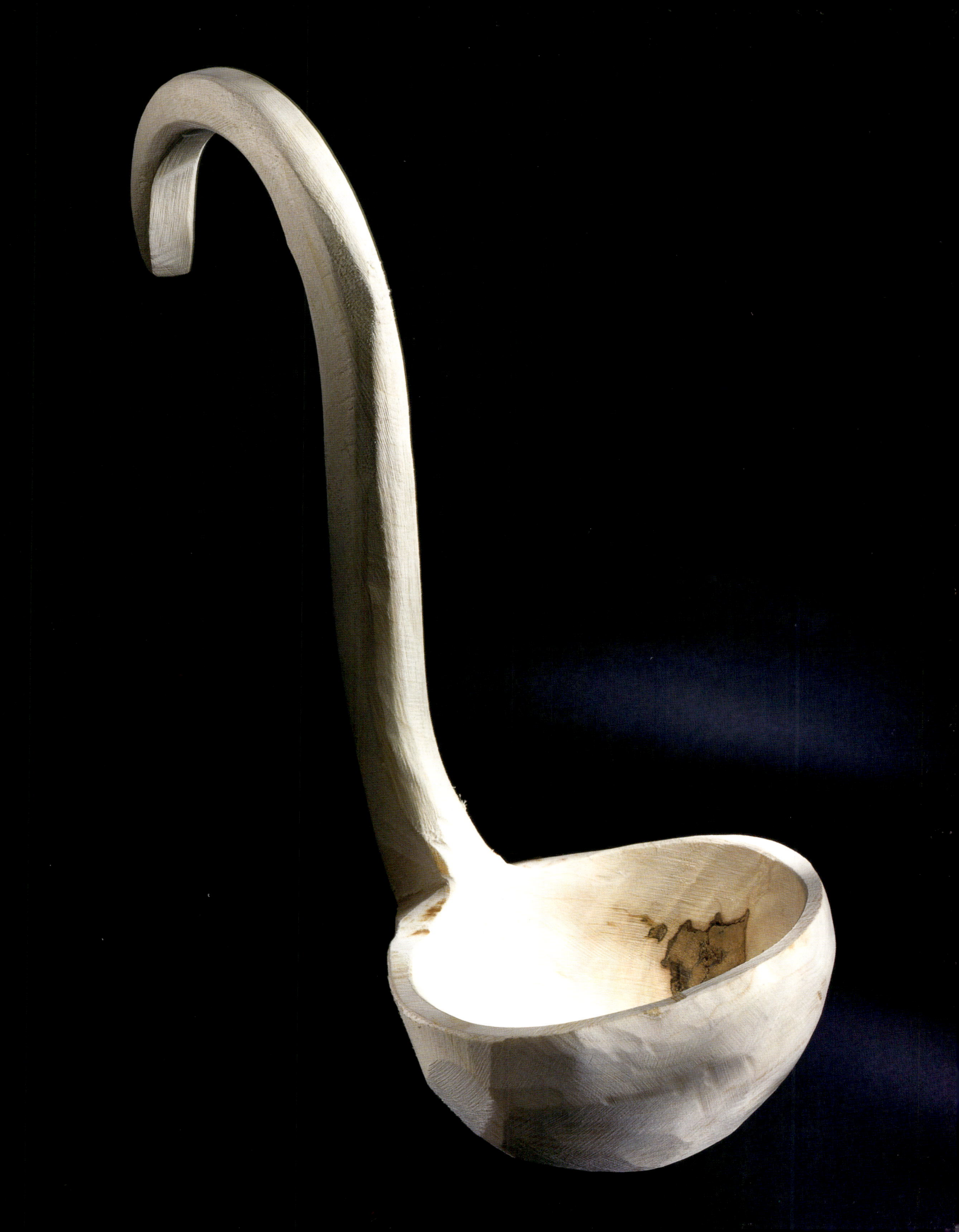

MANY TYPES OF WOOD, MANY LIVES

MAKING TOOTHPICKS is another traditional woodcraft connected with the production of *suha roba* products which has been preserved to the present day. Several craftsmen still make toothpicks using traditional procedures. This emphatically seasonal craft started in the 19th century as a winter pastime, and was often connected with socializing during long winter evenings. In addition to the important income earned by selling their products, the makers also cultivated a specific form of socializing.

Toothpicks have always been made of hazel wood, dogwood, barberry and beech wood sticks sharpered by hand. This special *suha roba* craft also demands a distinct division of labor. First, the crafters cut the stick bushes, which are afterwards split into small stakes. These are then further cleft to form thinner stakes, which are sharpened at both ends with a knife. Finally, the toothpicks are tied into small bundles and are ready to sell. Modernity has also brought technological developments to the manufacture of toothpicks; today, toothpicks are also produced by an entirely automated process. But their functional quality cannot compare with their handcrafted equivalents. Today, making toothpicks mainly rests in the hands of elderly or retired members of rural families. This activity is their additional source of income.

As part of its mercantile activities, the Habsburg Empire developed many handicrafts, especially by organizing various courses on handicrafts, and introducing and teaching craftsmen the principles of crafting technologies and design. Thus, some handicrafts spread to other areas where additional sources of income were needed, because the primary economic activity brought too little for a region to survive.

Alojz Cej's products (picture 1) represent the last remains of the tradition of making wooden dishes. They are distinct from others because all the component parts are crafted from spruce wood. Classic suha roba *items (picture 2) are also crafted at the Marolt workshop in Sodražica, but using modern tools, which enable the craftsmen to work in the finest details when finishing the products.*

MANY TYPES OF WOOD, MANY LIVES

The villages and isolated settlements in the wooded area of Trnovski gozd were in one such region. Very little historical memory of woodcrafts common in this area has been preserved to the present day. One of the few master craftsmen who continue to make milk pails and butter tubs of spruce wood is **ALOJZ CEJ** from Lokve. His products, although only of two types, are made entirely of wood, using traditional procedures. The rims connecting the staves into the shape of a vessel are joined in the traditional way: by a special wooden clasp. This special construction distinguishes Cej's products, and gives them a special, unconscious artistic dimension. They mediate a spontaneous but re-evaluated message from the heritage of our ancestors.

In my description of modern *suha roba* products I first mentioned those crafts and artisans whose products are based on a repetition of historical memory. There are very few modern solutions, especially original ones. There was an undergraduate thesis at the Ljubljana Academy of Arts in 1997 in which the author proposed designs for a modern line of wooden items, which could represent the turning of modern *suha roba* products into a new, creative direction. Hers was one of the first attempts, however. A number of self-taught craftsmen of *suha roba* products have themselves tried to design such items. If we disregard ideas copied from foreign models, we have very few good solutions. The modern wooden articles made by **ANTON MAROLT** from Sodražica are some of the better exceptions to this rule.

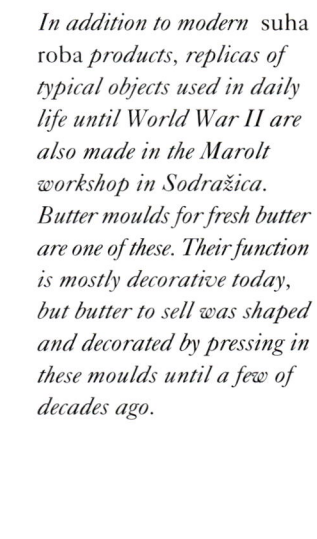

In addition to modern suha roba *products, replicas of typical objects used in daily life until World War II are also made in the Marolt workshop in Sodražica. Butter moulds for fresh butter are one of these. Their function is mostly decorative today, but butter to sell was shaped and decorated by pressing in these moulds until a few of decades ago.*

21

HANDICRAFTS OF SLOVENIA

MANY TYPES OF WOOD, MANY LIVES

TURNING WOOD is another woodcraft which evolved from producing *suha roba* products. The first lathes used were hand- or foot-powered, and the *suha roba* craftsmen produced a variety of wooden bowls, plates, parts of spinning wheels and other products. After World War II, the turning of wood continued predominantly with the turning of wooden plates and trays. The trend of designing unique, turned wooden bowls and other utensils declined in quality during that period.

Today, turning wood is a completely independent handicraft in terms of design and technology. The first person to venture into the unexplored territory of designing turned wooden products was the architect **JANEZ GOLOB** from Ljubljana, who is today recognized as a master craftsman of turned wooden bowls. Golob's bowls are classic examples of the synthesis of exceptional wood-turning skills and extensive knowledge of wood types, ennobled by expert design.

BORUT KARNAR from Podgorje near Slovenj Gradec is another wood-turner. He has limited himself to producing three basic types of product, which vary in size, type of material and color glazing: wooden turned bowls; bowls with a space for cracking nuts; and gourds with a hollowed centre. The latter are a variation of the traditional gourds, used predominantly by shepherds.

Lovrenc na Pohorju started turning wood many years ago, still using a foot-powered lathe. Bowls made from birch, alder, ash, elm, beech and rowan tree wood are his main products.

Golob's turned wooden bowls (Pictures 1, 2) are the finest of their kind in Slovenia. All are unique items. Golob gives his bowls a special value and perfect shape by manually checking the form of the bowls during the turning process.

MANY TYPES OF WOOD, MANY LIVES

MAKING CASKS is another classical *suha roba* woodcraft; over time it has evolved into a highly developed independent trade. Such a course of development was possible because of the high level of development of viticulture and viniculture, supported by related crafts such as nail-making and iron-forging. Casks of various sizes were used for transporting goods on horseback, even to very distant markets. workshop of cooper **FRANC MARIN** from Boreci near Križevci (near Ljutomer) is exceptional. His products are distinguished by superb modern crafting technology. The traditional farm-style, egg-shaped casks, the front sides of which are adorned by carved ornaments, are still made in his workshop. The carvings naturally reflect every customer's, i. e. wine-maker's, personal preference- to have his personal motifs carved on the front sides of his casks. However, the outward, representative appearance of the casks is not of crucial importance in cask-making.

In the past, this handicraft was widespread in Slovenia, and true cask-making centres evolved around individual coopers' workshops. Based on these workshops, particularly in the 19th century, real cask-making centres developed, for example, in Selška Dolina in the area of Škofja Loka, around Črni vrh nad Idrijo, and in Tacen near Ljubljana. In addition to these centres, casks were made in several smaller workshops. Making casks even reached places outside the wine-growing regions. Today, there are still several such minor coopers' workshops, and there are individual coopers who craft classical oak wood casks and work with other types of wood as well. Some vine-growers and wine-makers still use acacia wood casks, crafted predominantly by coopers such as **JOŽEF LOZEJ** from the greater Karst region.

Fornezzi's bowls (Picture 3) are mostly replicas of historical memory. The same description also applies to the cooper's products of excellent quality from the Marin workshop in Prlekija (Picture 4), in which the heritages of shape and function are successfully combined with modern production technique.

There are few turners in Slovenia today. Some are trying to establish new, functional products. Borut Karnar, for example, turns wooden dishes for breaking nuts and hazelnuts, and wooden gourds.

MANY TYPES OF WOOD, MANY LIVES

Jožef Lozej from Ivanji Grad in the Karst region specializes in creating casks of acacia wood.

Besides straw, **WOODEN SHINGLES AND PLANKS** were Slovenia's most common traditional roofing material. In the past, even town buildings were roofed with shingles (in Novo mesto, for example, this was the case even after 1900). Roofing with wooden shingles is restricted to dairy-farming stations in the highland regions, and to buildings presently protected as items of value in the architectural heritage of Slovenia. In the past, shingles were not made in workshops but by homeowners, who had to supply, keep and restore all roofing material on their own. One has to bear in mind that wooden shingles were much more durable when farmhouses were still warmed by stoves and food was still cooked in open fireplaces, allowing the smoke to lift up towards the roof and into the open air. The shingles were thus smoke-impregnated on the bottom.

There are two basic types or kinds of shingle in Slovenia: the wider and longer Gorenjska type, and the narrower Koroška type called *šiklni* or *šintlni*, which are hammered onto the gable in several layers and in alternating order. Making shingles is a very demanding task, only worthy of a master craftsman, because they are made from parts of tree trunks using a splitting technique called *kalanje*. Some craftsmen, for whom this craft represents an additional activity, still make them today. One such craftsman is **BOJAN KOŽELJ** from Stahovica near Kamnik, who makes wooden shingles and also roofs buildings with them. His demonstrations of the art of shingle-making and roofing techniques at various fairs and exhibitions are particularly useful. This area of his work is also of great educational and promotional importance.

Wooden shingles are one of the traditional roofing materials in Slovenia. The ways of life and culture only allow such roofing materials on certain buildings. These are often buildings whose original image needs be retained with expert care for the preservation of historical memory. Wooden shingles today are less durable than they were in the past, and thus merely help keep up the visual and decorative image of a building. Their durability can only be achieved by also restoring all other functions of the building.

MANY TYPES OF WOOD, MANY LIVES

The wheel is not a simple product of the wheelwright but represents a synthesis of knowledge of wood types and their growth with knowledge of assembling and strengthening the wheels, in which the wheelwright is joined by a blacksmith, who makes the wheel firmer by forging. The development of wheel-making is connected with the development of the road infrastructure and the driving conditions, which were decisive in determining the and diameter of the wheel.

The origins of **WHEEL-MAKING** go back to the 15th century. This craft started to develop as an independent handicraft when carts were first used in farmstead households and transporting goods by horse and cart became widespread. Wheelwrights were among the greatest connoisseurs of individual types of wood and their characteristics. Wheel-spokes or *špice* were usually made of well-dried dogwood, while the shafts and parts of the wheel frame were hewn from ash wood. Making wheels is not very popular today, and is preserved to only a very modest extent. It is connected with the upkeep of older work or holiday carts, which is the consequence of a slightly increased interest in sport and amateur horse-rearing, and the use of old carts for tourism purposes. Different clubs and societies of friends of these activities are being established. **FRANC BRENČIČ** from Petkovec near Logatec is one of the rare Slovene wheelwrights who not only makes wheels in his workshop but often demonstrates the crafting of the central product of his craft, the wheel, at various public events. This is of crucial importance for all handicrafts which have only a very small number of still-active craftsmen, because they help preserve historical memory. Such "live" performances are kinds of moving museums, and perhaps motivate individuals to learn more and possibly even take up the craft of wheel-making themselves.

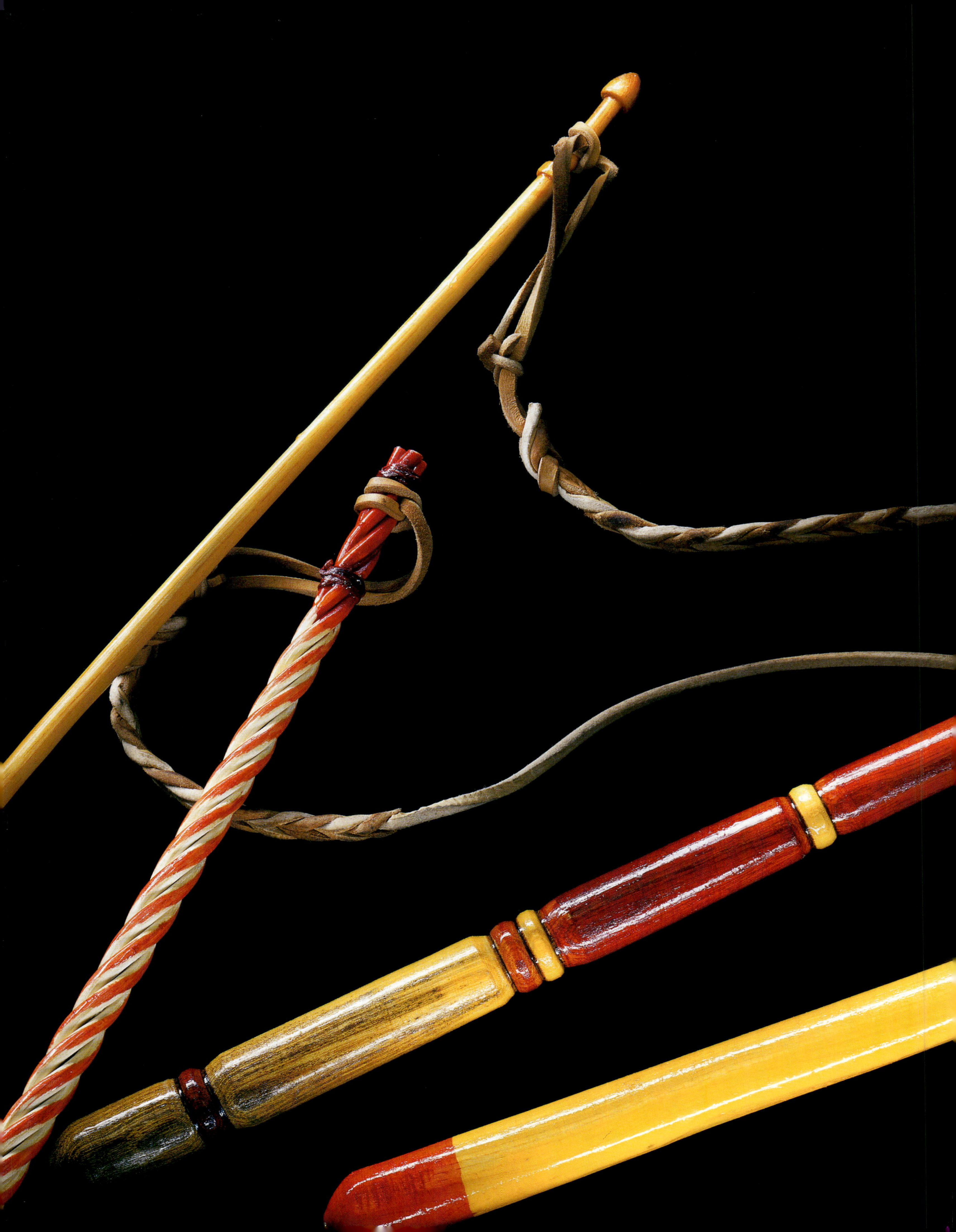

MANY TYPES OF WOOD, MANY LIVES

In relation to harnessing horses or oxen, and with transportation by horse and cart, the crafts which produce the equipment necessary for all three appeared. **WHIPS** are part of this equipment. Wood-turners often made whips from various types of flexible wood. The making of braided wooden whips called *bičevniki* has been preserved to this day. Two of the best-known makers of braided whips are **MARJAN SEMOLIČ** from Brestovica near Sežana and **ALOJZ SEVER** from Vrtača near Semič. Their technique is the same. First, they split a suitable stick spliced into four strips down to the handle. They then plait the strips into a thick braid. Such whips are very flexible. Semolič uses a local Karst wood type called *kropince* or *kroprivnice (Céltis australis)*, which was the most common type of tree found on vineyard and field borders in the past. It is very rare today, however, and not many whips are made from it, especially since 1990 when Semolič stopped trading with the Balkans. Making whips, locally called *škarabac*, was once popular in Brestovica and its surroundings; since 1960, however, Semolič has been the only whip-maker in the area. Each of the whips he makes is handled at least fifty times before completion, which takes about a month. Alojz Sever from the Bela Krajina region uses chestnut wood for his whips because it is just as easy to split. Whips have always been symbols of the drivers, a part of their overall outward appearance. Precisely because of this, whips were dyed and adorned with ponpons and leather fringes. Until World War II (i.e. when driving by horse and cart was a widespread economic activity) there were many whip-makers in the regions around Brestovica, in Opatje Selo in the Karst region, and in the *suha roba*, areas of in Ribnica, Velike Lašče and Cerknica.

MARJAN SEMOLIČ

In the centuries and decades of developed horse-breeding and the related discipline of driving with horse and cart (furmanstvo), *whips were the status symbols and trademarks of the drivers. That is why whips were adorned in various ways.*

Hunting dormice - those cunning denizens of the forest - in autumn is one of the exceptional, centuries-old hunting disciplines still practised today. Only its economic significance has changed. The Slovene polymath/scholar Janez Vajkard Valvasor first described dormouse-hunting and the ways to use the prey in *The Glory of the Duchy of Carniola* (1695). He also described the hunting apparatus: **WOODEN DORMOUSE TRAPS** with a bow, which are still produced by hand today and which constitute a separate craft discipline. Today, hunting dormice is more of a social, tourist and culinary event than one of economic necessity, which is the reason why the hunts were nicknamed *polharija*. But in autumn nights, modern hunters still use the wooden traps developed from older, traditional models. Dormouse-hunting was very popular, especially in the Notranjska region and in the forests of western Dolenjska. Even today, dormouse hunts are still the best-developed forms of tourist entertainment and socializing in these two regions. One of the few remaining trap-makers is **BOJAN ŠTEFANČIČ** from Pudob in the Notranjska region, where merry parties of dormouse hunters gather annually, in the forests around Snežnik Castle, to enjoy the sport and to later taste delicacies such as roast dormouse, dormouse stew and dormouse goulash. As mentioned earlier, the traps used are traditional models which have been partly improved. They are known under a variety of local names: *poušne, škrince, škrlupi, škatle, samojstre* or *toplarce*. Attention was focused upon improving the spring mechanism, where the older wooden bows or manually forged springs were replaced by metal ones.

The symbols of dormouse-hunters (polharji) *are wooden dormouse traps, which often bear their owners' insignia, since dormouse hunting is a social, group event.*

27
HANDICRAFTS OF SLOVENIA

MANY TYPES OF WOOD, MANY LIVES

Wood was the basic building material in the highland regions of the Alps, which means it was also used for making various tools and equipment. It played an important role in the pastoral culture of the Alpine world, which developed around dairy-farming stations built amidst the central or highland pastures, grazing areas and mountains in the Alps. The stations provided shelter for shepherds and cattle, and were also places where dairy products were made. Little of the dairy-farming heritage has been preserved, and the few remaining dairy-farming stations now house holidaymakers and tourists.

Despite that, some craftsmen still make excellent replicas of objects once used by shepherds and dairymen, and which are part of the Alpine and shepherds' heritage. The youngest, **DEJAN OGRIN** from Bohinjska Bistrica, deserves to be mentioned first. He makes excellent imitations of **DAIRYMEN'S CLOGS**, which are one of the oldest extant items of footwear. The young craftsman uses as many as three types of wood in the making of these special clogs, similar to those which were also popular in other parts of Slovenia until World War II. Ogrin's clogs are made entirely of wood. The sole is of popular wood, even though other craftsmen also use *maklen (Acer campestre)* or maple wood. The upper parts are made of thinly cut and interwoven spruce or larch wood strips. Clogs, with straw or leather uppers, also appear as part of the Slovene clog-making heritage. They are of more recent origin, however, and some craftsmen also lined the leather parts of clogs with felt. The making of such clogs was preserved longest in the Pohorje Massif. Some craftsmen from Skomar and its surrounding area still make them today. The village was named *Cokelburg* (Clogstown) by the local folk poet Jurij Vodovnik. The late **JOŽE KOPRIVNIK** from Resnik was a well-known clog-maker. His son **MARTIN** carries on his work today. The late master Koprivnik also taught **JOŽE ŽLAUS** from Globoče near Vojnik how to make clogs. Students from the Lovrenc na Pohorju Elementary School concluded in their research project that the last pair of "traditional" clogs in the region was made in 1980. This example shows that such school research projects are essential even in the study of individual handicrafts. They represent the preservation and documentation of historical memory, which is essential for the development of handicrafts today as well as in the future.

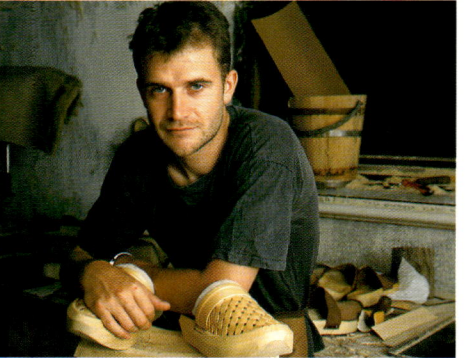

DEJAN OGRIN

Several traditional items of footwear are crafted in Slovenia, clogs being one of them. Jože Žlaus (Picture 3) and Martin Koprivnik (Picture 4) craft wooden clogs with leather uppers, while Dejan Ogrin (Pictures 1, 2) excels in making the entirely wooden bohinjske cokle *(Bohinj clogs), with uppers of interwoven osiers that also function as ornaments.*

28

HANDICRAFTS OF SLOVENIA

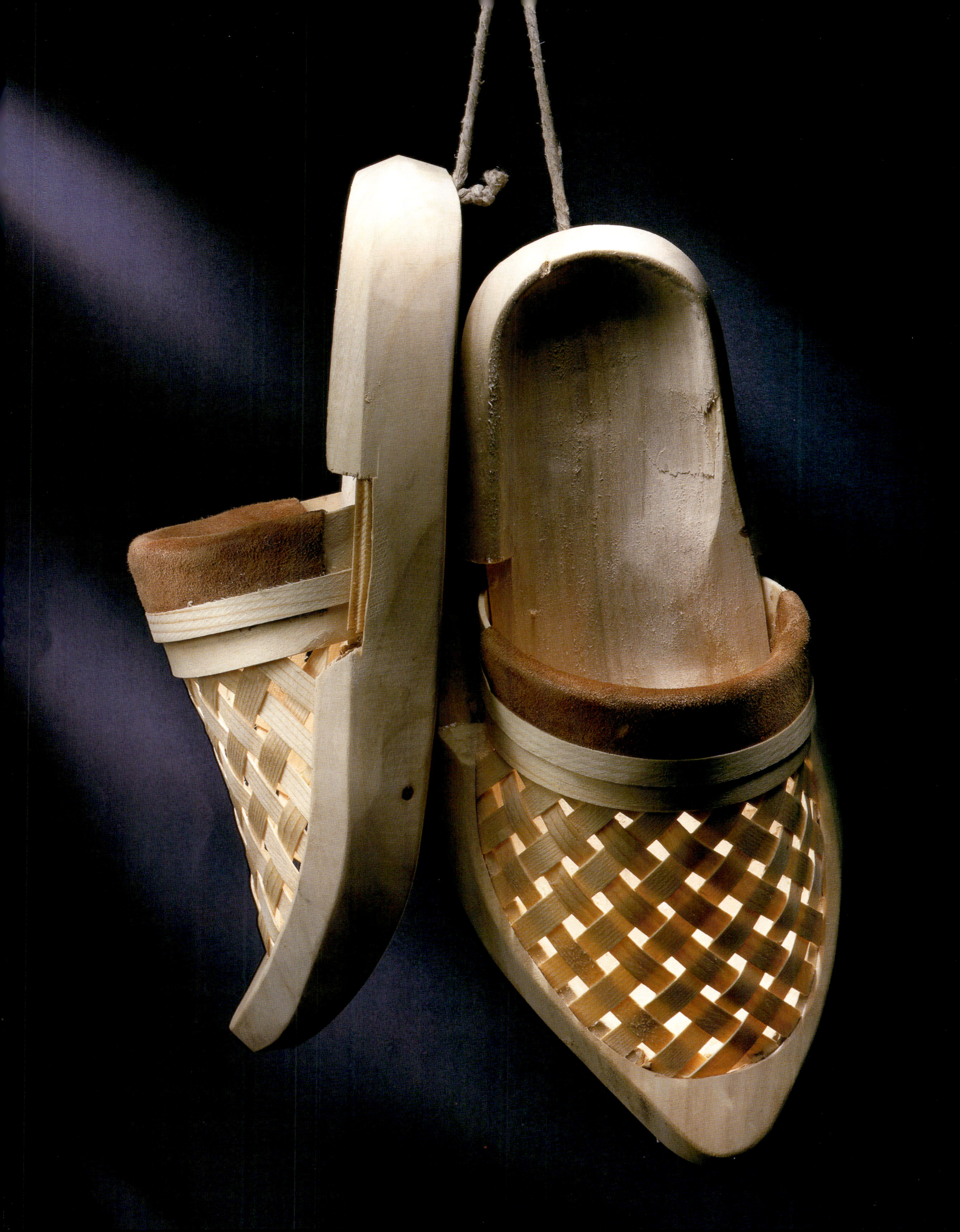

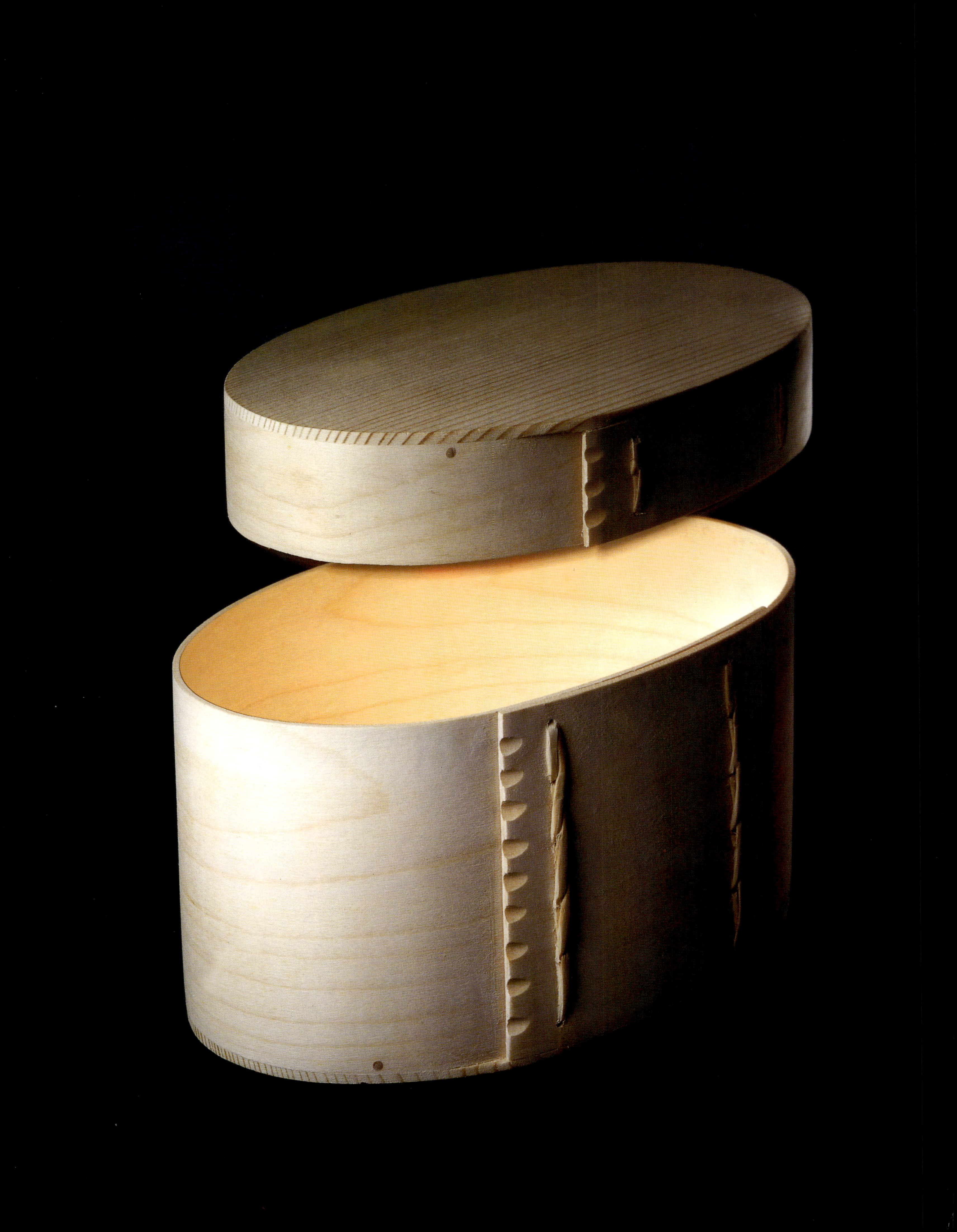

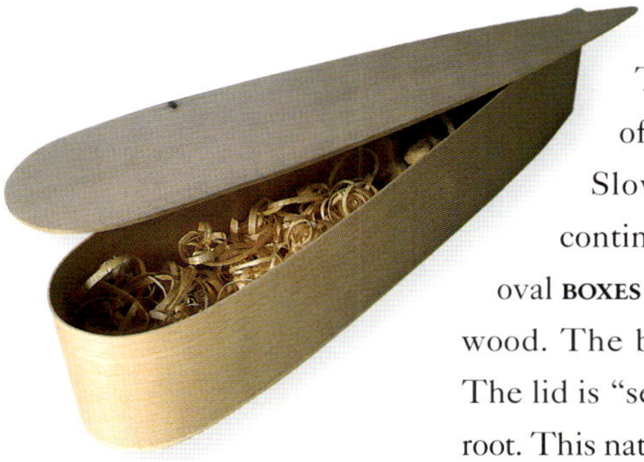

MANY TYPES OF WOOD, MANY LIVES

Two artisans, from the highland village of Gorjuše near Bohinj make important Slovene heritage articles. **IVAN JEKLAR** continues the tradition of making round and oval **BOXES WITH RIMMED LIDS** from spruce or larch wood. The boxes are made exclusively of wood. The lid is "sewn" to the box by a fresh spruce tree root. This natural "stitch" is the box's most beautiful ornament. Jeklar's boxes come in various sizes, just as they did in the past. They were used for storing documents, valuables and shaving equipment. Occasionally, they were used as handy lunch boxes, which were filled with chives, a piece of meat or a sausage before the ovner headed off to the fields or to the forest where the work needed to be done. Women often kept their sewing kit in rimmed boxes, and sometimes also seeds and spices.

IVAN JEKLAR

Ivan Jeklar also decided to replicate traditional wooden products. In his case, these are rimmed wooden boxes with lids. In addition to these, Jeklar also designs some new products and uses technological elements he learnt about when studying old craft techniques.

31

HANDICRAFTS OF SLOVENIA

MANY TYPES OF WOOD, MANY LIVES

Another local craftsman, **ALOJZ LOTRIČ**, is the only pipe-maker still producing the famous Gorjuše pipes called **FAJFE**. Lotrič continues formerly very popular, mostly winter activity, which most likely started in the 18th century. The Gorjuše pipe-makers developed a range of pipes differing in size, shape and ornamentation. Many of the pipes are made from pear wood and decorated with mother-of-pearl, silvered tin or brass. The most famous of all Gorjuše pipes is the stocky-shaped *čedra*. Ornamentation of the pipes with bits of mother-of-pearl was called *štikanje* - which, technologically speaking, is a fine form of wooden mosaic-making. When the trade started to decline at the beginning of the 20th century, the pipe-makers still produced over 3,500 pieces a year. Today, pipe-making is only a continuation of historical memory, a reminder of a once popular handicraft that provided an important additional source of income for the shepherds of the mountainous Alpine regions.

ALOJZ LOTRIČ

The role of wood in rites, customs and habits is described in the chapter on wickerwork. **MAKING WOOD CHAINS** is also an interesting woodcraft which deserves to be mentioned in this chapter. These chains of different lengths with flexible links are carved from a single piece of lime wood. The craftsman uses a technique by which the links are already intertwined upon completion. Two spoons are attached to the chain, one at each end, so that the chain binds them. Such chains are highly symbolic, representing married life. This is a fine handicraft whose course of development is relatively short. It is one of the many secrets common to craftsmen of all trades. Some of these secrets were included in special tests for obtaining apprenticeship or the title of master craftsman. Others were developed in the long hours of military service, in the peaceful hours on the battlefield of the Soča (Isonzo) Front, or while working in the pastures.

JANEZ GOLOB from Zagorje ob Savi learned about the craft of making woodchains by watching TV in the 1970s. The narrator, an elderly man from the Gorenjska region, described presenting newlyweds with these special and symbolic spoons on a chain. Golob considered the craft an interesting creative challenge, and started making wooden chains by hand regularly in 1982. Among his handcrafted products, which became popular wedding gifts (especially because of the spoons for the spouses), we find many varieties, based on the original, predominantly technological concept.

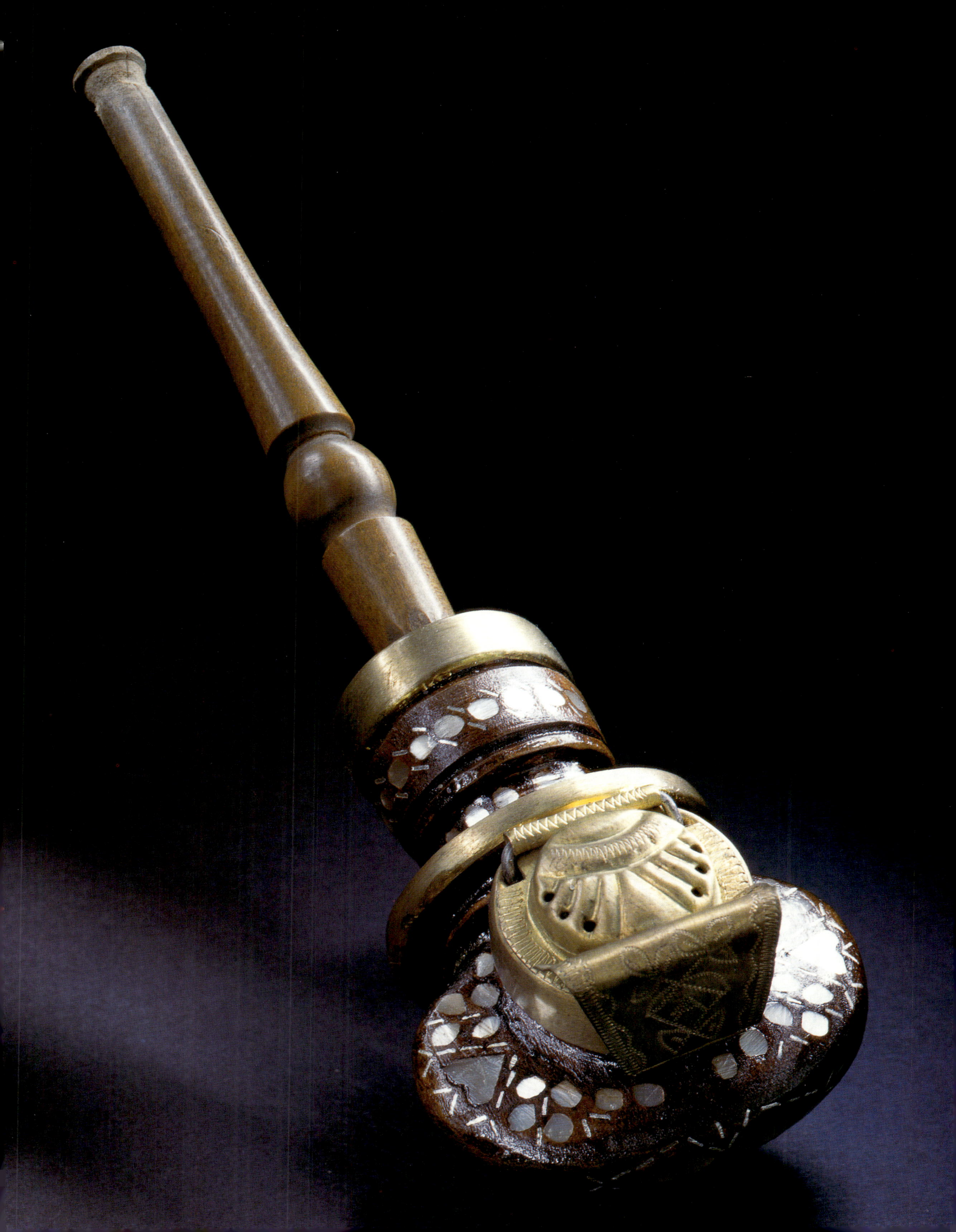

Many types of wood, many lives

Changes in the design of business, promotional and state gifts - especially from the mid-1980s onwards - naturally encouraged craftsmen from various wood-working crafts to start replicating wooden objects from the Slovene heritage. I am referring to the production of **REPLICAS OF WOOD PRODUCTS FROM THE SLOVENE HERITAGE;** I am also, of course, talking about items assembled as exhibits in museums and in private collections which are perfect copies items from history. Some craftsmen only specialize in replicating one or a few traditional objects. The workshop of **Jernej Kosmač** from Bistrica near Tržič is exceptional in this respect. Replicas of over seventy different traditional products are made here. He started carving coats-of-arms twenty-five years ago, and he has been making various replicas in his own workshop since 1990. The number of his products is less important than the fact that Kosmač has also trained his son **Matej,** who helps to replicate old wooden objects. The Kosmač family business is an example of the importance of knowledge, not only of the basic technologies but of traditional materials, eagerly tracked down in museums and private collections by Jernej Kosmač. Select traditional products first have to be subjected to thorough technological research, and then adapted to modern approaches. Some of the seventy types of items crafted in the Kosmač workshop - especially those through which the father and son have developed their trademark - will be mentioned here. A replica of the heritage of their hometown is first: a typical Tržič cobblers' lamp consisting of glass bowls filled with water, which for centuries made it possible for the Tržič cobblers to work at night. It no longer serves its primary purpose. A substantial number of buyers use it as a quality source of artificial light, created from the light of a candle or a petroleum lamp dispersed through the water-filled balls. At the end of this century, the cobbler's lamps represent a certain quality in our homes, in spite of all the high technology. That is why it is hardly surprising that the Kosmač lamps have been taken as presents to countries as for away as Japan. Another great specialty of the Kosmač workshop is used in this area: the pocket sundial, replicated from those originally used by shepherds in the past to measure time at Velika planina in the Kamnik Alps. It consists of a palm-sized piece of wood, a small wooden pole and a dial. It was a splendid invention, a local variant of the personal, portable, pocket sundial once used throughout Europe. It is noteworthy that even the shepherds, most of whom were uneducated, considered the measuring of time a necessity. In addition, Kosmač also replicates various objects used in farmhouses and borough households. These include cases, scores, carving sticks for cheeses, crucifixes, Nativity scene figurines, spoon-holders, bowl racks, replicas of toys, and numerous other items formerly used in daily life and during special occasions in Slovenia.

Jernej Kosmač and son Matej

Spoon-holders used to be essential items of furniture. Replicas of spoon-holders kept in Slovene museums and private collections are created at the Kosmač workshop (Picture 1). Replicas of the Velika planina shepherds' pocket sundials (Picture 2) and the Tržič cobblers' lamps (opposite page).

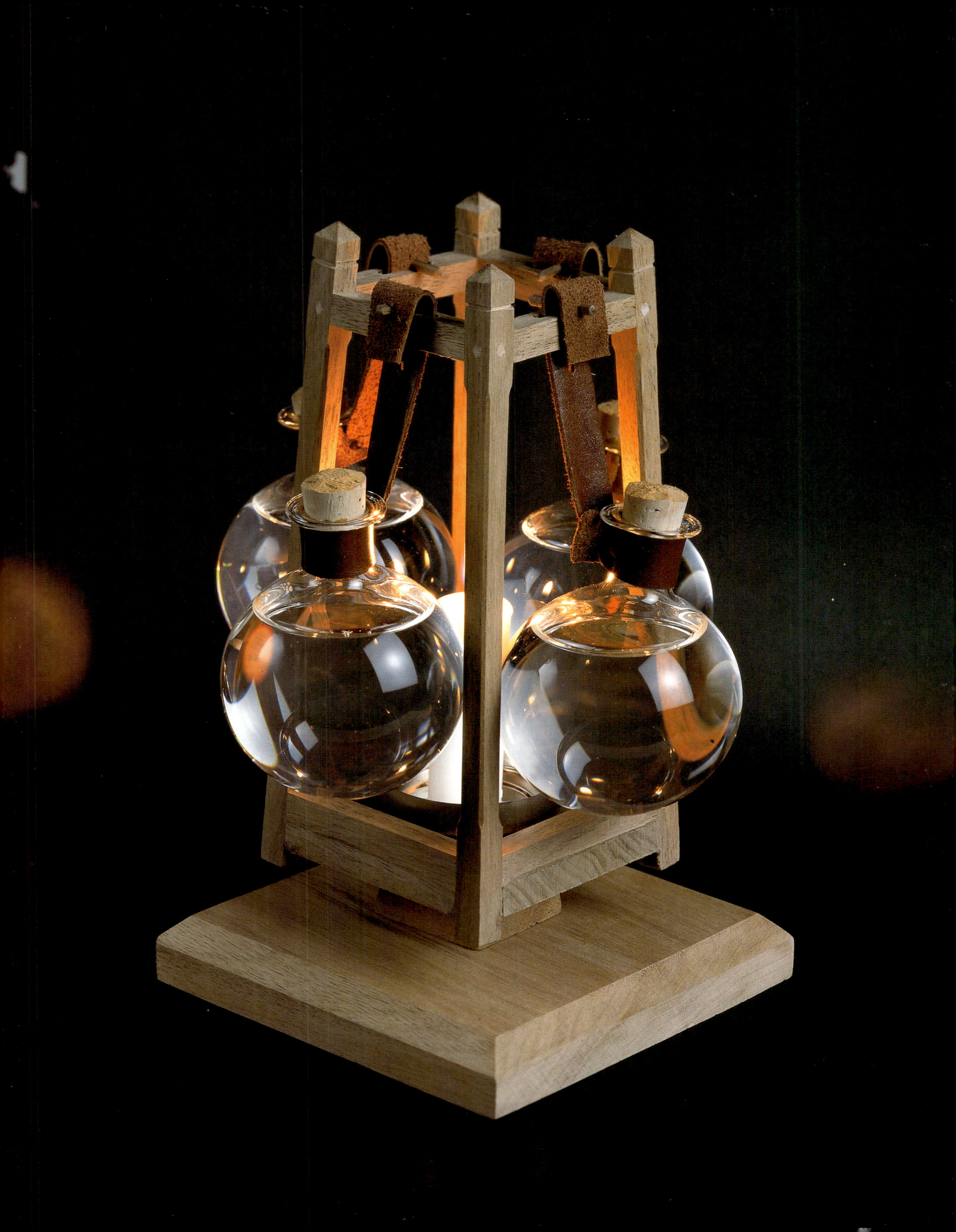

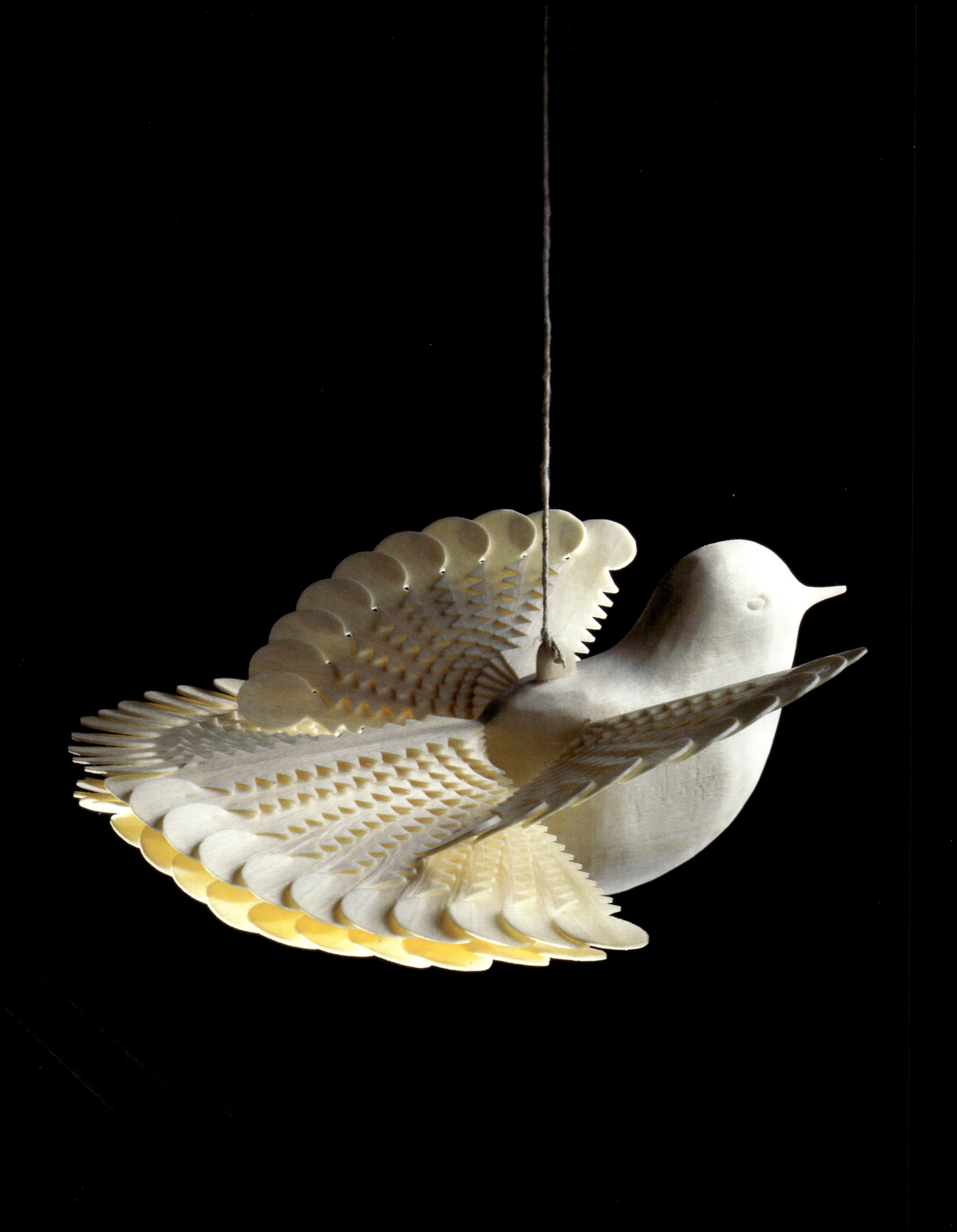

MANY TYPES OF WOOD, MANY LIVES

MAKING WOODEN DOVES, symbols of the Holy Ghost, is a long-neglected part of the handicraft heritage of the Slovene Alpine regions. The dove was normally hung above the table in the *hiša* - the central room in the house. It was attached to a string connected to the main entrance; whenever the door opened, the doves above the table would swing vertically and announce a visitor to the house. Carving doves from spruce wood is a craft typical of the European Alpine world. The dove's wings and tail are carved from separate pieces of wood, which are first cut and then spread out in a fan to create the impression of being spread in flight. Unfortunately, only a few wooden doves are found in Slovene museum collections, but they are still carved by craftsmen like **BOGOMIR SAMEC** from Litija, and his student **ROBERT PERKO** from Breznica near Žiri. They use the few surviving traditional doves as models.

MONIKA KLEMENČIČ AND ROBERT PERKO

Different sculpted renditions of the image of the Holy Ghost were hung above the table in the central room of the house throughout Central Europe, especially in the Alpine world. Little figurines of the Holy Ghost are true monuments to self-taught wood-carvers, and to their extensive knowledge of their material.

37

HANDICRAFTS OF SLOVENIA

MANY TYPES OF WOOD, MANY LIVES

ANDREJ OZEBEK, from Mošnje near Podvin, has made some truly artistic samples of doves, symbolizing the Holy Ghost. Ozebek carries on the family wood-carving tradition in his father's workshop, where he also makes miniature replicas of household items such as butter tubs. His products are highly suitable additions to the range of souvenirs from the Gorenjska region.

Carved pigeons representing the image of the Holy Ghost, made by Andrej Ozebek from Mošnje near Podvin in the Gorenjska region, are superior to similar products of other carvers primarily because of their overall level of artistic representation. The basic technology of wood-splitting remains the same in all products, but their form differs depending on varied artistic approaches to the shaping of the tail and wings.

MANY TYPES OF WOOD, MANY LIVES

Wooden carved moulds for shaping gingerbread from honey dough mostly have a decorative function today. Petra Plestenjak-Podlogar from Škofja Loka continues this challenging form of carving moulds, which is a tradition in her family. The reason why carving moulds is a difficult task lies in their characteristic function, since all the motifs and ornaments need to be carved as "negatives". The final pattern only appears after the imprinted honey-dough is turned into gingerbread. Such gingerbreads were given a local name in Škofja Loka mali kruhki.

The first European **GINGERBREAD MOULDS** for shaping honey-dough appeared in the 15th century. Honey and mead sellers and chandlers used them to shape gingerbread dough into figurines and decorative breads by pressing the dough into the moulds. Over many centuries, local variations of recipes for dough preparation evolved, and local mould-carving workshops appeared. Škofja Loka was famous for its local carved moulds. The gingerbread was nicknamed short bread or *mali kruhek*. **PETRA PLESTENJAK - PODLOGAR**, a native of Škofja Loka, carries on the rich family tradition of carving gingerbread moulds from pear wood. Besides replicating traditional motifs, Plestenjak designs her own, always remaining within the traditional artistic framework characteristic of mould-carving. Her carved moulds today are not only intended for the production of gingerbreads but are also frequently used as decorative items.

MANY TYPES OF WOOD, MANY LIVES

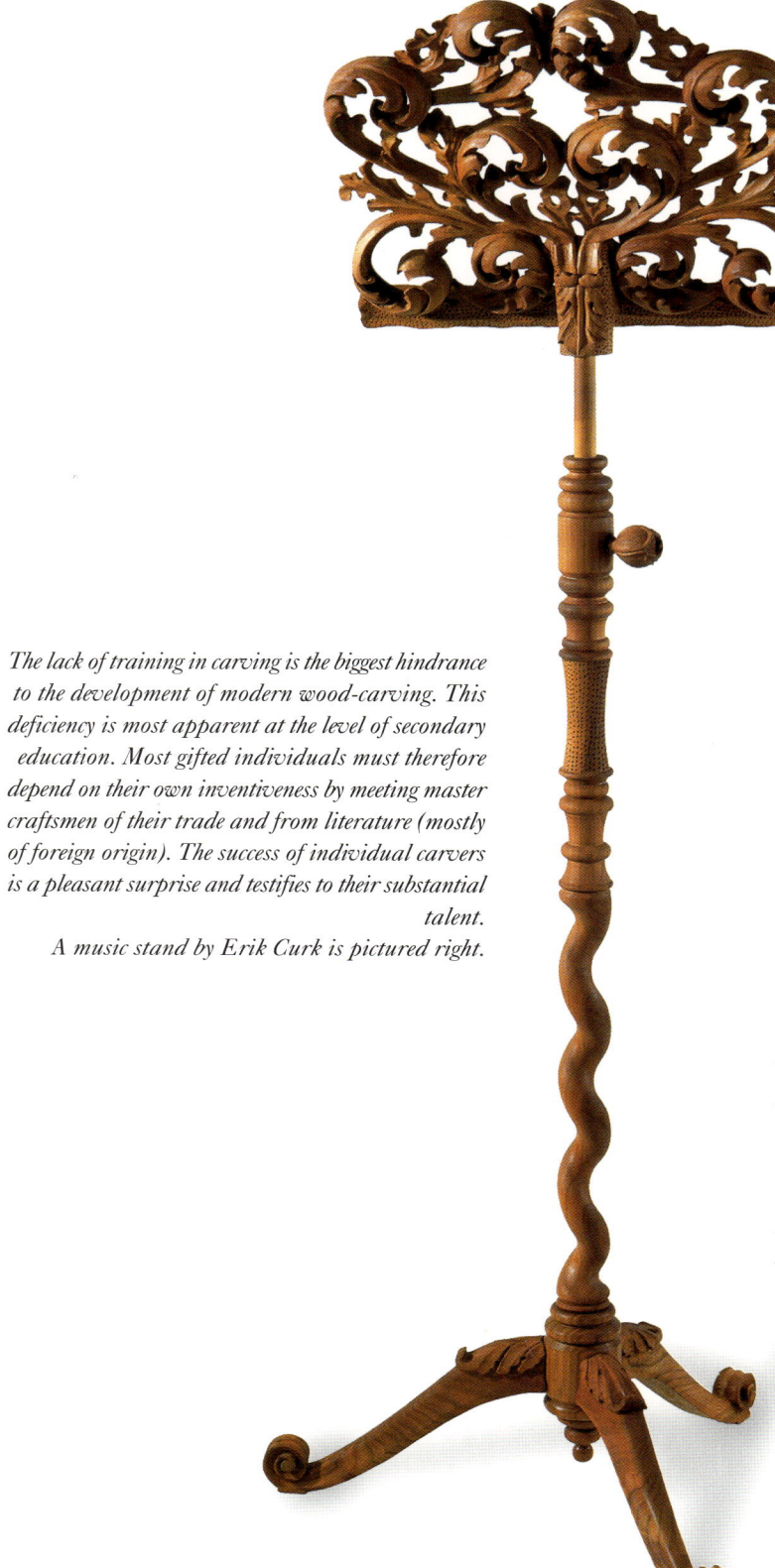

The lack of training in carving is the biggest hindrance to the development of modern wood-carving. This deficiency is most apparent at the level of secondary education. Most gifted individuals must therefore depend on their own inventiveness by meeting master craftsmen of their trade and from literature (mostly of foreign origin). The success of individual carvers is a pleasant surprise and testifies to their substantial talent.
A music stand by Erik Curk is pictured right.

The story of modern craftsmen who have chosen wood as the basic medium for their artistic expression is gradually coming to its end- or, more precisely, to the products which represent the culmination of the finest woodcraft. The rich heritage of wood-carving ended around the end of World War II. Interest in classic wood-carving and related crafts fell sharply in the late 1940s, and has only begun to rise again in recent years. The Slovene wood-carving and gilding heritage culminated in the "golden altars" of the 17th century, which are the most beautiful monuments to the numerous fragments of wood-working knowledge possessed by Slovene craftsmen. Altar-gilding reached its peak of quality and popularity in the 1770s. Between the 18th and 19th centuries, many self-taught folk artists appeared who took up the carving and gilding of sculptures and images. Their work is the corner stone of Slovene folk art. After World War II, only a few carvers continued this trade. Today, their work is mostly limited to commissioned restoration projects. **JOŽE LAPUH** from Ljubljana is the central figure in post-war Slovene carving. I should also like to mention several craftsmen who are educated artists and who specialize in woodcarving.

MANY TYPES OF WOOD, MANY LIVES

Woodcarving is, in fact, a synthesis of artistic and crafting endeavours. In some historical periods wood-carving was extremely popular and one of the best-developed crafts, with individual artisans as well as numerous workshops employing a large number of expert carvers. Wood-carving culminated in the Baroque and Rococo periods. Carved masterpieces from these two periods still inspire modern carvers, who continue and further develop their craft expertise. In addition to repeating heritage or historical memory, some craftsmen also see historical experience as a motif for the creation of new ideas and techniques based, neverteless, on historical models.

In the modern replication of objects from the wood-carving heritage, modern artificial materials and copying techniques are used, and make possible simple replication of the originals. But mastery of classic craft techniques, i.e. manual wood-carving, coloring, gilding and so forth, still count as the true expertise of the carver. Jože Lapuh from Ljubljana is considered a master wood-carver. He carved and painted the wooden statues of St. George and Mary with Child.

Carving Nativity scene figurines is also a carving technique taken up by self-taught carvers the carving of wooden Nativity scene figurines was done by individuals and carvers' workshops in the 19th century. Today, there are few carvers of Nativity scene figurines in Slovenia today, Franjo Srnel from Vojsko near Vodice being one of them.

41

HANDICRAFTS OF SLOVENIA

MANY TYPES OF WOOD, MANY LIVES

Today, **FRANJO SRNEL**, from Vojsko near Vodice, represents the self-taught branch of the craft. The young craftsman **MIHA LEGAN**, from the village of Stranska vas near Žužemberk, specializes in carving premium-period replicas (Baroque, for example). With the appearance of skilled individual wood-carvers and a renewed interest in wood-carving, the need for the organized training of carvers is becoming evident. Slovene carving is slowly returning to the position it occupied more than fifty years ago, i. e. on an equal footing with the carving of other European, particularly Alpine countries. Several young amateur carvers, such as **ERIK CURK** from Bled, have matured into exceptional masters of their craft. Curk studied the principles of wood-carving in great detail. He designs superb candlesticks and attractive wooden frames, as well as replicas or original interpretations of period styles, especially the Baroque.

MIHA LEGAN

The Legan workshop in Stranska vas near Žužemberk in the Dolenjska region is an excellent place to see a complete range of typical carvers' products, from gilded Baroque frames to candlesticks and various depictions of saints. All these are products of classical carving, which includes expertise in gilding, patina-finish, painting, and other features of technology and expression belonging to the wood-carving heritage.

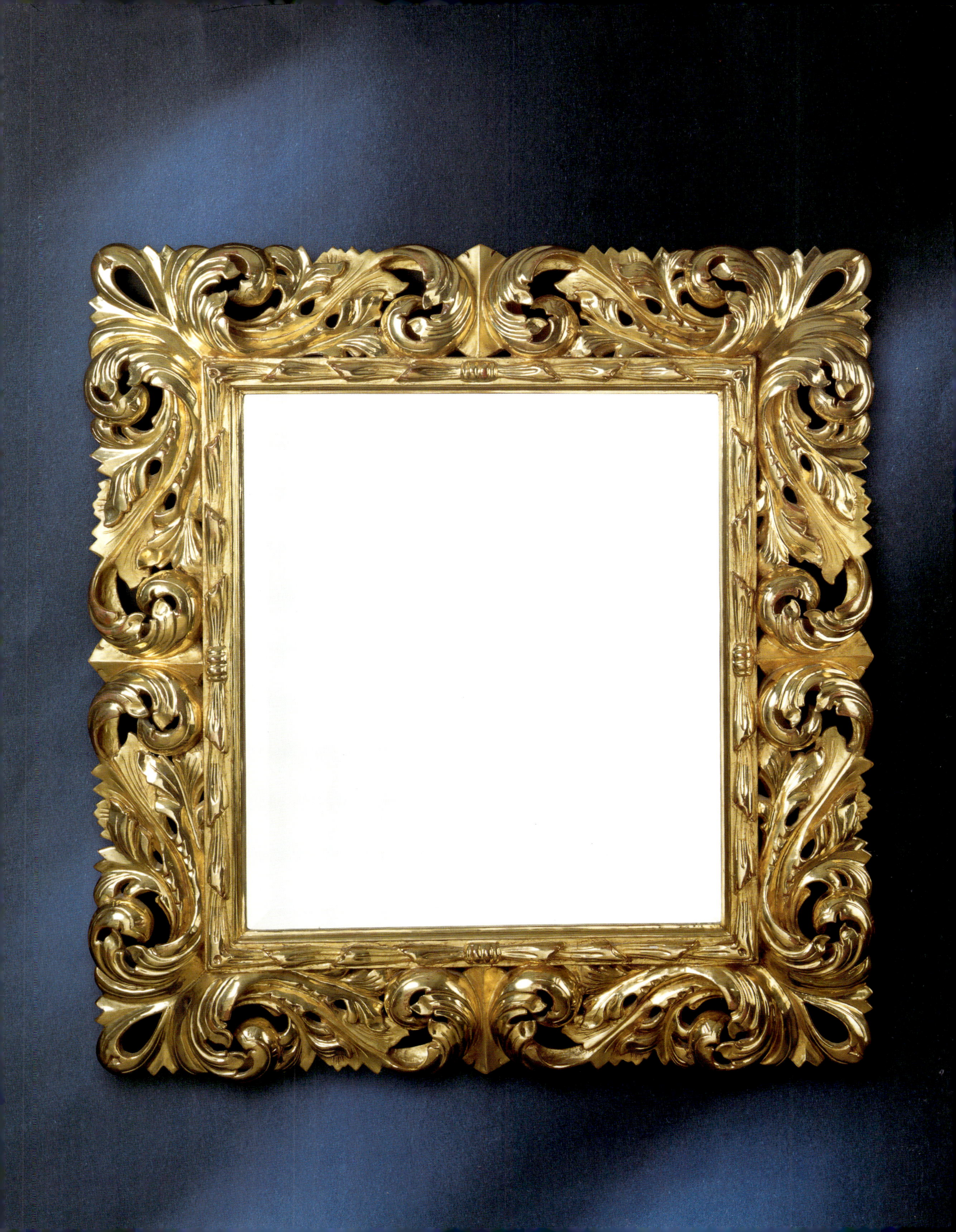

MANY TYPES OF WOOD, MANY LIVES

INLAYING (MAKING WOODEN MOSAICS or INTARSIAS) is a self-taught craft with a long tradition reaching far back into history. It was exceptionally well developed, and culminated in the Renaissance and Baroque periods. It is a common hobby in Slovenia today, but the artistic quality of the products mostly remains at an amateur level. It is a technically very demanding craft for which, an extensive understanding of wood, the characteristics of wood and craft technologies is necessary. The best Slovene maker of wooden mosaics is **STANISLAV ŠALAMON** from Maribor. He took it upon himself to transfer traditional Slovene ornaments into wood. It must be emphasized that he consciously chose the more challenging way of drawing his models from patterns found in traditional embroidery and lace, instead of using models of wooden chests with inlayed parts from the second half of the 18th and 19th century. Transferring the model to wood is a challenging task. His wooden mosaics are evidence of skilled craftsmanship, and are distinguished by superb colour and composition. Šalamon uses numerous natural veneers to achieve a variety of colour tones on his products.

The wooden intarsias created by Stanislav Šalamon are products of the highest class and are based on combining veneers of various colours into the desired compositions. In his work, Šalamon derives his inspiration from folk ornaments. The compositions of his intarsias supersede the decorative-functional character, and can function as independent images or works of art, as far as the materials and craft techniques allow.

44

MANY TYPES OF WOOD, MANY LIVES

Design is often assumed to be a process of discovering, planning and creating more or less perfect forms of products. But design is only parallel to craft procedures, detailed expertise of craft materials, and the final product. Franc Oblak's bows represent a synthesis of all these. They are modern products with a long history. In the past, bows were multi-purpose items used as hunting devices, weapons and in sports activities.

The making of **COMPETITION** and **SPORTS BOWS** - which is indeed an exceptional handicraft, demanding extensive knowledge of wood and wood-working procedures - has been perfected by **FRANC OBLAK** from Radovljica. He possesses the vast knowledge of wood necessary for his trade. An archer himself, he tests all his products. One of his bows was made in collaboration with designer Oskar Kogoj, and is now a part of his *Nature Design* collection. In addition to bows, Oblak also makes other technically accomplished wooden products, such as wooden cases.

MANY TYPES OF WOOD, MANY LIVES

JOINERY and CABINET-MAKING are not described in this book because they belong to the so-called "regular" trades, which are considered different from handicrafts for legal purposes. Slovene joinery, with its rich, centuries-old tradition and development, has always been recognized and admired at home and abroad for its outstanding quality. Two major joinery centres developed in the first half of the 19th century. One was Vižmarje near Šentvid pri Ljubljani (in the first half of the 19th century) and the other was in Solkan near Gorica (in the second half of the 19th century). They organized cooperatives in which numerous superb products were crafted. Interestingly enough, the activity of the cooperatives also extended to the organization of a rich social and cultural life. But these are only memories of the past, which has already been sufficiently researched and adequately presented. Their heritage still lives on in select workshops. Some of them have become true joiners' businesses, such as Mizarstvo Zalokar in Šentvid pri Ljubljani. A special discipline in joinery is cabinet-making. The few cabinet-makers still active mainly work on period furniture restoration; they also make complete or partial replicas of objects. The Zupan workshop in Žabjek near Ljubljana prides itself on a long cabinet-making tradition.

Because this is a book about handicrafts, the truly creative products of architect Janez Suhadolc, Professor at the Faculty of Architecture in Ljubljana, cannot be omitted. Suhadolc makes unique chairs in his own workshop. Each chair is a creative research project for Suhadolc. In addition to designing his products, he also takes into account the special needs of individual customers. In other words, he custom-makes each and every chair for its future owner. In this respect, Suhadolc continues and develops the basic concepts of the great Slovene architect Jože Plečnik. Suhadolc shows perfect mastery of his craft, since he pays attention to all aspects of production, from the concept, through technology and design, to the final product. Such mastery of all production phases by one individual is an exceptional phenomenon. In this day and age, more people often work in partnership to make first-class products.

The creation of original unique products with artistic value (from the concept to the final product) in the same workshop. These are unique items, as is further emphasized by their names and the fact that they were custom built for specific customers. ASTOL (Picture 1) is distinguished by an exceptional synthesis of shape and construction, HELIX (Picture 2) by prominent decorative details.

MANY TYPES OF WOOD, MANY LIVES

Individual periods of art have left their mark on historical memory, and even on specific items of the heritage testifying to the tastes of certain social groups. Individual art styles are thus also reflected in period furniture, which is still popular today. To some, living surrounded by items of a certain period style in this day and age is a challenge; for others they are part of their aesthetic horizon or a continuation of the family tradition. Some use them as status symbols to emphasize their social prestige. These are the reasons why cabinet-making concentrates on renovation, as well as the replication of period furniture (Zupan workshop, Ljubljana).

MANY TYPES OF WOOD, MANY LIVES

One of the peak achievements of traditional Slovene woodcrafts is the making of fiddles or other stringed instruments such as violins, violas and cellos. In this craft, extensive knowledge of the properties of wood must be topped by knowledge of its finest property - resonance. To gain this knowledge, the master makers of stringed instruments must have a detailed understanding of how the wood lives and knowledge of its growth. The first craftsmen to make stringed instruments were fiddle-makers, who first appeared in Slovenia after 1750. Between 1932 and 1940, a department at the former School of Arts and Crafts in Ljubljana specialized in making violins. A modern master fiddle-maker is Vilim Demšar from Ljubljana, who builds on his father's experience and carries on the fiddle-making tradition. His father, Blaž Demšar (1903 - 1981), was born in Selce near Škofja Loka, which at the time was a centre for coopers. Like his family, Demšar lived in the natural environment of wood and wood-working, and learnt all about the careful selection of spruce wood and its characteristics. This knowledge later proved useful for fiddle-making as well.

VILIM DEMŠAR

When talking about the quality of violins and other stringed instruments, mention is often made of high-quality wood that resonates. Of course, it is an important component of every instrument, but not the only one. As the saying goes, it is not the flour but the hand that makes the bread, and this also applies to violins, violas, cellos - in short, stringed instruments - which are created in the internationally acclaimed Demšar workshop in the centre of Old Ljubljana.

48

HANDICRAFTS OF SLOVENIA

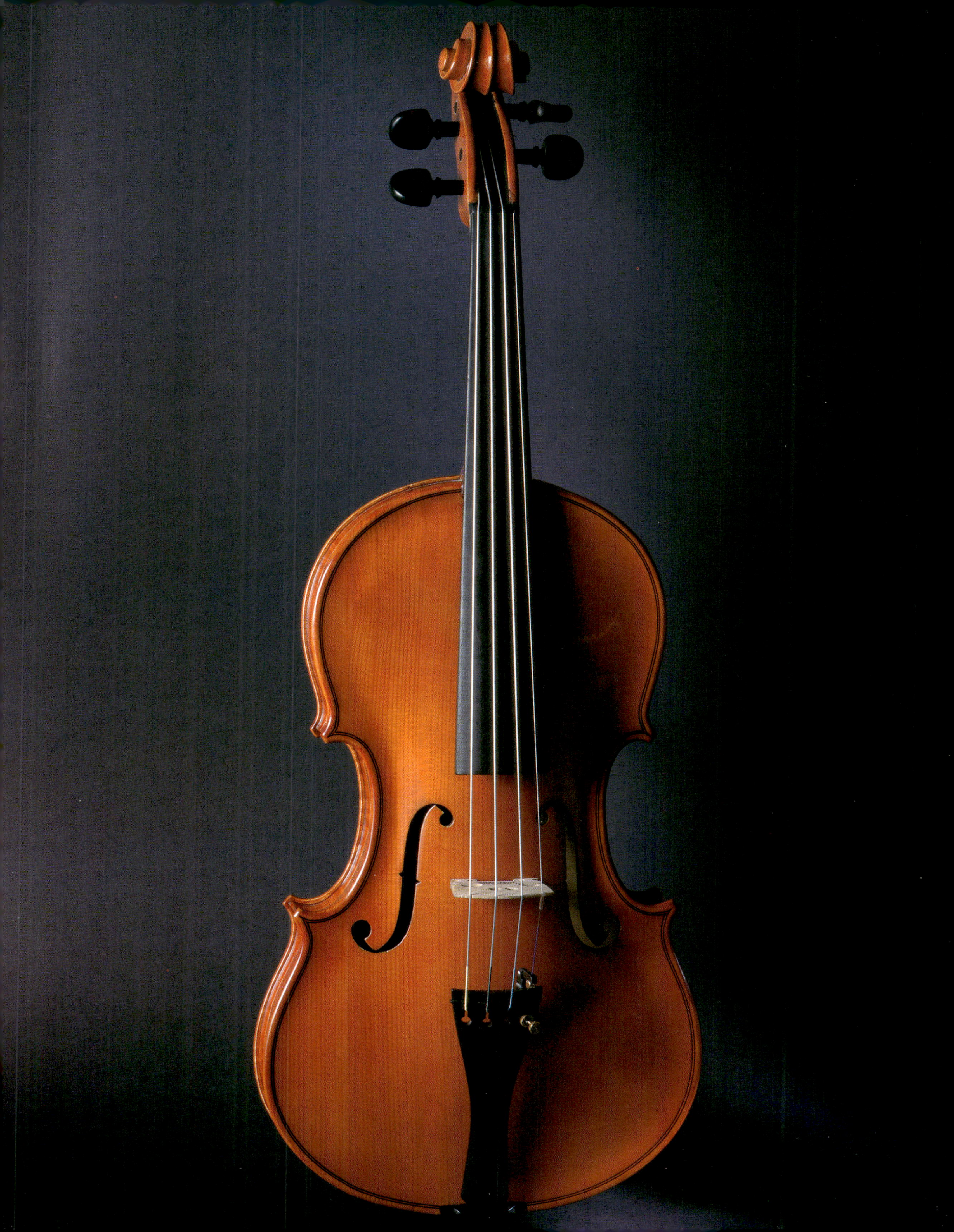

MANY TYPES OF WOOD, MANY LIVES

He started his professional life as a carpenter, and only later turned to making violins. Over the course of his life, Demšar made over six hundred stringed instruments, all of which produced the refined, particularly appreciated Italian sound. His son Vilim (b., 1937) learned the trade at his father's knee, and now excels in making not only violins but also other stringed instruments. His speciality is making small stringed instruments for children. He continues to perfect the sonority of the instruments by continuously introducing many original innovations. The latter make his instruments suitable even for soloist performances. One of his recent products, crafted in collaboration with designer Oskar Kogoj, must be mentioned here. On the 300th anniversary of the birth of the great violinist and composer from Piran, Giuseppe Tartini, Demšar and Kogoj designed a new type of violin. Kogoj's design concepts and Demšar's alterations in the inner construction resulted in a superb instrument in terms of quality of tone. Although completely new, the violin produces a sound equivalent to that of the most refined, two-hundred-year-old instruments.

Many types of wood, many lives

Time often seems to stand still in the modern, rushing world whenever we hear the wonderful sounds of a violin played by a virtuoso. Music relaxes us and makes us observe new dimensions and qualities we would normally never have noticed because of our busy daily lives. But do these thoughts not apply to violin-making, too? In the process of making a violin, time stops too, while the violin-maker discovers the stories and melodies already written in the wood of even growth in the individual elements, which he is assembling into a fine instrument. Making violins is a fascinating craft in which new sounds are born and gradually increased in intensity from the initial stages to the moment when the instrument comes alive in the hands of virtuosos. But the musicians only continue the work of geniuses of another type - the violin-makers.

Searching for resonance has been in the Demšar family for as long as they have worked with wood. The late Blaž Demšar learned about the sonority of wood from the local tradition of making casks in Selška dolina. Later, he used the extensive knowledge he had accumulated over the years to produce excellent stringed instruments.

And what exactly do cask-making and making violins have in common? If nothing else, coopers tested cask quality by knocking on it and then listening to the resonance, which was the only and the best indicator of wood quality.

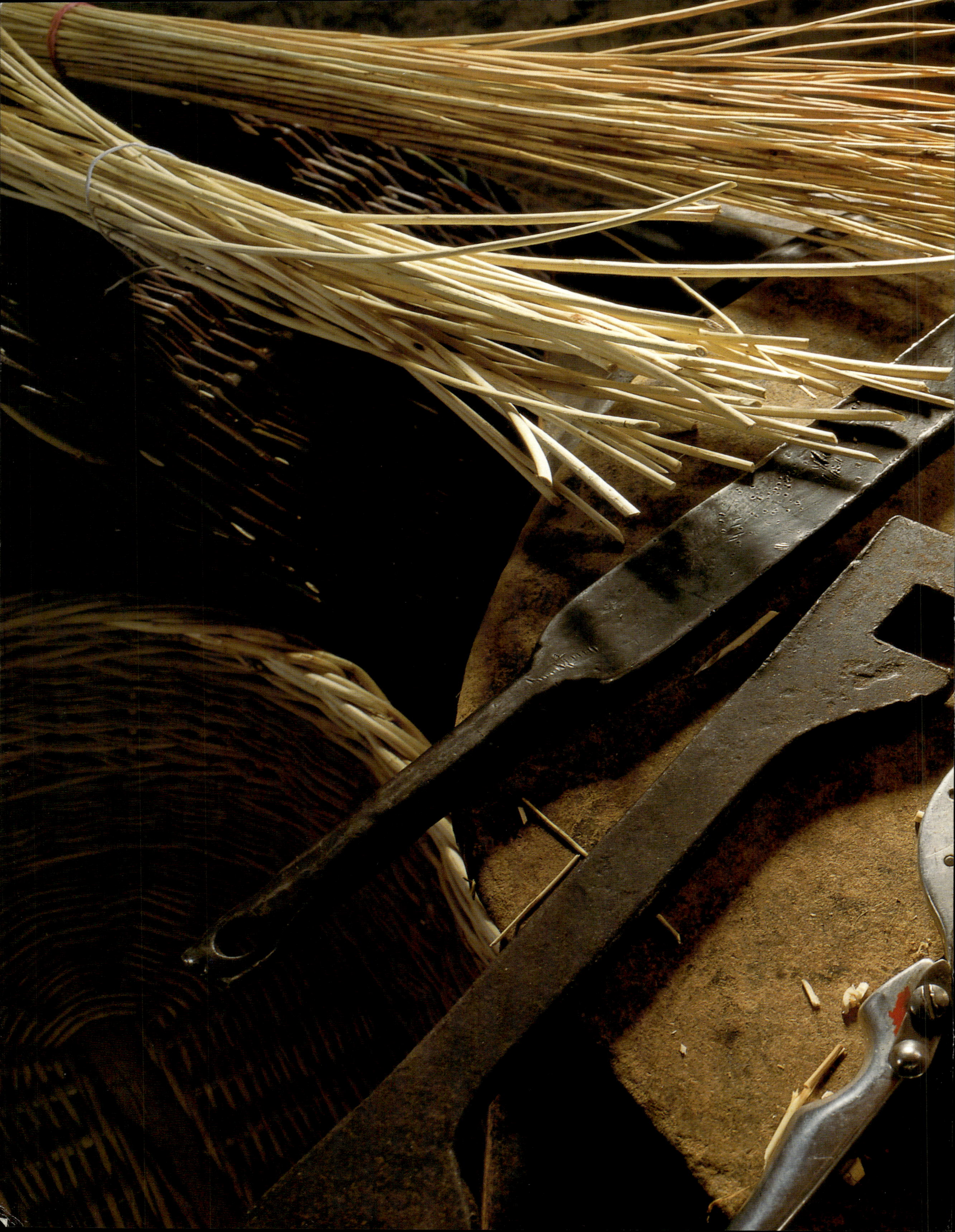

Cut by the Brook, Split Across the Knee

There is no finer example of man's symbiosis with nature than seeing the beauty of fresh osiers cut by a stream, woven in magnificent wicker products of highly varied patterns. Their rhythmic latticework creates a sense of measure, proportion and shape. In addition, weaving is a relaxing activity.

CUT BY THE BROOK, SPLIT ACROSS THE KNEE

Various types of rod, cane and wood shaving are the basic wickerwork materials in making wicker products and in Palm Sunday bundles at Easter time. The role of wickerwork in Slovenia today is somewhat paradoxical. There are actually many Slovene weavers who use natural materials to produce traditional wicker products. Nevertheless, the trade in general is poorly organized - in fact, it is the most unorganized handicraft in the country, despite its rich heritage. There are no organized weaving schools or courses, no expert research into its technologies, and no systematic plans for its improvement and development. Weaving is not included in the arts and crafts curriculum of primary education (there are less than a handful of weavers' clubs organized in Slovene primary schools). However, all these boast a vast experience and rich tradition in Slovenia. The extreme functionality of wicker products, which makes them useful in daily life, the relative simplicity of the basic weaving techniques, and systematic education in schools until World War II and some years after are the main reasons why weaving is still popular today. It is interesting to note that weaving wicker products is evenly distributed all over Slovenia due to the variety of materials available. One can even find weavers of wicker products in towns because of the availability of the raw products and even of the basic material – osiers require fairly little storage space. Because of its paradoxical, unorganized state today, however, the trend in the popularity of this craft might soon become negative, and weaving might start to decline.

CUT BY THE BROOK, SPLIT ACROSS THE KNEE

Modern Slovene artisans of this vital handicraft can be divided into two groups. The smaller includes the fairly rare weavers who gained their knowledge at special schools and courses before World War II and immediately after it. Most weavers, however, belong to the second group. They are amateurs who have learnt the trade from their predecessors through observation and imitation. Weavers from the first group are elderly, and their unused potential as media for transferring knowledge to younger weavers will soon be lost. In sharp contrast to the periods before World War II, there are no weavers' workshops in Slovenia today.

Earlier, I mentioned the rich heritage of Slovene weaving, especially regarding various forms of training for weavers. Most attention was paid to the development of handicrafts in the 19th century Habsburg Empire. Numerous regular weaving courses were organized in all of its many provinces, and training was supported by specialized textbooks and related literature, which has, sadly, not been saved to the present day. Along with these forms of education, a department for weavers was opened at the former Ljubljana School of Woodcrafts in the 1894/95 academic year. From 1908 to 1935, there was a National Weavers' School in Radovljica, and an institution with the same name continued work in Ptuj from 1928 to 1939. The latter was re-opened briefly after World War II, but eventually closed. Apart from these, there were also some smaller schools for weavers in Slovenia, and "travelling" courses in weaving. In the period between the two world wars, several businesses for the production of wicker products were established by trained weavers. Corresponding to the development of weaving, the growing of willow trees was also organized because one of the essential factors for the quality of wicker products is the quality of willow osiers. Willow trees were grown in special plantations to produce suitable material for weaving. We shall return to this subject later.

In the chapter on modern Slovene wicker craftsmen, selected artisans, famous for a wide selection of products of exceptional quality, are presented. Many of these weavers have exhibited their work in exhibitions of modern handicrafts in Slovenia and abroad. This means that we will not be discussing the usual, ordinary baskets, but a wide range of wicker masterpieces, superb in their crafting technology and design.

CUT BY THE BROOK, SPLIT ACROSS THE KNEE

Two types of basket: košara *and the two-handled* koš, *by Jože Javšnik, are typical wicker products of unwhitened willow osiers. Different natural bark colors enable the craftsman to create effective color patterns.*

The basic weaving materials of Slovene craftsmen is represented by a versatile selection of rods and pre-prepared wood. For domestic use, artisans use willow wood, cut from willow trees growing on the banks of brooks and rivers. This shows how individual handicrafts can positively contribute to the natural ecological balance. In the past, the cutting of fast-growing willow trees on the banks of brooks and rivers for weaving material took place annually. With cutting, the crafters also cleaned the riverbanks, thus preventing water from accumulating and flooding during periods of abundant rainfall. With the decreasing popularity of weaving, the banks of Slovene rivers and brooks are again overgrown with bushes.

Quality willow osiers, harvested from willow trees grown in special plantations, are essential for making good wicker products. A special farming discipline – growing willow trees - developed from growing willows for wicker products. Sadly, this belongs to history. The town of Notranje Gorice, on the outskirts of the Ljubljana marshes, was famous for its willow plantations, of which the Kozler plantation was the largest. Smaller willow tree plantations, scattered across Slovenia, mostly belonged to individual weavers' workshops or to the weavers. From the end of the 19th century, when the art of weaving baskets was at its peak, individual growers turned out annually as much as 15 tons of select willow osiers. These were also exported to Spain and Italy. The Slovene willow growers won a gold medal for the exceptional quality of their crop at the 1935 Thessaloniki exhibition. Since today Slovenia is trying to become recognizable by its specific trademarks, we tend to forget that even awards won in the past can contribute sigifreantly to gaining a modern reputation with a historical dimension.

The basic Slovene weaving materials are osiers cut from bushes and trees. Willow wood and hazel are most common, but weavers also use chestnut wood, spruce, beech and birch trees. Materials from plants such as cane or clematis are also used, and occasionally wheat straw and corn husking are used as well. Products from the last two materials are described in the following chapter. Thinner willow rods are used just cut, split or cleft. These semi-products of mostly willow or hazel wood are called *vitre (*osiers). Furthermore, some types of osiers are used plain (in their natural state, with bark retained), while others are whitened in a mechanical or heat-induced process. Harder varieties of wood or osiers (beech, chestnut, dogwood and others) are used for designing the basic frames in wickerwork products, and also for handles and connecting elements. Osiers from these varieties of wood are also used in their natural state or whitened, i. e. with their bark peeled off.

CUT BY THE BROOK, SPLIT ACROSS THE KNEE

Traditional weaving is one of Slovenia's most widespread handicrafts. But individual weavers mostly repeat historical memory-that is to say, they craft select, regionally different types of wicker product. Attempts to create new products of original design with consideration for traditional craft procedures are an exception to the rule. At present, this area is covered by amateur attempts, in which the products of Jože Javšnik represent the pinnacle.

JOŽE JAVŠNIK from Celje prefers plain, unwhitened willow osiers, and has developed weaving in this material to a high standard. Using different types of willow, he creates products of various colors resulting in ornamentally effective linear latticework. Whitened willow osiers are also used for weaving larger wicker products such as baskets for potato, fruit, seed, hay or leaves. Osiers are also used in two varieties: with a natural, white color, or browned by steam. That is why the latter type of osier is referred to as steamed willow osiers. Using dyed, whitened willow osiers is a recent fad, more popular abroad than in Slovenia, where it is only occasionally used by certain craftsmen.

CUT BY THE BROOK, SPLIT ACROSS THE KNEE

Heather, Indian millet and birch are also used for making brooms. Birch and heather brooms are used for the quick sweeping of surfaces of barns and yards, while those from Indian millet are used for sweeping indoor areas. In the surroundings of Ljubljana, **ALOJZ JERMAN** from Senožeti makes excellent birch brooms. **JOŽICA KONČAR** from Vnajnarje near Ljubljana is another well-known broom-maker. **FRANC KOŽELJ** from the village of Reva above Trebnje is one of the best-known wicker-weavers and weaving teachers in the Dolenjska region. In addition to other wicker products he also crafts brooms of Indian millet.

Franc Koželj from Reva above Trebnje in the Dolenjska region makes various types of basket, the most representative of which are: korba, *(a larger basket),* poltr *(an oval, two-handled basket) intended for carrying firewood, and* koš *(a larger strapped basket) for carrying hay and leaves. Today, all three products are assigned new functions outside of the environment in which they were originally made and used.*

CUT BY THE BROOK, SPLIT ACROSS THE KNEE

1

2

Brooms of Indian millet and birch branches are also typical wicker products. These ancestors of modern vacuum cleaners are still universal devices for indoor and outdoor sweeping. For the latter, sturdy birch brooms are used. Their quality depends on how well the branches have been tied or fastened together, their elasticity and branch-length. The brooms were crafted by weavers Alojz Jerman (Picture 1), and Jožica Končar (Picture 2).

CUT BY THE BROOK, SPLIT ACROSS THE KNEE

Slovene wicker-weavers offer a wide selection of products. I have already pointed out the variety of materials which contribute to this versatility. However, the different forms and uses of these products must also be mentioned. Many traditional wicker products are assigned new functional meanings and roles today. At the turn of this century, a chronicler of Slovene handicrafts contended that **JERBAS** (round baskets with a flat bottom and small handles) and **KOŠARA** or **KORBA** small baskets were the most typical products of Slovene wicker-weavers. Of course, this statement is inaccurate. Slovene weavers also commonly crafted different types of basket, furniture and other elements for interiors (such as hangers), and even prams and bassinets. Making wicker-covers for bottles was another typical weaver's craft, which is not surprising in a country with a well-developed viniculture and viticulture. Wicker-covered bottles appear as craftsmen's supplements to wine production, just as in making casks. Today, the range of wicker products is much smaller than in the past, but it is still wide enough to reflect various local and regional differences.

Wreathed products by Alojz Možina from the village of Sabonje near Ilirska Bistrica.

CUT BY THE BROOK, SPLIT ACROSS THE KNEE

Branko Jazbec connects beke, *the elements forming the bottom of a basket* (žbrince), *with metal rings. These rings were originally made of dogwood.*

The typology of wickerwork products from the Karst region is fairly modest, but not lacking in quality. All Karst wicker products are extremely durable. That is due to the types of plant endemic to the Mediterranean which are used for weaving. The Karst weavers make excellent baskets and wicker-covered bottles. **ALOJZ MOŽINA** from the village of Sabonje near Ilirska Bistrica specializes in making wicker-covers for bottles, while **BRANKO JAZBEC** from the village of Sveto near Komen makes *žbrince* - strapped baskets for carrying on the back, formerly used in every Karst household for gathering hay and leaves. Such baskets are woven from hoops of fresh ash wood, but he also uses hazel, elm or white beech wood. The hoops are fastened in place by *beke*, willow osiers normally used for binding vines.

Cut by the brook, split across the knee

Several excellent weavers are still active in the Gorenjska region. This relatively large number of weavers is connected with the local weaving tradition, which culminated in the national Weavers' School in Radovljica. A native of this town, **Marjan Golmajer**, weaves superb wicker baskets from osiers of different colors. **Matija Zupan** from Srednja Bela near Preddvor is a master weaver, too. He makes wicker products typical of his region. These include baskets with two handles called *cambohi*, other types of wicker baskets such as *korbe* (larger wicker baskets), *škundre*, and strapped baskets, carried on the back, called *koši*.

Marjan Golmajer

Marjan Golmajer from Radovljica weaves top-notch wicker products from osiers of various colors. He makes baskets for different shapes and purposes, small one-handled baskets, umbrella stands, laundry baskets and shallow baskets called peharji *among others. With his sense of design and the balanced, rhythmic variations of weave, Golmajer is a master weaver.*

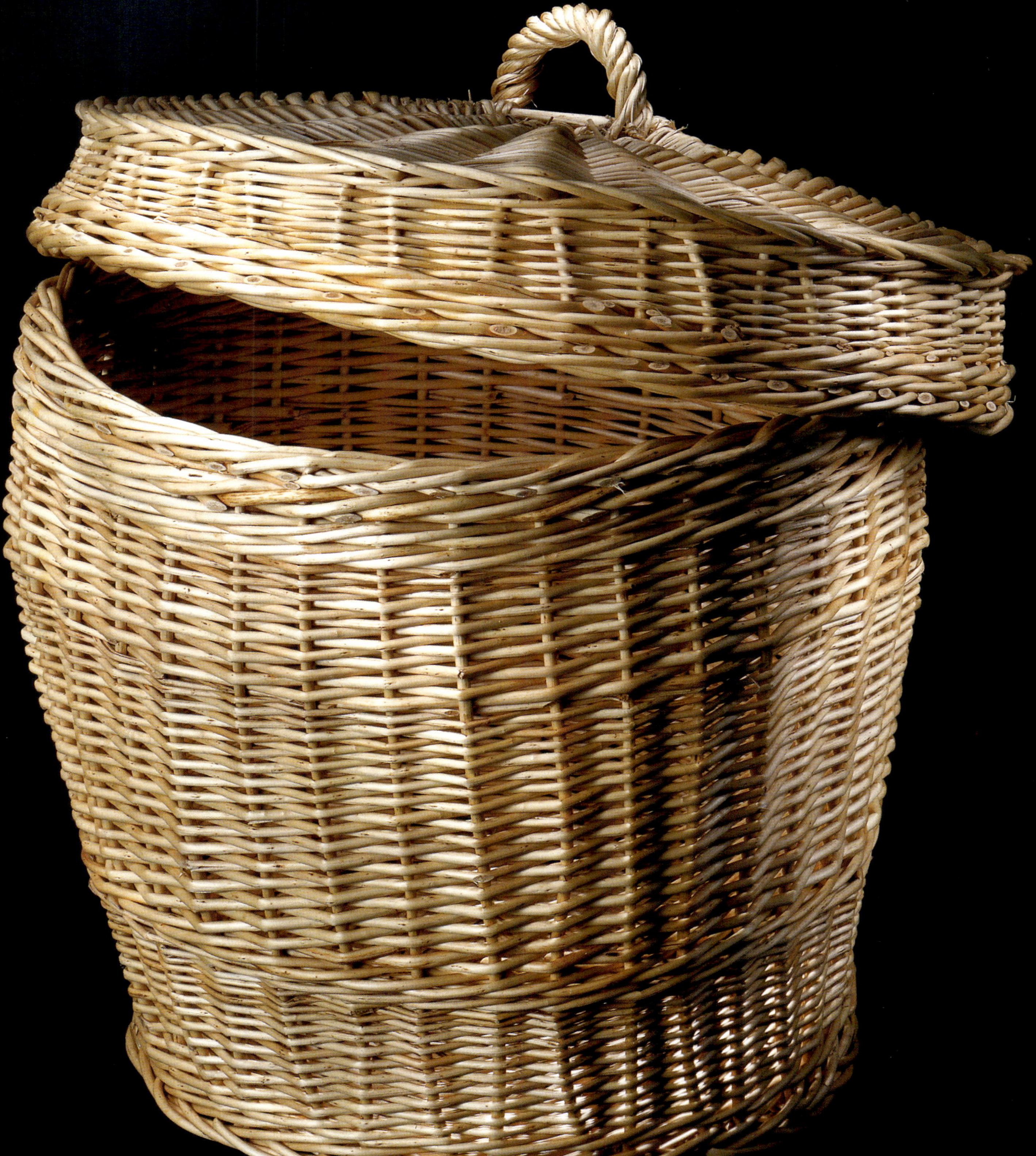

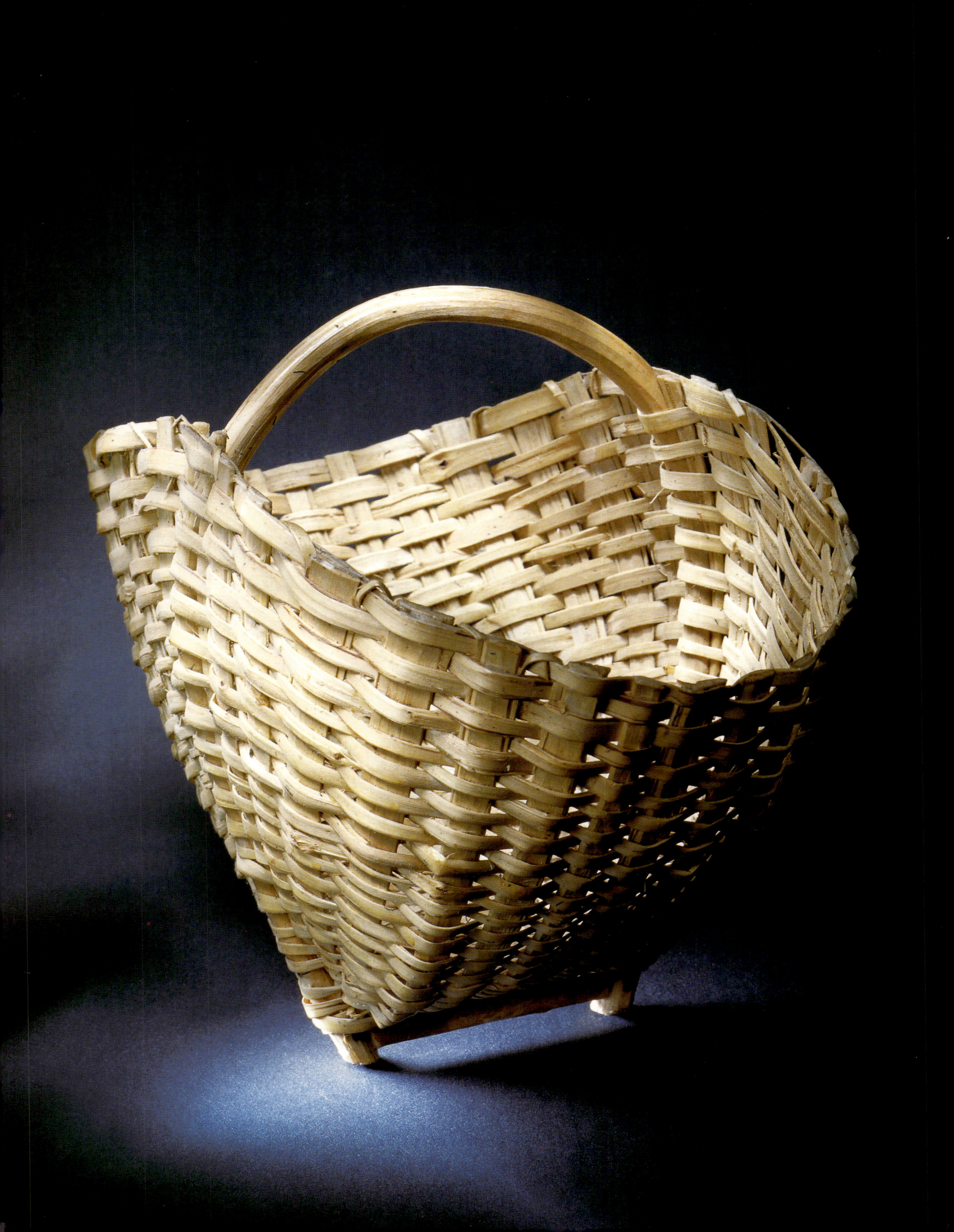

CUT BY THE BROOK, SPLIT ACROSS THE KNEE

MATIJA ZUPAN

Matija Zupan from Srednja Bela near Preddvor also teaches weaving to future young weavers as part of his career. He occasionally heads a weavers' club at the local primary school, organized for children eight years old and above. In 1990 the school's weavers' club was 24 pupils strong, which is a very encouraging number if we keep in mind the general neglect of handicraft training in Slovene schools.

CUT BY THE BROOK, SPLIT ACROSS THE KNEE

There are many weavers even on the outskirts of Ljubljana, especially in the rural hillsides towards the north-east. The exceptional weaver **TONČKA JEMEC** lives in a small village called Petelinje near Dol, on the road towards Litija. She commands an extensive knowledge of her craft, and was the first weaver to start courses of weaving at the local primary school more than a decade ago. That was unique in Slovenia for some time, but eventually more schools followed suit. In 1996 Jemec made an enlarged woven rosary for Pope John Paul II. Exceptionally skilled, Jemec can weave more demanding wicker products such as *cekarji* (two-handled bags), cases and similar products. **ALOJZ ZAVIRŠEK** from Šmarje–Sap also creates a wide selection of wicker products. Several other weavers from the Ljubljana region craft excellent wicker products. Their modern wicker masterpieces can be seen at the annual exhibitions in Zadvor near Sostro; however, they are very difficult to find in specialized gift shops in Ljubljana or its surrounding area. Several weavers from the wider Ljubljana area use wheat straw as their basic weaving material. Their work is presented in the next chapter.

Tončka Jemec uses evenly split, handled, whitened willow and hazelnut osiers in weaving. She usually adorns her wicker products with a line of osiers dyed in shades of red or green. She learned weaving from her parents, who in turn learned it from their parents, who still had the opportunity to get special weavers' training at organized weavers' courses headed by state-employed weaving teachers who traveled through the entire Habsburg Empire. Thus Dolsko and the surrounding areas developed into strong weavers' centers, and weaving was a welcome additional source of income of the local rural populace.

CUT BY THE BROOK, SPLIT ACROSS THE KNEE

Various types of one- or two-handled basket, differing in shape and, even more, in name can be found in Slovenia. As a consequence of many regional dialects, several local names were given to the same type of basket. Alojz Zaviršek from Šmarje–Sap makes all basic types of basket, (korba, ritaša, pleter, polter, cajna) characteristic mainly of the eastern and south-eastern parts of Slovenia.

CUT BY THE BROOK, SPLIT ACROSS THE KNEE

Weaving osiers around bottles (or wreathing) has a functional as well as decorative value. It has developed along with wine-growing in areas with well-developed viniculture. The quality of wreathed bottles is determined by judging the firmness of the weaving, which protects the fragile glass bottles from breaking. Some weavers make small openings in the weaving just below the neck of the bottle to make pouring easier. The picture shows Štefan Kalšek, master weaver of wreathed bottles.

Many local weavers still work in the hills around Litija and Zasavje. A whole range of weaving techniques has been preserved in the predominantly rural Posavje region. **ZVONKO KOSTEVC,** from Planina near Sevnica outside the Posavje region, makes various wicker baskets, and I have already mentioned Celje weaver Jože Javšnik from the central part of the Štajerska region. **ŠTEFAN KALŠEK** is a weaver from Žiče, a town also renowned for its monastery. Kalšek's wicker products could effectively round up the range of local souvenirs connected with the renewal of the monastery. The importance of this institution in the Middle Ages was internationally recognized in 1997, when the entire project for monastery renovation project was awarded the Henry Ford European Conservation Award.

CUT BY THE BROOK, SPLIT ACROSS THE KNEE

Janez Zupan from Zaloka near Šentrupert in the Dolenjska region proves that weaving is suitable for the disabled, too. His the wicker products are of exceptional quality. In addition to the wicker products presented in the picture, he also makes various types of custom-woven baskets. These include small baskets for filtering wine, and baskets for carrying fire-wood. His most interesting product is a basket intended for picking blackberries and other forest fruits: it has a pointed bottom, which allows the picker to thrust it firmly into the ground.

The suggest that weavers of traditional wicker products mostly ply their craft in the remote, underdeveloped parts of Slovenia is inaccurate. Zvonko Kostevc from Planina near Sevnica (see the picture) is one of the many craftsmen from one such region, but a substantial number of weavers also work in boroughs and on the outskirts of larger towns.

69

HANDICRAFTS OF SLOVENIA

CUT BY THE BROOK, SPLIT ACROSS THE KNEE

1

2 3

Prlekija is a region where several good craftsmen live. Some of them are exceptional masters of weaving, who build upon their extensive knowledge in attempts at "design", even though only by alternating weaving styles and the colour of osiers. Janko Zabavnik's baskets, called korpe and korpflaše - wreathed wine bottles (Pictures 1, 3), and Jože Duh's miniature wicker products (Picture 2) are often displayed at arts and crafts and tourist exhibitions.

CUT BY THE BROOK, SPLIT ACROSS THE KNEE

Weaving is also well developed in north-eastern Slovenia, in Prlekija. There, and in Prekmurje, wicker products are sold in the souvenir shops of local health resorts. Three of the numerous local weavers deserve to be mentioned because of their outstanding products. They are: **JANKO ZABAVNIK** from the vicinity of Ljutomer, **MILAN PETEK** from Bučkovci, and **JOŽE DUH** from Grabe. The latter is famous for excellent miniatures of wicker baskets.

Milan Petek from Bučkovci is a master weaver. In addition to crafting traditional wicker products (baskets), he also continues to develop by making wicker furniture (tables, chairs). Making wicker furniture was a highly evolved craft in Slovenia up until World War II, and the techniques used in weaving furniture were taught in weaving schools and courses. After World War II, this type of weaving was completely neglected, and no attempts were made to work according to the trends of modern design.

The traditional exhibitions of arts and crafts in Slovenj Gradec are important for the wider Slovene area, but also exert a strong local influence. This tradition has encouraged several individuals from the Mislinjska valley, the wider Koroška region and Pohorje to again take up wickerwork, either as an additional source of income or a sole occupation. Weaver **Ivan Kašnik** from Slovenj Gradec weaves excellent baskets from hazel osiers, modelling them after traditional baskets. Two other craftsmen, **Ignac Kustec** and **Jože Omerzu** from Lovrenc na Pohorju, are also master weavers. Kustec annually weaves about eighty wicker baskets from rods of *pintavec* trees. Omerzu learned weaving in his birthplace of Bizeljsko, where weaving baskets and other wicker products was a typical winter pastime for men. While the men wove baskets, women kept them company by singing. Around Easter, baskets for carrying food to church in order to be blessed, called *žogjenki* or *žognjiči*, typical of this part of Pohorje, are still made. They are oval baskets with concave centers, wooden bottoms, spruce wood frames, and sides shaped from whitened hazel osiers.

Ivan Kašnik from Slovenj Gradec makes baskets of varied sizes (košare), *and round baskets with flat bottoms and small handles called* jerbasi *from whitened hazel osiers. He achieves a great artistic and decorative effect by alternating the weave of the osiers. From the technological aspect, his wicker products are also distinguished by strong firmness, which is one of the key factors in their durability.*

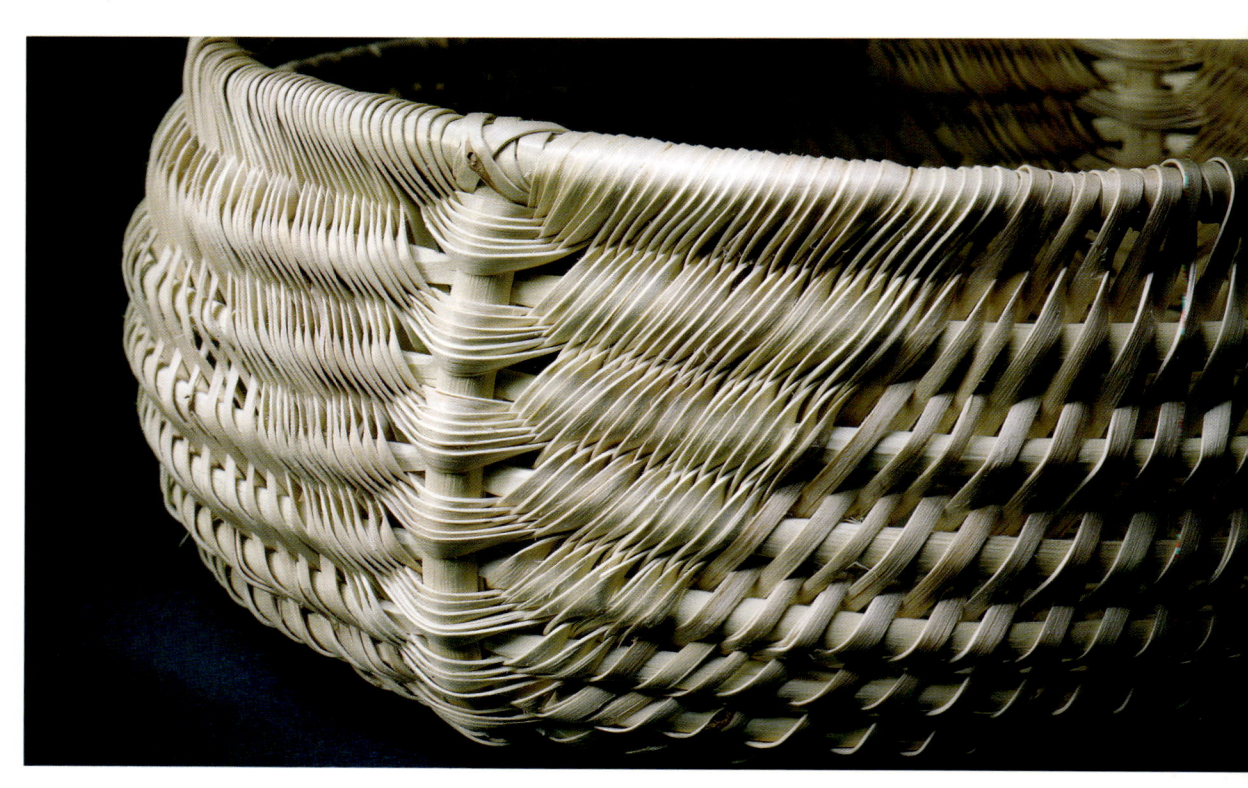

CUT BY THE BROOK, SPLIT ACROSS THE KNEE

Weavers Ignac Kustec (Picture 1) and Jože Omerzu (Pictures 2, 3) find enough weaving materials for their products locally, on the Pohorje Massif.

CUT BY THE BROOK, SPLIT ACROSS THE KNEE

Finally, we come to the Dolenjska region, where weaving is still best developed and preserved. The weavers from Trebnje and Mirna have founded a local weaver's society, which organizes several weaving courses and clubs, which successfully train younger weavers. There are many master-weavers in the vicinity of Trebnje, which is one of the important local weaving centers. The weavers include: **Franc Koželj** from Reva, already mentioned; **Ana Marija Klančičar** from Dolenjske Toplice who wreathes bottles and weaves excellent baskets, locally called *procke)*; **Janez Hočevar** from Škocjan; **Anton Gorenec** from Dolenja Nemška vas near Trebnje, and **Janez Zupan** from Zaloka near Šentrupert. These are all masters of their trade.

Ana Marija Klančičar weaves procke (baskets with one handle, used for picking fruit, potatoes and diverse garden vegetables). In addition to this traditional use, her products are given new functions in other, especially urban milieus today.

CUT BY THE BROOK, SPLIT ACROSS THE KNEE

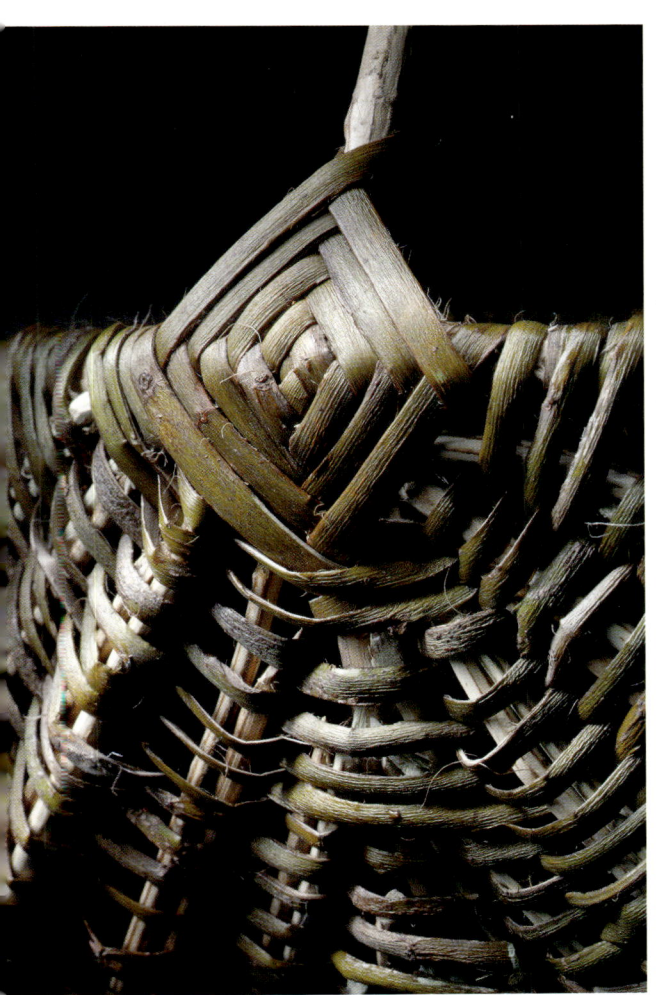

The wicker products of individual weavers often reflect the natural and working conditions of a region. Larger baskets used for transporting hay, grass or leaves are often adapted to the natural surroundings they are used in, which also conditions the manner of carrying them. Those with straps can be carried on the back, while one- or two-handled baskets are used to carry goods over shorter distances. Anton Gorenec from Dolenja Nemška vas near Trebnje makes such baskets.

CUT BY THE BROOK, SPLIT ACROSS THE KNEE

Janez Hočevar from Škocjan in the Dolenjska region makes excellent cekarji *(narrow two-handled bags), baskets with one handle, and* jerbasi *(shallow, wide baskets). All three types are distinguished by admirable material preparation and craftsmanship, and are suitable for use on special occasions, especially at Eastertime, when the baskets are filled with Easter food and taken to the church to be blessed. These and other quality wicker products are frequently used as packaging for original business and state gifts.*

76

HANDICRAFTS OF SLOVENIA

Several local names were given to the same types of basket. Thus, convex baskets made in the Ribnica valley were nicknamed *ritaše* because of the two bulges very similar to the human backside (in colloquial Slovene called *rit)*. A popular type of basket in this region is the square-shaped basket with woven handles, and with rims painted in floral motives. They are called *holandarce* (Dutch baskets). The origin of the name has not yet been satisfactorily explained. It is possible that such baskets were imported to these parts through trade with Holland, or that this particular basket shape was invented in the Netherlands.

Rods are also the primary materials used for making **Palm Sunday bundles**. Fresh green rods are combined with other decorations and assembled into bundles rather than woven. These bundles have different regional names: *butara*, *potica*, *prajtelj* and *beganca* to name a few. The bundles were normally crafted at home and then taken to church to be blessed on Palm Sunday. This custom is rooted in pre-Christian times, when our ancient ancestors believed in demons of fertility which demanded offerings every spring. Among the many types and shapes of Palm Sunday bundles, those from the surroundings of Ljubljana are special, even though they are the most recent in origin. The bundling technique used is so intricate that one can justifiably call it a handicraft. Several families on the outskirts of Ljubljana make them for sale. This started in World War I and reached a real boom in the 1930s. The uniqueness of the **Ljubljana bundles** (*Ljubljanske butarice*) lies in the material they are made of. The locals from the villages of Dobrunje, Sveti Urh, Janče and Sostro make them from fresh spring greenery and adorn them with natural or dyed wood shavings. The established colors of the wood shavings are red, white and blue, which are the colors of the Slovene flag; but today, other colors are also introduced. There are two ways to make a Ljubljana-style Palm Sunday bundle from wood shavings. Each piece of wood shaving is either rolled into a cone or simply bent in a semi-circle and then attached to the bundle. The craftsmen of the **Mrvar family** from Dobrunje are famous for their superbly crafted and decorated Palm Sunday bundles. They have developed new wood-shaving decoration techniques. They use spruce wood shavings to make other decorative items, such as bowls, Christmas tree decorations, signs for wine-shops, high-quality packaging shaped like beehives called *koši*, used for storing mead bottles, and so on.

Cut by the brook, split across the knee

In other parts of Slovenia, Palm Sunday bundles are only made in small numbers for home use and are not sold for profit. Their size and shape vary greatly. The bundles from Ljubno on the Savinja river, nicknamed *potice*, are most extraordinary. They are types of sculpture, depicting farming tools and objects, objects for personal use, sketches from daily life or religious motifs. They are made from fresh greenery, rods, bark, fruits and other natural materials available in springtime. The motifs differ every year, making the bundles a gallery of Easter season folk art.

Of course, there are many rules-of-thumb regarding the number of types of wood which make up the bundles in most of Slovenia. In certain parts of the country, seven types of wood are used as a reminder of the seven sacraments. Elsewhere, it is customary to include in the bundle rods of all types of trees growing on a particular estate. Making Palm Sunday bundles is an exceptionally vivid and constantly evolving activity. Therefore, it is impossible to say that the shaping and techniques of making bundles represent replication or a repetition of historical memory; but, as a craft, it is constantly and vitally improved by new approaches.

The Mrvar family were the first makers of Palm Sunday bundles (picture left), and almost the only craftsmen who have tried to adjust their ample expertise in preparing, assembling, rolling and bending wood shavings to the design of new products. They first studied and tested the new technologies and the application of them in crafting new products. Today, they craft functional objects such as baskets and dishes from bent wood shavings, as well as Christmas tree decorations and exquisite business gifts, which introduce the receiver of the gift to the richness of, the noble material of wood.

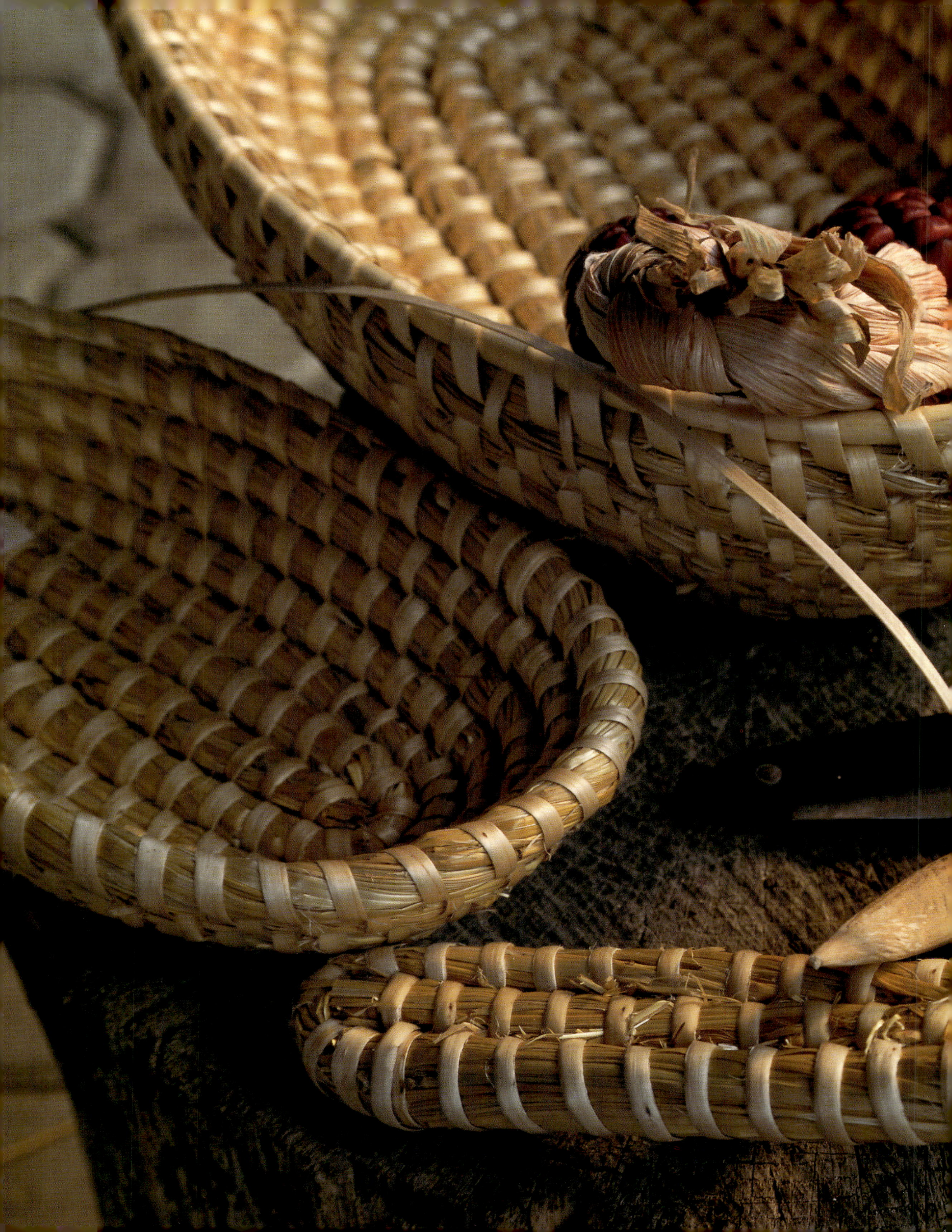

Straw is Woven, the Grain Turns into Bread

Wheat straw can also be used as a primary material for craftsmen. But modern harvesting techniques (types of wheat and ways of storing it) often see straw as waste material. Formerly a typical by-product, straw must be specially processed to be suitable for weaving products today. But, all in all, bread has also changed…

STRAW IS WOVEN, THE GRAIN TURNS INTO BREAD

In describing the changes in growing and harvesting wheat, we must not unduly generalize. The above thought may hold true only for the crafting of individual products. Such products are, for example, straw dishes and other household items. However, straw used for handicraft purposes is a totally different matter. It is represented by a purposeful, directed handicraft discipline - making straw-hats. High-quality straw is necessary for the production of quality straw products. This was first realized and recorded at the end of the 18th century. At that time, a special variety of straw was grown in Tuscany exclusively for weaving.

Various types of straw, especially rye and wheat straw, are used in weaving straw dishes, bags and hats. **THATCHING ROOFS** is a discipline directly linked to the use of straw because both use the same material. Today, the covering of straw roofs is a handicraft which demands the special preparation of the material because of the changes in agricultural technology. Thatching has become an independent craft only in the last few decades. As was the case with shingle-roofing, thatching was once considered a chore each house owner had to do on his own or in collaboration with his neighbors. Today, thatching roofs also demands special straw preparation. The wheat must be harvested at the right time, and the sheaves must be threshed manually with a flail. Straw trusses are then ready for thatching.

Classical roof-thatching is carried out on certain special buildings which belong to the national architectural heritage. The demand for thatchers' services outside of this domain is connected with the special wishes of clients who would like to have their garden sheds or country houses thatched.

STRAW IS WOVEN, THE GRAIN TURNS INTO BREAD

There are only a few modern thatchers in Slovenia. Through their actions they help to preserve older buildings which form part of architectural heritage of Slovenia. Furthermore, these thatchers also satisfy the demands of those who wish to have their holiday homes, garden sheds and "meditation" huts thatched. Of course, these actions and wishes often have more of a status than a functional nature. The tearing out of just one element of culture from its historical and functional context (in this case, a thatched roof) is extremely irresponsible behaviour. Thatching the roofs of houses - where straw is used as a noble material, used to form wholesome, above all different, alternative living concepts - is an entirely different matter. Over the centuries, at least three or four different techniques for thatching roofs have developed in Slovenia. The differences are in how the edges at the gutters are formed, and in how the roofs are waterproofed at the ridges. As has already been mentioned, roofs is a unique handicraft skill or profession today, which only few individuals still master. They include **Franc Barbič** from Hrastek near Podbočje in Dolenjska, who regularly works on restoration and maintenance projects for buildings which form part of the Slovene architectural heritage.

STRAW IS WOVEN, THE GRAIN TURNS INTO BREAD

Weaving straw is part of the weaver's craft. Various products used to be made from straw trusses tied together with thin hazel osiers. According to some experts they were made using one of the oldest weaving technologies. In this way, sowing baskets, oval bread baskets, baskets for storing grains and fruit *(bednji)*, beehives, measuring cups for grain other products were made. The range of woven straw products is much less extensive than it was in the past, but there still are some craftsmen around Slovenia who have mastered straw-weaving. Master craftsmanship in weaving straw is not only exemplified by the shape or size of the products but also through their firmness, and through the way in which the straw is tied in specific shapes. There are known examples in which some weavers have tested their products by filling them with water. Water should not leak from quality woven products.

There are several master craftsman of straw products in the wider Ljubljana area. **FRANC JERIHA** from Prežganje makes various types of basket, such as *sejalnice* (round or oval straw baskets used for sowing), *peharji* (shallow, round, straw baskets) and *stručnice* (oval, straw dishes used to raise bread). **FRANČIŠKA VRBINC** from Dobrunje regularly displays her products at arts and crafts exhibitions in Zadvor near Ljubljana.

The pehar *(a shallow, slightly convex basket) and* stručnica *(a shallow, oval basket) are the most representative straw products, made of tightly tied or bound wheat stalks. Traditionally, both were used in bread preparation. The* pehar *was also used for storing various fruits, seeds or grains, and dried fruit. Jožef Mišica from Črnomelj in the Bela krajina region is a proficient maker of these products.*

STRAW IS WOVEN, THE GRAIN TURNS INTO BREAD

Experienced weaver Franc Jeriha from Prežganje near Ljubljana makes shallow, slightly convex baskets – peharji *and* štručnice *(formerly used for raising bread), and* sejalnice *(oval sowing baskets). The latter are bulged at one side, and used for sowing the field, as their name suggests. Their distinctive shape, which in its basic form reminds us of a grain of bean, is remarkably ergonomic, and is adapted for carrying in one hand, leaving the other free for sowing.*

STRAW IS WOVEN, THE GRAIN TURNS INTO BREAD

Frančiška Vrbinc

Frančiška Vrbinc crafts peharji *and* sejalnice *in Dobrunje near Ljubljana. Today, the sowing baskets have been given alternative uses because sowing has mostly become automated. Sejalnice became decorative objects because of their exceptional shape, and are often found in specialized gift shops and shops for interior decoration items.* Peharji *are also used for decoration today, in addition to their primary function as baskets in which bread dough was raised.*

86

HANDICRAFTS OF SLOVENIA

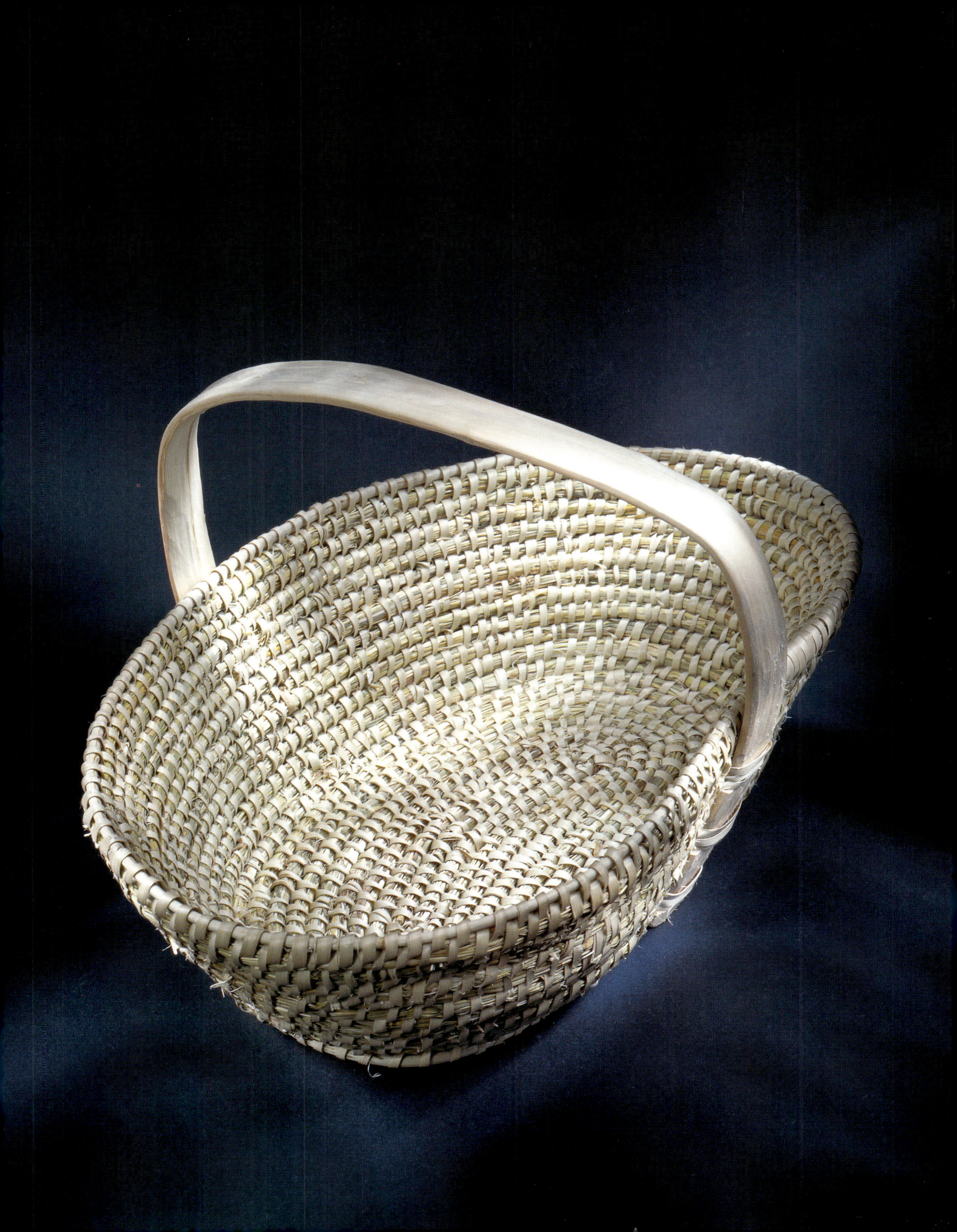

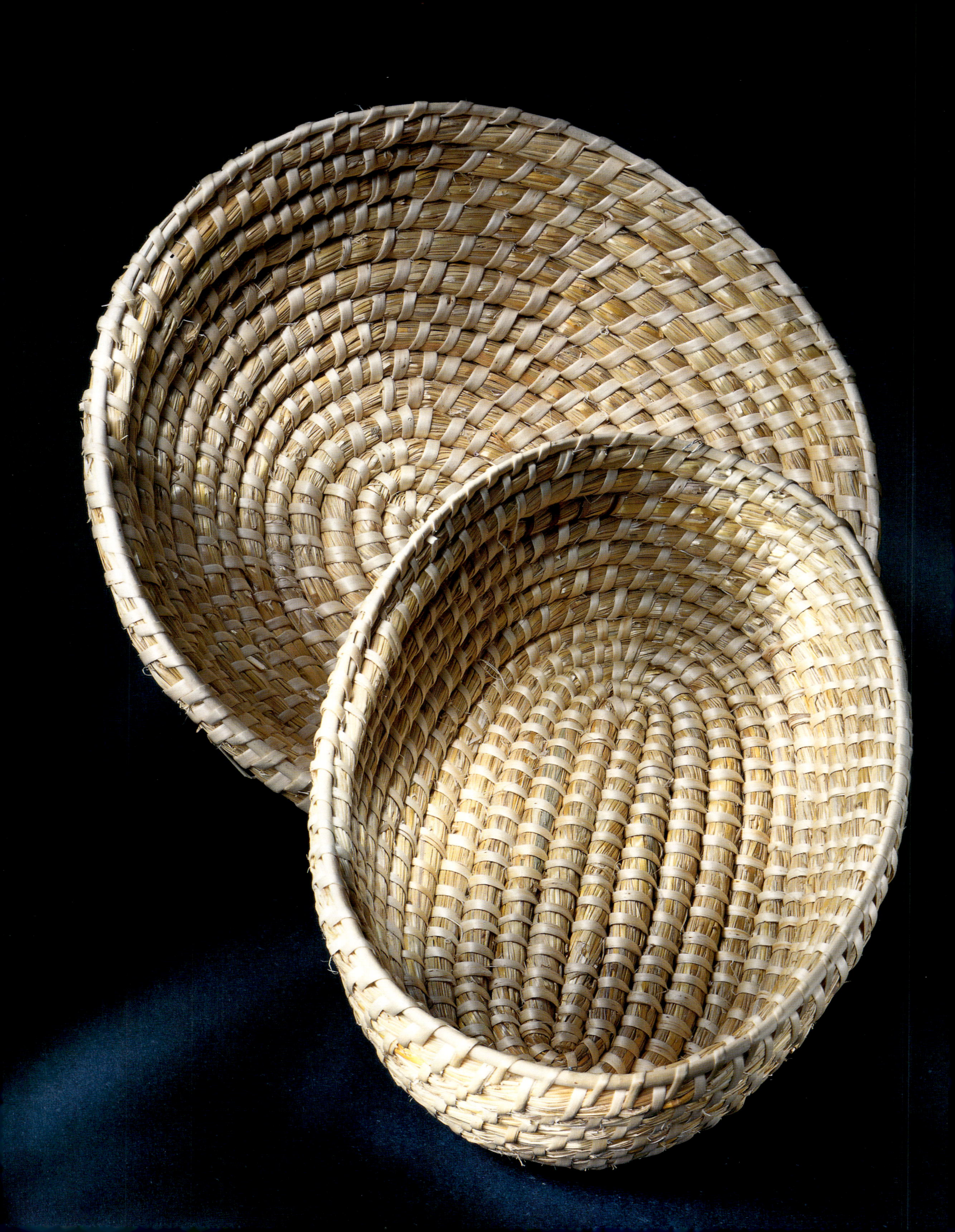

STRAW IS WOVEN, THE GRAIN TURNS INTO BREAD

Two more excellent craftsmen weave straw products in Dolenjska and Bela krajina.

Anton Zakrajšek from Migolica near Mirna in Dolenjska makes superb straw products, including containers with lids, which were once used for storing grain, beans, nuts and various other crops.

Jožef Mišica from Črnomelj is famous for his *peharji* - shallow, round, straw baskets of different sizes.

Anton Zakrajšek

Anton Zakrajšek (born in 1960) belongs to the younger generation of weavers. He has greatly contributed to the revival of straw-weaving in the regions of Trebnje and Mirna. Some years ago, Zakrajšek was one of the founders of the local Weavers' Society, the only one of its type in the country. Establishing craft societies is necessary and appropriate for the future preservation of other handicrafts. Zakrajšek's straw products are indeed superb. The prime feature of these woven products is the design of straw dishes, which centuries ago proved indispensable for storing grain and various crops.

89
HANDICRAFTS OF SLOVENIA

STRAW IS WOVEN, THE GRAIN TURNS INTO BREAD

VERONIKA STARIN from Bišče near Domžale and **MATILDA PROSENC** from Vir near Domžale are the last makers of straw hats, a trade that developed in the 18th century as a supplementary economic activity carried out at home. It consisted of two basic phases. The first phase was the plaiting of straw braids; the second involved sewing and designing the braids into straw hats and, later, straw bags. The making of straw hats first started in Ihan and then spread to the neighboring areas of Kamnik, Menges and Domžale, as well as to some villages in the Zasavje region. Most of the local populace in these areas had been involved in making straw hats and bags in the past. The rapid development of this handicraft must have been influenced by extensive contacts with the Tyrol region, where straw hat-making developed before it reached Slovenia. Later, straw hat-making factories appeared, which preserved a part of the domestic production process because the people plaited straw braids at home. During the period between the two wars straw-weaving began to decline, and after World War II it completely died out. Therefore, Starin and Prosenc are the last weavers of straw who make only one type of straw product, which is still much appreciated and is a renowned Slovene feature known abroad. This is known as *kranjski*, *domžalski* or *mengeški cekar*, a narrow, two-handled bag, made by plaiting straw braids of varying colors into characteristic patterns.

VERONIKA STARIN

The owner's insignia, or Christ's initials, are also plaited into the pattern on the bag. This bag (*cekar*) was already a regular part of the Slovene national costume or formal attire in the period between the two world wars. Due to the lack of expert care after World War II, it became something of a national stereotype. Because of this, various popular folk music bands make it part of their wardrobe image. We have also missed a great opportunity in this handicraft field because no one has yet attempted to design new, modern, fashionable, familiar solutions which would be based on products from the Slovene heritage of straw-weaving.

Cekarji (narrow two-handled bags) made of straw braids of various colors are comparable to straw hats, because both were perfected by weavers of straw products. Making straw braids, bags and hats was formerly one of the most popular handicrafts in farming households around Kamnik, Menges and Domžale. Today only two makers of straw products continue the rich local tradition. Veronika Starin is one of the most esteemed weavers for the preservation of this craft to the present day.

Matilda Prosenc is one of the older makers of narrow, two-handled straw bags, which are known as kranjski, domžalski *or* mengeški cekar. *This type of bag has become a necessary accessory of Slovene folk costumes, but sadly no modern design approaches to crafting it have yet been developed.*

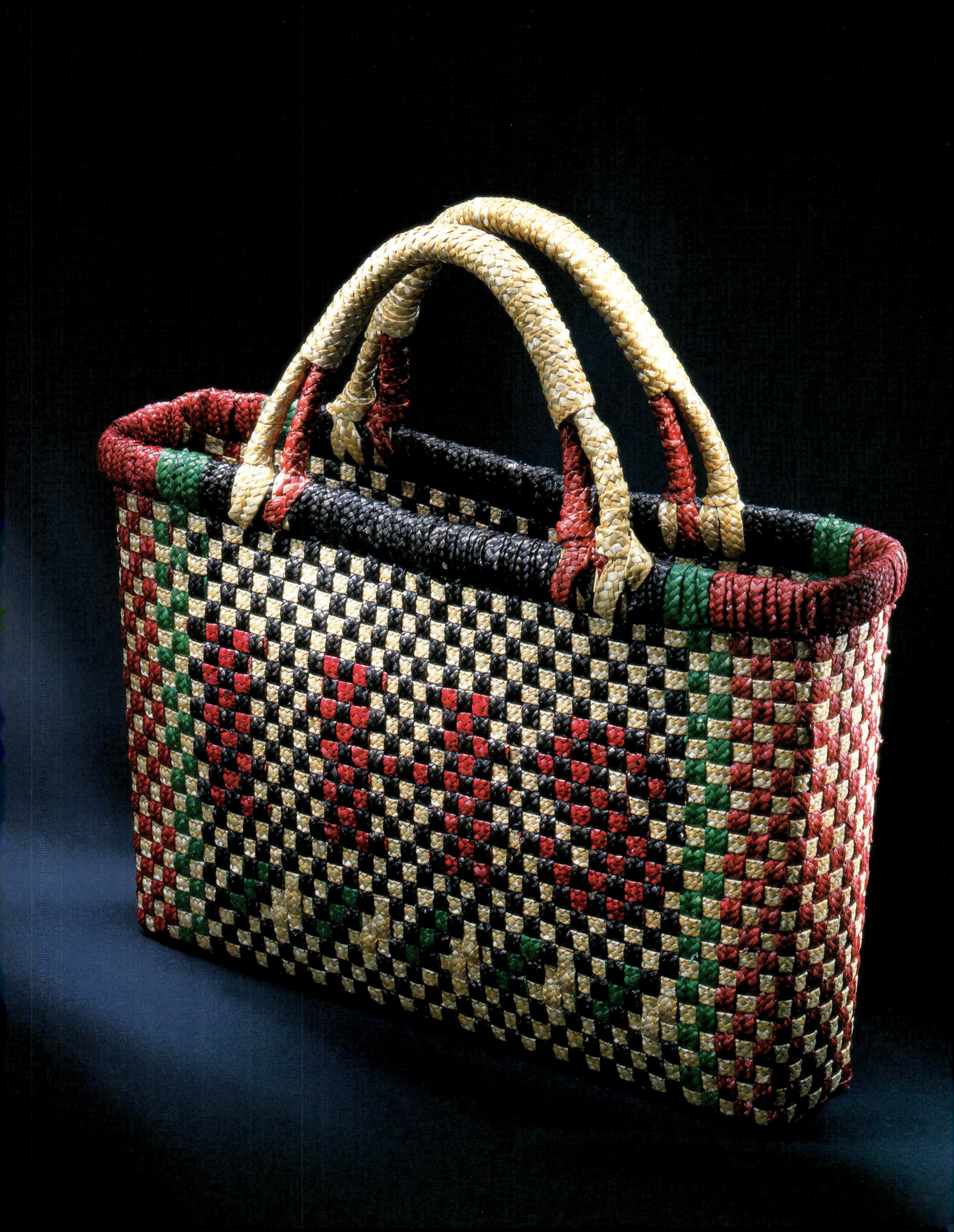

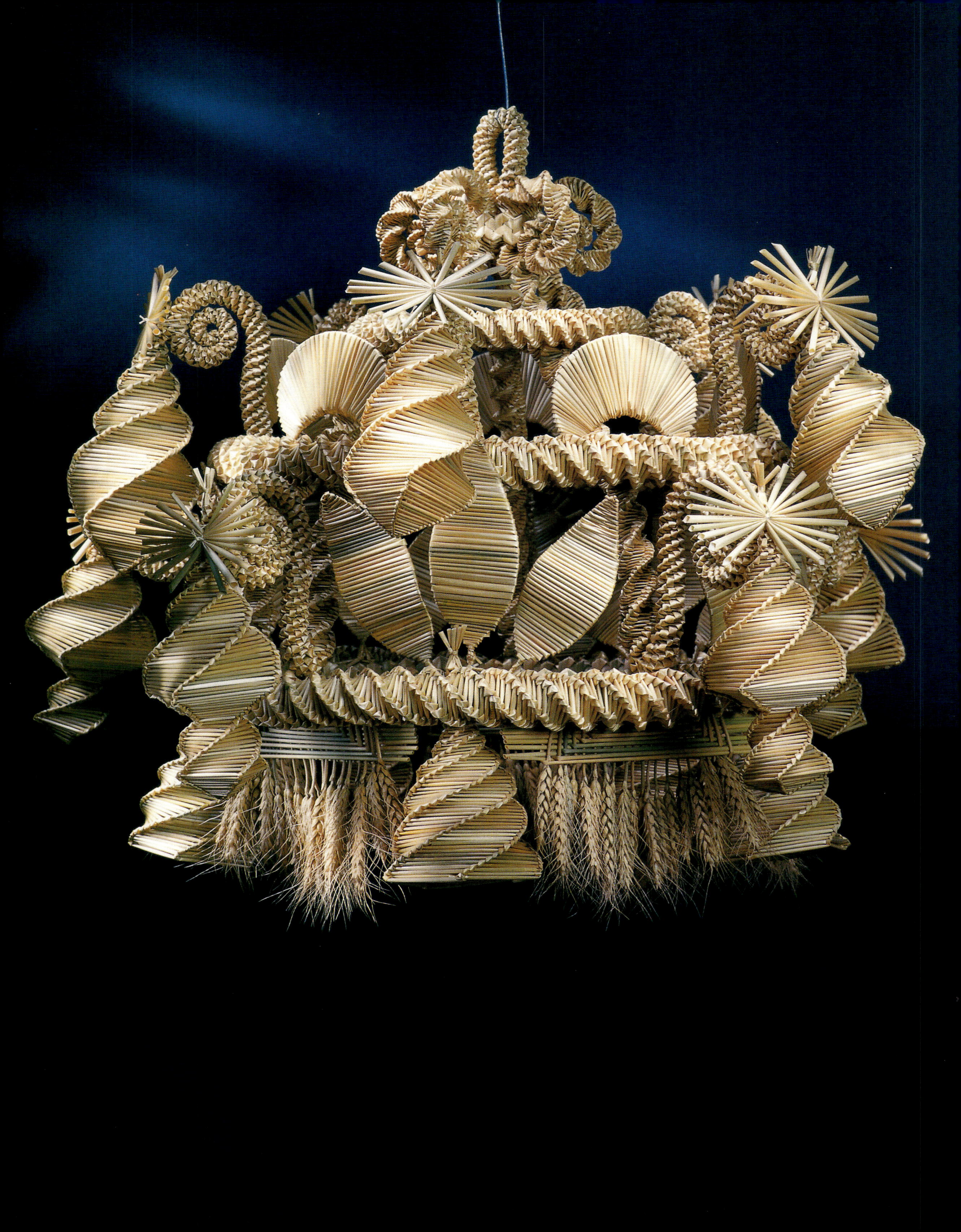

Straw is woven, the grain turns into bread

Straw has always been used for weaving decorative lampshades and other interior decorations for holiday occasions. This type of weaving and assembling of wheat ears was best developed in the north-eastern parts of Slovenia, especially in Prekmurje. Decorative straw lampshades are called *do(v)žnjeki*, *doužjeki* or *lüjstri*. Their origins have not yet been researched, but there are indications that they are connected with old rites at the end of harvest time. Even the name *do(v)žnjek* could be a derivation of *do-šeti* (to finish reaping), which was always a festive occasion. Lampshades and other straw objects for hanging were often decorated with colorful or silver paper, and bean or maize grains. These decorations were used at other special occasions, including weddings and Christmas festivities. In order to produce straw lampshades and other decorative hangings, suitable straw is necessary. There are only a few craftsmen who still master this art, amongst whom we must mention **Brigita** and **Jani Smodiš** from Lipovci "Beltinci". **Bernarda** and **Ivan Žižek** are also well-known producers of straw decorative hangings from the same village.

Brigita Smodiš

Brigita and Jani Smodiš from Lipovci make decorative straw lampshades, thus continuing the long tradition of crafting straw products within the Jakob family. Bernarda Žižek also comes from this tradition. Together with her husband Ivan she also makes straw lampshades called doužnjeki *or* lüjstri, *and diverse other decorative straw products in Lipovci.*

Straw chandeliers are made of a variety of straw elements, woven in different ways and ultimately assembled into the final product. This is precisely planned and highly systematic work. Bernarda and Ivan Žižek, and Brigita and Jani Smodiš all adorn their chandeliers with decorative components of woven straw, and incorporate the most beautiful wheat ears into the final product.

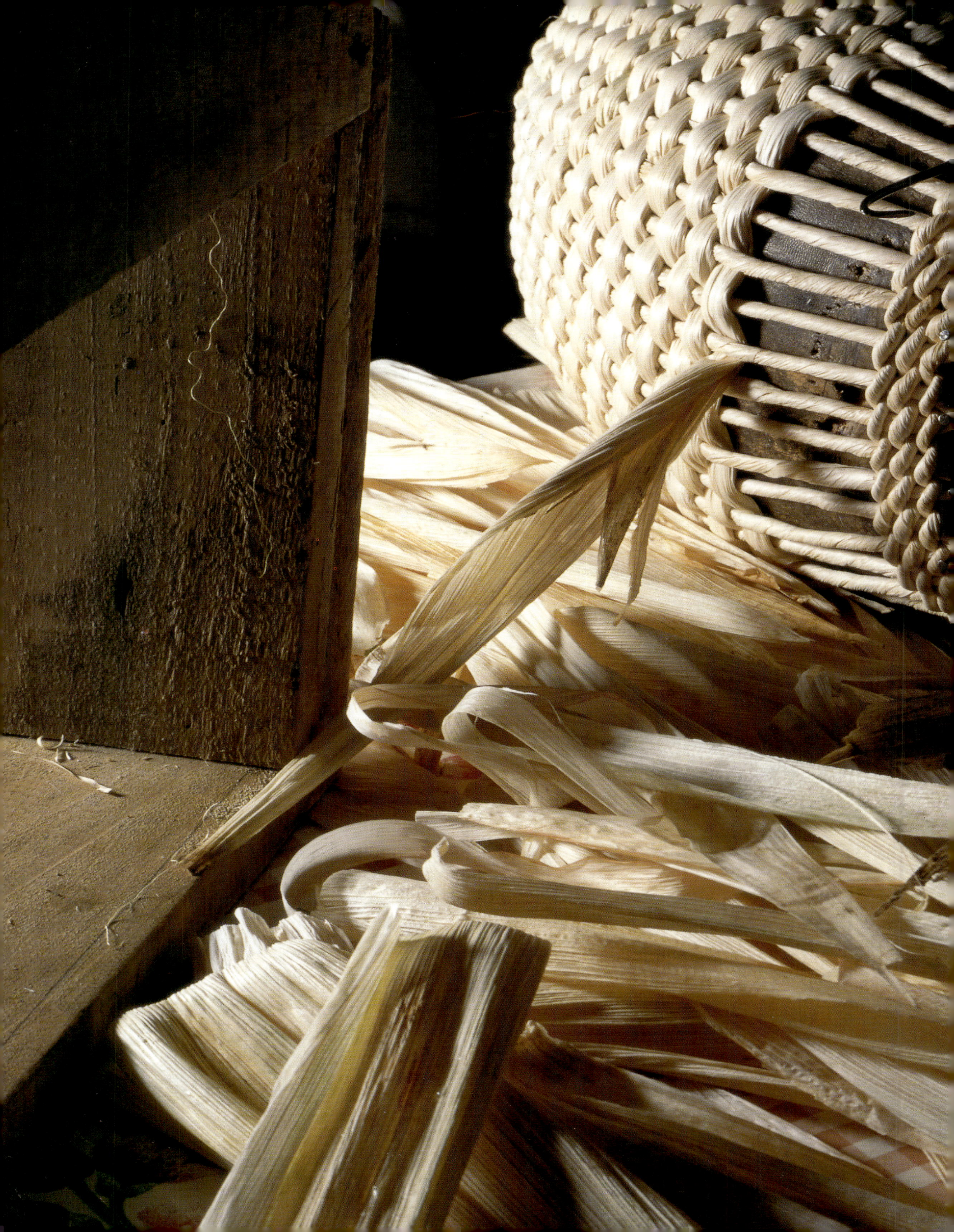

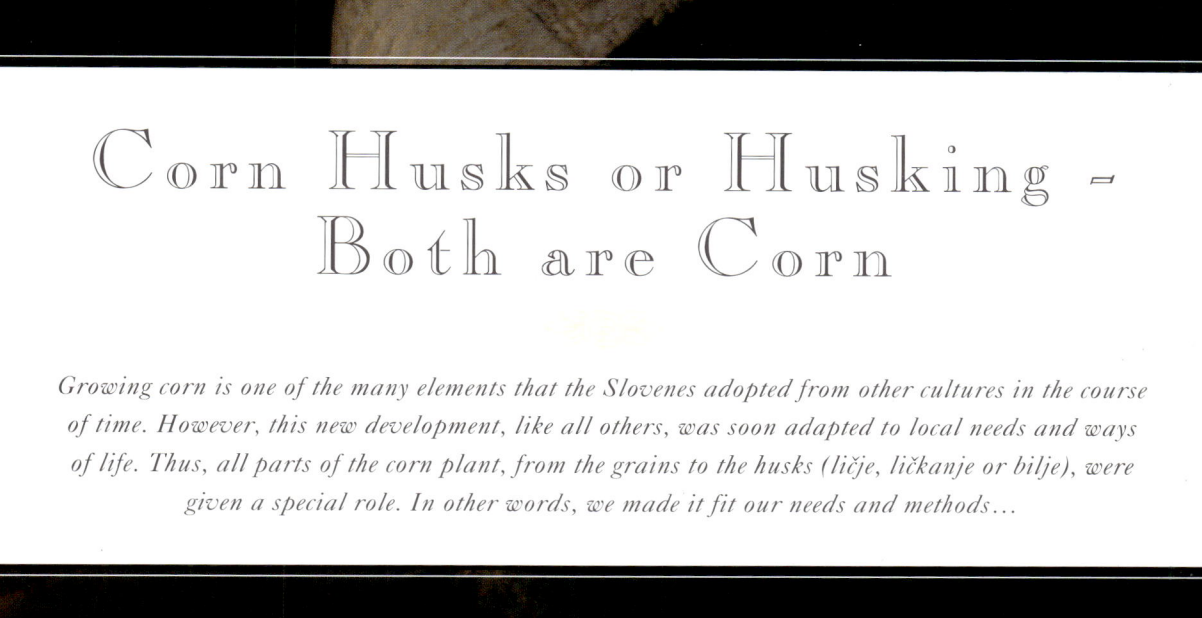

Corn Husks or Husking – Both are Corn

Growing corn is one of the many elements that the Slovenes adopted from other cultures in the course of time. However, this new development, like all others, was soon adapted to local needs and ways of life. Thus, all parts of the corn plant, from the grains to the husks (ličje, ličkanje or bilje), were given a special role. In other words, we made it fit our needs and methods…

CORN HUSKS OR HUSKING - BOTH ARE CORN

Corn husks - *ličje*, *ličkanje* or *bilje*, which is the Prekmurje name for them - are also used for weaving. The process of removing the husks from dried cobs is called *ličkanje*. Another, more illustrative Slovene term to describe the same process is *kožuhanje* (skinning). In the past, this group activity was a chore but also an opportunity for socializing. This aspect has, to a lesser extent, been retained in the present day. Dried corn husks - *bilje* - were used for weaving doormats, mattresses (especially for babies and children), clog-like slippers, bags and long plaited braids, which were placed on door and window frames in houses and barns as padding, to seal them off and prevent draughts in winter time. The use of corn husks for weaving was best developed in the Prekmurje region. A Hungarian teacher introduced the craft to the area during World War II. Dried corn husks first had to be whitened and made flexible enough for weaving. Many women from the region eagerly took up this craft. Soon, making slippers, bags, spreads, ladies' handbags and boxes from corn husks was a popular handicraft in the Lendava area. The craft was also part of the school curriculum. It was very popular throughout the 1950s, but then started to decline. Today, only a few weavers contribute their products to the Prekmurje souvenir range. **MARIJA RAJTAR** from Turnišče and **TEREZIJA BENCE** from Genterovci are major contributors to the souvenirs of the region.

CORN HUSKS OR HUSKING - BOTH ARE CORN

*Weaving products from corn husks (*ličje *or* bilje, *as the husks are called in the Prekmurje region) was introduced to the district after World War II. In those times, such products were relatively modern because they were independent of historical or traditional models. Weavers used readily available material, abundant in the fields. In time, the number of weavers started to decline, and they could only depend on their own creativity regarding the design of their products, which slowly became the heritage of the post-war era. Terezija Bence from Genterovci still makes products from woven corn husks.*

CORN HUSKS OR HUSKING - BOTH ARE CORN

MARIJA RAJTAR

Dried corn leaves make excellent weaving material which, however, needs to be specially prepared and sorted by size and quality. Many products are woven from corn leaves, including articles for personal use (bags and purses), useful household items (baskets, decorative planters), and excellent slippers. The latter are also the masterpieces of Marija Rajtar from Turnišče in Prekmurje.

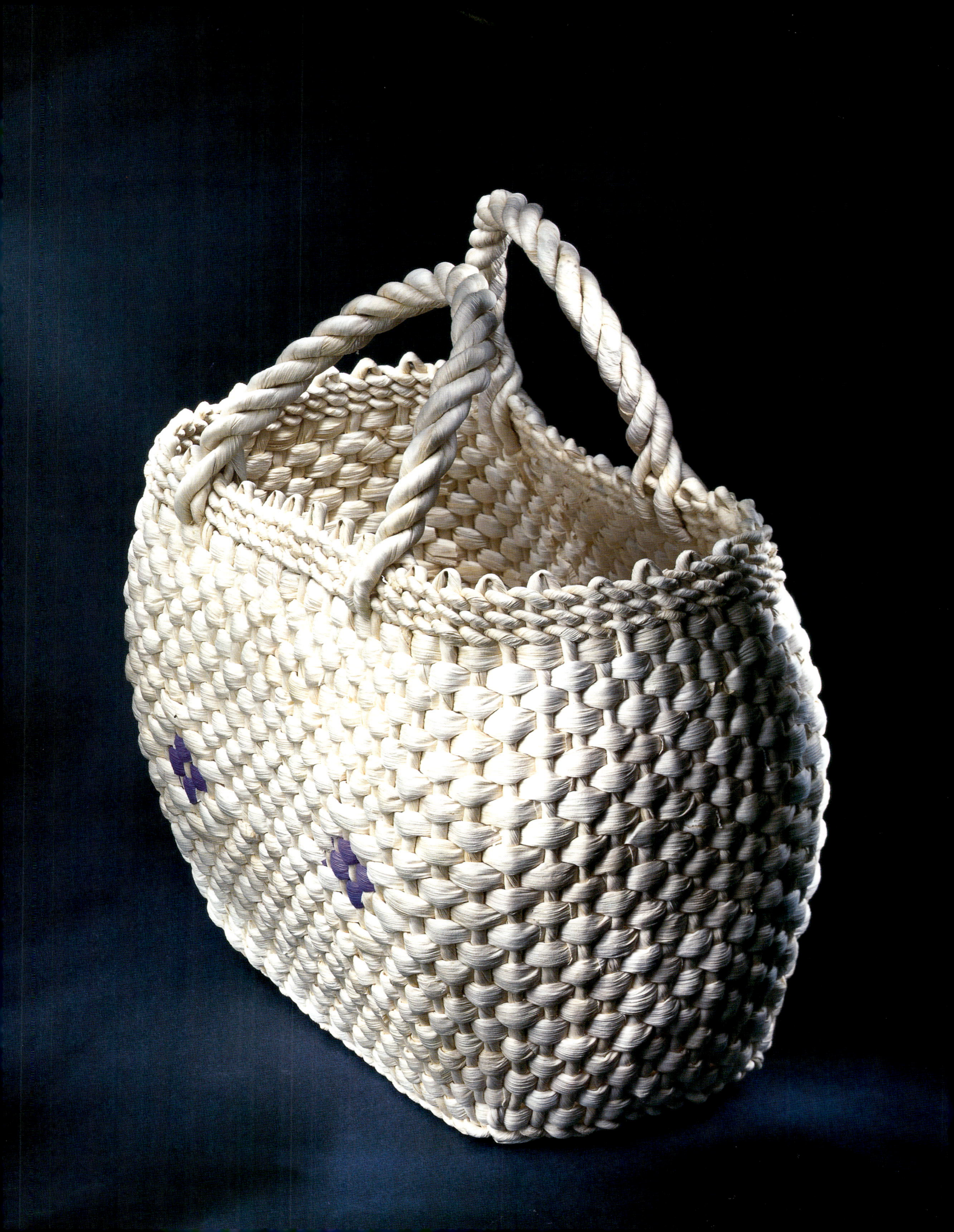

CORN HUSKS OR HUSKING - BOTH ARE CORN

Sadly in this area of handicrafts too the same conclusion applies that technological knowledge has not been developed further, particularly in terms of modern design tehniques. A truly brilliant exception to the rule is **STANISLAVA VAUDA** from Ptuj, a young graduate from the Department of Design and Textiles at the Faculty of Sciences and Technology of the University of Ljubljana. In 1998 she created a line of tapestries and clothes made of corn husks, a material that has shaped her rural hometown in a special way. Her project is innovative in terms of production technology and design. This points to a certain trend in modern design, which builds on recognizable models from the Slovene crafts heritage, with completely redefined combinations and meanings of course, retaining or returning to the local and regional tradition-which is what is needed for the future of the modern world.

I am convinced that the work of Stanislava Vauda from Ptuj truthfully represents a turning point in understanding the enormous abundance of materials, working technologies and creative possibilities which are mediated to us through individual handicrafts. Perhaps Vauda's important step towards working with and recognizing the creative possibilities in the domain of corn husks was coincidental. Such a superstructure should be striven for in all the handicrafts we have inherited as "live" historical memory. Her approach to crafting is a model which should be followed in other crafts.

CORN HUSKS OR HUSKING - BOTH ARE CORN

Dried corn leaves - until recently merely material for doormats, numerous other woven products and health-friendly bed mats - were turned into clothes in the creative hands of Stanislava Vauda. Her introduction of corn to clothes manufacture should not be interpreted as a simple alternative approach to making clothes, or as a provocative insertion of this material into garment design. There is an alternative flair to her products, hidden in the exciting encounter of the body with the masterpieces of nature. The latter takes one back to the furthest historical memories, when man was protected only by plant leaves or the skins of slaughtered animals, and yet distinguished as a different group because of them.

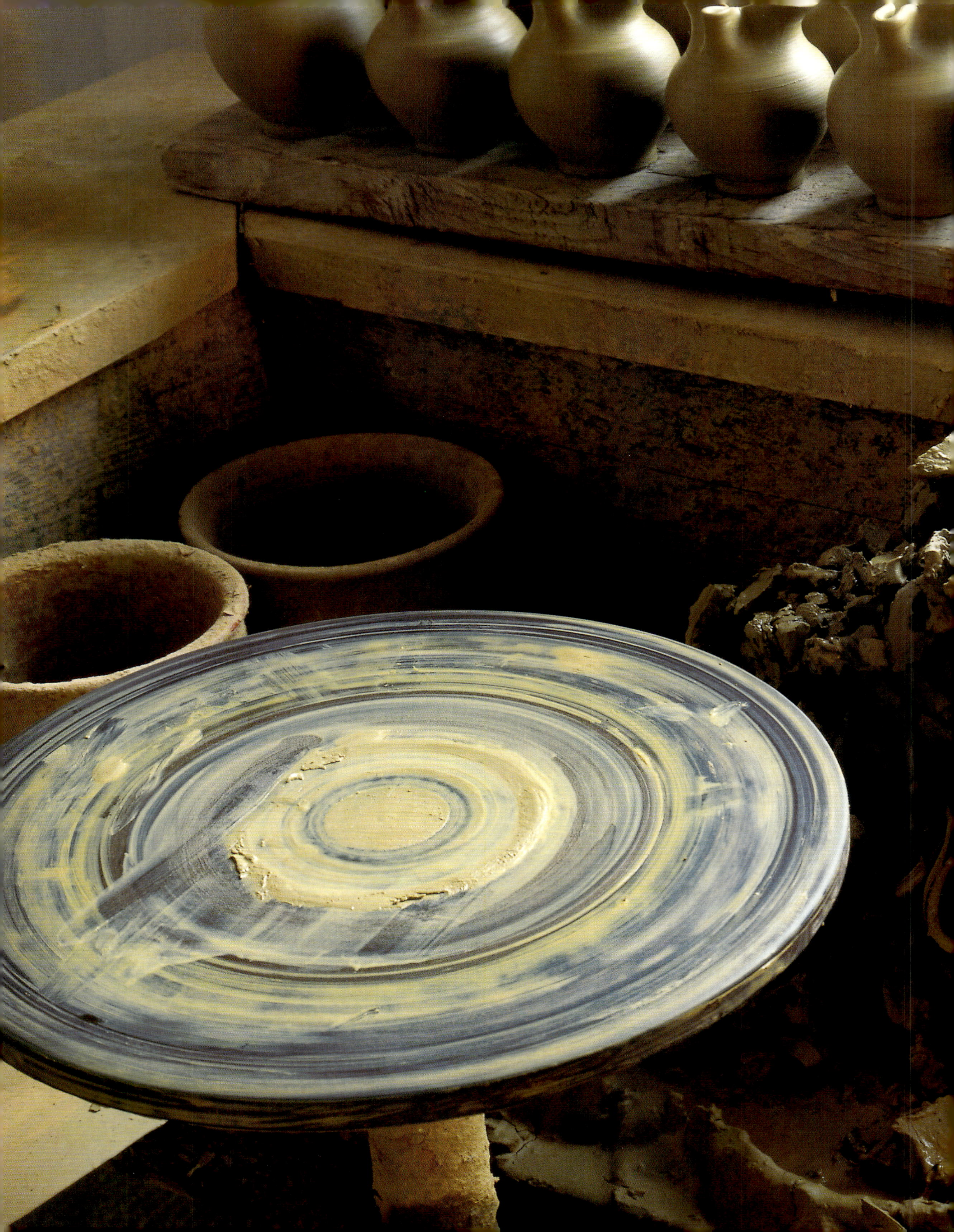

Hand Traces in Clay

It is said that clay is the most suitable and adaptable material for sculpting and creating new forms. However, it is the sculptor's hand that gives life to clay and not the clay itself. It has been so for centuries, as is evident from the oldest pottery remains, preserved to this day and covered by soil - its original home. These objects, uncovered by archaeologists, testify to the tradition of pottery and ceramics, which still enrich our everyday life today...

HAND TRACES IN CLAY

The potters' heritage has inspired modern design. The classical wine pitcher, also called a majolika *was given a new appearance through the expert approach of a designer (architect Matjaž Deu), but retained the traditional, mostly positive aspects of its functionality (i.e., comfortable pouring, keeping the wine cool, retaining the traditional mood at the table etc.).*

Clay is the basic material for two handicrafts: pottery and ceramics. Today, we often come across products in which the technology and design techniques and procedures of both are combined. Slovenia is, or rather was, a country of potters. Pottery was well developed in Slovenia in line with its rich natural clay resources. Today, there are many imported materials for pottery and ceramics readily available in shops to complement domestic clay. However, even the amounts of locally quarried clay would satisfy the artisans' need to explore their creative, design and artistic potentials. The vast heritage of potters, who relied exclusively on locally quarried clay, testifies to that. Clay from different regions had certain specific characteristics which were retained in local types of earthenware.

There are two predominant trends in handicrafts that use clay as the basic material in Slovenia: pottery and ceramics. There are several types of clay suitable for pottery and ceramics in Slovenia. The potters carry on the rich tradition of their trade, adapting it constantly to suit the needs of modern man. In ceramics, the dominant trend is that of making unique items and of exploring original artistic concepts. Pottery is part of the national heritage, despite the fact that the number of potters and pottery workshops has declined drastically. Ceramics has only begun to grow in recent years. It is also popularized by the mass of Slovene and foreign textbooks on ceramics.

The influence of modern potters, or rather families of potters, is still most strongly felt in the traditional pottery centers or near local clay quarries. New potters are trained at various pottery courses. Their work is mostly limited to imitating models and only few can pride themselves on truly original pieces. This confirms international findings that a large quantity of skilled craftsmen in any trade does not ensure quality products. Only a few craftsmen possess the combination of skill, artistic talent and expertise essential for developing new products. Sometimes it takes generations before a truly exceptional craftsman is discovered.

Hand traces in clay

This may be the reason why experts from several related disciplines often collaborate on the production of a line of pottery or ceramic products today. Artists, designers and technicians work on the design and concepts needed to make a prototype sample. Once it is made, skilled potters replicate it further. In Slovenia, such an interdisciplinary approach to pottery and ceramics is still a rare exception to the rule; perhaps this has to do with the individualistic national character. I know of only one example of collaboration in the production and design of a pottery product. A modern version of a *majolika*, a traditional wine pitcher, was designed by architect **Matjaž Deu** from Ljubljana in 1997 and crafted in a limited edition by potter **Franc Kremžar** from Gmajnica near Komenda.

Individual families of potters still continue the tradition of crafting earthenware in former potters' centers. Their numbers notably decreased during the period between the two world wars, but those that remain continue to craft various regionally typical products, distinguished by specific ornamentation, colors and even figural shapes. The little horse-shaped whistles, made by the Bojc family from Dolenja vas near Ribnica, are typical of such products.

HAND TRACES IN CLAY

The Ribnica valley was once also famous for its *suha roba* craftsmen and potters. The **Nosan** family from Prigorica and the **Bojc** family from Dolenja vas are master potters from that area. Three generations of the Nosan family create and develop the figural pottery of Ribnica, and many new thematic products as well. They preserve Ribnica-style pottery by the use of transparent glazing and the application of various natural brown clay tones.

THE NOSAN FAMILY

Three generations of the Nosan family come together in Prigorica near Ribnica in the Dolenjska region. Jakob Nosan, the family elder, specializes in making traditional Ribnica clay whistles, shaped like animal figurines, while his son, grandson and his son's son-in-law make products more modern in content and function. They remain faithful to the traditional Ribnica-style pottery by using simple brown and green shades of glazing, baking the clay in a wood-heated kiln, the manual shaping of clay, and the use of the modeling mould. The products of all three generations of the Nosan family have often represented traditional and modern Slovene pottery in Slovenia and abroad.

106

HANDICRAFTS OF SLOVENIA

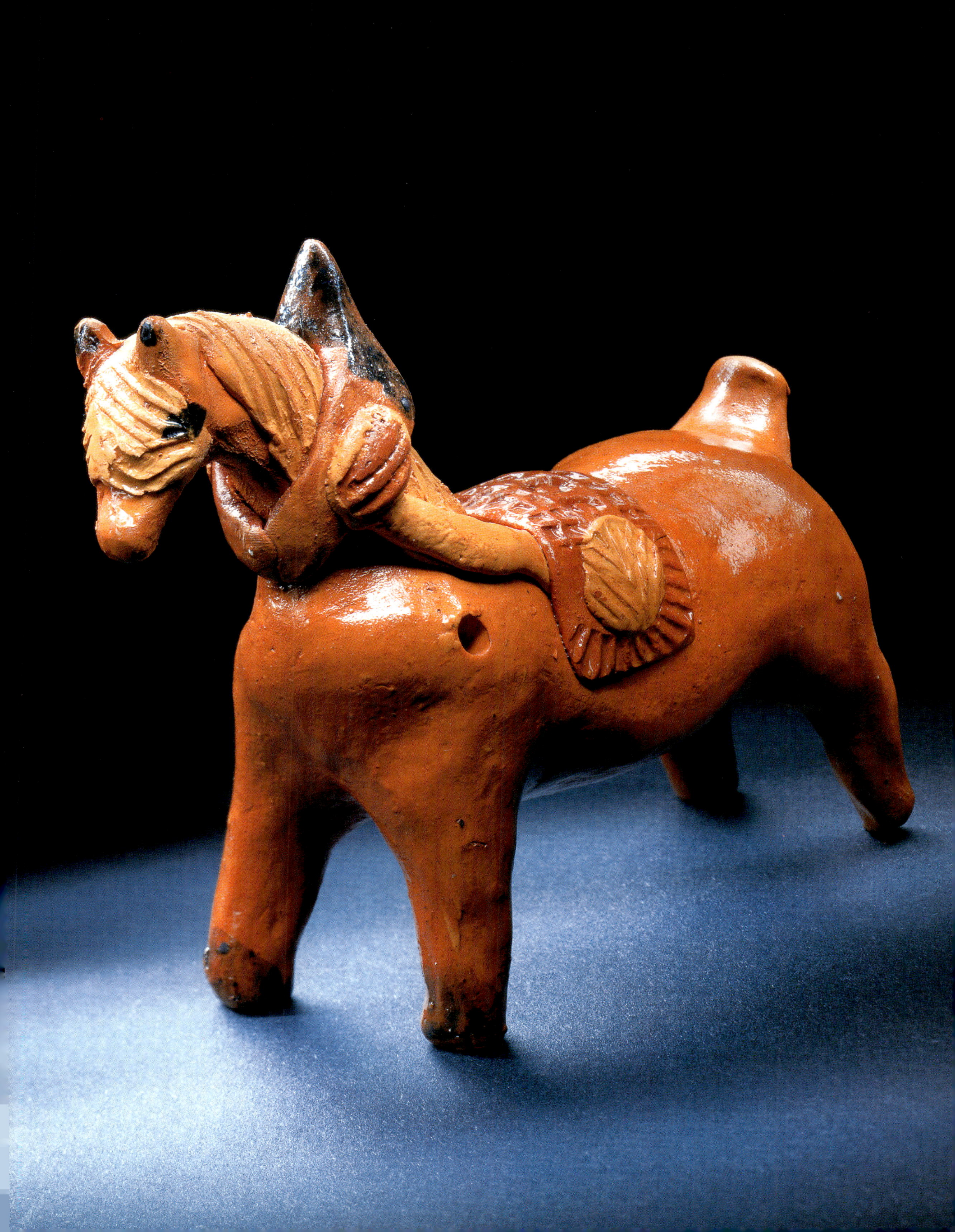

HAND TRACES IN CLAY

The Bojc family continues to make typical Ribnica clay sculptures, ranging from a little horse with a whistling rear *(konjiček, ki piska v riti)* to statues of St. George and other saints. **JOŽE KRŽAN** from Zaloke near Raka is also a master potter. **JOŽE PUNGERČAR** from Gruča near Šentjernej took over the pottery workshop from his father, who was known as one of the best makers of decorated bowls. Besides bowls, Pungerčar makes pots for baking poultry, other types of pot, typical Dolenjska wine pitchers *(majolike)* adorned with verse inscriptions, and rooster-shaped *majolike*. The rooster is a symbol of Šentjernej and the neighboring areas.

Another important former pottery center is Komenda near Kamnik. The local potters of this town established their cooperative in 1929; this became a pottery business, still in existence today **KOMENDA POTTERY COMPANY**. They specialize in the production of commercially successful products.

St. George, mounted on a horse, fighting a dragon (Picture 2), and a woman with her hands raised in prayer - similar to the Oranta in the art of the Old Christians (Picture 1) - are two typical statues in clay by Bojc, the style of which is difficult to define. According to one hypothesis they were created with the aid of "expert" tutors in the period between the two world wars. Such collaborative efforts should be models for modernity we often fail to combine various expert approaches (conceptual, design, technological and artistic), for the production of quality modern products.

Potters from the Šentjernej plain also came up with a regional type of earthenware which differs from that of other regions in shape and ornamentation (Picture 3). Clay bowls, crafted in the Pungerčar workshop in Gruča near Šentjernej best exemplify the Šentjernej style. Aside from making bowls, the crafting of wine pitchers in the shape of roosters has also been preserved in this region. In the past, clay roosters were crafted manually on the potter's wheel. Today, they are made by pressing the clay into two-piece plaster moulds(Picture 4).

HAND TRACES IN CLAY

*In Komenda near Kamnik the local potters established their own Potters'
Cooperative in 1929. In 1932 they built large facilities for drying and storing
earthenware, and a kiln for baking clay. The workshop continued work after
World War II and evolved into a proper, now privately-owned, potters' business.
Today, they specialize in the production of larger artistically and decoratively
consummate products, including some traditional Slovene and international
ornaments introduced to Slovenia from areas such as Friuli or Veneto
(Picture 5). Thus, old ornaments are revived for new items of tableware used
in food preparation and serving.*

Cel teden se trudim
in žulim roke,
v nedeljo si z vincem
ogrejem srce.

Hand traces in clay

The Kržan workshop continues the vast potters' tradition in the area of the Krško plain. The shape and ornamentation of their products greatly resemble those from the Šentjernej plain, which is understandable considering their close geographical position and similar cultural prerequisites. Most of the products crafted today are intended for practical use, as in the past. Bowls with rhythmically shaped ornaments (Picture 2), various types of dishes, baking moulds and flower-pots are still traditional Slovene potters' products, which are also crafted in the Kržan workshop. Because the area between the margins of the Krško plain to Bizeljsko is a wine-growing region, majolike (wine-pitchers) are also produced in the Kržan workshop (Picture 1).

Jože Kržan

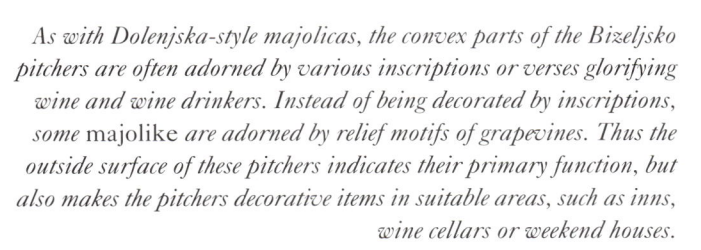

As with Dolenjska-style majolicas, the convex parts of the Bizeljsko pitchers are often adorned by various inscriptions or verses glorifying wine and wine drinkers. Instead of being decorated by inscriptions, some majolike are adorned by relief motifs of grapevines. Thus the outside surface of these pitchers indicates their primary function, but also makes the pitchers decorative items in suitable areas, such as inns, wine cellars or weekend houses.

1

2

HAND TRACES IN CLAY

Members of the **KREMŽAR** family from Gmajnica near Komenda are the only potters to continue the local pottery tradition. **FRANC KREMŽAR** is one of the most outstanding Slovene potters. He has designed several lines of excellent products such as *potica* (walnut roll) moulds and meat baking pots, bowls, pitchers and even sacral dishes from baked clay. The latter make original gifts for newly-ordained priests or other clergy. He has exhibited his products in Slovenia and abroad, and headed several pottery workshops and courses for all generations. The rich heritage of Komenda pottery has been enriched by his expert knowledge and technology, and by the creation of a modern pottery workshop.

FRANC KREMŽAR

The potica *mould, or* potičnica, *is only one of the supreme products crafted by master Franc Kremžar. Having formed, dried, glazed and baked the mould in his kiln, Kremžar wreathes its outer side with wire. This manner of protection was the task of specialized craftsmen -* piskrovezi *- in the past. They went from door to door offering their services. Kremžar's earthenware is both decorative and functional. He has adapted many traditional shapes to modern needs. His fine dishware ennobles the preparation and serving of food, adding spiritual and aesthetic pleasure to eating and turning it into a ritualized act.*

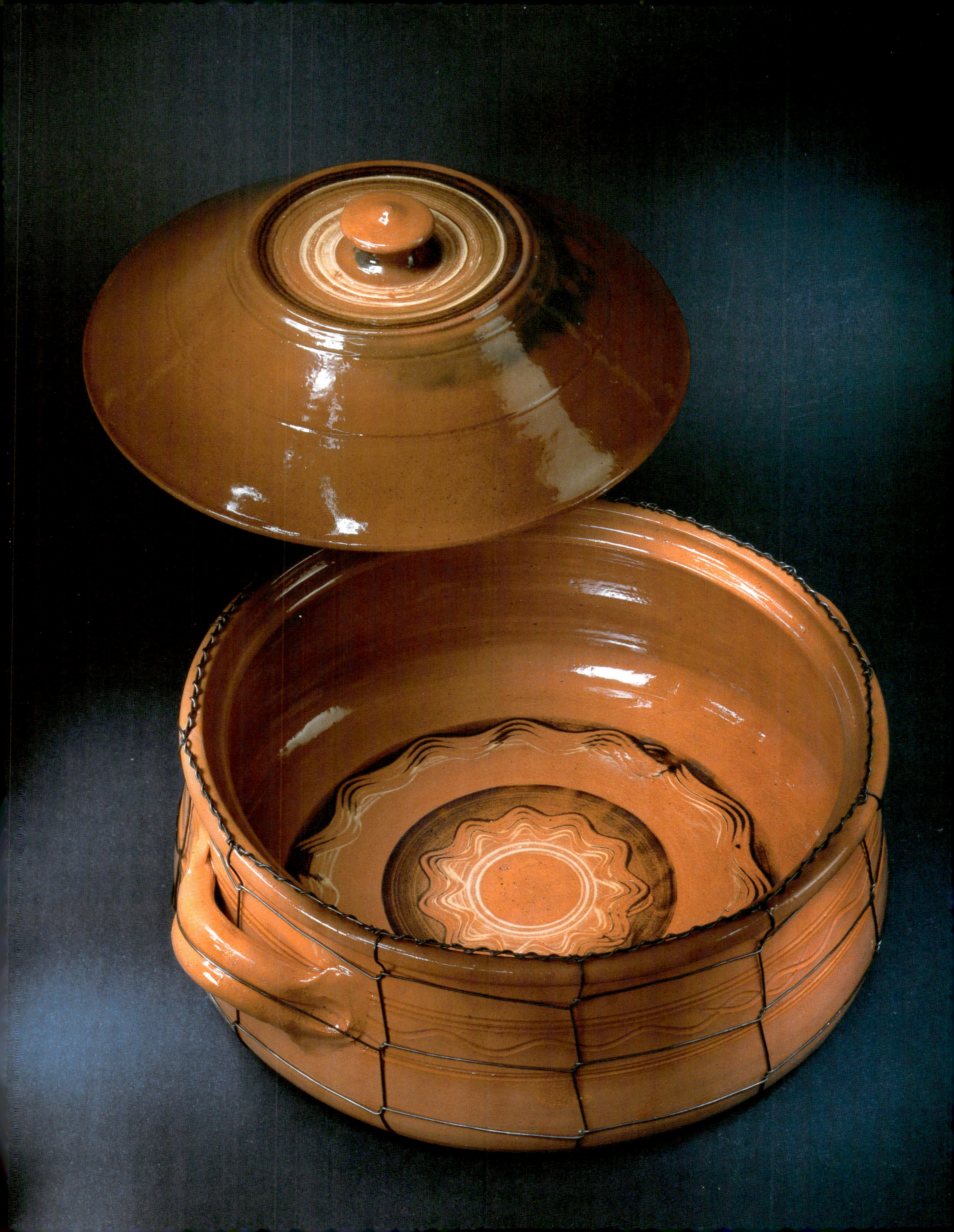

Hand traces in clay

Sašo Žuman continues to work in his grandfather's pottery workshop in Ljutomer. His products, like those of his grandfather, continue the tradition of Prlekija-style earthenware, which still has many potential uses today. The earthenware sift, used for drying cottage cheese, is one of these highly practical products (Picture 1).

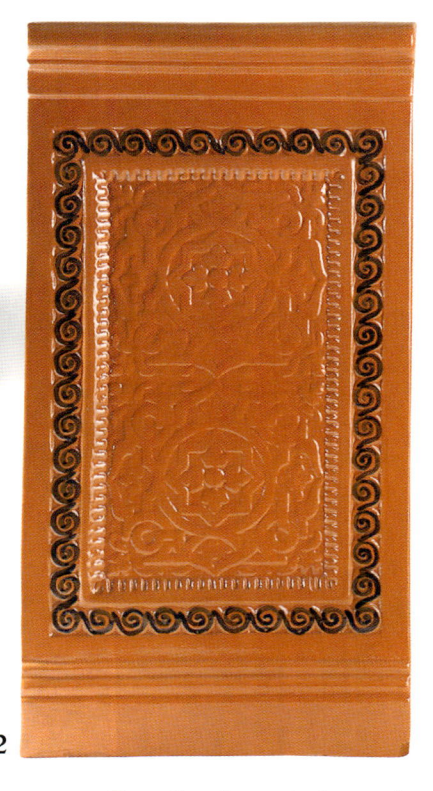

Even though some potters make earthenware ovens or even stoves for baking bread, both of these activities remain the province of stove-makers. Stoves used for warming the house or baking bread have again become popular. In accordance with the customer's wishes, modern stove-makers will build traditional stoves or replicas from national heritage (Picture 2), or even design completely modern ones.

One craft parallel to pottery and ceramics was **STOVE-MAKING**, which also uses clay as the basic material. As their name suggests, stove-makers make stoves and ovens. The craft has become very popular in recent years. Perhaps this is because of the renewed interest in stoves and open fireplaces. **MARKO AVGUŠTIN** from Komenda makes modern and traditional farm-style stoves. He designs them in collaboration with various Slovene sculptors and painters, which has proved successful in other handicrafts as well. **FRANC BUSER** from Prožinska vas near Štore is the only active potter in the Celje and Liboje regions, where pottery and ceramics used to be widespread. From here we move past Ormož to Ljutomer, the "capital" of Prlekija. There, **KAREL ŽUMAN** created superb earthenware until his death in 1977. He was the first Slovene potter to build a specialized gift shop and gallery next to his workshop to exhibit and advertise his best pieces. Nearly every visitor to Ljutomer stopped at his workshop. His most important legacy is the fact that he also trained his son **BRANKO** and grandson **SAŠO**. Sašo is one of the youngest Slovene potters today. Together with his father, Sašo carries on the Žuman family pottery tradition, also developing new earthenware products.

HAND TRACES IN CLAY

3

5

4

Franc Buser's earthenware is distinguished by superb craftsmanship and a wide range of types from traditional functional items such as bowls and potica *moulds (Pictures 4 and 5) to other traditional products which have been assigned new decorative functions in addition to their basic purpose. Pitchers (Picture 3, far left), originally used for storing vinegar or carrying water, are today often used as wine containers to decorate the table on special occasions.*

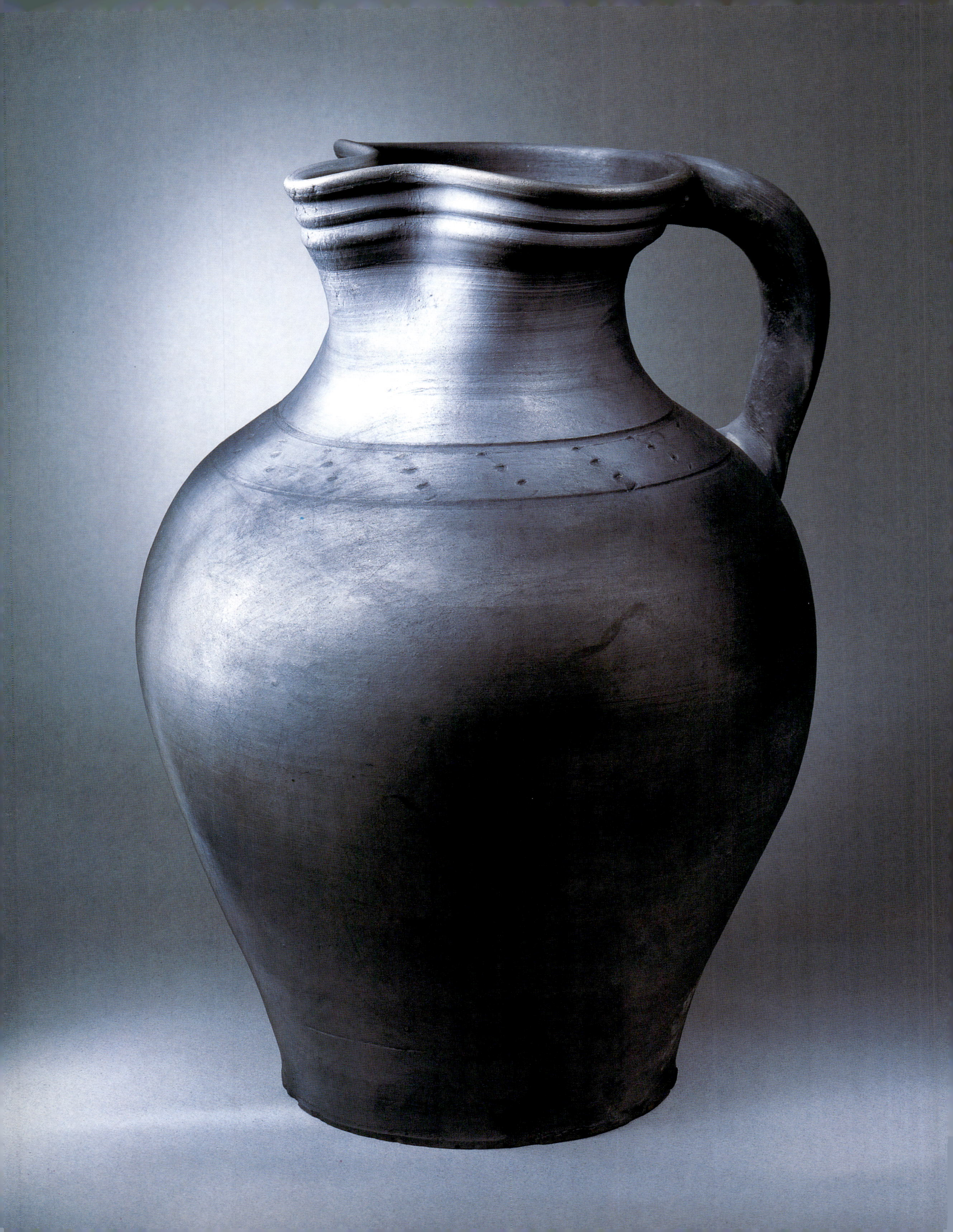

HAND TRACES IN CLAY

In the period after World War II, pottery in the Prekmurje region developed without appropriate expert attention. Thus the quality of some products has declined drastically. Despite such products, traditional Prekmurje earthenware has survived, and is now the foundation for the discovery of new design techniques.

ALOJZ BOJNEC AND HIS GRANDSON TOMAŽ

Over ninety potters occupied the neighbouring villages of Bogojina and Filovci in the second half of the 19th century. They established a local Potters' Cooperative in 1923, but by the 1950s the number of potters had fallen to thirty. Today, the local potters' tradition is still continued by the Bojnec family. The Prekmurje potters also have special kilns which are either of a mound or oval shape. They are situated in the open or in special sheds.

117

HANDICRAFTS OF SLOVENIA

HAND TRACES IN CLAY

Franc Zelko is a potter from Goričko in the Prekmurje region. He comes from a family of potters-his father was also a potter. The family tradition is continued by his daughter who, since graduating from at the internationally acclaimed School for Potters, Ceramists and Stove-Makers in Stob, Austria, has widened the range and improved the quality of products crafted in the Zelko family workshop.

Finally, the road brings us to Prekmurje, where pottery was best developed in the past. In Filovci, for example, a local potters' guild was active until 1912, while the first local potters' cooperative was established in 1923. In addition to its old tradition, Prekmurje pottery is also original in terms of the technology used. The typical Prekmurje kilns have seven or eight air vents called *sopihi* through which the smoke exits and enters on top. Typical Prekmurje black pottery is baked in these kilns. The color is the result of the baking technique rather than the color glazing. Logs with high resin content are fed into the kiln during the baking process. They emit a very thick, dark smoke. The potter seals off all air vents to keep the smoke in the kiln and allow it to "pass all the dishes," as the process is called in potters' jargon. **ALOJZ BOJNEC** from Bogojina, **FRANC ZELKO** from Pečarovci and **ŠTEFAN GOMBOC** from Tešanovci still make traditional Prekmurje earthenware.

Pottery has completely disappeared from many former pottery centers. This happened in the Bela krajina region with predominantly female potters till first World War, in Ljubno in the Gorenjska region, in Pištanj, in the area of Savinjska dolina, in the vicinity of Grobelno, and in Zadrečka dolina. The latter is also the place where the oldest written records about potters (from 1359 and 1493) were found.

HAND TRACES IN CLAY

Narrow-necked pitchers for wine or other beverages, with a hollow handle in which there is a hole, are a peculiarity of pottery from the Prekmurje region. Such pitchers helped keep the liquids cool and clean because drinking was only possible through the hole in the handle, while the neck of the pitcher remained sealed. The typical dark graphite color of Prekmurje earthenware is achieved by mounting pine logs with a high resin content into the kiln, after sealing off its air vents with clay. The smoke, rich in resin, is thus kept in the kiln to pass the earthenware (as the process is called in potters' jargon). Potter Štefan Gomboc also uses this technique to color his earthenware.

Hand traces in clay

Archeological remains confirm pottery to be one of the oldest handicrafts known to man. Studying such remains inspires craftsmen to search for new creative solutions rather than replicating ancient pottery. Barbara Plevnik from Ljubljana searches for ways to modernize and improve ancient models. The results of her creative endeavors are unique pottery and ceramic products.

Pottery and ceramics have become increasingly popular in recent years. Some credit for that should certainly be given to the Ljubljana-based Society of Potters and Ceramists. They organize various forms of training for potters, and contribute to raising the technological and artistic quality of both handicrafts, which was quite poor for some time. Today, there are several potters who make superb pottery and ceramic products. They do not replicate traditional models but instead attempt to find new solutions by studying items from the national pottery and ceramics heritage. Only select craftsmen, whose originality distinguishes their products from those of other potters, are mentioned here. Possibilities for contemporary pottery and ceramic creation are unlimited. One such artisan is **Barbara Plevnik** from Ljubljana. She bases her products on models of ancient earthenware uncovered in archaeological excavations, and then searches for ways to modernize and improve them. Her products are permeated with the spirit of ancient cultures, making them somewhat mystical. **Snežana Sotlar** from Ljubljana started working with ceramics in the period of stagnation of the handicraft. Today, she can pride herself on an original portfolio. Something similar can be said of **Tanja Smole-Cvelbar**, whose superb ceramic products are also used as high-level business gifts. **Nataša Prestor** from Laze in Planinsko polje is also a master of her craft. She mostly makes witty and caricatured ceramic figurines in her studio. She has designed some thematically well-rounded collections like Nativity scenes, a selection of Slovene folk costumes, characters, professions, traditional national heroes and motifs from the folk tales in which they appear. She carries on the Ribnica tradition of figural pottery, which she has taken to a new, higher artistic level.

HAND TRACES IN CLAY

The ceramic figural compositions of Nataša Prestor offer an insight into her "Castle Snežnik among Memories, Tales and Reality" project. In it she attempted to revive the tradition and memories of the castle in ceramics. She recreated the personal bathroom of Herman, the Noble Prince of Schönburg and Waldenburg (Picture 1), which in its time was a true oddity, in painted and glazed ceramics (terraglia). She was inspired to make a composition of the castle children standing in the castle alley of giant rose bushes by an old photograph with the same motif (Picture 3). A gardener tended the castle garden, orchard and apiary. Prestor used an old photograph of the gardener and his family to render an interpretation of memories connected with life in the castle (Picture 2).

HAND TRACES IN CLAY

Some potters and ceramists attempt to permanently record some elements of the Slovene handicraft heritage in more durable materials. One of the most successful individuals in this regard is **MARJETA PIKELJ** from Črnuče near Ljubljana. She uses the patterns from moulds originally used for making a honey sweetmeat called *loški mali kruhek* to make decorations of baked clay.

Some artisans attempt to use more permanent materials to record some products that were historically or are still used in completely different contexts. Figural sweetmeats were made from honey dough. Such gingerbread figurines were very important, and also edible gifts which people exchanged at various holidays. Marjeta Pikelj replicates loški kruhki *in a more durable material (baked clay) which assigns a purely decorative function to her products.*

122

HANDICRAFTS OF SLOVENIA

HAND TRACES IN CLAY

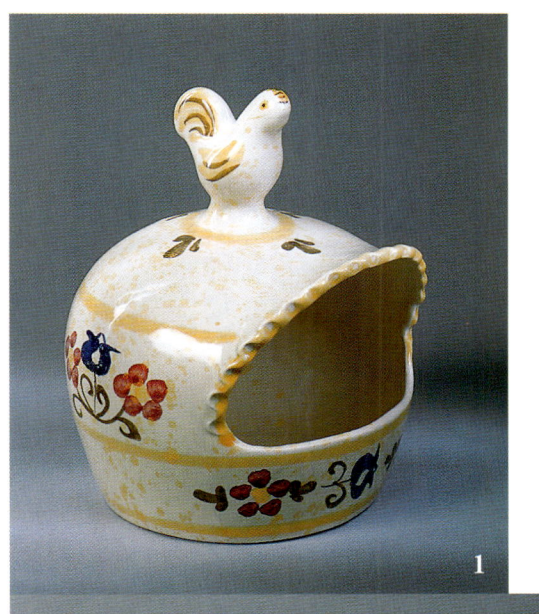

The style of the saltbox by Brigita Vogrinec (Picture 1), and the group of spice containers by Sašo Rus (Picture 2) are reminiscent of the design of kitchenware and kitchen utensils after 1900. The products designed by Rus are much more consistent since their artistic form closely approaches the characteristics of the originals. The wide range of products crafted by Brigita Vogrinec is designed like rural earthenware and decorated (with types of glazing and colors) using techniques closer to those used in ceramic kitchen products in wealthy houses in the early 1900s.

123

HANDICRAFTS OF SLOVENIA

HAND TRACES IN CLAY

HEDVIKA-VIKA ČIPAK from Ljubljana also makes decorative figurines in ceramics with a great degree of originality. Her mobiles of bell-shaped porcelain figurines are unique. **SILVA DRAVŠNIK** from Kozjak in Mislinjska dolina also makes these. Photographs of two of her figurines were featured on the posters and other advertising material for the 12th annual Exhibition of Home and Applied Crafts in Slovenj Gradec and Ljubljana in 1998.

The bell-shaped porcelain dolls by Silva Dravšnik are based on assembling individual elements into a whole. After shaping and baking, the individual elements are assembled on a string. In this manner, a caricatured hanging doll is made. Her products are of a decorative nature, while her design techniques and procedures result in markedly unique dolls.

HAND TRACES IN CLAY

Clay, as a craft material, allows for many creative possibilities resulting in both functional and decorative products and objects. Making caricatured figurines as witty interpretations of people - their characters, particularities, vices and virtues - is one such possibility. Renditions of these motifs in clay are widespread in all cultures, so special figurines with a high amount of originality are of particular interest. Hedvika-Vika Čipak from Ljubljana strives to find her own original artistic expression.

HAND TRACES IN CLAY

After decades of stagnation (with minor exceptions), Slovene ceramics have started to develop again in recent years. Although there are some pottery schools and courses, these alone do not suffice for the true advancement of this handicraft. There are some remarkably gifted individuals whose attempts to find original creative styles and expressions enter relatively virgin territory for the craft. Like some other ceramists, Danica Žbontar is trying to go beyond the imitation of models by other authors or of those found in (mostly foreign) literature.

Some modern ceramic products are extremely functional. Ljubo Blagotinšek makes decorative ceramic whose lights shape reminds one of bottomless, shiny vases. Parallels with the basic function and light effects of these lamps can be found in lamps created in the oriental world.

HAND TRACES IN CLAY

Lorna Novak's products follow the tradition of the classic crafting of products on a potters' wheel. After crafting, Novak adds her original designer's touch, retaining all the typical characteristics of earthenware: the alternating rhythm of baked clay with polished (glazed) elements, functionality, and so forth.

Božena Blanuša's ceramics express the decorative-functional design trend, and are in fact a mix of two elements: the designer's talent, and the skill she acquired when studying at the Famul Stuart School of Applied Arts in Ljubljana.

Mojca and Stane Božič have developed an exceptionally interesting design approach in creating their products. They use the motifs of peepholes - found predominantly on farm buildings in the countryside - which are ingeniously decorated with patterns assembled from bricks as the central decorative and artistic motif.

HAND TRACES IN CLAY

Modern pottery and ceramics are not equally represented in all Slovene regions. **MAJK MULAČEK**, **JANA MIHELJ**, and **STANE** and **MOJCA BOŽIČ** are the best-known artisans in the Primorje region, even though the number of local craftsmen and women is the smallest in the country. They use the wide selection of clays, glazings and other materials available in neighbouring Italy to make top-class ceramics. The best craftsperson from northern Primorska is **ALENKA GOLOLIČIČ** from Gorenji Log near Most na Soči. She crafts using the *raku* technique, and also makes replicas of locally-unearthed archaeological of earthenware remains with the purpose of introducing them to a wider audience. The ceramic products of **LJUBO BLAGOTINŠEK** from Cerklje are also most original. **BOŽENA BLANUŠA**, **ANICA MIHORKO**, **URBAN MAGUŠAR** (who heads the renowned Magušar workshop for pottery and ceramics), **MAJDA GREGORIČ-TROST**, the sculptor **MOJCA SMERDU**, **DANICA ŽBONTAR** and a number of other artisans make fine products from clay and ceramics in Ljubljana. **MATJAŽ MATKO** from Novo mesto first learned about ceramics in the monastery of Pleterje. In the years since, he has invented an exceptionally original style. His products are therefore comparable to international ceramic masterpieces. The products of **SAŠO RUS** from Petrovče near Celje are comparable to Matko's, while **BRIGITA VOGRINEC** from Miklavž and **LORNA NOVAK** from Maribor continue to produce replicas and interpretations of traditional Slovene pottery and ceramics. **LJUBICA KOČICA** from Rogaška Slatina is a well-known designer and crafter of ceramics and unique of glassware items. The quality of her work has been recognized by numerous Slovene and international awards.

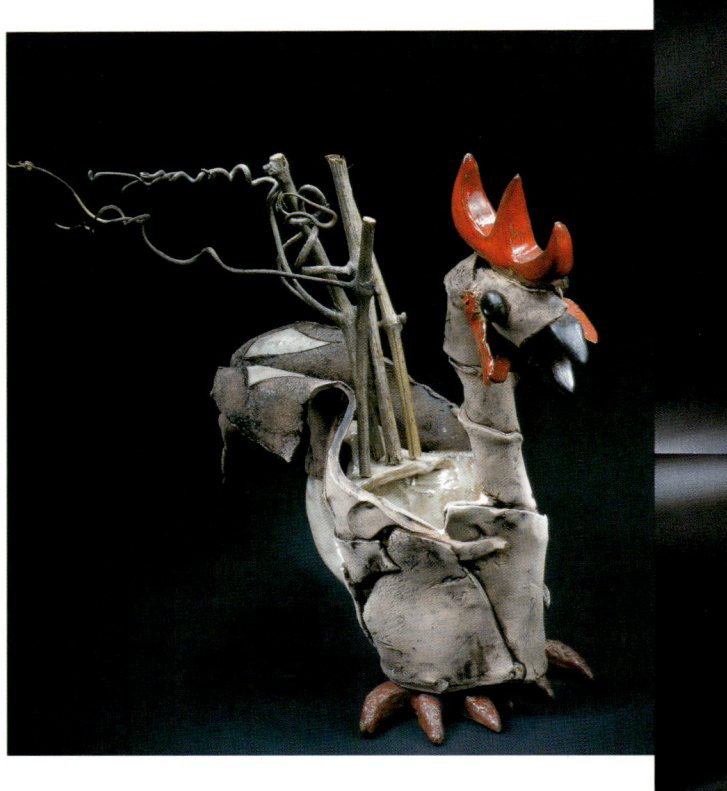

Matjaž Matko continues to work towards new trends in shaping clay at his studio in Novo mesto. He calls his unique sculptures - which are creatively and technologically distant from other established forms of ceramic product - zgnetenke (kneaded things). In the creation of his sculptures, he combines various materials in addition to clay, such as dried grapevine stalks and vines.

The ceramic products of Ljubica Kočica are, in fact, unique sculptures in ceramics, and are often used as special awards and select gifts.

HAND TRACES IN CLAY

Anica Mihorko is modernizing the shape of established products such as trays, plates, dishes and bowls by giving them a new, wavy and versatile form. She uses clay to capture and present the effects characteristic of other materials (such as crimped or undulated cloth and so forth).

Replicating traditional earthenware objects is also developed in Slovenia. Alenka Gololičič has made a name for herself in this field by crafting excellent replicas of archeological finds of ancient pottery. She studies these pre-historic remains to find new means of creative expression.

HAND TRACES IN CLAY

Tanja Cvelbar Smole's functional and decorative products are of the highest quality. They are distinctly original due to their intelligent artistic concept, the synthesis of shape and the touches of color glazing. Her functional products thus play the role of three-dimensional sculptures.

Snežana Sotlar merges design with "graphical" drawings. Her products are very similar in expression to types of ceramics found in archaeology and from exotic cultures.

130

HANDICRAFTS OF SLOVENIA

HAND TRACES IN CLAY

The ceramics of Majk Mulaček and Jana Mihelj transcend into sculpture. In this manner, "once" functional and decorative objects are given new meanings and even spiritual emphasis.

Urban Magušar's glasses are only one of his successful lines of products. His basic concepts resemble those found in glasses and bottles made in old glassworks (glažute).

131

HANDICRAFTS OF SLOVENIA

HAND TRACES IN CLAY

The superb technology of ceramics and intelligent (philosophical) model of content are the ingredients which mediate the introspective messages of Majda Gregorič Trost. Her personal talent has been enhanced by further training in Japan.

HAND TRACES IN CLAY

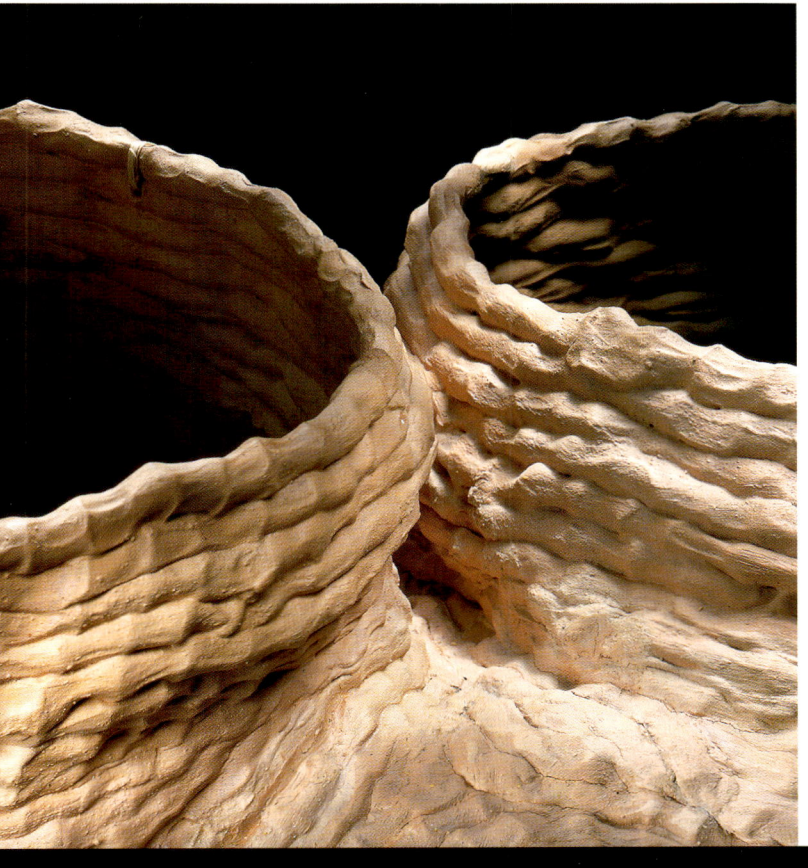

This has been a presentation of the creativity of modern Slovene potters and ceramists. Some sculptors who also make products in ceramics and clay were not mentioned here because they work outside the framework of handicrafts - presently categorized in Slovenia as home and applied crafts, which are regulated by suitable legal norms. Discrepancies in the field of terminology also separate the otherwise organically-connected forms of artistic creation which ought to work side by side to find new concepts and creative solutions.

Mojca Smerdu from Ljubljana builds her potter's the sculptor's expression on the ancient technique of assembling earthenware by the spiral layering of rolled clay strips. However, this technique is only a means to give deeper meaning to her clay masterpieces. Her clay statues take us beyond an admiration their form and surface structure. They are a means by which we establish contact with our psyche. They touch upon questions of our inner void, and the emptiness of the world we live in. Placing her products at the end of our chapter on clay was not coincidental: she adds a new, intellectual dimension to functional, decorative or traditional clay products. This touches upon the communicative role and meaning of the masterpieces present here.

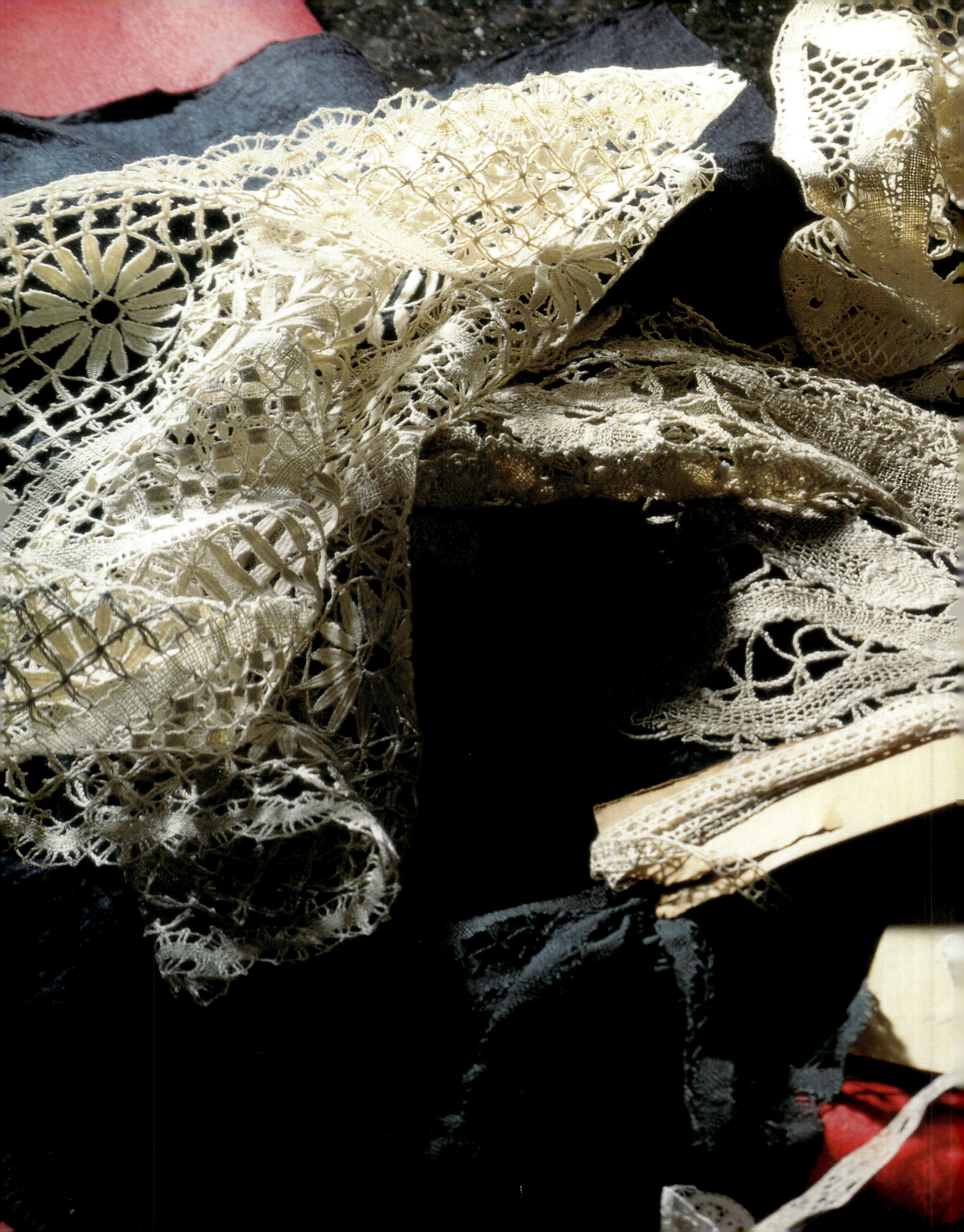

Thread Over Thread is Woven into a Lovely, Colorful Pattern

The introduction of modern weaving, knitting, embroidery and bobbin lace-making is a rather complicated affair. All of these handicrafts are extremely popular. The limits between craftsmen and home weavers are very indistinct. Both groups of crafters frequently resort to stock models and pattern books, while the original creative process from the concept, via pattern, to the final product is often more of an exception than the rule...

THREAD OVER THREAD IS WOVEN INTO A LOVELY, COLORFUL PATTERN

Although nearly every weaver, embroider or bobbin lace-maker could be mentioned here, only a few selected artisans whose work exceeds mere skill are presented below. These individuals perform their craft not only to satisfy their creative urge to decorate their living spaces or clothes, but also to create a handicraft which has more or less positive economic influences. The number of textile handicrafts practised in Slovenia is exceptionally wide, ranging from older, traditional ones to some that are relatively new to Slovenia, like patchwork. Some, such as crocheting and tapestry-making, have been completely omitted in this book because their quality does not exceed the aesthetic average. Of course, the number of craftsmen using these technologies is exceptionally wide, and unfortunately they all consider themselves artists.

MARICA CVITKOVIČ

Traditional Slovene weaving has, so to speak, died out, judging from the small number of weavers still struggling to preserve the national weavers' heritage. The last weaver of linen and linen-ware is **MARICA CVITKOVIČ** from Adlešiči in the Bela krajina region, where linen weaving was preserved the longest, i.e. until the late 1940s. Flax is still sown annuallyin the Cvitkovič fields and spun into linen threads. These are later woven into linen on Marica's weaving loom (called *krosne*), and finally turned into fine linen products. This is adorned by *tkaničenje*, a typical Bela krajina-style cross-stitch embroidering technique in which red and blue threads are used. The most representative examples of Cvitkovič's linen-ware are the embroidered woven towels called *otirači*, which supposedly first came into use in the 15th century. In recent times, *otirači* have been assigned new functions. In some households they are used as curtains, for example. Marica Cvitkovič also makes individual pieces of Bela krajina folk costumes, tablecloths, napkins and curtains. She also paints Easter eggs called *pisanice* with wax, using a technique characteristic of the region.

Modern weaving can first be seen as the continuation of historical memory in which replicas of models from the Slovene heritage are made. In its beginnings, weaving was not considered a handicraft but a regular, mostly winter, domestic handiwork activity in rural areas. It was preserved longest in Prekmurje and Bela krajina, but today one can count the number of the still active traditional weavers on the finger of one hand. The Cvitkovič family from the Bela krajina region owns a workshop and gallery in which you can admire and buy their products.

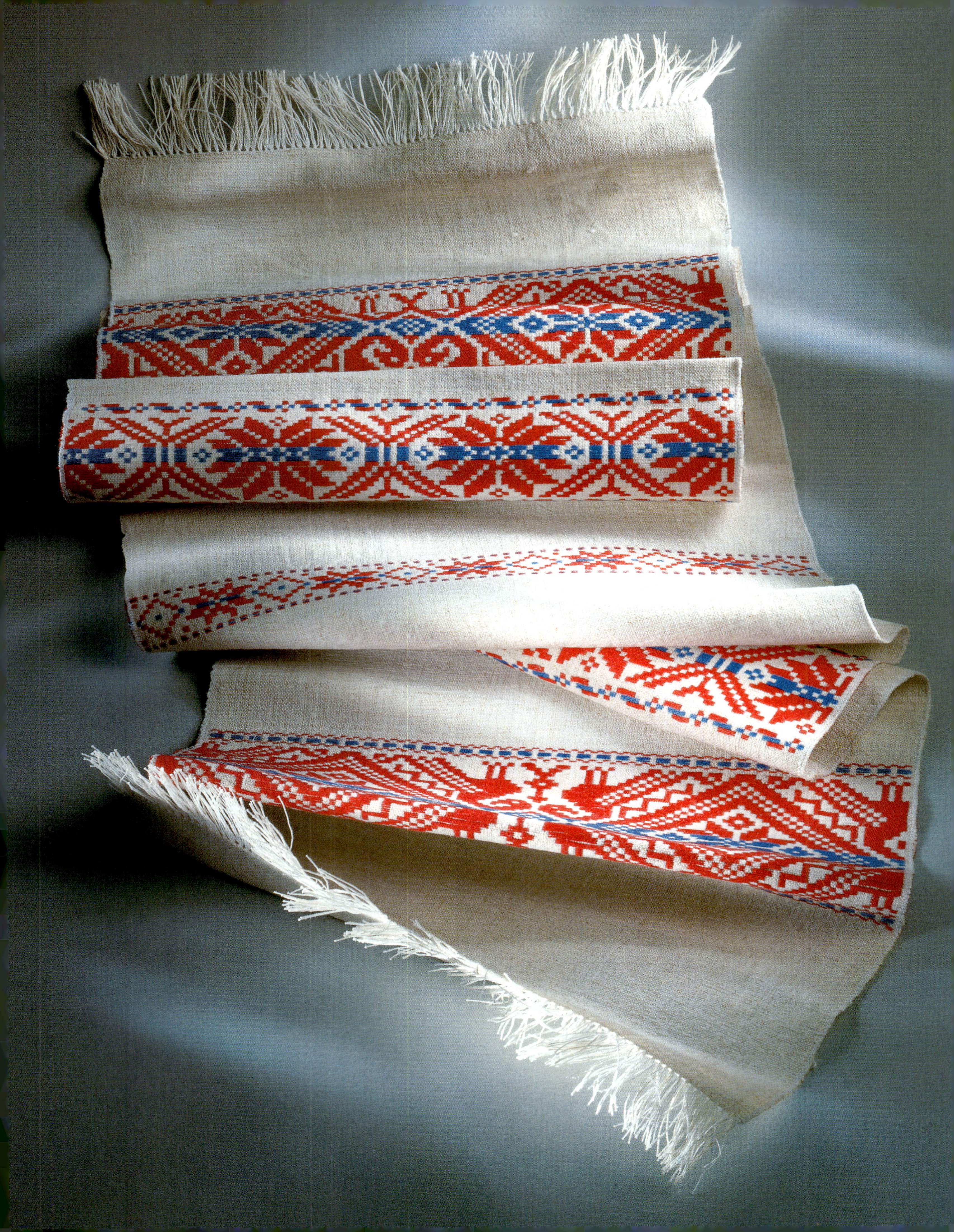

THREAD OVER THREAD IS WOVEN INTO A LOVELY, COLORFUL PATTERN

JERNEJ RUČIGAJ from Bohinjska Bela continues the weavers' tradition of the Gorenjska region using slightly modernized techniques. **MAJDA MRZELJ** from Vrhnika is also an influential weaver of unique modern woven products. She began weaving modern products in the specialized weavers' workshop at the former Dekorativna factory, where many tapestries designed by Slovenia's finest painters were created. Since the closure of this workshop, Majda Mrzelj has continued to craft unique products in her own workshop. **MARJETA SIEBERER** and **ZVEZDANA KRŽIČ** from Ljubljana have each produced creative and original works.

Today, weaving (especially modern weaving) is a predominantly a women's chore. In the past, weaving was also a predominantly female activity in the division of labor. In some better-developed Slovene regions (primarily Gorenjska), however, the weavers were mostly men. They produced various types of linen, but also used woollen threads, preparing the base from which cloth was made in special manufactures called valjkalnice. *Jernej Ručigaj from Bohinjska Bela continues the weaving tradition of his ancestors. His products, however, are much more demanding and of higher quality, created with far greater skill than is needed for the production of linen sheets for example.*

THREAD OVER THREAD IS WOVEN INTO A LOVELY, COLORFUL PATTERN

Modern cloth is produced in Slovenia as a result of home experience and weavers' knowledge imported from abroad. In the former Dekorativna factory in Ljubljana, Majda Mrzelj (Picture 3) developed a specialized workshop in which unique, experimental samples of cloth were produced. The workshop was also the place where large tapestries - designed by leading Slovene painters - were made, which influenced modern Slovene weavers. Of the latter, Marjeta Sieberer (Picture 1) and Zvezdana Kržič (Picture 2) are the most outstanding.

THREAD OVER THREAD IS WOVEN INTO A LOVELY, COLORFUL PATTERN

Vesna Hrovat from Novo mesto has developed a highly intelligent and artistic approach to designing her woven products. She draws from the fundamentals of the weaving heritage of linen products, which she combines with products of related handicrafts in which threads are worked into finished products, such as lace.

The embroideries of Neda Bevk are marked by the pure "architecture" of weaving. With elementary but intelligent combinations of thread and color, she creates perfected and sensual textiles.

Weaving on modern vertical or horizontal weaving looms results in products that are completely different from traditional ones. Such products are unique, and are the result of conscious artistic creation. **VESNA HROVAT** from Novo mesto mainly draws from the Slovene weavers' heritage in creating her woven masterpieces. She appreciates traditional weaving as a model and motivation in developing new, modern techniques. Her unique woven products are often combined with bobbin lace crafted at the Primožič workshop in Žiri. Such combinations are made for the *Lanka* trademark. Architect **NEDA BEVK** from Ljubljana develops completely original, creative weaving techniques. She makes wonderful scarves, bedspreads, and curtains, distinguished by purity of form and an intelligent use of textiles, woven into numerous well-balanced color combinations.

THREAD OVER THREAD IS WOVEN INTO A LOVELY, COLORFUL PATTERN

MAKING EMBROIDERED ITEMS (EMBROIDERY), is a very common needlecraft. Embroidery by needle and thread only started developing in the 19th century, but spread rapidly to become the most widespread handiwork of women. Its popularity was further enhanced by its inclusion in the school curricula, and by numerous regularly organized courses. The embroiderers of the past did not depend solely on their own creativity but also on screen prints on linen or paper. The patterns printed on paper were transferred onto cloth by punching. The organized efforts of agricultural advisors to encourage parallel economic activities, and the growing popularity of farm holidays, have contributed to a revival of embroidery in rural parts of Slovenia. The embroiderers mentioned below were chosen for illustration only, since the format of this book does not permit us to mention all of them. The Bela krajina-style embroidery of **MIROSLAVA RITONIJA** from Črnomelj is of outstanding quality. Besides embroidering, she also paints Easter eggs *(pisanice)* using the typical wax-drawing technique. Other embroiderers specialize mainly in embroidering tablecloths, curtains and decorative cushions. Some of them are: **JOŽICA GROBELNIK** from Velenje, **ROZALIJA STROJAN** from Zgornje Pirniče near Medvode, and **ANAMARIJA DIJAK** from Jesenice. **MARIJA LAPANJA** from Daber near Slap ob Idrijci also makes fine embroideries. These embroiderers regularly exhibit their products at the biannual Exhibitions of Home and Applied Crafts in Slovenj Gradec and Ljubljana.

THREAD OVER THREAD IS WOVEN INTO A LOVELY, COLORFUL PATTERN

Embroidery is a very common form of needlecraft and is mostly taken up by women. Male embroiderers are rare exceptions to the rule. In the course of time, various embroidery styles and techniques have evolved, depending on the type of the basic material used. They used a linen, cotton or silk base, threads of different types of material and different color combinations in the working process: the function of the final products - tablecloths, small cloths for decorating kitchen walls, curtains or embroidery on blouses - reflected the differences. Embroideries with floral motifs are becoming increasingly popular and often appear in modern Slovene farmhouses, some of which also cater for tourists. The products of Jožica Grobelnik (Pictures 3 and 4 on the previous page), Anamarija Dijak (Picture 1), Rozalija Strojan (Picture 2) and Marija Lapanje (Picture 3) are of the highest quality in Slovenia, but there are many other Slovene girls and women in the rural areas, as well as in towns, who are true masters of embroidery, endowed with exceptional creative powers. It is important to emphasize, however, that modern embroidery is reduced to the repetition of historical memory from different historical periods, dominated by the last decades of the 1800s and the first years of the 1900s. More attention should therefore be paid to the creation of modern embroidery in the future, for which the craftsmen and women need not only their skill but also some knowledge of art and design.

THREAD OVER THREAD IS WOVEN INTO A LOVELY, COLORFUL PATTERN

Embroidery and tkaničenje, a special embroidery technique, are rooted strongly in the Bela krajina region. Miroslava Ritonja from Črnomelj belongs to Slovenia's master weavers of otirači (typical Bela krajina towels), curtains and various tablecloths.

THREAD OVER THREAD IS WOVEN INTO A LOVELY, COLORFUL PATTERN

There is a white spot in the creative field of modern embroidery, which cannot be said of any other ancient handiwork with a rich heritage: knitting. The conditions for the development of this handiwork were excellent in Slovenia, since rearing sheep was a popular form of farming, especially in Slovenia's Alpine areas, providing the knitters with the basic material for their work (woollen yarn). Machine-made products, knitted in modern knitters' workshops - some of which even use computerized knitting machines - are legally not considered handicraft products. This is a great deficiency and limits the creativity of the knitters. Opposing the technical and general changes of the modern world and favouring old crafting methods is of little use in Slovenia, or anywhere else. Certain knitters are attempting to manually craft unique knitwear. Some of them still replicate the traditional models available, while others see each knitted item as an independent work of art which can also be worn. Mojca Kavčič (Picture 4) is one such knitter, while knitwear made by Helena Pratnekar (Pictures 1, 2) and Marija Pezdirnik (Picture 3) demonstrate greater connection with classic knitted items.

THREAD OVER THREAD IS WOVEN INTO A LOVELY, COLORFUL PATTERN

4

KNITTING is a much older needlecraft in which clothes are produced from woollen yarn by needles. The basic conditions for the development of this craft were excellent in Slovenia, since wool production was one of the most common farm activities. **WOOLLEN SOCKS** have always been the most representative items of knitwear, along with gloves, caps, sweaters, cardigans and, in recent times, coats and two- or three-piece ladies' ensembles. A new needlecraft, hosiery, has developed from knitting socks for domestic use. It was best developed in the upper valley of the Sava river, and in the area between Tržič and Jesenice. Knitting socks for sale was also known in Višnja Gora and its vicinity. The main hosiers' center was Tržič, with a hosiers' guild numbering 600-700 knitters. Knitting socks was a craft that employed men, women and children, but started to decline at the turn of this century. However, diverse knitting techniques have been preserved in various parts of Slovenia. The knitting tradition is also carried on in several big factories, such as Almira in Radovljica or Rašica in Gameljne near Ljubljana, and in numerous smaller and medium-sized knitwear workshops. As part of home crafts, knitting woollen socks has been preserved in the Gorenjska region. **MARIJA PEZDIRNIK,** from the village of Mojstrana, and **HELENA PRATNEKAR,** from Mežica in the Koroška region, are well-known knitters. **MOJCA KAVČIČ** from Ljubljana considers knitwear a work of art in itself. For her, every knitted item is a piece of art, and not only a base for further ornamental or appliqué decoration. She has achieved notable results in expressing her own artistic ideas on knitwear.

THREAD OVER THREAD IS WOVEN INTO A LOVELY, COLORFUL PATTERN

BOBBIN LACE-MAKING is a unique phenomenon in Slovenia in several respects. Even though it is known in several Slovene towns, it has developed best among the mining populace in the Idrija area. From there, it gradually spread elsewhere, mostly because of the organized training of prospective lace-makers. Until the interwar period, lace-making was the main or many additional source of income. The first lace-trading firms appeared in Slovenia in the late 19th century. The two most outstanding with respect to production, organization and trading in Idrija are: **STUDIO KODER** and the **FRANC LAPAJNE** firm. The **ANTON PRIMOŽIČ** firm from Žiri is also very important for lace trading. Bobbin lace-making has seen a sharp decline since World War II, so today, hand-made lace is becoming an exception. A true renaissance in bobbin lace-making started in the 1980s, and still continues today, when the craft is once again becoming popular. This might be due to a renewed interest in the Slovene heritage, seen as one of the ways of re-establishing national identity. Nowadays, lace products are popular business, promotional and state gifts because they bear the mark of Slovene creativity. The other aspect of Slovene lace-making is its typology. There are two distinct lace-making schools in Slovenia: the Idrija and Žiri schools. The trend is to differentiate Idrija lace *(idrijska čipka)*, and Žiri lace *(žirovska čipka)* by name. The differences between the two have been much over-emphasized, sometimes quite euphorically. Of course, both types of lace have unique, typologically distinctive characteristics, but using the name Slovene lace for both is more appropriate, since to a casual visitor to Slovenia the entire country seems like a town. Emphasizing the local varieties of Slovene lace, on the other hand, gives the impression of great creative variety throughout the country, which is also done in other fields of culture and life.

TADEJA PRIMOŽIČ

Together with Idrija, the town of Žiri is one of Slovenia's biggest lace-making centers. The trademark of the Žiri lace-makers in connected with the well-known lace-making and lace-trading business, A. Primožič (founded in 1888), whose lace you can admire and buy in their gallery in the center of Žiri.

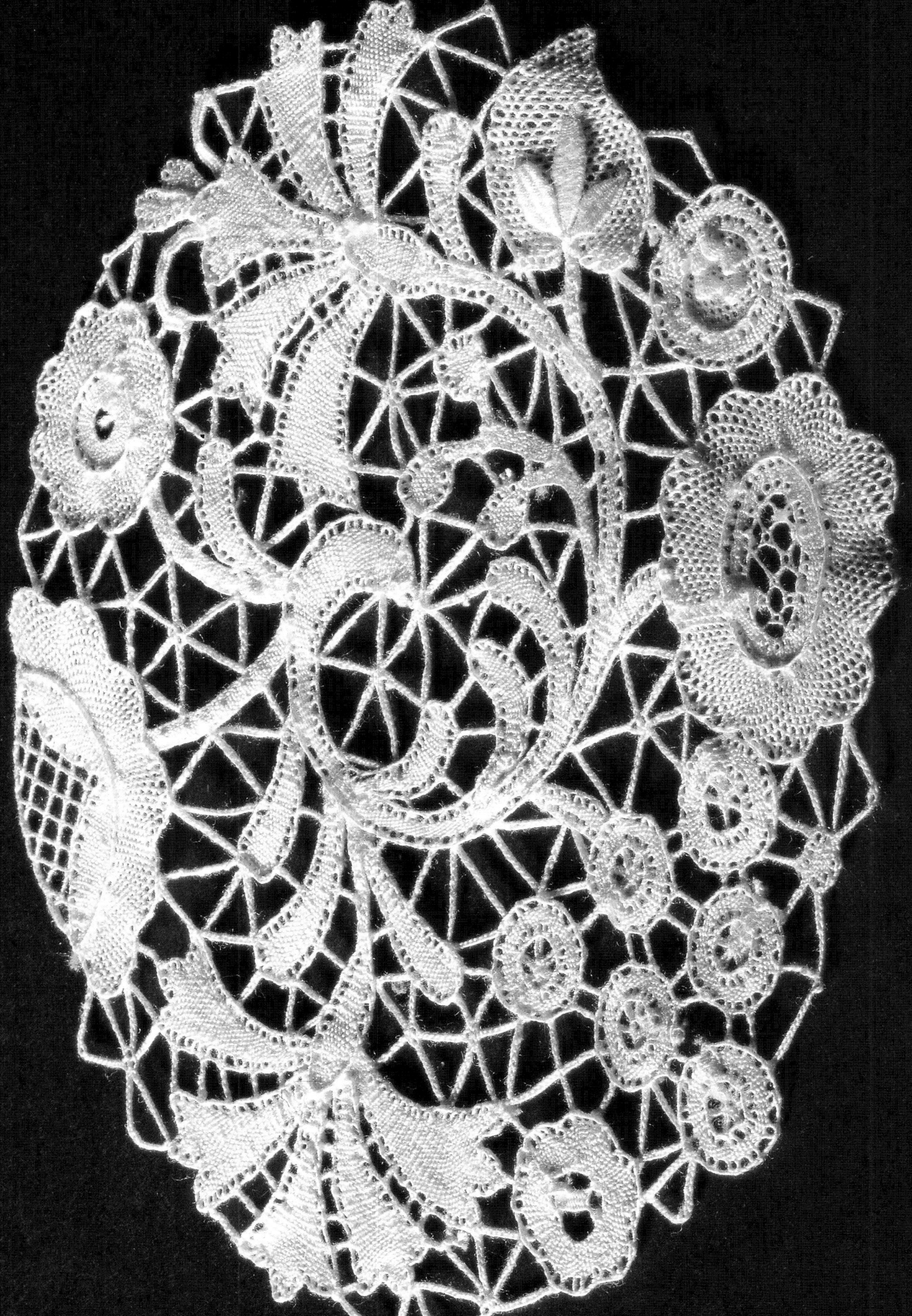

THREAD OVER THREAD IS WOVEN INTO A LOVELY, COLORFUL PATTERN

After decades of oblivion, lace again became popular in the mid-1980s. Such renewed popularity is the consequence of increased interest in Slovene creativity and the national heritage related to diverse areas, including that of business and state gifts. Lace products had to be specially adapted and functionally developed to be suitable for this purpose. The Primožič firm from Žiri (Pictures 1, 2) has achieved some notable results.

The third aspect of the phenomenon is the education of lace-makers. The **Lace-making School** in Idrija was established in 1876 and has continued work uninterruptedly to the present day. Several other lace-making schools were opened later, and in 1995 the first textbook on lace-making was published. This textbook, entitled *Klekljanje* (Bobbin Lace-Making), is the only Slovene textbook on handicrafts. This introduction was necessary to show the importance and extent of bobbin lace-making. Modern bobbin lace-making also develops in town areas, and is no longer connected with certain social groups, who saw the craft suitable for earning additional income. Many craftssmen and women find lace-making a relaxing hobby and a useful skill, confirming the saying: "The more you know, the more you are valued".

There are many lace-makers in Slovenia, which is why I will limit myself to the presentation of select key practitioners here. The **Lace-making School** in Idrija contributes the lion's share in terms of training lace-makers. There are also lace-making schools in Železniki and Žiri and, in addition, regular courses are organized throughout Slovenia as part of various courses.

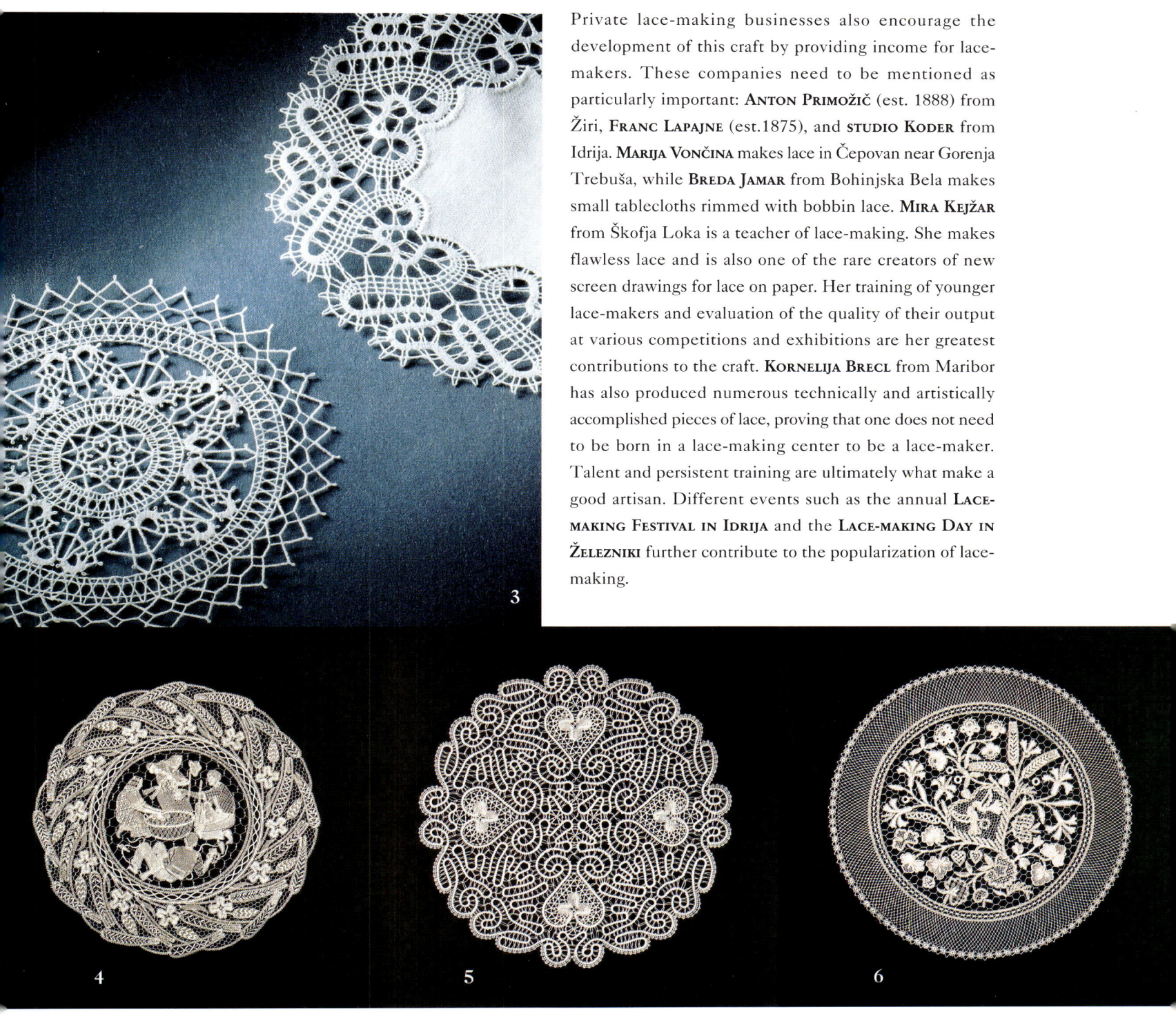

THREAD OVER THREAD IS WOVEN INTO A LOVELY, COLORFUL PATTERN

Private lace-making businesses also encourage the development of this craft by providing income for lace-makers. These companies need to be mentioned as particularly important: **Anton Primožič** (est. 1888) from Žiri, **Franc Lapajne** (est.1875), and **studio Koder** from Idrija. **Marija Vončina** makes lace in Čepovan near Gorenja Trebuša, while **Breda Jamar** from Bohinjska Bela makes small tablecloths rimmed with bobbin lace. **Mira Kejžar** from Škofja Loka is a teacher of lace-making. She makes flawless lace and is also one of the rare creators of new screen drawings for lace on paper. Her training of younger lace-makers and evaluation of the quality of their output at various competitions and exhibitions are her greatest contributions to the craft. **Kornelija Brecl** from Maribor has also produced numerous technically and artistically accomplished pieces of lace, proving that one does not need to be born in a lace-making center to be a lace-maker. Talent and persistent training are ultimately what make a good artisan. Different events such as the annual **Lace-making Festival in Idrija** and the **Lace-making Day in Železniki** further contribute to the popularization of lace-making.

The Lace-Making School in Idrija, Slovenia's oldest, has continued work uninterruptedly since 1876, thus contributing the lion's share in the preservation and popularization of bobbin lace-making. It is the only school in Slovenia in which pupils are trained in one of the handicrafts. The identity of the lace-making tradition and modern creative trends are also preserved in the model lace products of the school's pupils (Pictures 4, 5, 6). In addition to this school, there are several other schools, courses and individuals teaching bobbin lace-making to young aspiring lace-makers. Kornelija Brecl from Maribor is an excellent lace-maker (Picture 3).

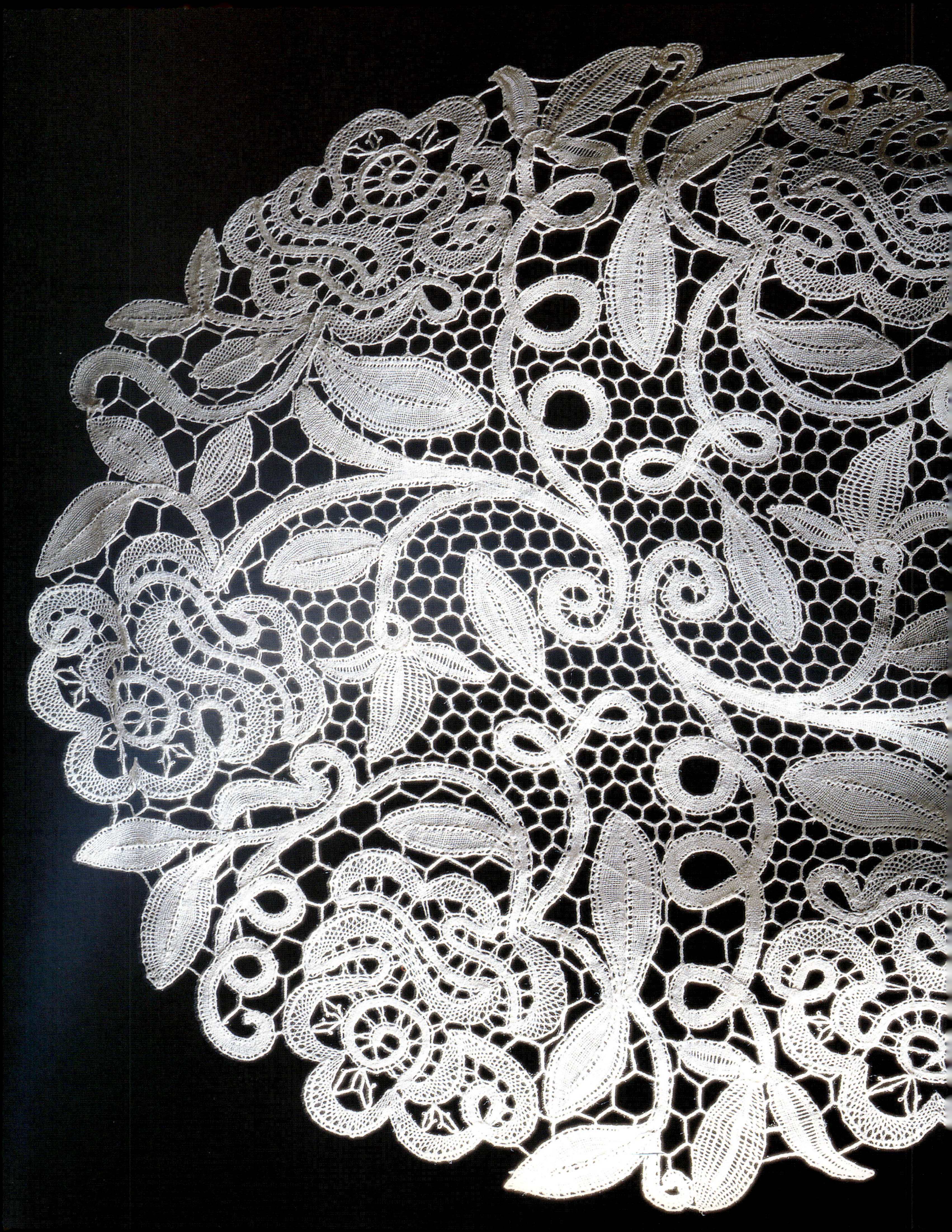

THREAD OVER THREAD IS WOVEN INTO A LOVELY, COLORFUL PATTERN

Mira Kejžar

The lace-making teacher Mira Kejžar has educated several generations of lace-makers. In addition to successfully transferring her technical knowledge to young lace-makers, Kejžar has also translated her personal talent onto paper by drawing numerous plans and drawings of lace patterns. The strongly-rooted belief that lace-makers invent the pattern as they go along is completely wrong. Bobbin lace is made following a precisely-drawn pattern pinned onto the bun. The originatirs of countless patterns remain anonymous. Some of them came to Slovenia from abroad, from all arcas of the former Habsburg Empire. Mira Kejžar and some other lace-makers contribute to lace-making in three ways: by drawing lace-making patterns, by making lace, and by transferring their knowledge to the younger generations. These help preserve and continue bobbin lace-making, but are also essential for the preservation of any handicraft.

151

HANDICRAFTS OF SLOVENIA

THREAD OVER THREAD IS WOVEN INTO A LOVELY, COLORFUL PATTERN

Bobbin lace-making has spread strongly in the last decade, not only geographically but also with regard to the number of lace-makers. With the popularization of this craft, tendencies to protect lace (especially that from Idrija) have appeared. Some people seek to clearly define the particularities of specific regional types of lace (Idrija lace, Žiri lace). Such endeavors are charged with unhealthy regionalism at times. The increased popularity of lace-making is nevertheless most welcome, and it is a pleasure to state that Slovene lace-making continually develops within and outside traditional lace-making centers. Marija Vončina is a lace-maker from Gorenja Trebuša above Čepovan (Picture 1); Breda Jamar makes lace in Bohinjska Bela (Picture 3); and Vanda Lapajne continues the family lace-making and lace-trading business in Idrija (Picture 2). Studio Koder (Picture 4, 5), also located in Idrija, has introduced more innovative approaches in the conceptualization, making and selling of bobbin lace. You can view and buy their refined lace, or lace elements incorporated in to other products for home and personal use, in their shop gallery.

THREAD OVER THREAD IS WOVEN INTO A LOVELY, COLORFUL PATTERN

THREAD OVER THREAD IS WOVEN INTO A LOVELY, COLORFUL PATTERN

In discussions of individual handicrafts, one must always take into consideration their future development. In most cases, the efforts of craftsmen go no further than replicating traditional products of their trade. More attention needs to be paid to changing this mentality to one that emphasizes the necessity of developing concepts for new products and new functions for them. Lace was mostly considered an addition to be incorporated into classic products. Most of the lace pieces produced still remain at the level of the replication traditional models. However, the need to create modern lace was also recognized. There have been some attempts to produce original modern lace. But most pieces of bobbin lace created today are, in fact, repetitions of historical memory and variations thereof. But the notion that we do need modern as well as traditional lace is derived exactly from this historical development. **Saša Pušnar** from Ljubljana not only produces useful and decorative objects in the manner of modern bobbin lace but also makes her lace paintings part of her artistic research.

ANDRAŽ DEBELJAK

In the mid-1980s the phenomenon of framing lace appeared, giving lace a new decorative function similar to that of paintings. This is a positive way of emphasizing the exceptional mastery combined in numerous pattern switches and alternations, raising it above the level of edges for tablecloths or collars on blouses. More over it seems that a good knowledge of heritage opens up new horizons in the field of craft techniques and expression. The young lace-maker **Andraž Debeljak**, a student of landscape architecture at the Ljubljana Faculty of Biology, has not only designed original lace-making patterns but also introduced new materials to the craft. Instead of the traditional cotton, linen or silk thread, he uses thin gold or stainless wire. Working with such materials demands complete mastery of the craft because the thread must never be torn. If this happens, the pattern is interrupted and the artistic and aesthetic quality of the piece is ruined. Debeljak's products are original masterpieces, made for business and state gifts under the family trademark Anars. They are presented as lace paintings or appliqués in the glassware of **Ljubica Kočica** and **Tanja Pak**, both renowned Slovene designers of glass.

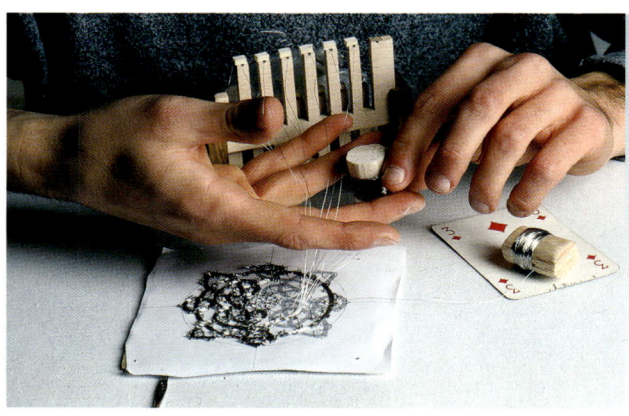

Andraž Debeljak's production of bobbin lace made of wire and incorporated into glassware is a model example for the future development of handicrafts. His final products are the result of a creative symbiosis between two artists: a lace-maker and a designer of glass. Most of Debeljak's products were incorporated in glass products crafted by designer Ljubica Kočica from Rogaška Slatina. Tanja Pak from Ljubljana also collaborated with Debeljak by using his metal lace as elements in her glassware. In the development of these combined products, corresponding technological analyses were performed, thus making the final products not only artistically but also technologically accomplished.

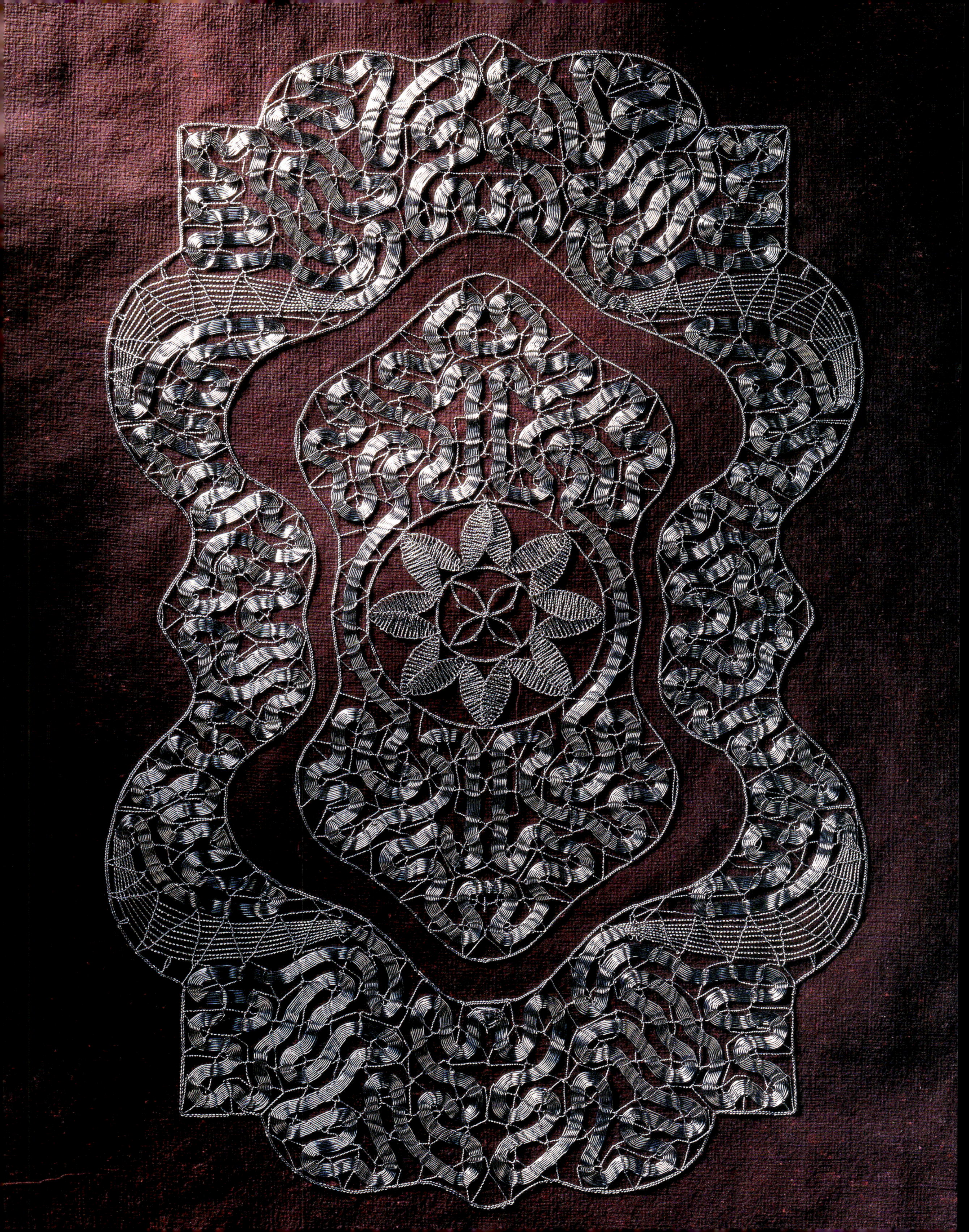

THREAD OVER THREAD IS WOVEN INTO A LOVELY, COLORFUL PATTERN

The extended use of various materials in bobbin lace-making also has a history of its own. Saša Pušnar first introduced wire to bobbin lace-making. Pušnar was also one of the first lace-makers to make modern, original bobbin lace. For her, lace is not part of a tablecloth, pillow or piece of clothing but a painting, a modern work of art. Such trends are essential for the further development of Slovene lace-making on the foundation of the rich tradition, towards new, modern creative directions.

THREAD OVER THREAD IS WOVEN INTO A LOVELY, COLORFUL PATTERN

One of the textile design. Handicraft is **PATCHWORK**. This came to Slovenia through foreign influence. Decorative bed spreads and quilts are sewn by alternating patterned parts of cloth combined in varied correct geometrical patterns. **MARGARETA VOVK-ČALIČ** from Kranj, who has found her own original crafting style, is the best patchwork artist in Slovenia.

Patchwork products are also created by a specific set of laws and rules. Many patchwork courses are organized on the basis of foreign models and literature. Despite the firm rules for the identification of patchwork products, the set of standards for judging and evaluation, and the differentiation of influences from different world patchwork centers, Slovene patchwork artists should strive towards developing their own technologies, and above all to original expressions in color and composition.

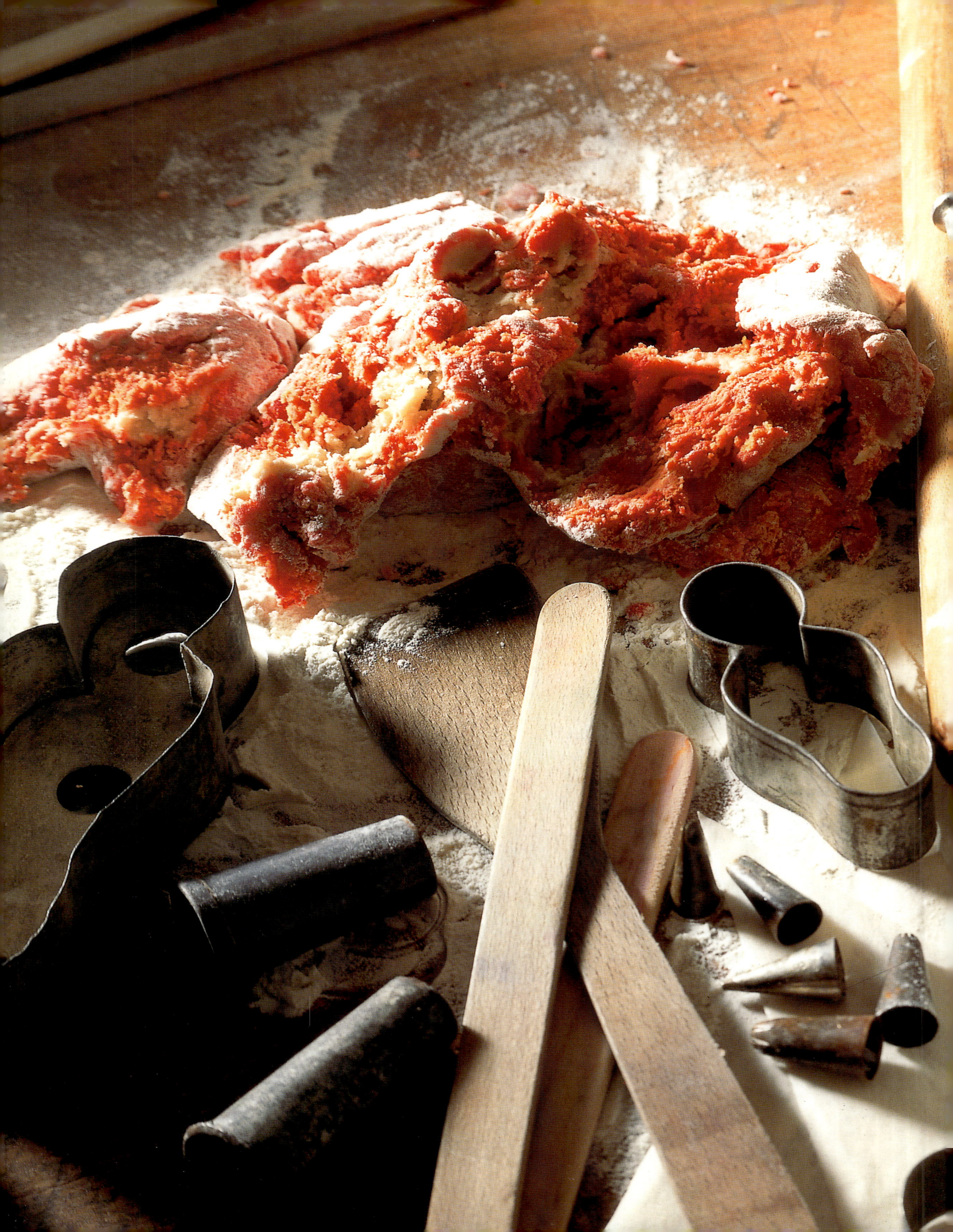

Honey, Wax and Dough

Three important goods are connected with man and his natural environment - wax and bread. All three have always influenced our lives and were used for daily or different special occasions. Because of the ties with these goods, certain forms of expression and skill appeared in handicrafts...

Honey, wax and dough

Apiculture, with its venerable history, is not just another simple economic activity in Slovenia. The Slovene contribution to European apiculture helped lay the basic foundations for modern beekeeping. When modern apiculture began to evolve in the mid-19th century, the first teacher at the apiculture school in Vienna was a Slovene, Anton Janša from Breznica in the Gorenjska region. Peter Pavel Glavar from Komenda was his contemporary. He wrote the first European beekeepers' treatise for the improvement of European apiculture. At the same time, the first painted beehive panels appeared, which were exquisite and only found in Slovenia. Today, they represent the most comprehensive gallery of Slovene folk painting available. People's emotions, scenes from daily life, folk superstitions and philosophy from the mid-19th century to the beginning of the 20th century are depicted. More on will be said later this subject.

First, we shall introduce some craft materials which contain bee products. One of these is **HONEY DOUGH**, which has been made for centuries as part of the **MEAD-, HONEY-,** and **CANDLE-MAKING** craft, carried out by mead-and honey-sellers. The term *lectarstvo* (gingerbread making) is often used to describe it. It is derived from the name of the final product *lect* or *lecet* (gingerbread), which is a semi-permanent sculpted and decorated sweetmeat. The technology of gingerbread-making changed in the 19th century with the introduction of cheaper honey substitutes such as sugar. All three original gingerbread-making techniques have been preserved to the present day, and include the free manual shaping of the dough, pressing the dough into special wooden moulds, and making simple gingerbreads later decorated with glazings squeezed onto the base from decorating bags. Although the term "gingerbread-making" was originally used to refer to all three techniques, it is used to describe only the last of them today. The most famous of all glazed and decorated gingerbread sweetmeats is the gingerbread heart, with a mirror and a verse to fit every occasion in its center.

Some authors hypothesize that sculpted and decorated gingerbreads were part of the ancient ritual of the preparation of breads and votives, used as aids to evoke affection or love in a person of the opposite sex, and also in rites at festive occasions like Christmas or Easter. A sense of proportion and manual skill has always been necessary for free-hand gingerbread making, resulting in unique gingerbreads.

The origins of this technique of shaping honey-dough remain unknown, though it is likely that it was developed in nunneries. From there it spread elsewhere. It was taken up by women in the countryside and later, to a lesser extent, by women in the towns as well. Making gingerbreads was also a pastime of noble ladies in castles. This craft was preserved longest in Dražgoše and its surrounding areas, which is why they are still called **DRAŽGOŠKI KRUHKI** (Dražgoše breads) today. They are often used as promotional gifts. The makers stick to traditional motifs (hearts, half-moons, hosts, images of St. Nicholas, buns), but also design new ones, which is commendable. One of the best-known makers of *dražgoški kruhki* is **CIRILA ŠMID** from Železniki.

CIRILA ŠMID

The manual shaping of honey dough in Železniki, Dražgoše and their surrounding areas is an activity that has helped keep the historical memory of mead- and honey-sellers alive. According to some theories, this craft spread to the countryside from local monasteries and convents in certain parts of Slovenia.

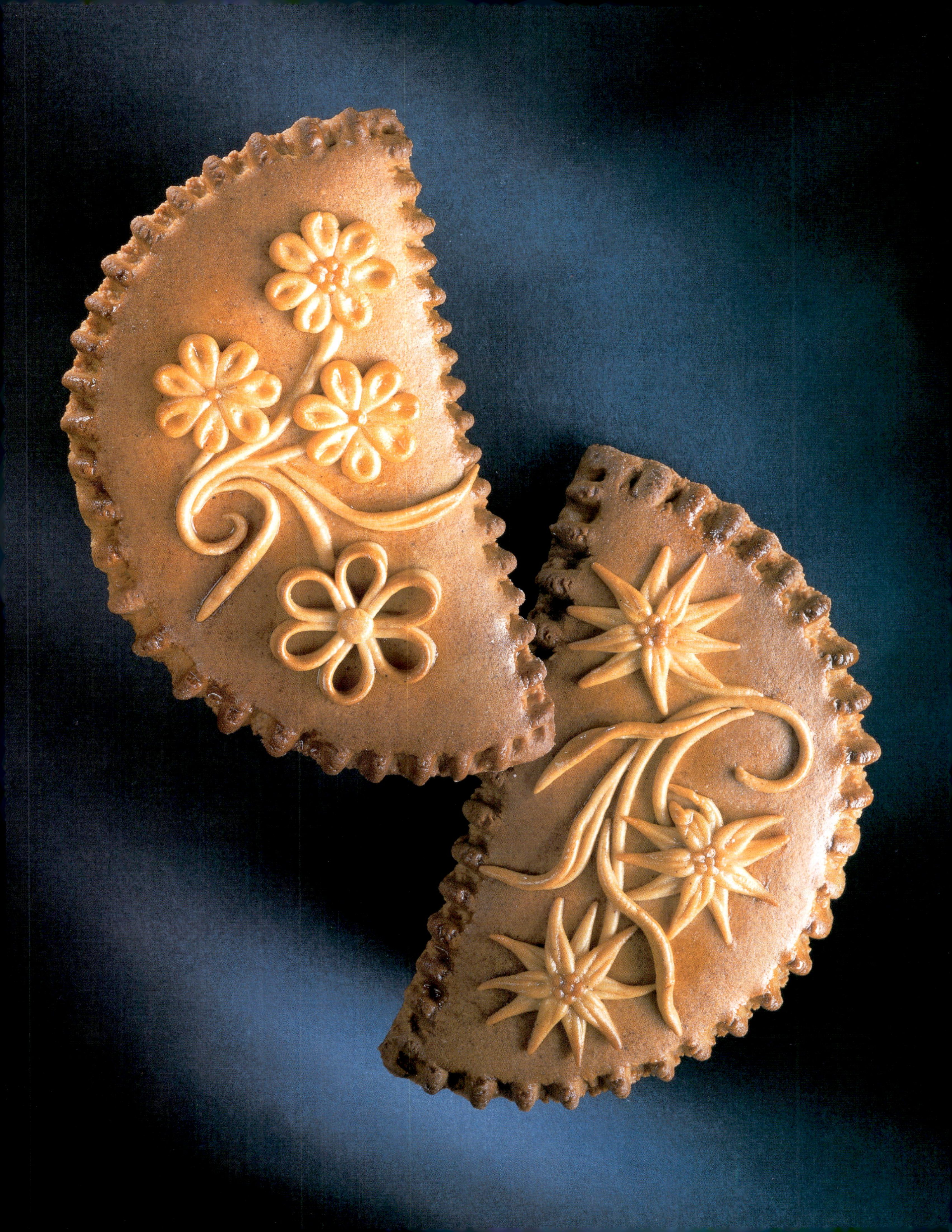

HONEY, WAX AND DOUGH

Crescent-shaped gingerbreads (krajčki) *are the oldest type of manually-shaped gingerbreads, but stars and hearts are also forms in which they commonly first appeared. Today, some craftsmen and women are experimenting with new shapes and motifs, but their efforts remain at an amateur level. Another crafter who also specializes in baking this sweetmeat is Frančiška Zalaznik, who works in Vrhinka, outside the primary territory of the craft.*

Outside the Škofja Loka region, there are two more makers of this sweetmeat: **FRANČIŠKA ZALAZNIK** from Vrhnika and **ANA SELAN** from Ljubljana. The latter learned the trade from her mother in Dražgoše. She started researching materials and techniques of gingerbread-making. Her accomplished masterpieces, with refined ornamentation, make high-quality gifts for every occasion. They are used as personal and business gifts, and to decorate walls in private houses. This exemplifies how the roles of some products of the craft heritage change over time. In the past, all gingerbread sweetmeats, made manually or otherwise, were useful presents that one could also feast on. Today, they are mostly used as decorations. Some individuals even replace the honey dough (used to make figural breads by being pressed into special moulds) with clay to make decorative objects.

162

HANDICRAFTS OF SLOVENIA

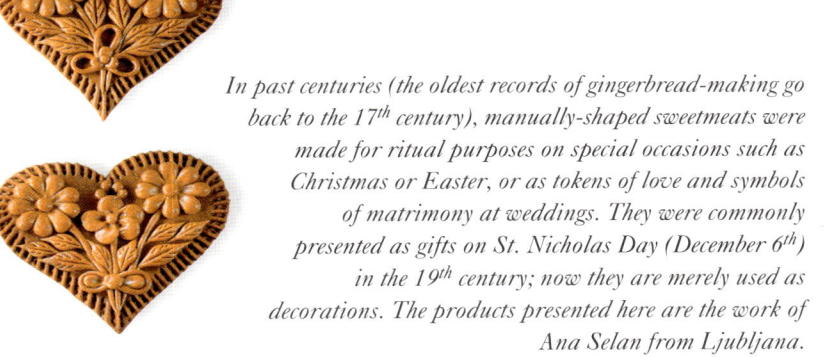

Honey, wax and dough

In past centuries (the oldest records of gingerbread-making go back to the 17th century), manually-shaped sweetmeats were made for ritual purposes on special occasions such as Christmas or Easter, or as tokens of love and symbols of matrimony at weddings. They were commonly presented as gifts on St. Nicholas Day (December 6th) in the 19th century; now they are merely used as decorations. The products presented here are the work of Ana Selan from Ljubljana.

Dekle poglej me prav,
da t' ne bo jutri žal,
da ne boš rekla,
da sem te golj'fal.
pa eno tako ženo 'met
le enega srca.
Ljubezen še bo,
ko tebe in men
Najslajša radost je srca,
ko vsko si delita dva.
(A. Aškerc)
On, ki ptice pod nebom živi,
naj ti da srečne, vesele dni!
(F. Prešeren)

Honey, wax and dough

The workshop of **Hrabroslav Perger** from Slovenj Gradec carries on the two-hundred-year-old family honey-making tradition, based on Štajerska motifs. It is one of the oldest honey and mead workshops in Slovenia. In addition to a wide range of gingerbreads, Perger also makes baptism, confirmation and wedding candles, adorned by traditional ornaments from the 19th century and earlier. In working with *lect*, Perger makes red gingerbread hearts, rimmed in white and decorated in various colors. A small mirror is attached to the center and a verse or saying (normally concerning love or friendship) is placed below. Perger is famous for his gingerbreads with rhythmically flowing ornamentation patterns. He also designs bigger heart-shaped gingerbreads for special occasions and purposes. In recent years, Perger has been experimenting with new color combinations and new ornaments. Amongst the new successes is the Slovenj Gradec gingerbread heart, which has become the most recognizable town souvenir and gift.

THE PERGER FAMILY

Candles were also mentioned. The primary candle-makers' material is, of course, wax, which is produced by bees. Today, of course, the use of beeswax is limited because it has been replaced by cheaper materials such as paraffin. Producing candles from beeswax signifies a special value. Some candle-makers and workshops, like **Čebelarstvo Božnar** from Polhov Gradec, still make candles of pure beeswax.

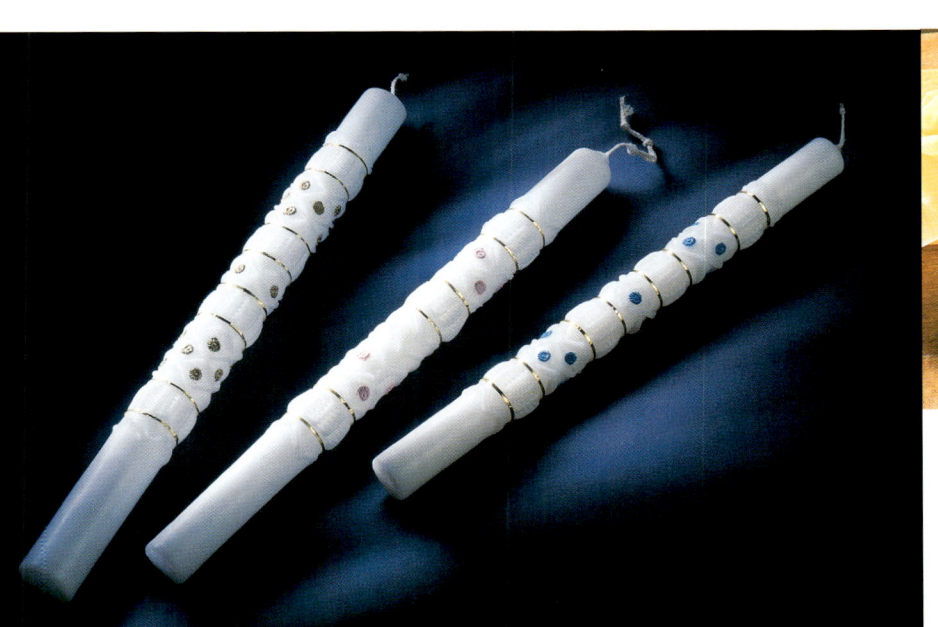

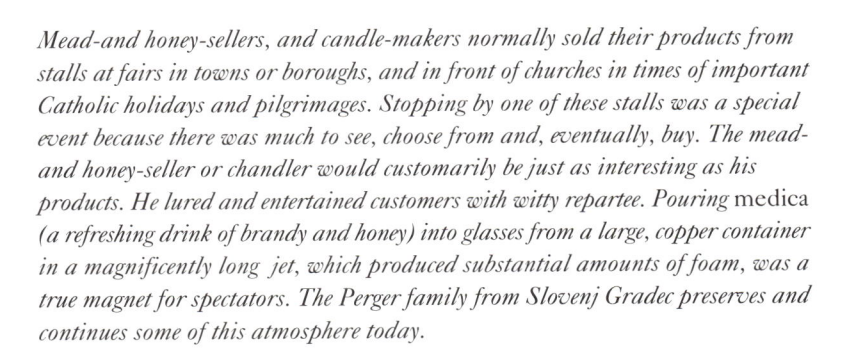

Mead- and honey-sellers, and candle-makers normally sold their products from stalls at fairs in towns or boroughs, and in front of churches in times of important Catholic holidays and pilgrimages. Stopping by one of these stalls was a special event because there was much to see, choose from and, eventually, buy. The mead- and honey-seller or chandler would customarily be just as interesting as his products. He lured and entertained customers with witty repartee. Pouring medica (a refreshing drink of brandy and honey) into glasses from a large, copper container in a magnificently long jet, which produced substantial amounts of foam, was a true magnet for spectators. The Perger family from Slovenj Gradec preserves and continues some of this atmosphere today.

Honey, wax and dough

In the past, candle-and honey-makers made classic candles for lighting, holiday and ritual purposes. The great Slovene architect JOŽE PLEČNIK took up the design of original candlesticks for interior church decoration. In collaboration with the Kamnik-based candle-maker STELE, he produced a number of unique candles. They were colored and decorated with wax figures, created by pouring hot wax into wooden gingerbread moulds. Many of these can still be seen at the Stele workshop, which has a long tradition. It is the only surviving classic candle-makers' workshop with all the architectural particularities. Its attic and roofing are adapted for the natural whitening of beeswax by sunlight.

Although predominantly crafted for secular use, candles were also made in convents and monasteries. The candles made in the CARMELITE CONVENT IN SORA NEAR MEDVODE are the products of master chandlers. Wax proved to be an excellent material for designing modern decorative candles. These often function as decorative sculptures rather than as simple sources of light. Here, modern candle-making merges with sculpting, especially if the candles are unique items not produced by pouring wax into moulds (as used in serial production).

RAFAEL SAMEC from Ljubljana created his first line of decorative candles several years ago. Besides colored wax, Samec introduced other materials to candle-making. His candles, made from wax and other materials - products of combined collaborative efforts with designer STANE TURŠIČ - increasingly resemble sculptures. SONJA and BOGDAN KOGOVŠEK from Ljubljana also make decorative candles, trying to synchronize the possibilities of wax shaping and color.

HONEY, WAX AND DOUGH

Candles designed by the Carmelites in their convent in Sora are unique items. Each of the candles is decorated with manually-shaped colored wax (Picture 1). The Stele workshop still preserves the memory of its collaboration with architect Jože Plečnik by producing candles based on his concepts (Picture 2). In Čebelarstvo Božnar in Polhov Gradec, candles are made by the simple technique of bending waxed honeycombs. Made of beeswax, a completely natural material (Picture 3), they burn exceptionally well. Making modern candles is very widespread today, but relatively few original and quality products appear on the market. Svečarstvo Kogovšek (Picture 4) and Svečarstvo Samec (Picture 5) were the first chandlers' workshops to design original products independently from foreign models.

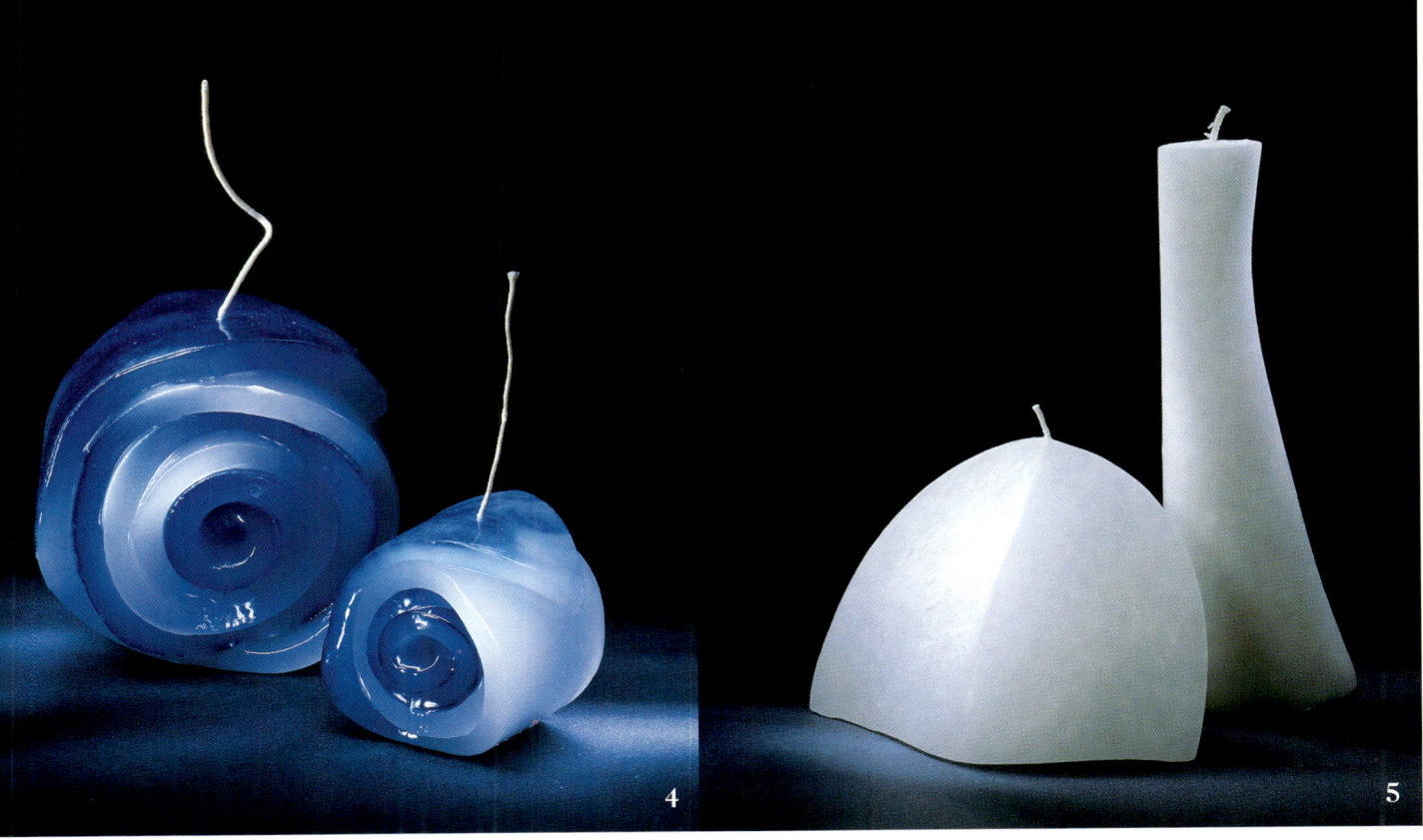

3

4

5

167

HONEY, WAX AND DOUGH

Another natural material must be given attention in this chapter-dough, made from various types of flour. Because they are some of the most beautiful examples of the symbiosis of man and nature, dough, bread and flat-cakes have always played an important part in folk customs and rites. They were nutritional but also symbolic. Dough is an excellent material for different types of home craft. It is connected with professional bread preparation carried out by bakers and bakeries. In some rural households, breads for special occasions, marking the cornerstones in the lives of everyone (births, christenings, weddings), are still baked today, thus preserving this home craft.

It is easy to convince oneself that baking is a well-developed handicraft in Slovenia by visiting the annual exhibition of Slovene farm delicacies in Ptuj. In this competitive exhibition, one can note a rich creative variety of dough masterpieces that soothe the stomach as well as the soul. Singling out individual bakers would therefore be most unfair. When and on what occasions do the Slovenes shape their daily bread and flat-cakes in particular forms? The first two occasions for which bread is given are births and christenings. **CHRISTENING-BREADS** and **FLAT-CAKES** are made from white wheat flour. There is a wide selection of such breads and flat-cakes called **BOTRINA**. This ornamental bread is made from plaited dough braids. It is presented to the newborn by the godparents. It has different names in different parts of Slovenia. In the region of eastern Štajerska it is called *bosman*, a name that also appears in other rites and customs. **WEDDING-BREADS** or **FLAT-CAKES** are made with even more effort and attention. The one we are already familiar with is *bosman*. It is sometimes seen as a symbolic infant. In the past, it was placed in the bride's lap before she and the bridegroom retired to their room. Sometimes mock baptisms of this bread were performed at wedding feasts. In the Koroška region, wedding-bread was completely different. It was called *podirjanca* in Rož and *dirjenca* in Zilja. It was named after the characteristic hole in its center, and was decorated with dried fruit and cigars. It was tossed into the crowd of wedding guests during the wedding celebrations and everyone attempted to catch it. Today, these breads occasionally appear at weddings or baptisms as reminders of a once-popular custom, but they no longer have such a strong symbolic meaning as they had in the past. They represent an attempt to break away from of the uniformity of modern times.

The plaited heart is also a common form of wedding-bread. Two doves, intertwined rings and other symbols of matrimony adorn the heart. The ornaments are also made of dough and then attached to the base as appliqués. **MARJANCA DOBNIKAR** is a master baker of heart-shaped wedding-breads. She learned the craft at her birthplace of Artiče in Bizeljsko. Another type of wedding-bread (similar to that from Koroška) can be found in Prekmurje and Bela krajina. Here, the bread is known as *vrtanek* or *vrtanj*, and is wheel-shaped like the *podirjanca*. The hole in the center is rimmed with a bread braid. Smaller varieties of this bread were baked in Prekmurje during reaping and harvest time as presents for the best reapers. Today, *vrtanjki* are popular sweetmeats at various gatherings and receptions.

Honey, wax and dough

Bread plays a symbolic and not only a nutritional role in rites connected with Lent, Easter or Christmas time, but also on All Saints' Day. Today, numerous preserved local and regional varieties are mostly baked for Easter and Christmas, as the preservation of historical memory. These breads usually consist of dough braids, and are surprisingly well-regarded and loved in urban areas. Their typology is also a subject of research in urban areas, too. In the Primorska and Dolenjska regions, breads called *menihi* (monks) are baked at Easter time. They are breads of various sizes, with a whole egg inserted in their centers before baking.

Of course, *potica* (walnut roll) is the central Slovene cake. Initially, it was only baked at Easter and Christmas, but it is the most popular sweetmeat today. When talking about it, one should use the plural *potice* because the taste of the cake depends on the filling. The outward form of *potica* is relatively new-the ribbed, round, clay baking-mould with a hole in its center has only been known for the last two hundred years. The technique of shaping the *potica* has also changed in this relatively short period, and this can be seen in the origins of its name. The word *potica* originally derives from the word *povitica*, which signified a pastry of rolled dough with a filling inside. Slovene potters, who invented the *potica* mould, are credited with the form by which we know this Slovene sweetmeat today.

A type of wedding-bread or flat-cake, the "wedding heart" is a typical product made by Marjanca Dobnikar and, with its local characteristics, belongs to the Bizeljsko region. Its iconography is directly related to the wedding ceremony. The base of the bread (pletenica) is made of dough of mixed yeast, white flour and milk, while the decorations are crafted from a mix of white flour, egg white and water. In addition to making the bread, Dobnikar also crafts traditional decorative paper napkins onto which she then places her products of exceptional quality. Another who specializes in baking this sweetmeat is Frančiška Zalaznik, who works in Vrhnika, outside the primary territory of the craft.

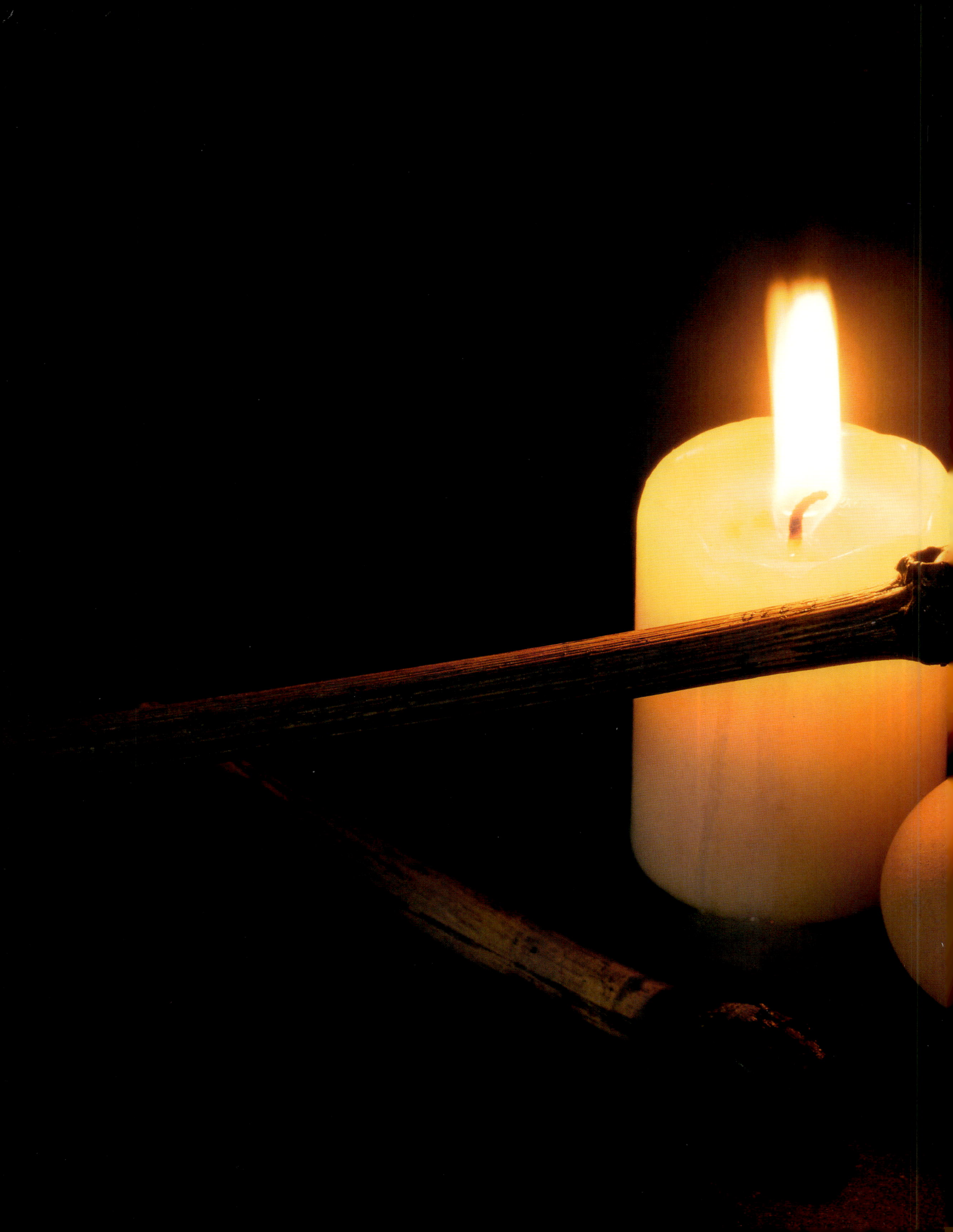

Images of Fertility

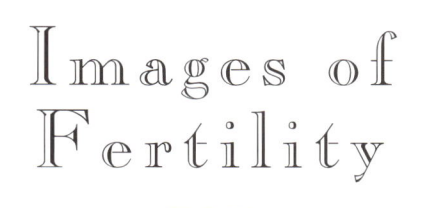

Spring after spring nature comes to life. Hundreds and thousands years ago, people saw spring as a time of re-birth, and created their own symbols to commemorate the occasion. This included the egg, which symbolizes fertility and the source of new life in spring time. This ancient Indo-European symbol was adopted by Christianity and is symbolically connected with Christ's resurrection.

Images of Fertility

Easter eggs made by Milena Starešinič from Ravnac near Suhor. The ornaments are made by scraping the egg surface.

To this day, eggs are a traditional Easter dish in all Christian nations. Coloring and decorating *pirhi* (Easter eggs) is an example of an activity related to seasonal rites. In addition to its spiritual dimension, painting eggs is a vital form of art and one which occurs annually. One must naturally differentiate between two areas of egg decoration: making Easter eggs at home from eggs decorated according to various techniques, and making eggs for sale. Each of these techniques has a special name. Thus there are *pisanice, pisanke, jermenke* and *remenice*. This second sphere - decorating eggs - is a special handicraft which craftsmen consider an artistic challenge. Some experts disagree on when painting Easter eggs first appeared. Some place it in distant pre-Christian times, while others think it first appeared in the 18th century. Regardless of this discrepancy, painting Easter eggs is an interesting phenomenon with its own history, development and future.

Some older, traditional egg-painting and decorating techniques are still used in Slovenia today. The first presented are *remenke* or *remenice* from Prekmurje. Their name suggests that they were first painted red. In the Prekmurje dialect the word *rumen* means "red". The characteristic of contemporary Prekmurje *remenke* is their bright red color base - egg shell - onto which predominantly floral motifs are incised with a sharp object (a needle or knife). The base color today may occasionally vary to other color tones as well.

In applying of ornaments onto Easter eggs with a special pen and melted wax, one half of the egg is colored first. When the wax dries, the pattern is drawn onto the other part. To prevent the oval-shaped eggs from rolling and ruining the ornaments, the eggs were laid into a basket full of wheat until the wax dried. This is the oldest technique of decorating eggs with wax (products by Milena Starešinič).

IMAGES OF FERTILITY

For ornamenting eggs, Mihaela Gregorčič uses a special pen - pisalka - a wooden stick with a small, cone-shaped metal trough, which she heats on the candle flame.

She then inserts a piece of wax into it to melt. When the wax melts, it enables her to write with the bottom, narrower part of the trough. The basic technique in wax painting is founded on protecting the color that must not be painted with darker colors. This means that she first starts applying wax to the lightest parts of the ornament, those in the natural color of the egg shell.

When Mihaela Gregorčič has drawn the first ornament on the egg shell with wax, the procedure of painting the egg with the next color follows. Where applied, the wax prevents the color from taking hold. The process is repeated in this manner to the darkest hues, first dark red and brown to almost black shades. Decorating eggs demands a well-prepared plan and an even better preconception about making a pattern using wax coatings.

IMAGES OF FERTILITY

Another technique of egg decorating originates in Bela krajina. The local variety of Easter eggs called **PISANICE** is suggestive of the decoration technique used, also because of the manner in which the artists apply heated wax onto the egg by a special pen. First an ornament (that ought to remain in the original color of the egg) is drawn. Then the eggs are immersed in other color coatings from the brightest to the darkest. The technique resembles the batik technique of textile dying in Asia and Africa. Two of the many makers of Bela krajina - style Easter eggs (pisanice) are **MILENA STAREŠINIČ** from Ravnac near Suhor and **MIHAELA GREGORČIČ** from Metlika. These eggs have already become a traditional Slovene souvenir. Starešinič and Gregorčič have both won numerous awards and prizes in competitions, which are very common at Easter time. One of these is organized annually by the newspaper *Slovenske novice*. There are normally many contestants attempting to win the prize for the most beautiful set of *pirhi*. Every year, more original decoration techniques appear, which are not just repetitions of historical memory, thus proving that there are no limits in egg painting except the artisans' imagination. Painting eggs in innovative ways has a considerable tradition. For example, available historical sources testify to the fact that around Easter time numerous fine Slovene painters painted and sold Easter eggs in shops and even galleries in the period between the two wars.

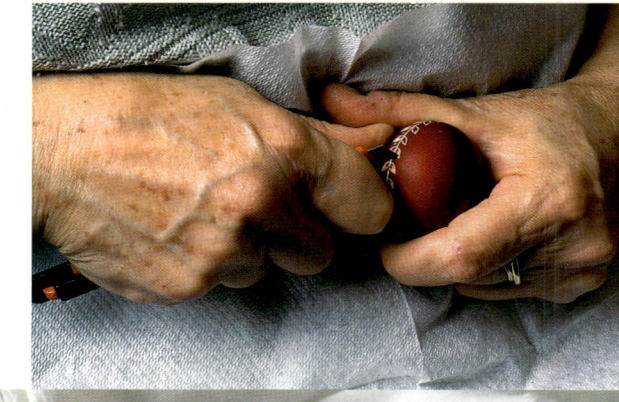

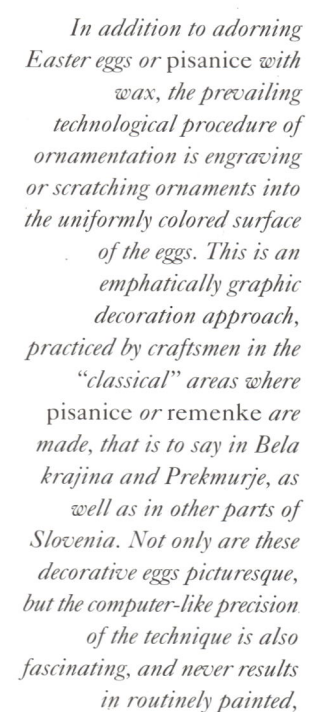

MILENA STAREŠINIČ

In addition to adorning Easter eggs or pisanice *with wax, the prevailing technological procedure of ornamentation is engraving or scratching ornaments into the uniformly colored surface of the eggs. This is an emphatically graphic decoration approach, practiced by craftsmen in the "classical" areas where* pisanice *or* remenke *are made, that is to say in Bela krajina and Prekmurje, as well as in other parts of Slovenia. Not only are these decorative eggs picturesque, but the computer-like precision of the technique is also fascinating, and never results in routinely painted, stereotyped items.*

174
HANDICRAFTS OF SLOVENIA

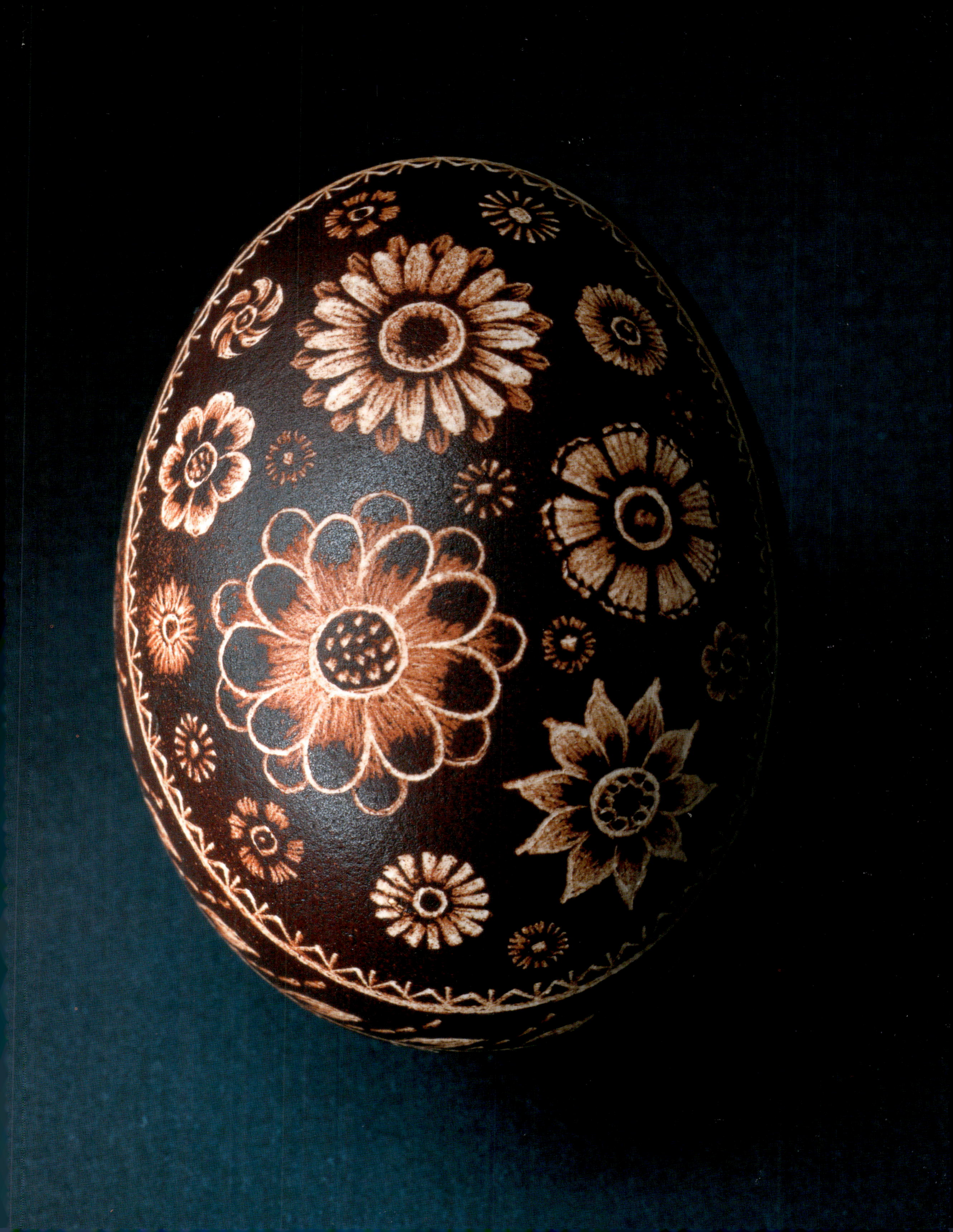

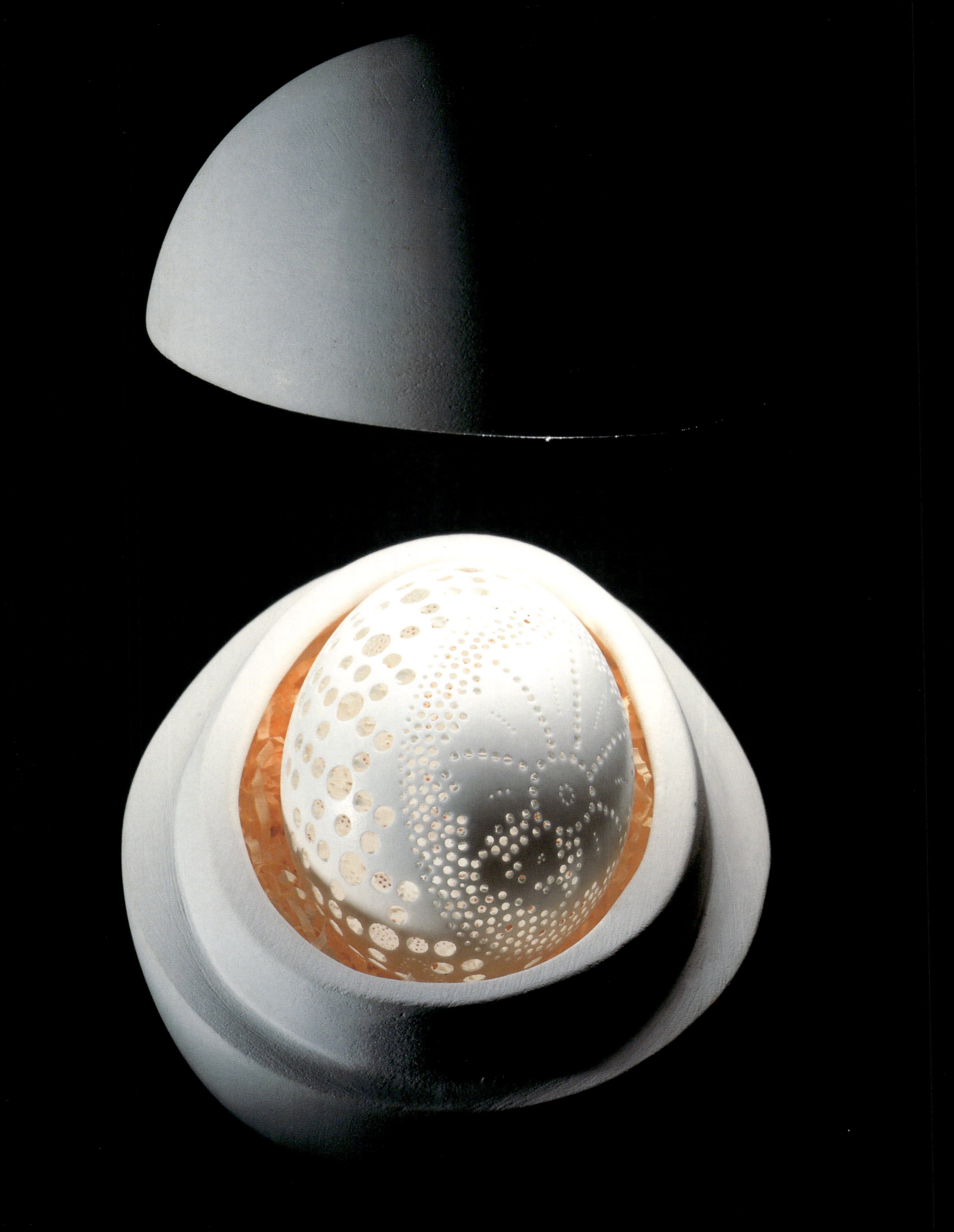

IMAGES OF FERTILITY

Some modern craftsmen discover high-quality craft technique with their creative attempts. This happened to **Franc Grom,** an exceptional craftsman from Vrhnika who, several years ago, created a truly exceptional set of Easter eggs. Today his *pirhi* are known as *vrhniški pirhi* (*pirhi* from Vrhnika), and are a local trademark. Grom's technique and creativity are exceptional. He drills minuscule holes (from 3,000 to 17,000 per egg) into the emptied eggshells - of course, not in random order but in special lace patterns and decorations to make true lace-like masterpieces. Such work requires enormous patience and an exceptional sense of proportion and rhythm, important for transferring ornaments and individual ornamental elements onto the eggshell. He draws patterns from the Slovene national handicraft heritage of ornaments in the creation of his products.

Franc Grom

Perforating eggshells by a drilling machine is a unique way of decorating emptied eggs. It is one of the modern fashions of artistic expression on Easter eggs, to which considerable attention is also paid elsewhere in Europe (in Bern, St. Gallen, Winterthur, Nyon), where workshops, fairs and other domestic and international creative events are organized.

IMAGES OF FERTILITY

The most distinguished creative feature of Franc Grom from Vrhnika near Ljubljana is his refined transferral of the traditional patterns of bobbin lace and embroideries onto the eggshells by perforation. This gives the eggs a completely new artistic dimension, and also makes his eggs differ from those less common in other European countries. Because of their distinctive ornamentation, Grom's products were justifiably named "vrhniški" because Grom lives and creates in this Slovene town. Other typological variants created in Bela krajina or Prekmurje are likewise named according to the region in which they were made. Grom's example shows that local names can be used to refer not only to traditional products but to modern ones as well. Grom also experiments with perforating in original patterns, entirely separate from models found in the heritage of lace and embroidery. In this last feature, Grom's creativity is comparable to that of similar European artists (such as the Swiss Walter Fehr).

IMAGES OF FERTILITY

The refined lace patterns on perforated eggs come to life fully with additional lighting. Grom achieves interesting artistic effects in combining the patterns with diverse color coatings on the inner and outer side of the egg shell. His products have naturally exceeded their primary, Easter significance. Today they are regular business or state gifts, as symbols of superb creativity, distinguished by a sense of balanced composition, rhythmic ornamentation and exquisite crafting.

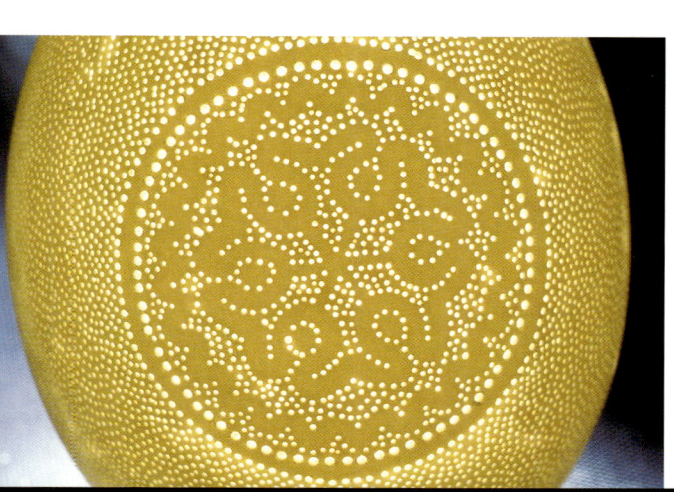

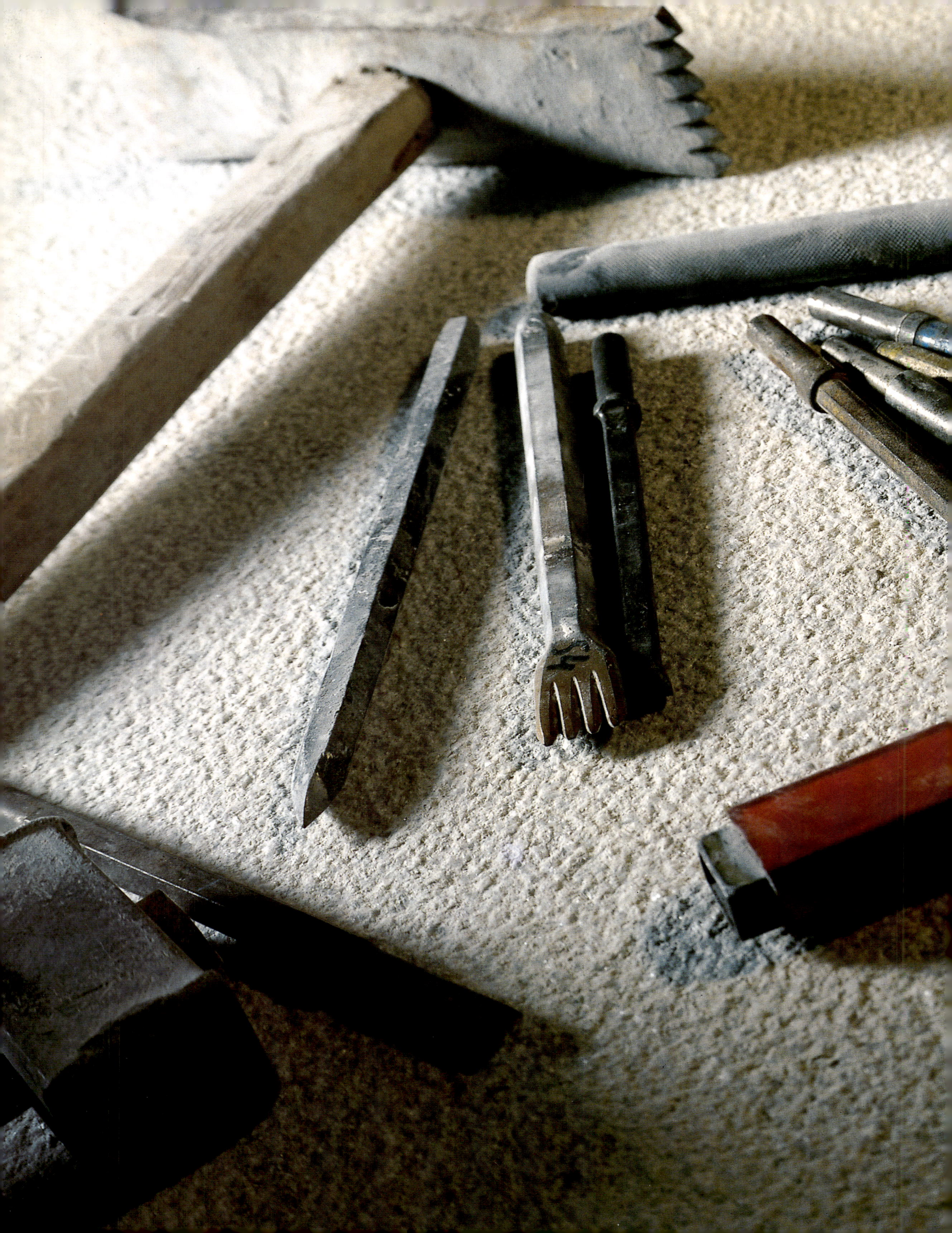

The Manuscript of the Millennia

Stonemasonry has a rich tradition in Slovenia, and various types of stone are used as its basic materials, not only in the Karst region, where working with stone has been a way of life for centuries, but also in other parts of the country. There, various softer or harder types of stone have always been and still are used as material, to which the hands of skilled masons give new meaning...

THE MANUSCRIPT OF THE MILLENNIA

The regions of Primorska, the Karst and Istria have the richest tradition in quarrying and dressing stone. Stone was the main building material, but many smaller objects for interiors and household items were made of it as well. The craft developed between the 17th and 19th centuries, which was the period when master stonemasons from the regions of Friuli and Veneto came to Slovenia to introduce new knowledge and stone-dressing techniques. These craftsmen naturally used different varieties of locally available stone. For example, Podpeč marble and *gliničan* are typical of the Ljubljana region, *Hotaveljčan* (Hotavlje stone) and the green tuff from Peračica are typical of the Gorenjska region, while black stone is predominant in the hillside regions of Litija and in western Dolenjska. Some wonderful black stone farmhouse portals hewn of this stone can still be found in that region. Schist for roofing is quarried in Selška dolina, Poljanska dolina, and on the slopes of Pohorje. Various types of softer sandstone suitable for dressing are also quarried there. From the conglomerate found on the shores of the Sava river, called *labore*, high-quality "white" millstones were made. The best "black" millstones were hewn from Kočevje stone. Building links and smaller constructions were made from gray sandstone from the Rogatec region, while whetting stones were made from a type of sandstone with a higher content of flint. In Slovenske gorice, numerous underground shafts (true mines) are preserved, where sandstone, particularly suitable for building homes, churches and wine cellars, was quarried and transported by carts and oxen to places where building material was needed. Stonemasons from the Karst region have always used several types of stone (Cretaceous limestones), ranging from those suitable for exterior use (Repenje stone), to softer ones used for the dressing of buildings and equipment for the interiors (Lipica stone). Stone of high quality quarried in the Trieste region (Nabrežina and its vicinity) was used for finer products and building details. This is only a brief review of the natural resources that were the foundation for the development of Slovene stonemasonry.

Modern methods and techniques of working stone are predominant in modern stonemasonry. But the heart of this craft still begins and ends with hammers, boasters, mallets and polishing devices. Slovene stonemasons continue the rich tradition of dressing stone in diverse new directions, while their knowledge remains indispensable in the renovation and preservation of objects of the stonemasons' heritage.

Hewn stone mortars were among the most typical utensils and appliances for food preparation in the Primorska region. In modern times, mortars have been assigned mostly to decorative functions because of the purity of their shape, which is an example of the misunderstood positive value of heritage objects and their functionality. We often come across mortars used as flowerpots. Today, hewing stone mortars is a continuation of traditional stonemasonry. In the past, this was a rather common home-craft, which has evolved into an independent craft of exceptional quality. This quality is also exemplified in the work of Zvonko Čehovin.

The Manuscript of the Millennia

Despite favorable natural conditions, a rich tradition and excellent knowledge of stone-dressing, the popularity of stonemasonry slowly started to decline after World War II. The conditions started to improve only after the extensive promotion of stonemasonry as a creative and economically promising craft. **Boris Udovč** from Naklo near Kranj, one of the leading Slovene stonemasons, has contributed a great deal to this. Until some years after World War II, "white" millstones were made in the-then renowned Puhar workshop in the same town. Today, Udovč accepts even the most challenging and demanding stone-dressing commissions, collaborates on projects connected with the preservation of the national architectural heritage, and makes various replicas. He thus continues the varied and accomplished work of Vodnik, the Ljubljana-based former stonemasons' workshop.

Boris Udovč

Kamnoseštvo Udovč (the Udovč stonemasonry) is a workshop where the artistic hewing of stone is carried out. They specialize in carrying out truly challenging orders, often related to the replication of traditional stone objects, and the renovation monuments, their stone architectural components and their accoutrements.

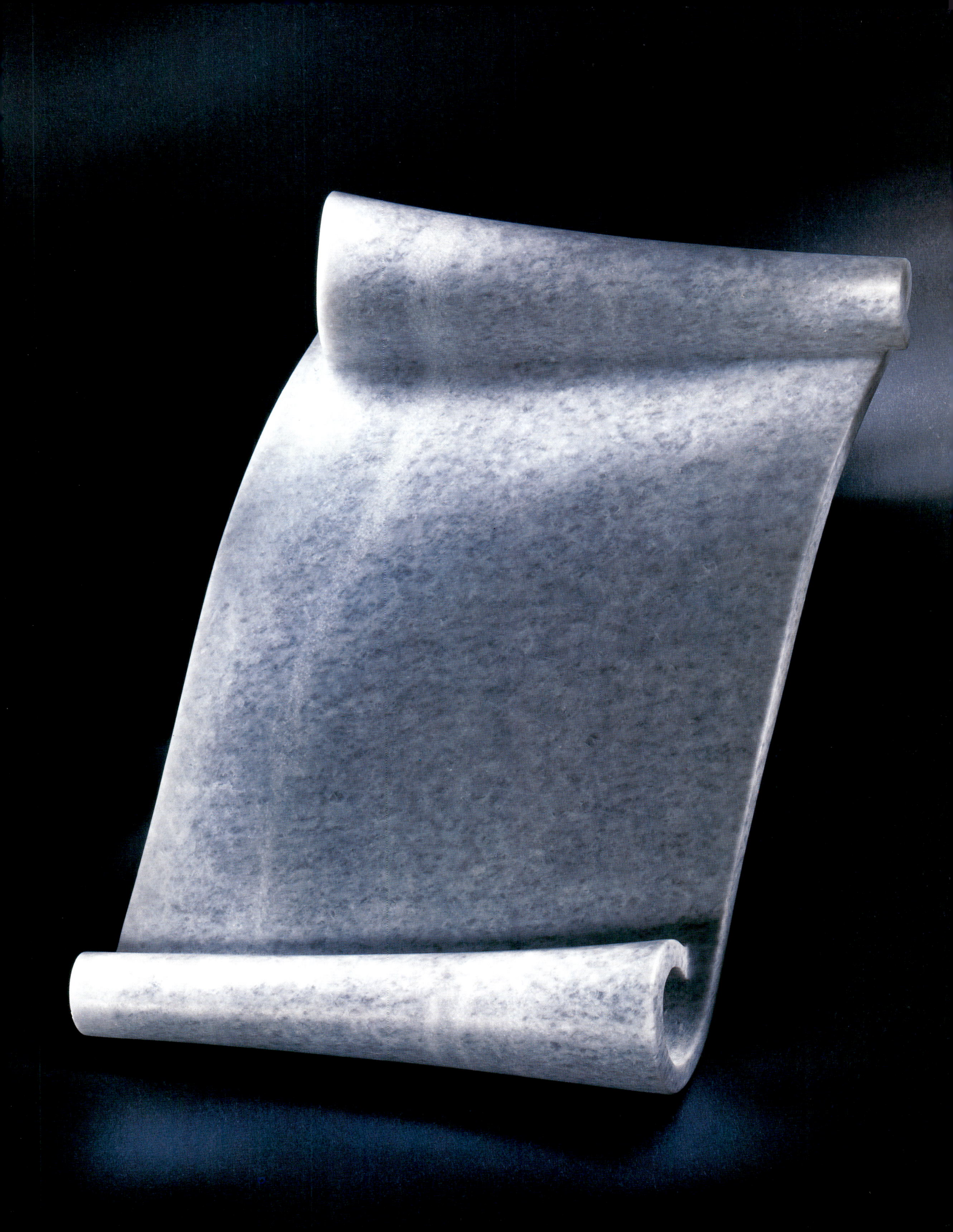

THE MANUSCRIPT OF THE MILLENNIA

The workshops of Mužina (Pictures 2, 3) and Tavčar (Picture 1) are deluged with orders. Both employ highly skilled stonemasons, and develop excellent technologies. By continuing the classical stonemasons' heritage, ennobled by new technological procedures, they create conditions for the further development of this typical Karst handicraft. They plan their products themselves, but they also craft creations by renowned designers, such as the well in front of the Oskar Kogoj Gallery in Miren, which was made at the Tavčar stonemasonry.

Several stonemasons' workshops of various sizes still exist today. Their main commissions are connected with making gravestones and decorating buildings. The firms of **MUŽINA** from Selo near Ajdovščina and **TAVČAR** from Povirje near Sežana are the best known stonemasonries in the Primorska region. The Mužina firm prides itself on top-notch modern technology, and the Tavčar firm has its own quarry and a wide range of products. Many expert stonemasons work in the Tavčar workshop. They make commissioned products, which mostly demand manual stone-dressing. They make unique staircases, fences, fountains and vessels. **PAVLO GULIČ** from Kopriva na Krasu, who excels in dressing the most challenging details, is one of them.

THE MANUSCRIPT OF THE MILLENNIA

Modern technology of the highest quality, combined with the use of various electronically-guided machines, cannot replace the mark of classical stonemasonry the manual shaping of products and details, which gives them their charm, exceptional form and excellence. The hands of Pavlo Gulič from Kopriva na Krasu can craft anything which modern technology fails to achieve.

THE MANUSCRIPT OF THE MILLENNIA

Two craftsmen – **Dušan Volk** and **Jože Gavez** from Bilje near Renče- use stone from the Soča basin and the Karst region for dressing their unique, hand-crafted products. **Zvonko Čehovin** from Ozeljan makes replicas of typical Karst or Mediterranean stone mortars, which were once indispensable items in every household. In the past, they were used in food preparation; today they are used as decorative items. In 1990 local Karst stonemasons sculpted a stylized statue of *morska medvedijca (Monachus albiventer)*, designed by Oskar Kogoj. This fountain sculpture was made of Lipica stone and was one of the biggest in former Yugoslavia. It was dedicated to the Mediterranean Games in Split.

The stone found in Primorje makes the products of local stonemasons exceptional. They craft a wide selection of exceptional products from Karst and Soča stone, which they know best. Dušan Volk dresses different types of decorative and functional stonemason's objects, which in this manner become parts of the environment we live in.

THE MANUSCRIPT OF THE MILLENNIA

Today, our preferences and tastes in art are often partial to products dressed from different varieties of imported stone, which may have been quarried and brought to Slovenia even from very distant quarris on other continents. Importing stone for bigger orders and larger surfaces is justifiable, but it is not an excuse for preferring it to Slovene stone. Even in material found locally, stonemasons and their customers can find a varied selection of colors and forms. Jože Gavez from Bilje near Renče uses stone from the Karst region and the Soča river.

In another part of Slovenia, **Jože Leva** (from Koritno near Oplotnica) hews or rather, splits schist slates, which are, together with wooden shingles, straw and stone slates from the Karst region, typical roofing material in certain parts of Slovenia. Besides their primary role, his schist slates have been given new roles today. They are used to plaster the exterior walls of buildings or stone fences, which is not the best use for them in my opinion. The manual production of whetting stones from gray sandstone, which contain more flint, is still carried out by **Marjan Antolinc** from Log near Rogatec.

Many of the once numerous workshops, quarries and stonemasons have become part of historical memory. In several areas, the revival of stonemasonry has been hindered by modern efforts to preserve the natural resources of the country, but these efforts are positive. One example is the basin of the Krka river. In its upper part, tuff is still deposited in the form of natural barriers. The locals know this stone as *lahki kamen* or *lahkouc* (light stone). In the past, most local settlements and other buildings were built from it. It was gathered during the summer, when the water level was low enough to allow the stone to be cut with special saws. The stone blocks were then transported to the building sites. Today, this local tuff is legally protected as part of the Slovene natural heritage.

THE MANUSCRIPT OF THE MILLENNIA

Splitting schist for roofing has been preserved to a limited extent. Its use is now restricted to the upkeep and conservation of roofs of buildings belonging to the national cultural heritage. Jože Leva makes schist slates for roofing (Picture 1). Quarries of gray schist are situated in the vicinity of Rogatec in the eastern part of Slovenia. Because of their high flint content, they are suitable for the production of whetting stones. Marjan Antolinc (Picture 2) crafts round whetting stones for spinning whetting machines, and also whetting stones called osli *for sharpening scythes and knives.*

191

HANDICRAFTS OF SLOVENIA

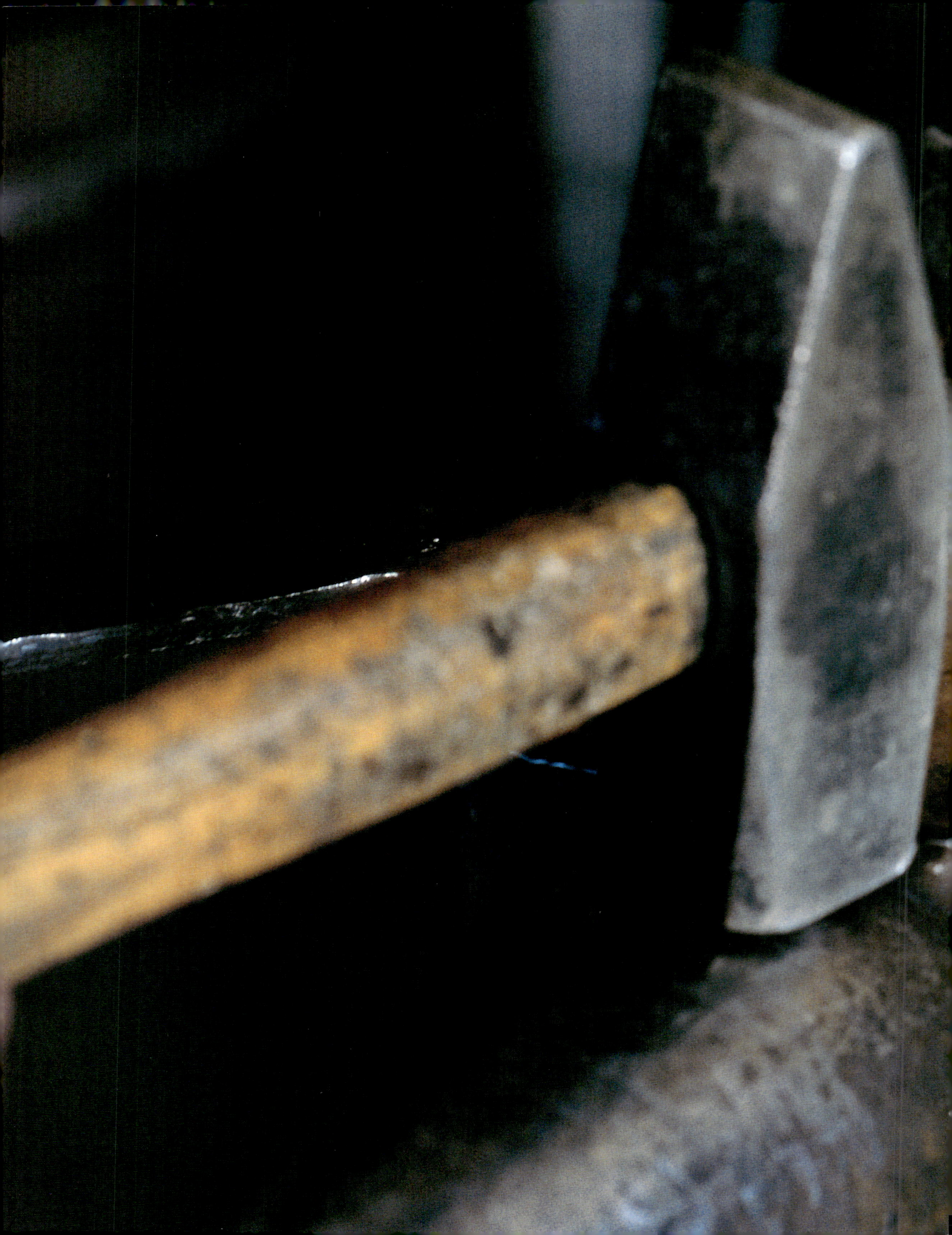

Between Hammer and Anvil ...

We normally label incomprehensible things as secrets. The harder they are to comprehend, the more secretive they seem. Our elders believed that people working with metals possessed supernatural powers. Such convictions were born out of ignorance and the inability to understand creative processes. Of course, the basic requirements for working with metals are skill and talent, and even today these are possessed by few...

BETWEEN HAMMER AND ANVIL...

The questions of the history and past development of Slovenian iron forging and its corresponding crafts (such as nail making) through different historical periods have already been satisfactorily researched and presented, so no further descriptions of the past of this craft seem necessary at this point. In the past, iron forging was one of the most important services in the countryside, boroughs and towns. Archeological finds from Slovenia and later historical reports testify to that, and in the subsequent historical periods, many workshops appeared. There were several regional centers where iron forging was especially widespread. These centers were in Kropa, Kamna Gorica, and the areas under the Pohorje massif. Individual blacksmiths appeared in virtually every town or regional center. Even today, when there is only a handful of classical blacksmiths, they still specialize in tool-making, shoeing horses or iron forging. These profiles within one trade ultimately resulted in independent trades. But the further one returns to the past, the less clear the boundaries between the three become, or the presence of specialists for each, in individual workshops, can be observed. In the field of **ARTISTIC METALWORK**, i. e. the forging of unique and serial products which have a specific utility or decorative value, we must today recognize that quality products can be achieved through the technically creative symbiosis between the designer and the creator and producer of the work - the blacksmith. This is not, of course, merely a sign of our times, for there are many examples from the history of this craft which lead to the same conclusion. During the recent past - e.g. the period between the two world wars, and following World War II - some of the greatest works of the so-called *kroparski* (i.e. from Kropa) "artistic metalwork" (the term used for this craft at the time) were created through a co-operation between the *kroparski* blacksmiths and exceptional architects and designers, such as Jože Plečnik, Špinčič, and Boris Kobe. Therefore, no theory of "genius loci" can come into consideration here. Indeed, although there existed a great legend of Kropa metalwork, it was in fact the late Joža Bertoncelj who essentially created his own, personal, expression from the interpretation of models by craftsmen already noted as top-quality creators.

Despite the rich heritage of Slovene blacksmiths, modern Slovene ironwork is rather scant. The scope of artistic ironwork remains unimportant, regarding the number of blacksmiths and their creative potential. With rare exceptions, the products that appear are average interpretations and "reminders" of the traditional models conceptualized by expert architects and artists who cooperated on making objects of iron in the past.

BETWEEN HAMMER AND ANVIL...

That does not diminish the meaning of products of artistic iron forging and the heritage of Slovene blacksmiths in the least. Even in the remote historical periods, products of wrought iron such as window bars, lattices, railings, bolts, and doorknobs were made in blacksmiths' centers. However, they were designed by specially trained designers. There were some exceptional blacksmiths, who combined skill and talent to create true masterpieces. Joža Bertoncelj from Kropa was definitely one of them. His works are exhibited at the Kropa Museum and in various other public places.

There are unfortunately no modern design solutions in the field of ironwork. The "experiments" of amateur blacksmiths, deriving from solutions, already known from artistic ironwork, are frequently of dubious quality. Most are amateur imitations of artistic ironwork, and are of average aesthetic quality. The cheese knives designed by **JURE MIKLAVC** from Škofja Loka are an exception to the rule. Miklavc produces them in his father's workshop. This is the perfect example of family cooperation, where traditional crafting knowledge meets exceptional design expertise.

The cheese knives of the Academic industrial designer Jure Miklavc from Škofja Loka, are crafted in his father Stane's workshop. The blades are made from stainless steel, while the handles are of cherry wood. They belong to a set for cheese, and were designed in collaboration with his mentor and professor, Vladimir Pezdirc. The main problem in the knife design was how to join the blade and the handle into a harmonic whole, accounting for the different materials which offered diverse possibilities of design.

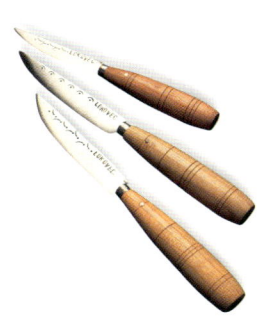

BETWEEN HAMMER AND ANVIL...

MAKING KNIVES was well developed in the area of Čepovan, however, this trade has all but died out today. **JOŽE RIJAVEC** from Zgornji Lokovec makes knives of various sizes, and tempers them into superb pieces. In the past, the Lokovec knife-makers also made a typical local variety of vine cutters called *fouči*, and other interesting products like drills, used for manual wood drilling called *črvarji*. We can see that few of the formerly numerous trades connected with iron forging in centers of such crafts have been preserved to the present day, and their tradition is carried on only by a few individual craftsmen. That is lamentable, because new handicrafts could develop on the base of the old ones, building on the tradition and identity, which are the fundamentals for establishing respectable trademarks. (In the field of making knives, one of such centers is in Maniago, Italy.)

JOŽE RIJAVEC

Jože Rijavec is the only blacksmith to carry on the rich tradition of blacksmiths from Lokovec, especially making knives and drills. In the 19th century forging iron was well developed in the wider area around Lokovec. The locals still boast about the fact that Empress Maria Theresa placed an order for twenty million nails for the purposes of the Austrian army. Even though this information may be only a fragment from local folklore, its contents testify to the well-advanced ironwork in the region.

196
HANDICRAFTS OF SLOVENIA

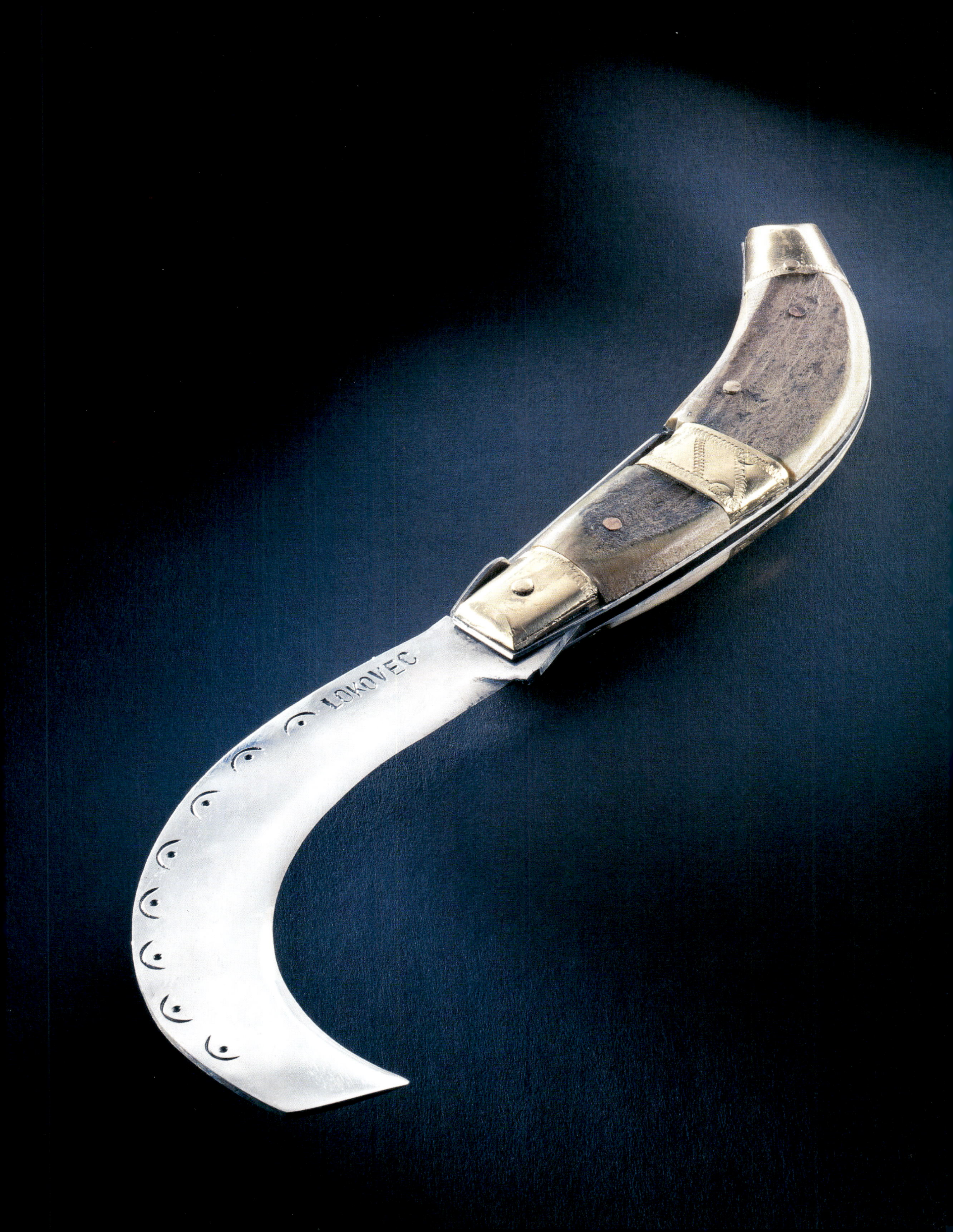
LOKOVEC

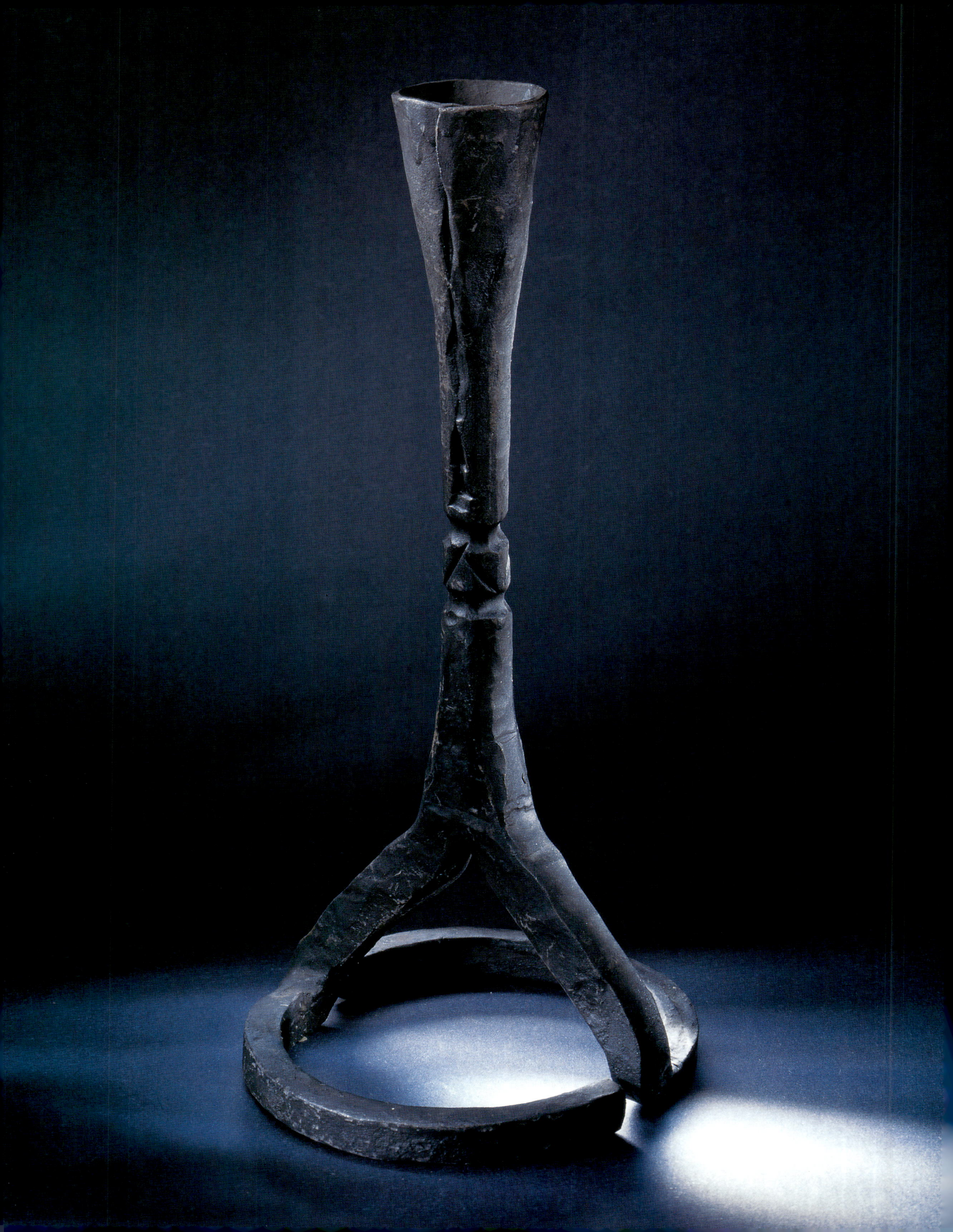

BETWEEN HAMMER AND ANVIL...

MIHA KRIŠTOF from Vinarje near Maribor makes unique items and products related to the national blacksmiths' heritage. His creativity is truly exceptional, and is divided between original, unique ironwork items, and working for the needs of the national blacksmith's heritage. He has won several awards for his original work, even though he is one of the youngest blacksmiths in Slovenia. Several years ago, he won a contest for altar equipment in Rome. He designed two candlesticks and a crucifix for one of the city's many basilicas. He has made several artistic objects of wrought iron for specific customers. Pope John Paul II, on his visit to Slovenia, was presented with a crucifix shaped in the form of a fruitful vine created by Krištof. In this crucifix, Krištof successfully combined the centuries-old local blacksmiths' tradition with the basic Christian and Slovene symbols of vines and viticulture.

MIHA KRIŠTOF

During his career of over twenty years, the products of Miha Krištof have improved immensely. He is one of the exceptional blacksmiths - born once in several generations - who can merge their crafting skills with their natural gift for forging iron.

BETWEEN HAMMER AND ANVIL...

Modern Slovene artistic iron forging prides itself on the masterpieces of **VLADO ZUPANČIČ** from Slovenj Gradec. He has developed his original style and is trying to find an independent personal artistic expression, different from the traditional (Kropa) stereotyped models. In an artistically vital town like Slovenj Gradec, this should not be a difficult task.

VLADO ZUPANČIČ

Blacksmith Vlado Zupančič works in Slovenj Gradec. His ironwork products are distinguished by great precision, but the design and outward image still exemplify influences from the Slovene iron forging heritage.

BETWEEN HAMMER AND ANVIL...

In discussion of the shaping of metal and related handicrafts, two other important trades - in which technical skill goes hand in hand with creativity and design - must be mentioned. One is represented by **GUN-MAKERS** and **ENGRAVERS,** and the other by **GOLDSMITHS**. We shall meet the gun-makers first. **MILAN ŠTEH** from Kamnik pod Krimom with his engraver (**CVETO FRELIH**) and carver of gun butts (**ROBERT FLERIN**) best represents the fine Slovene gun-makers' tradition. The engravers and carvers decorate individual gun parts with wonderful engravings of hunting motifs. But it takes more than engravings to create a good gun. Superb guns are made by expert gun-makers, who must master the mechanics and preparation of metals, as well as the blacksmith's skills. Mastery of these skills is not only connected with exceptional knowledge, but also with the rich gun-making heritage in the ethnic Slovene areas. The peak of this craft was thus reached at the old Slovene gun-making center - Borovlje (today's Ferlach, Austria), where the first traces of this trade go back to the smelteries and smithies of the Middle Ages. With the introduction of compulsory military service in the 18th century, the demand for guns and other firearms made in Borovlje increased. Guns, mainly to satisfy local demand, were also made in Ljubljana and Maribor. At the end of World War I, a gun-making plant was opened in Kranj, and a gun-making school in Ljubljana, where numerous top Slovene gun-makers were trained. Today a small number of excellent modern gun-makers carry on the rich tradition of this craft.

Superb technology and design, which must follow certain laws, are the basic components of gun making. This craft is a combination of diverse skills, working procedures and creative interventions. Gun maker Milan Šteh from Kamnik pod Krimom, is one of the best Slovene gun makers.

BETWEEN HAMMER AND ANVIL...

2

Besides numerous **GOLDSMITHS**, who produce many series of standard gold items, there are several crafters who continue the tradition of making unique items of gold jewelry, combined with precious and semi-precious stones. According to the old terminology, this trade belongs to the applied arts and crafts, in which the goldsmith designs each piece, according to the customer's special wishes, personal traits, and particularities. Such jewelry design supersedes the material value of the gold piece, making the latter an accessory, which helps promoting the personality of its owner. Working with gold has a rich tradition in Slovenia. The first goldsmiths appeared in Slovene towns during the Middle Ages. In these times, and some later periods, the goldsmiths also made practical and decorative metal objects from other metals.

Through time, **MAKING PRACTICAL, DECORATIVE METAL PRODUCTS** from metals, such as copper or brass evolved as an independent handicraft. Today it is best represented by the workshops of **PIRNAT**, **ŽMUC** and **PEZDIRC**. But let us return to goldsmiths.

1

The products of the top Slovene makers of decorative objects from metals other than iron, by Pirnat (picture 1), Pezdirc (picture 3), and Žmuc (picture 1) have already become a part of the natural heritage. Their collaboration with Jože Plečnik, and other Slovene architects has been decisive for the development of their craft.

3

203

BETWEEN HAMMER AND ANVIL...

Tine Šrot belongs to the group of Slovene goldsmiths who have directed their energy and knowledge into crafting truly unique items. The miniature rack-wagon in gold, created for one of his customers, is one such item.

Today, they are united in the Section of Goldsmiths at the Chamber of Trades of Slovenia. Several artisans, who produce unique jewelry in gold can be found in their ranks. A true veteran among them is **TINE ŠROT** from Ljubljana, who is also a kind of sculptor. He designs objects and figures, matched with the wholesomeness of a specific object, created for a specific customer. He made his name more than a decade ago by creating a miniature gold rack-wagon in correct proportions. The rack-wagon was intended as a business gift for a specific customer. It is safe to say that there are several exceptional Slovene goldsmiths, who annually display their work at various specialized exhibitions. The review of goldsmiths would of course be incomplete without **MIŠA JELNIKAR**, an expert designer of contemporary silver and gold jewelry. Her masterpieces are internationally recognized. She achieved international success decades ago with her distinctively original, personal style of design.

BETWEEN HAMMER AND ANVIL...

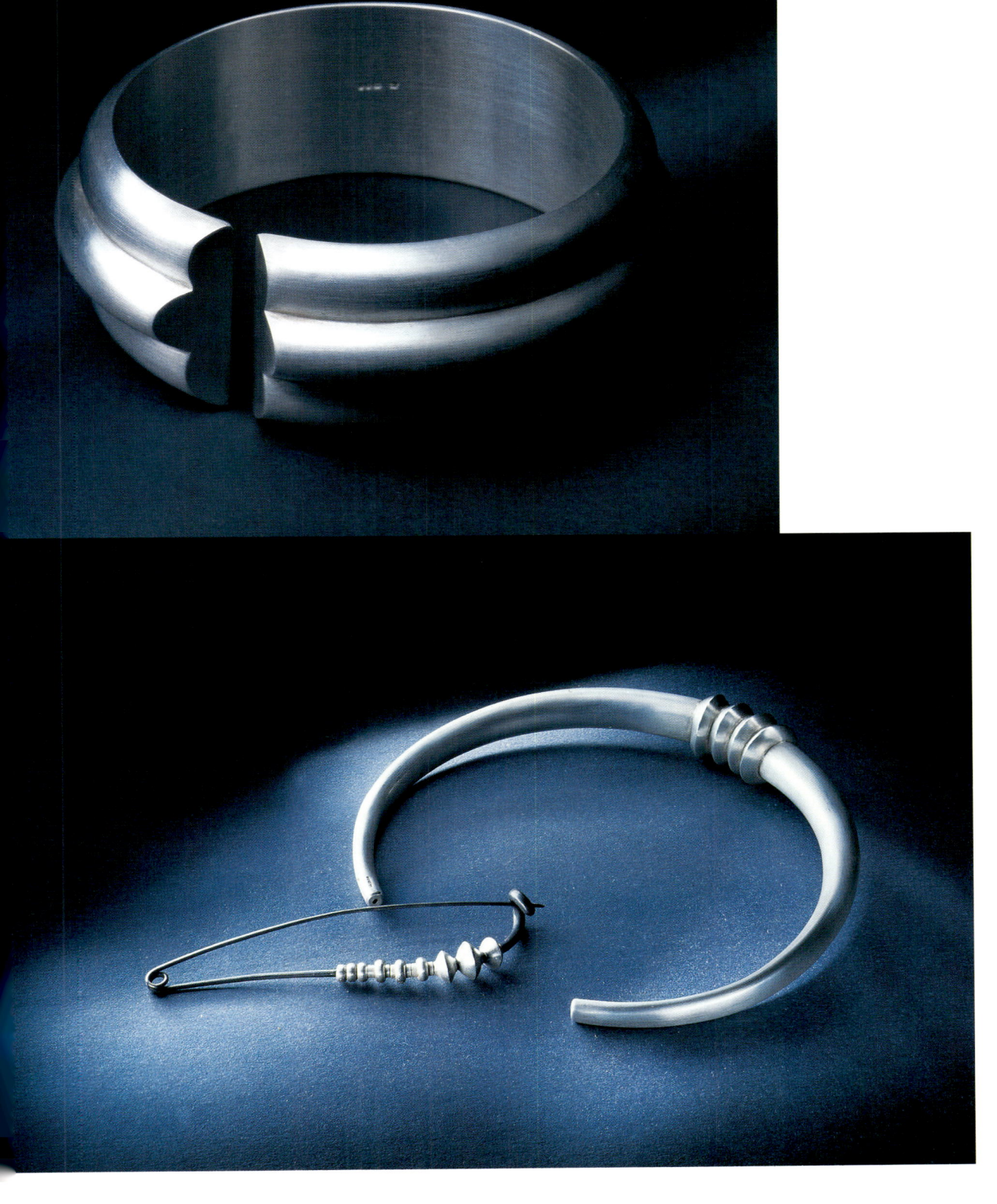

The specialty of the jewelry crafted by Miša Jelnikar is the perfect purity of its forms. This exceptional originality distinguishes her creations from mass products. The uniqueness of her jewelry is well recognized abroad.

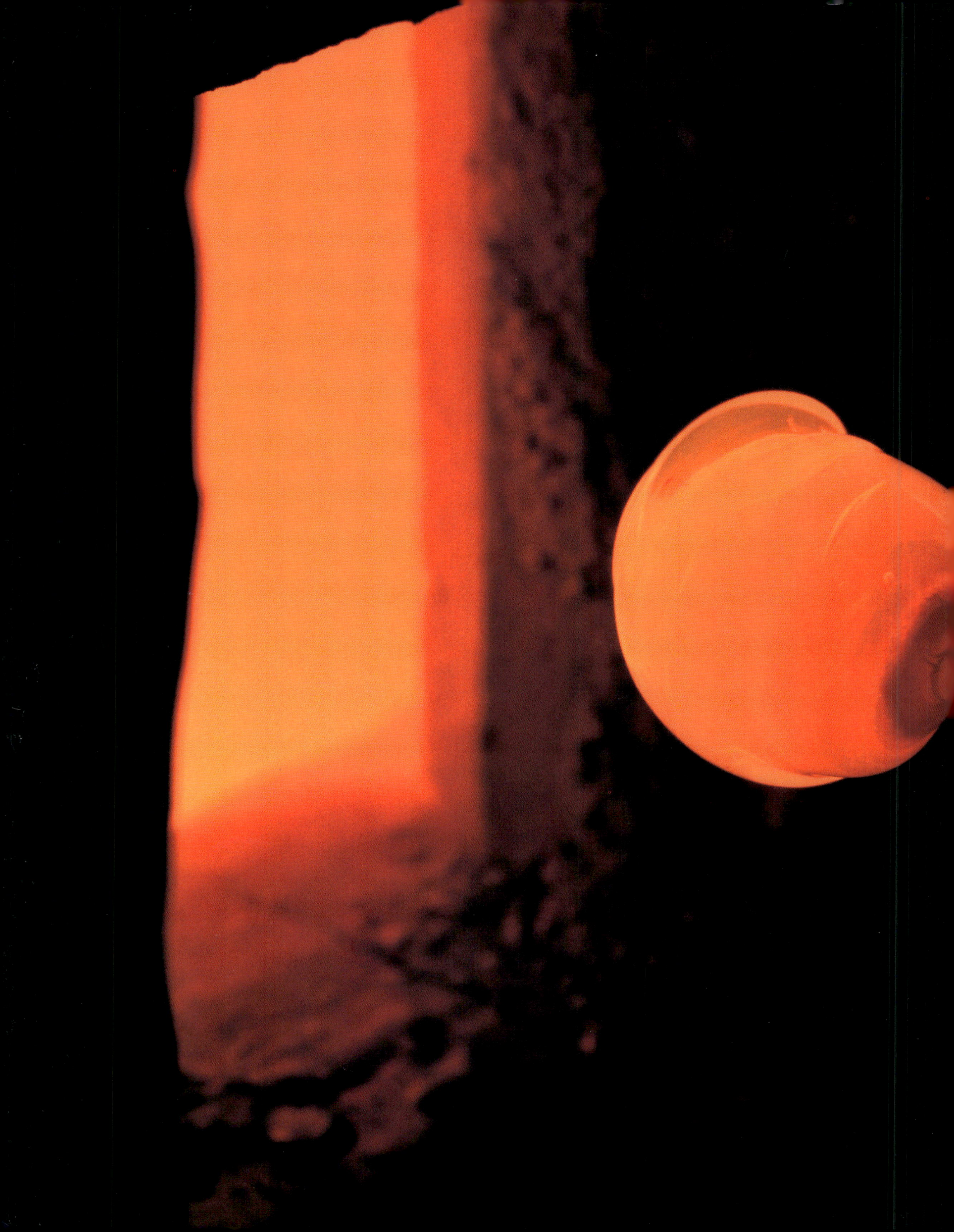

The Harmony of Form and Content

The natural conditions for the development of glass-making and related handicrafts in Slovenia were excellent. The first records of glassworks in Slovenia are from the 16th century. There is not enough tangible proof of earlier glass production. Most of the glassworks appeared between the 17th and 19th centuries in forested areas, where settlements for glass-blowers and glass-cutters were later built.

The harmony of form and content

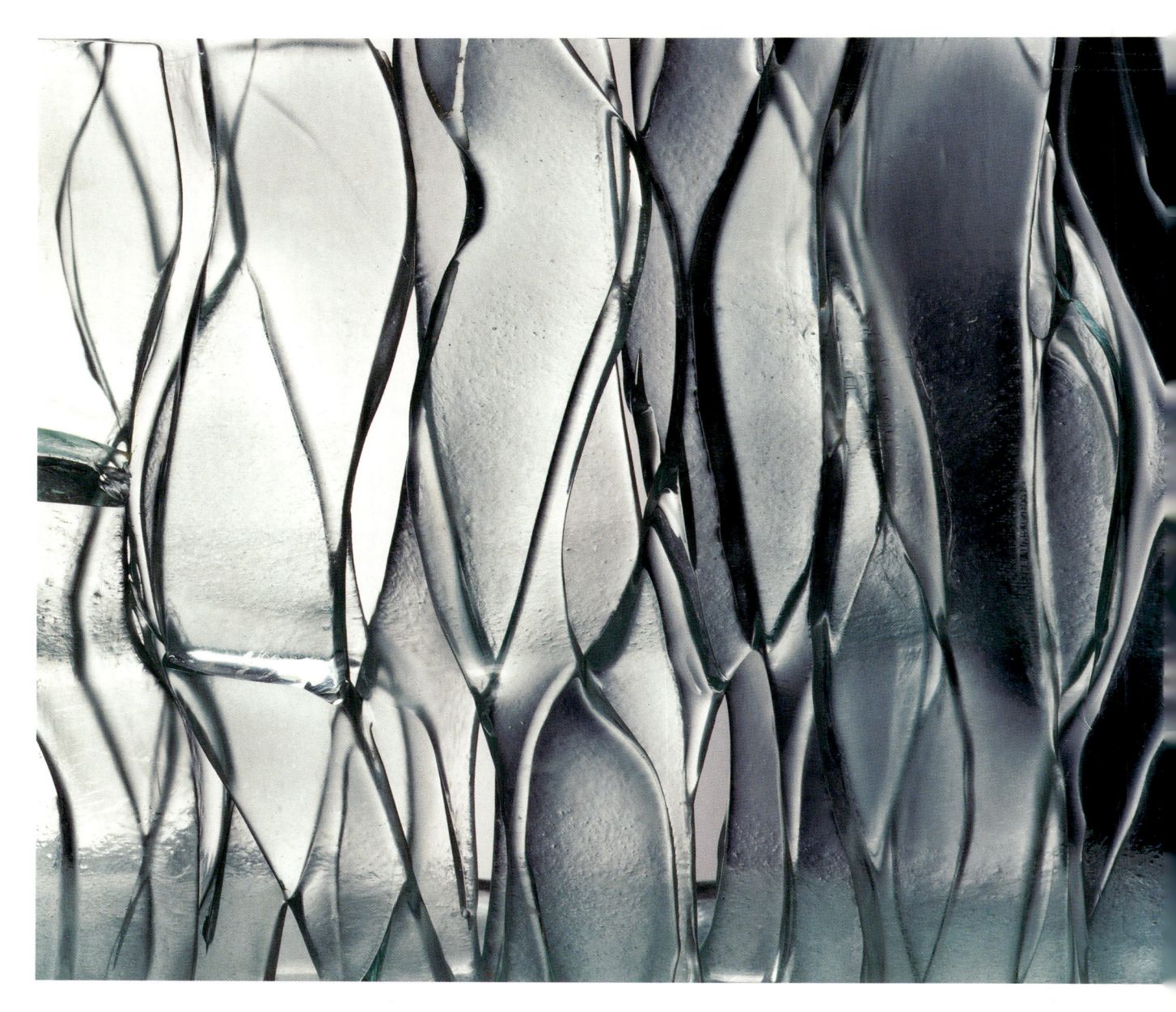

A brief glimpse into the history of Slovene glass production and related crafts shows how long and rich it is. Today it is carried on by large glassworks such as Rogaška Slatina, Hrastnik, and Hrpelje. The School for Glass-Cutters and Glass-Blowers in Rogaška Slatina educates new craftsmen and women. The school also has its own department where the students can also acquire practical experience, i.e. learn about the production of glass. In addition to these, there are several smaller glassworks and studios where unique glass products and blown glass items are created. Glass-cutters and glass-blowers use different materials. The latter work with glass mass or industrially made tubes and sticks made from laboratory glass. Glass-cutting, engraving and painting are special technical skills, as well as a means of expression, as are the making of stained glass and the decorative etching of glass, which also boast a rich tradition.

THE HARMONY OF FORM AND CONTENT

The rich heritage, consisting of products from small forest glassworks *(glažute)*, is preserved in some museums and private collections. The idea of making replicas of traditional glass products is relatively new, and many glass-makers and glass-cutters have not yet taken it up. The leading maker of glass replicas is **CIRIL ZOBEC** from Rogaška Slatina. He makes modern glassware as well as replicas of traditional *glažuta*-style items. He also makes minute replicas. Replication demands extensive knowledge of old technologies, and the precise execution of fine details on individual pieces. **FRANC SAJKO** and his son **MITJA** from Rogaška Slatina produce series of vases, bowls and stemware, as well as some unique replicas of *glažuta* products. They have their own business *(Kreativ)*, which they have been promoting with the slogan *Štajerska glažuta*, as a reminder of the tradition left by the small forest glassworks, which were at one time particularly common in the forests of the Štajerska region.

The highly-developed production of glass in Rogaška Slatina originates from the establishment of individual glassworks, which were originally designed to carry out all processes in glass-working. They evolved into recognizable businesses with their own trademarks. The Sajko workshop is one of them. In addition to stock glassware, they also produce replicas of traditional glassware, represented by items from forest glassworks.

THE HARMONY OF FORM AND CONTENT

Traditional Slovene glassware was made in glažute *(glassworks), situated in the forested areas of the country. Only a few traditional products have survived to the present day. They inspire replication, the preservation of historical memory, and the modern development of past technologies and design techniques. Ciril Zobec from Rogaška Slatina, makes traditional as well as modern glassware.*

CIRIL ZOBEC

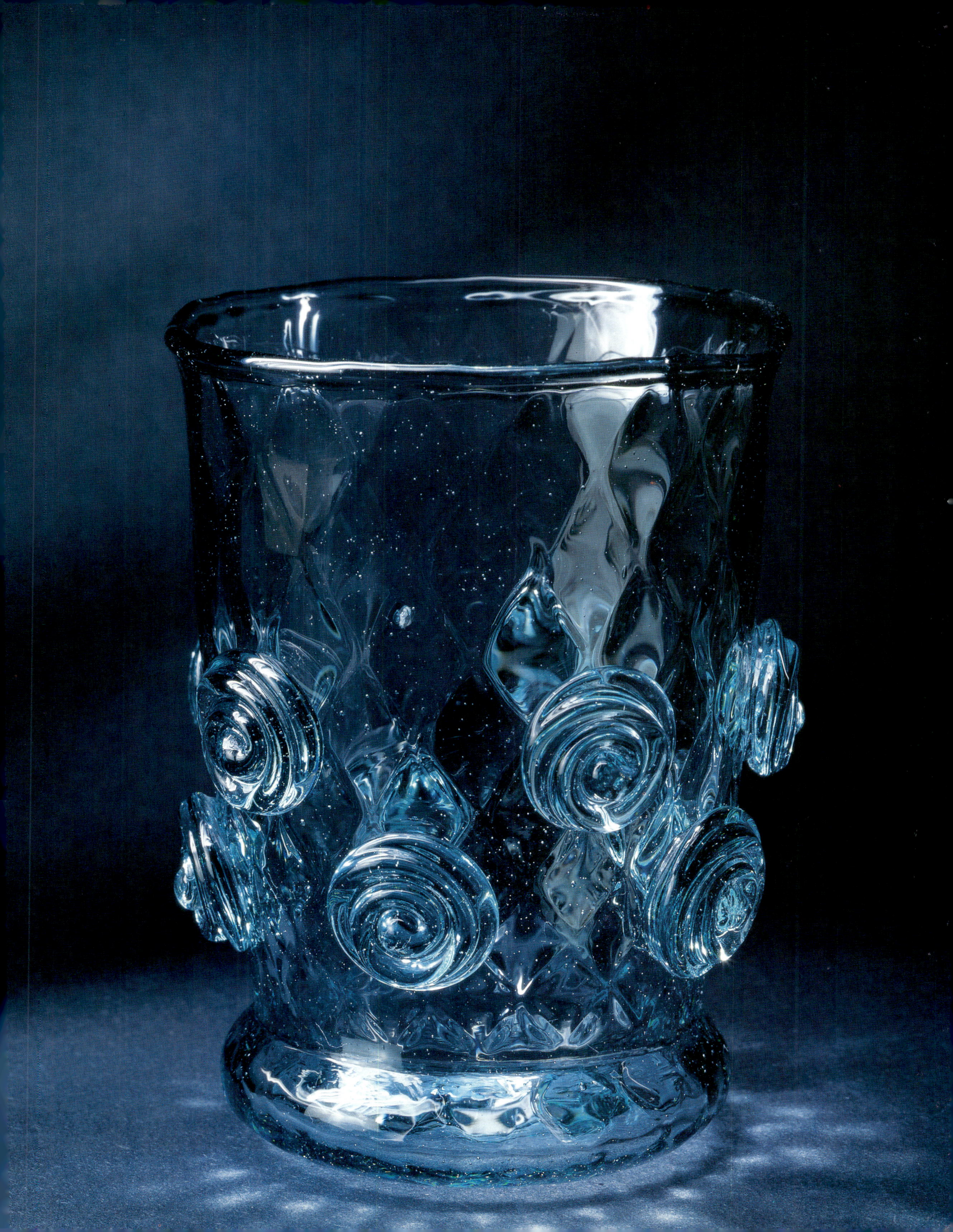

The harmony of form and content

The **Glass-making School in Rogaška Slatina,** an important glass-making center, was established in 1947 and still exists today. In addition to the general program, they established the production of serial products, as well as various masterpieces of blown and cut glass, which you can see and buy in their showroom. The internationally-renowned Slovene designer Oskar Kogoj has designed a line of glasses for them. These are made by **Stjepan Bukvić**, **Vlado Češnjaj**, **Leopold Miklavžič** and **Branko Zagorščak**. The glasses are a part of Kogoj's *Nature Design* collection, and are made from white (transparent) glass, or colored parts of individual elements. Together with the same artisans, Kogoj has designed several unique glasses as presents for certain Slovene and internationally-prominent personalities.

Master glass blowers from the Glass-Making School in Rogaška Slatina craft glasses designed by designer Oskar Kogoj. For his Nature Design *collection, numerous glasses for special purposes and for specific clients have been produced in collaboration. The special purposes of the glasses inspire Kogoj to derive inspiration from spiritual spheres, with which he combines glass iconography (Pictures 1, 2, 3). A well-known collection of glasses (Slovenska dvanajstija) (Picture 1).*

THE HARMONY OF FORM AND CONTENT

In addition to replicating models from the Slovene glass-making heritage, some craftsmen are challenging themselves interpreting traditional models according to the new trends in concept and design of recent years. Designer **Peter Ogrin** from Ljubljana was inspired by the traditional two-litre wine flask made from bubbled glass, called *štefan*. He designed a whole line of products, from the bottles to glasses and other tableware, which represent a continuation and a further development of traditional wine flasks. His line is produced at the Luminos glassworks in Slovenska Bistrica.

Peter Ogrin bases his glassware on blown-glass from the rich heritage of Slovene glass-making.

THE HARMONY OF FORM AND CONTENT

TANJA PAK

The young Slovene designer **Tanja Pak,** born into a family of glass-makers, also created her early glass items in Rogaška Slatina. Having graduated from the Department of Design at the Ljubljana Academy of Fine Arts, she continued her studies at the London Royal College of Art. She not only designs but also produces and manufactures some of her pieces herself. She designed a selection of products (candlesticks, glasses, bowls) using transparent glass in an effort to find the perfect shape. She combined transparent, green and bubbled glass in the wine glass, which was used as a top business and state gift for the City of Ljubljana in 1994 (the nation's capital also prides itself on the international award for the city of vines and wine, having been one of the most important European wine trading centers for centuries). During her postgraduate studies in London, Pak discovered new technological and design possibilities. In collaboration with the **Rokus Publishing House**, she designed an intimate, rotating light for the **design from Slovenia** line of modern handicraft products. Light, travelling through small glass plates of a varied structure, emits countless, changing artistic messages. Pak also experiments with melted pulverized glass to discover new means of artistic expression.

Tanja Pak continues the rich family tradition of glass design. However, she does not merely repeat the tradition but uses it as a foundation from which she builds her own modern creative style. Her expertise is the result of extensive knowledge, research and understanding of glass, and of the appropriate training undertaken in Slovenia and abroad.

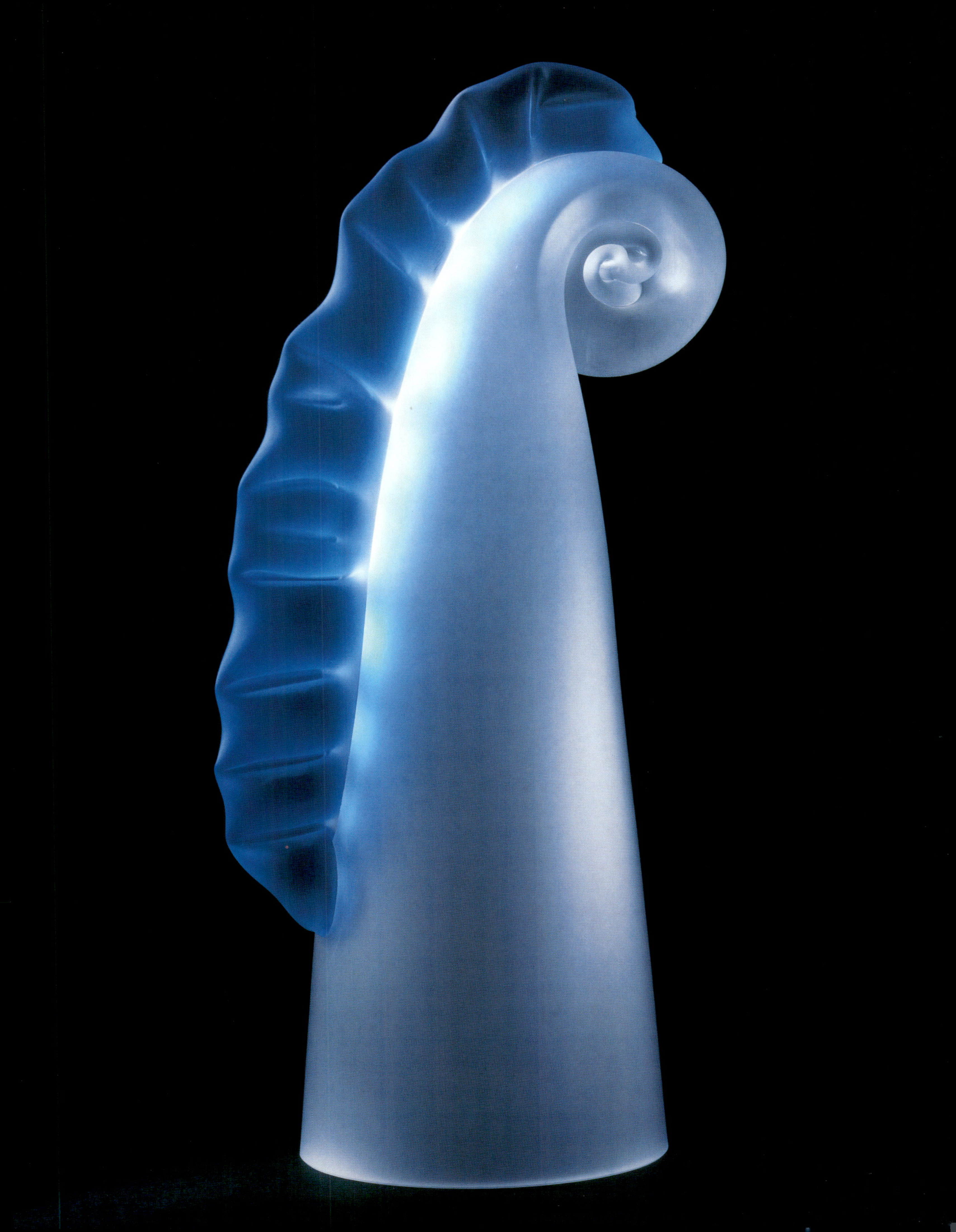

THE HARMONY OF FORM AND CONTENT

Tanja Pak introduces into her products stories from her imagination, which flourished in an environment where literally everything was connected with glass. She has developed a variety of technological and simultaneously creative possibilities, which enable her to bring all her ideas to life. Her glassware contains fluctuations, not only of thought but of water and air as well. Thus her products are not static but create an impression of being "alive", or, as she describes it, they are forms that flow.

THE HARMONY OF FORM AND CONTENT

The designer considers glass to be a living being. This is why her products, distinguished by purity of form evoke constant comparisons with the world around us, with nature, the undulating breeze and sliding drops of water.

THE HARMONY OF FORM AND CONTENT

Designing modern glassware is completely different. In addition to individual designers from larger glassworks, designer **LJUBICA KOČICA** from Rogaška Slatina was the first to reach peak quality in inventing, designing and producing excellent, original, unique items. She designs serial products as well. Besides being an expert glass-maker, Kočica is also a talented ceramist, and true glass masterpieces are created in her workshop. One of these masterpieces, created for the **ANARS** company from Ljubljana, is a technological and architectural achievement. For Anars, Kočica put Andraž Debeljak's bobbin lace, made of metal thread, into a glass mass. This procedure is a true artistic and aesthetic challenge, and rounds off the image of the product. Her original unique pieces, mostly made by whetting and engraving a glass base, are also outstanding. Kočica has already won a number of prizes at home and abroad.

Designer and sculptor Ljubica Kočica from Rogaška Slatina is one of Slovenia's top glass designers. She has already established her name and a distinctly personal style. Her products are unique masterpieces, created by diverse design, technological and artistic approaches.

THE HARMONY OF FORM AND CONTENT

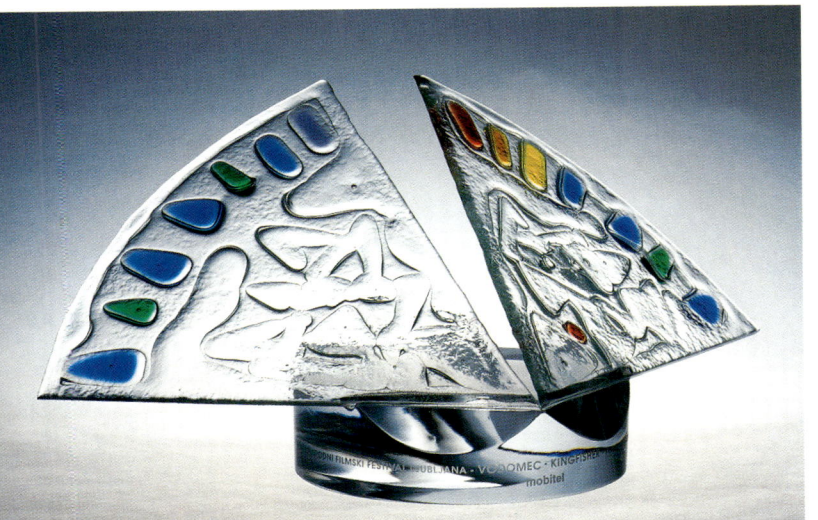

Designer **BARBARA DOVEČAR** from Nova Gorica also finds glass as her prime artistic challenge. She first crafted products using a combination of glass and ceramics, but she later devoted all her creative energy to the creation of high-quality glass jewelry and to various products for interiors. Her combined glass and wrought iron products are very interesting because they combine two extreme materials, which results in inventive and accomplished artistic solutions.

Barbara Dovečar's glassware often changes its basic, functional form to become three-dimensional sculpture. Glass thus becomes a means of expression, a material for creating special messages in space.

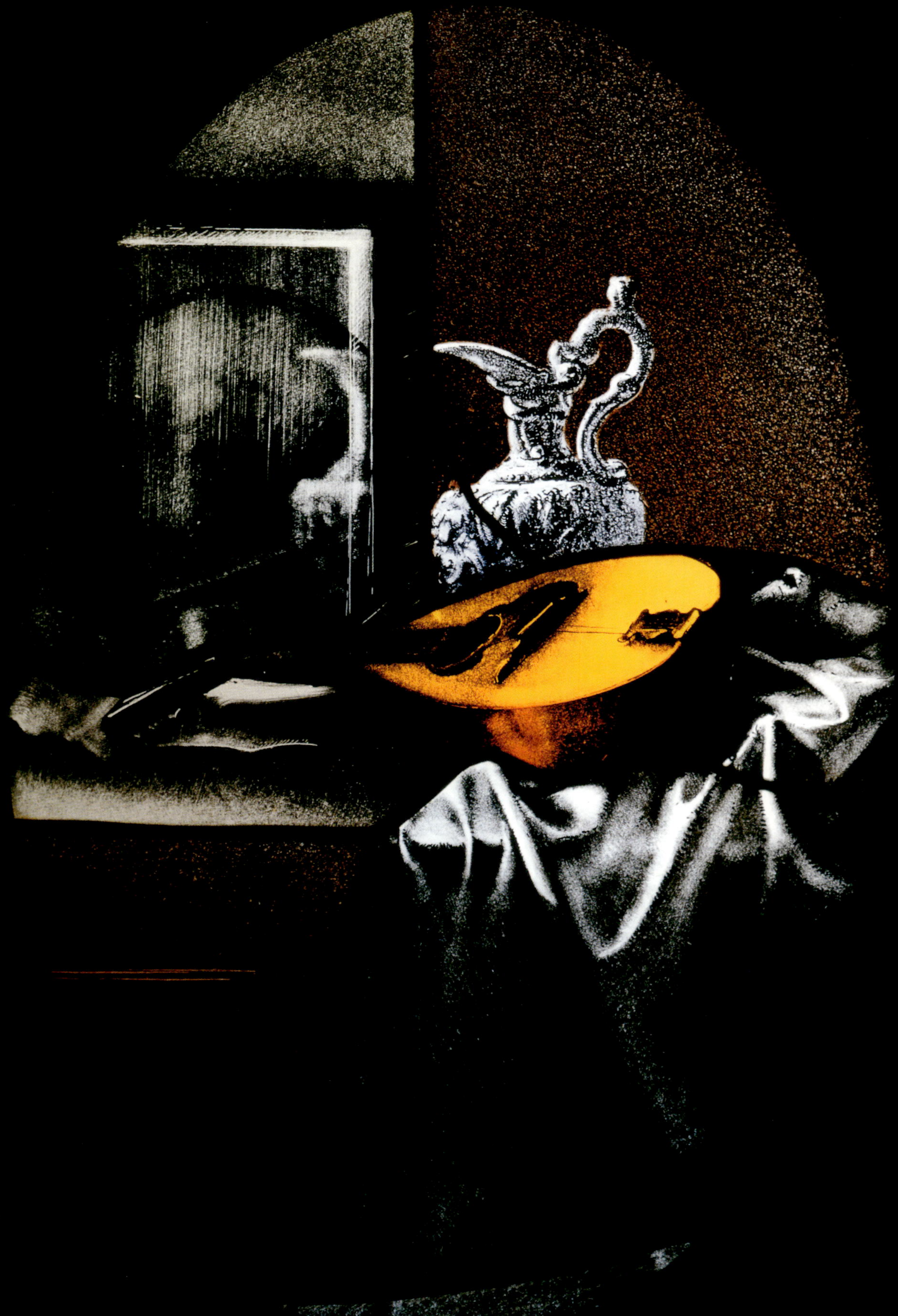

THE HARMONY OF FORM AND CONTENT

The period between the Middle Ages and the Baroque was the golden era of stained glass, also known as **VITRAGE**. Stained-glass windows were fashionable and were incorporated into the architecture of churches, castles and city houses. In staining glass, the natural pigments are applied to parts of glass, dried and, then burned into the surface. These compositions on windows of various sizes are composed of many glass pieces set in a lead framework, like a mosaic. The lead framework helps shape the basic outline and the contours of the whole composition. After the Baroque period, the popularity of stained glass fell sharply, so it had to be revived at the beginning of the 19th century. There was much demand for stained glass due to many renovation project and interest in new ones. **STOJAN VIŠNAR** from Zasip near Bled is a master maker of stained glass. He works with Academic painter **TOMAŽ PERKO**. Perko draws motifs on paper and transfers them to glass plates. Višnar then burns the plates in the kiln in his workshop, and sets them in their final form – the lead framework. His stained-glass windows adorn many churches and other public and private buildings both in Slovenia and abroad. In recent years, the foreign **TIFFANY** technique - or making objects and windows from colored glass pieces (or glass imitations) - has become popular. The pieces are arranged in various patterns or decorative color compositions, and then soldered in place by a copper tape. The technique was imported from the Anglo-American world but has not yet developed beyond imitations or interpretations of stock foreign models.

Stojan Višnar

Making stained glass or vitrages reaches back to the 10th century in European art and crafts. It reached its peak in the 13th century, when the magnificent French Gothic charterhouses were built. In later periods, people also started decorating secular edifices and rooms with vitrages.

THE HARMONY OF FORM AND CONTENT

With the decline of stained glass, a new demand for brightly ornamented or decorated glass appeared. **ETCHED GLASS** was thus born. The oldest extant example of it in the world dates from 1683. The oldest Slovene examples are preserved in Ljubljana and date from the period after the great earthquake of 1895. Mixes of fluorine substances are used for etching glass. The glass surface is coated with a protective layer. A needle is then used to draw various motifs and ornaments onto the glass. The glass is then coated with the fluorine mix, which eats away the upper part of the glass, exposed by the needle, leaving permanent patterns in the glass. **ALEŠ LOMBERGAR** from Ljubljana is an expert etcher who makes new decorative etchings. He is the only expert capable of carrying out the restoration and replication of etched-glass pieces in buildings which form part of the national architectural heritage. In the course of his fifteen-year-long career, he has made replicas of the old etched-glass doors of the Slovene Philharmonic Hall in Ljubljana, and created window and door decorations in several traditional inns.

THE HARMONY OF FORM AND CONTENT

Etching glass is not merely a technology but a means of expression. Diverse methods and techniques can be used to make replicas (also for the purpose of renovating buildings which are part of the architectural heritage), or for completely modern artistic creation.

THE HARMONY OF FORM AND CONTENT

IVAN JURJEVIČ   IRENA JURJEVIČ

With regard to glass, there exists another method of expression: **PAINTING ON GLASS.** It does not directly belong to the chapter in which the various techniques of shaping glass were presented. In this craft, glass is only a base for the painting, which is transferred onto it from a paper model by applying colors onto the face or back of the glass. True glass-painting centers developed between the 18th and 19th centuries, where paintings in glass, mostly depicting vernacular motifs, were made. As part of contemporary popular artistic culture and art appreciation, peddlers sold them throughout central Europe for the customers to decorate their houses, and to present to individual churches and chapels. In addition to selling imported glass paintings, some were made in Slovene workshops. A unique style of color and composition was developed in glass painting, as well as various procedures (the finishing procedures of color transitions, shading, simplification in depicting body parts or garments). Today, there are very few artisans capable of making high-quality replicas because this demands extensive studies of the glass-painting heritage, and great expertise in paints and painting technologies. **IRENA** and **IVAN JURJEVČIČ** from Ljubljana are truly the best Slovene painters of glass. They are the only ones capable of replicating glass paintings well enough.

Glass-painting in fact belongs to the chapter on the repetition of historical memory, but it is mentioned here because of its basic material. Vast expertise is required to make excellent replicas of painted glass, not only of motifs but mostly of the prerequisites of painting techniques. Something similar could be said for colors, which have to be similar to those which were fashionable at the time the original was made.

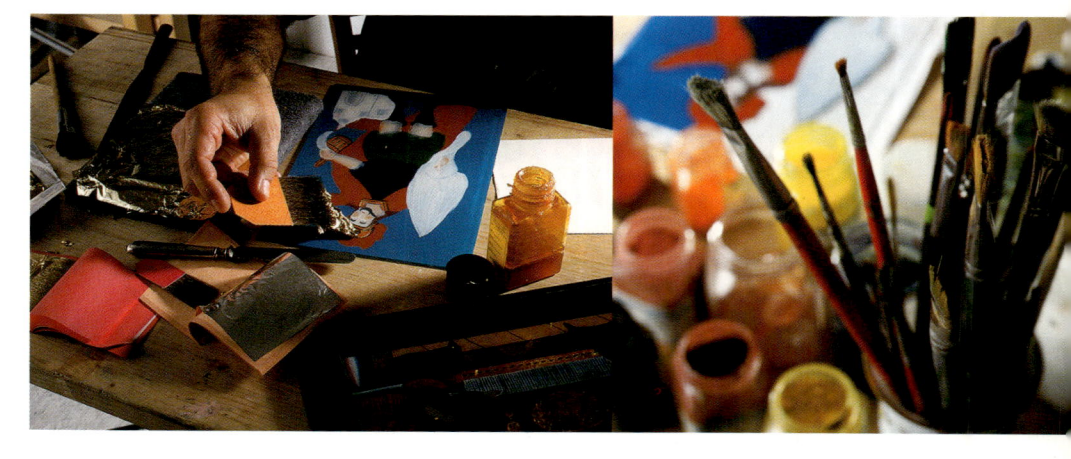

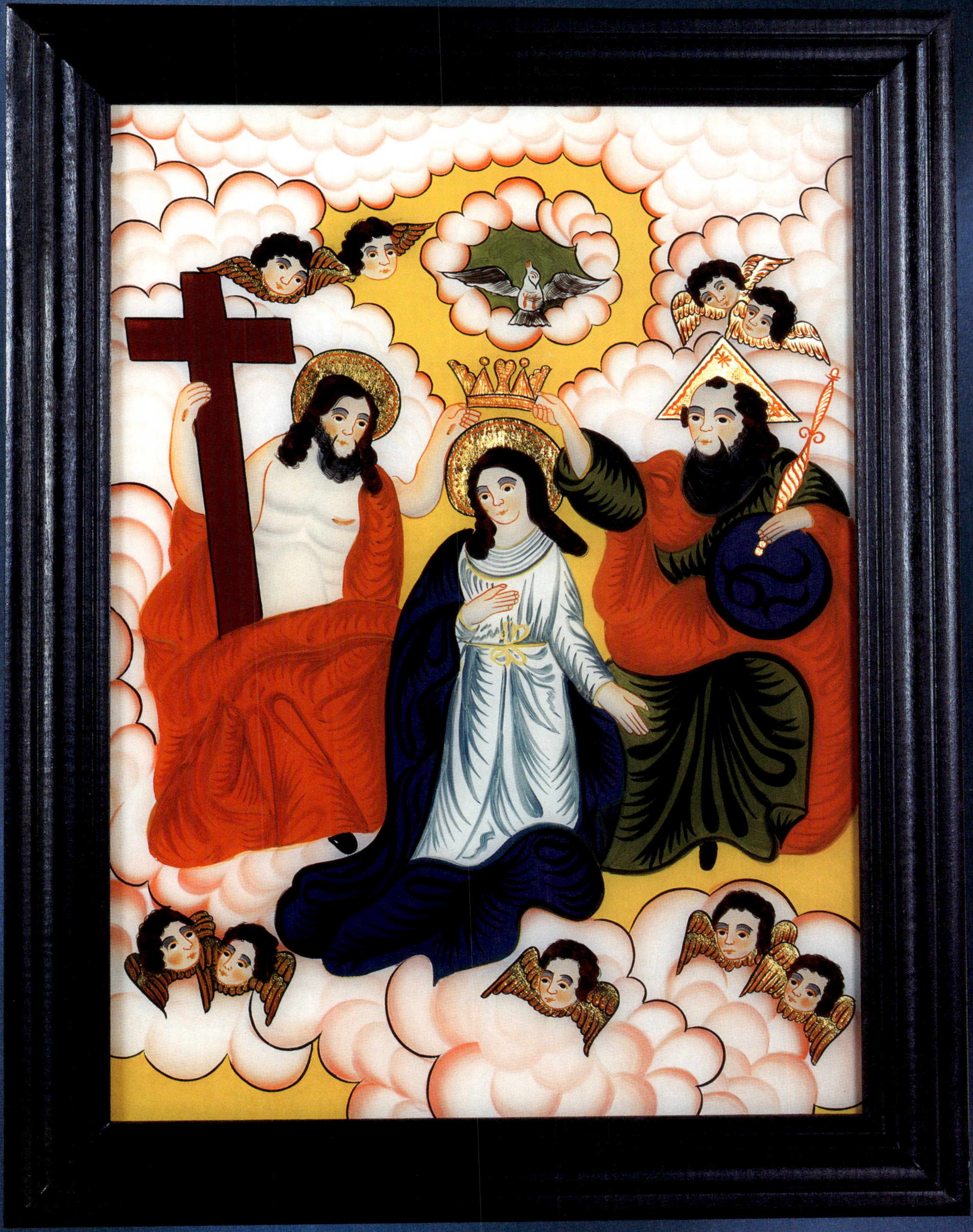

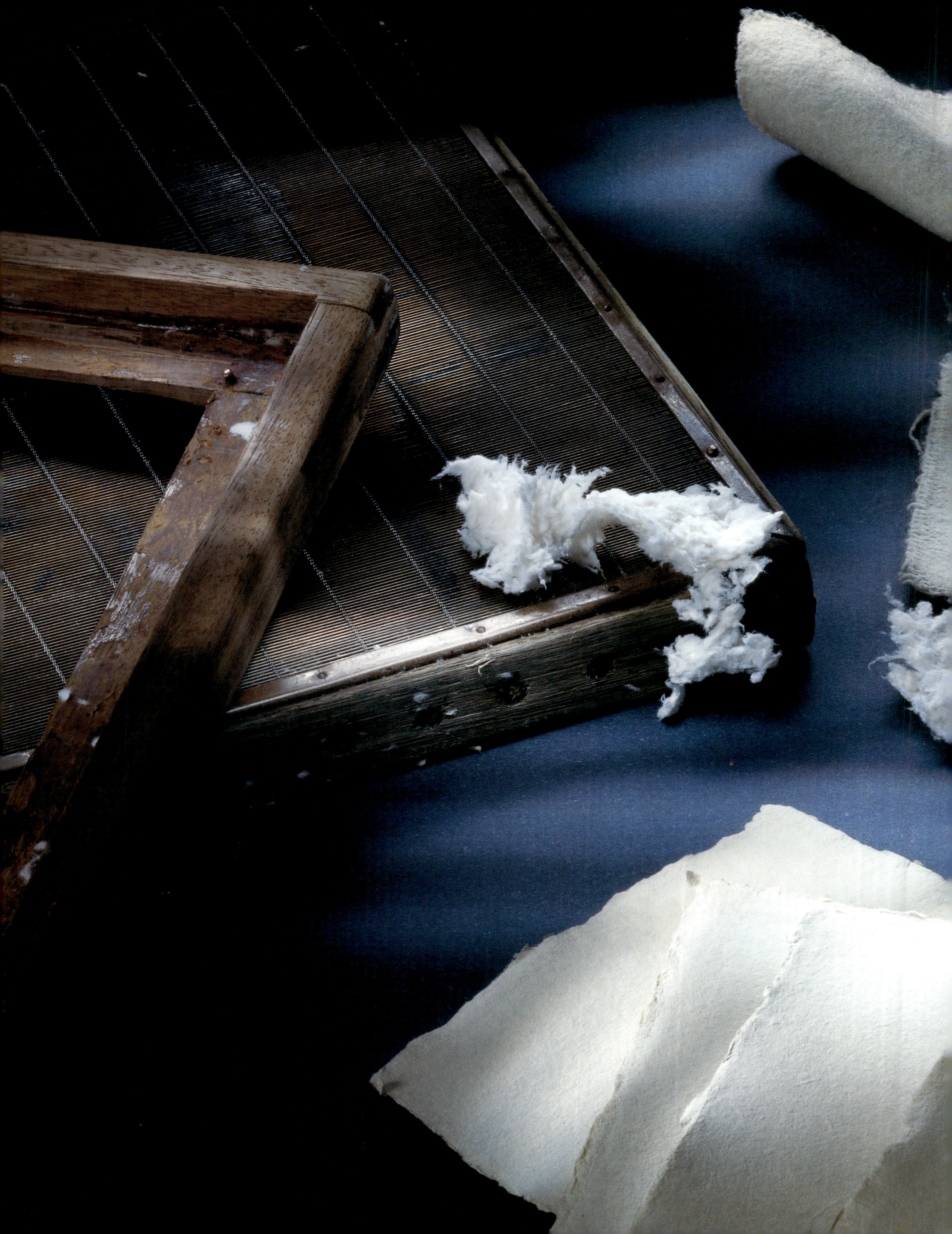

Masterpieces from the Paper Mill

The Chinese invented paper-making more than 1,900 years ago. The Arabs first brought it to Europe. There used to be several paper mills in Slovenia but only one of them has survived. This is the paper-mill at Fužine near Ljubljana, which was later turned into a large paper industry centered around Vevče. Hand-made paper crafted on the spot of the former paper-mill has been produced in Fužine since 1579…

MASTERPIECES FROM THE PAPER MILL

Even though the purpose of this book is not to describe in detail the history of individual handicrafts preserved to the present day, a minor exception needs to be made regarding the production of hand-made paper. This vitally-preserved procedure is one of the oldest in Europe. On the right bank of the river Ljubljanica, opposite Fužine Castle, a paper mill was opened in 1579. Its output was modest, but every single sheet of paper produced bore a water-printed coat of arms of the lord of the castle and of the paper mill with it. The activity at the mill and the castle came to a standstill between the 16th century and the first half of the 19th century, when Fidelis Trpinc, the son of a wealthy merchant, bought them both. Trpinc bought a nearby grain mill in 1840, turned it into an oil mill, and built a new paper mill next to it. When it first became operational, in 1843, it employed seventy people. Paper-making proved to be a lucrative business, and Trpinc bought more land to expand the mill and to add a power plant. In those days, the Vevče paper mill was a modern, partly-automated production plant. They continued to produce paper manually as a parallel activity. This represents the oldest preserved procedure for the making of hand-crafted paper by European standards. It is a sort of living museum, considering the wide range of products crafted from this paper, as well as the form of creative expression.

JOŽE VALANT from Vevče still continues the rich local tradition of manual paper-making in his private business. Years ago he and **JOŽE KRESNIK**, a foreman at the Vevče paper mill, took over their present workshop and turned it into a true paper-making studio. They manufacture many varieties of hand-made paper and various other paper products.

JOŽE VALANT

To touch hand-made paper actually means touching centuries of cultural development. Nearly everything recorded in historical memory rests on paper. This is why hand-made paper is especially valued and esteemed. It is most appreciated when it is used as something to write on, or as material in various fields of design.

228

HANDICRAFTS OF SLOVENIA

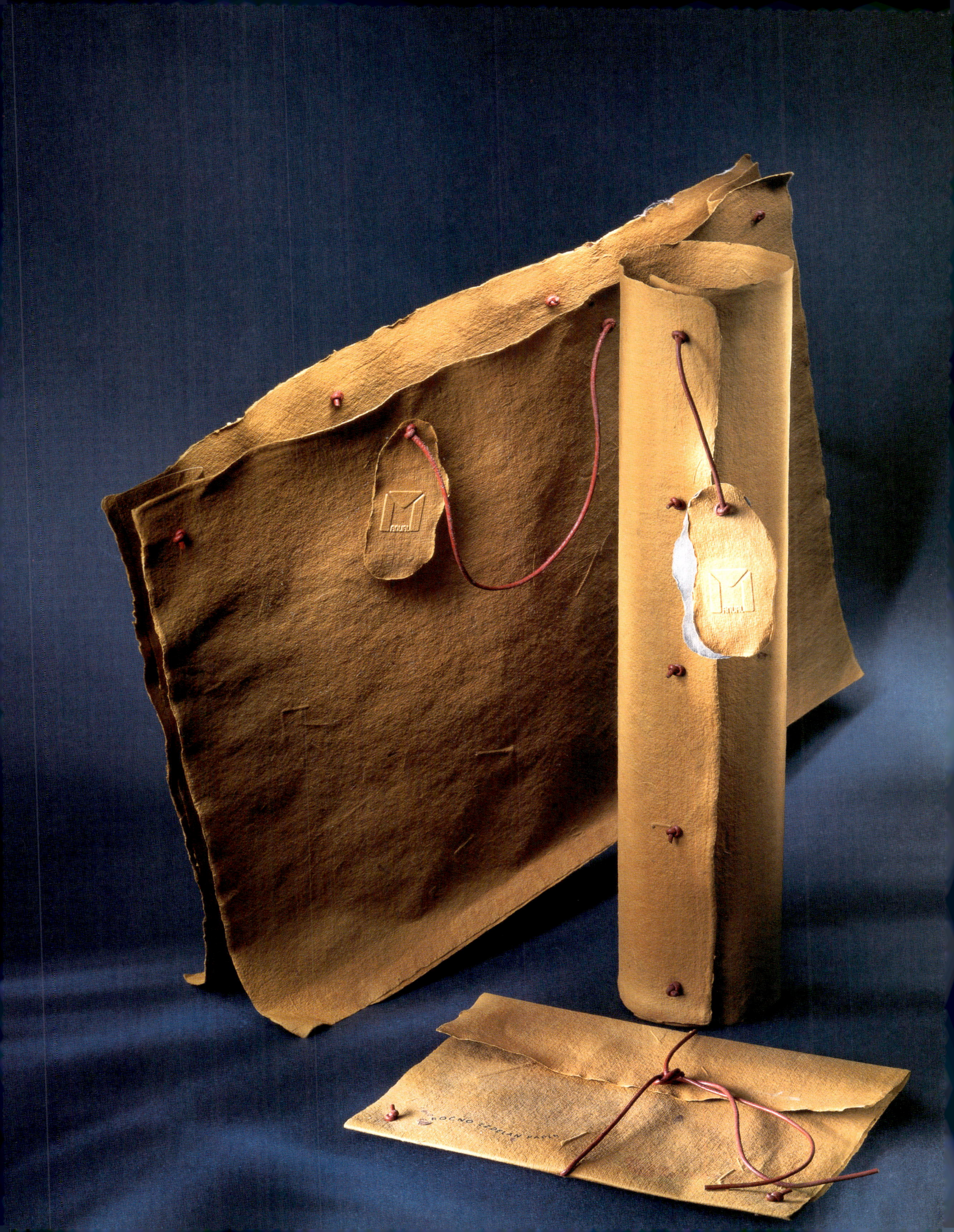

Masterpieces from the paper mill

Flax and cotton are still the basic raw materials for paper. The fibers of the two are first ground to the desired length. This was originally done with wooden stampers, but a Dutch grinder called a *holandec* is used today. In addition to cutting the fibers, paper pulp of the appropriate thickness is also formed. The manual production of paper represents a good example of the division of labor. A paper-maker (vatman) extracts some of it from the basin using a sift-like mould and lets the water run off. At the same time, he has to shake the mould in order to distribute the fibers as evenly as possible. This should be done in a single motion, which only the best craftsmen can perform. When the mass dries completely, a procedure called *gavčenje* follows. The second paper-maker or *gavčar* (coucher) takes the mould and removes the future sheet of paper by overturning the mould onto a felt lining. In the meantime, the first paper-maker has already made a new sheet of paper, and now passes it on to the *gavčar*, who hands him the empty mould in exchange. Thus their motions rhythmically complement one another. Sheets of wet paper accumulate on the felt lining one after another. When the heap is reasonably big, it is taken to the press to remove all water. After the pressing, the third paper-maker separates the wet sheets from the felt linings. Next, the paper is dried on special shelves. After that, it is glued to prevent excessive color or ink absorption and, finally, pressed and dried again. With this the paper-making procedure is complete.

Jože Valant also makes various water prints and seals. The image on the stamp is shaped from silver wire and then placed onto the sift. In the contoured spots, the paper layer must be applied more thinly than elsewhere. If we hold up such a sheet of paper towards the light, a clear print of the sign appears. Today, water prints are common on high-quality writing paper, and paper for state and other special occasions.

As is true of other domains of heritage, paper still has many new uses. We can discover countless particular features when studying its history. These particulars can help us find new shapes, technologies and artistic solutions. One of these is the production of diverse basic types of paper with many possible additions found in nature, especially in the plant world, where paper after all originates.

For the production of parchment paper substitutes (real parchment is made of animal skin), only flax fibers are used. These are transformed in an adapted Dutch grinder with more intensive kneading so that the fiber length is preserved. Thus we can see that the basic varieties of paper are all made from natural materials. For special varieties of paper used for decorative or art purposes, fibers of other plants are added, such as rush, hemp or other types of grass. A speciality among Valant's papers are those containing petals of different meadow flowers (saffron, daisies), herbs and leaves. They make paper of various colors, from plain white to bright colors and even black. Hand-made paper has been used in several facsimile editions of older prints. A true masterpiece is the hand-written monograph on the Lipica horse, which is a consummate work of art. Writing paper for offices, paper packaging for wine bottles, flowers and other gifts are also made in Valant's workshop. The speciality of this workshop for the manual production of paper is the occasional demonstration of old, traditional procedure of making paper. Paper-makers, dressed in the old working clothes with leather aprons, make paper with moulds, and also use old wooden paper press with a screw. These live demonstrations are not just a form of advertising but also a live demonstration, a sort of a "theater of history". They are not a nostalgic longing for the past but useful reminders of various creative options, of which modern man is often not aware in this day and age.

Masterpieces from the Paper Mill

Paper has always been used as a material for special handicraft skills connected with the manual production of paper. One such craft is **making paper flowers**, **bouquets** and **garlands**. Until World War II, this was one of the most popular handicrafts. There are several Slovene artisans who can still produce flowers from colored or crepe paper. The paper flowers, which are sometimes but not always waxed, are then tied together into bouquets, garlands and other flower arrangements. The declining number of paper-makers is connected with the lessened importance of paper flowers in our daily lives and rituals, such as weddings, the recruitment of soldiers, funerals and decoration of the interiors at Christmas and on other festive and holiday occasions. **Agneza Bezjak** from Ljutomer is a master paper-maker. She is one of the rare connoisseurs of the typology of various paper products, especially in marking their individual "roles" in the wedding ceremony.

The bridal wreath and bouquet, corsages for the groom, bride, best man and wedding guests, Confirmation or Holy Communion decorations, and recruitment bunches are the most representative traditional products made from paper flowers. The mastery of this craft, which also has some regional or local particularitias, is the craft best preserved in the areas of Pivka and in north-west Slovenia. One of the great masters of this craft is Agneza Bezjak from Ljutomer.

Masterpieces from the Paper Mill

Some amateur societies for the preservation of the national heritage and folklore also include some competent (mostly women) paper-makers. This is the case with the **women of Lašče** and **Pivka**. In the Pivka region, making paper flowers is still a visual part of the annual rituals connected with recruiting soldiers. The recruiting wagons are decorated with bright-colored paper blossoms. In nearby Brkini, women and girls still make a mass of paper flowers with which they festoon the high hats of male Lenten characters called *škoromati*.

Andreja Stankovič from Novo mesto is a well-known maker of paper flowers in the Dolenjska region. **Marta Kušnik**, from Ruta near Fala in Dravska dolina, is an expert maker of waxed paper flowers in this part of Slovenia. Until World War II, the uses of paper flowers were varied. In addition to the uses already mentioned, paper flowers were used to decorate festive breads and flat-cakes (*bosman*), and churches on special occasions, such as First Communion, Confirmation or the Ascension. The main reason for the popularity of making paper flowers in the past can be explained by the excellent textbooks of this home handicraft printed in the Habsburg Empire. The textbooks contained detailed drawings of the cut-out shapes, and instructions for assembling those into the desired blossoms. Making paper flowers was often part of the arts and crafts program in schools. Today, all that remains are memories of these times long gone.

Andreja Stankovič from Novo mesto bases her paper flower arrangements on the traditional production of paper flowers.

MASTERPIECES FROM THE PAPER MILL

The distinguishing feature of the work of Marta Kušnik from Ruta in Fala near Dravska dolina is that they are waxed by dipping them into melted wax. This gives the flowers and other parts of the plant – when they are shaped - a special, glass-polished glow. At the same time, waxing prolongs durability and resistance to heat and rain. Graveside wreaths were made of paper because they kept their shape and color longer than non-waxed ones. Waxed paper flowers were also used for making wedding decorations, altar decorations, signs and crucifixes for houses.

Despite all that, even today paper and its related product – cardboard – are still popular materials to work with amongst the younger generation. **CARDBOARD** is a factory-produced material, ennobled by creative hands which shape it into various products. **Dušan Pavšič** from Maribor has made an exceptional line of products from rippled cardboard. He has proved that wonderful products can be shaped from this simple corrugated surface and that noble products can be crafted from it. Soon, many others started imitating his work, which testifies to the lack of original creativity at the end of the 20th century.

Packaging made of corrugated cardboard by Dušan Pavšič from Maribor. The numerous varieties of paper and cardboard available have triggered the somewhat increased manufacture of paper packaging and other functional objects. Young designers often come up with innovative ideas. In addition to these new attempts, included in daily life-too slowly or never carried out and used-various amateurs are also taking up the crafting and shaping of paper.

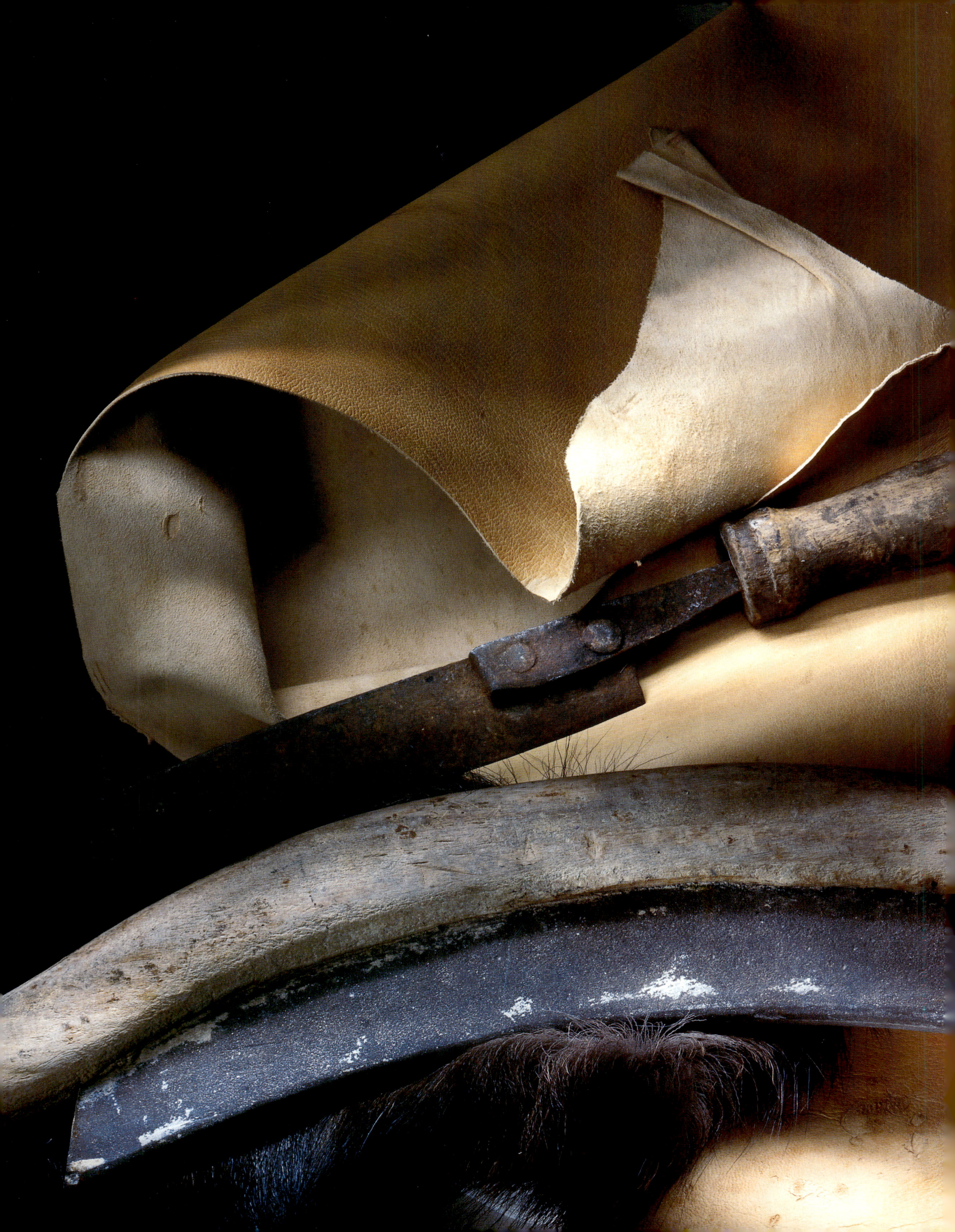

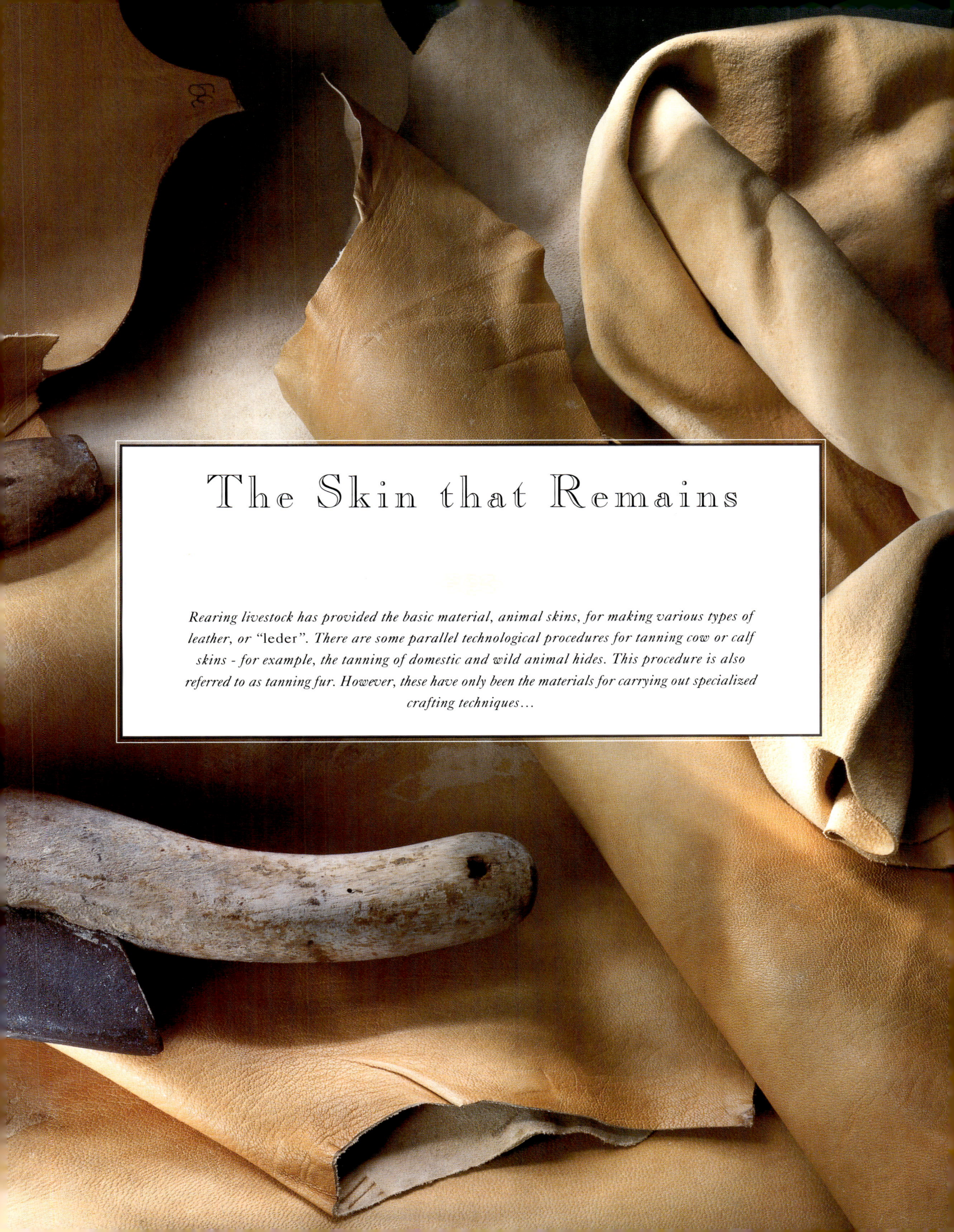

The Skin that Remains

Rearing livestock has provided the basic material, animal skins, for making various types of leather, or "leder". There are some parallel technological procedures for tanning cow or calf skins - for example, the tanning of domestic and wild animal hides. This procedure is also referred to as tanning fur. However, these have only been the materials for carrying out specialized crafting techniques…

The Skin that Remains

The history of the Slovene leather industry *(ledrarstvo)* is very rich. Various street names in towns and squares testify to that. There are names of places, homes and houses in Slovene towns and regions such as *Za čreslom* (which means "behind the tanning-bark") in Ljubljana. Architectural evidence proving the existence of the leather industry can be noticed by the presence of skylights on buildings where skins were once dried. The first reports of tanners' guilds are from the 16th century. The rich heritage of leather-tanning is best preserved in Radovljica where, not too long ago, the **Mali** tannery was still operational. It was known locally as **pri Bezulneku** and is situated in the city center - actually in the town hall, just opposite the apiculture Museum. In the tannery one can still see the complete tanning apparatus, together with the ancient tubs for soaking skins in tanning liquid.

Slovene tanners mostly tanned cow and calf skins to make leather. They also tanned sheep and goat skins used for bellows. Tanned sheep pelts were used to make winter coats. Two of the most famous, and also the best modern Slovene tanneries, are the **Grčar** tannery in Dragomelj near Domžale and the **Grad** tannery in Motnik. They represent the quality and technological peak of leather-tanning.

Janez Grčar

Tanning skins is a long and demanding process. After tanning has been completed, each skin is marked by a stamp, which is also the trademark of the Grčar firm.

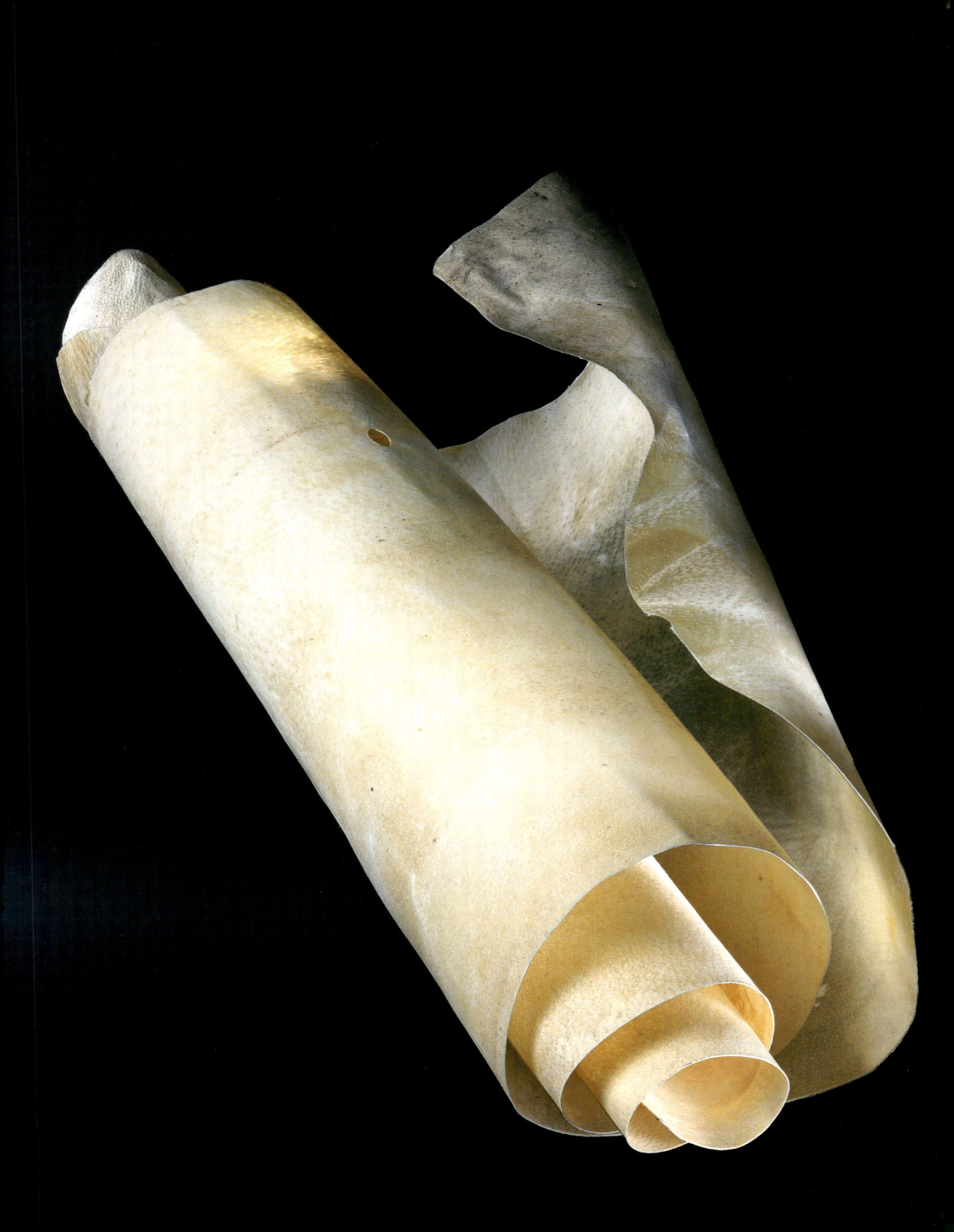

The Skin that Remains

There are many more workshops that tan the skins of domestic and wild animals and turn them into fur products. This is due to the great popularity of hunting in Slovenia. The skins of the hunter's prey are often tanned into trophies or other, more functional objects. Designing fur clothing and fur accessories is a special handicraft - furriery. Among the most renowned furriers are the **Eber** family in Ljubljana. A number of smaller furrieries still sew the traditional Slovene winter caps, called **POLHOVKE**, from tanned dormouse pelts, which is a special domestic fur-tanning discipline. Today, *polhovke* are a part of the traditional clothing style, but until only a couple of decades ago they were one of the most usual winter caps for men in the Alps and central Slovenia; today, however, they are seen only as a part of folk attire.

Superb tanned skins from the Grad company of Motnik (Picture 1). Tanned dormouse skins are used to make the traditional Slovene winter hat for men (polhovka) *at the Eber workshop (Krznarstvo Eber) (Picture 2).*

The Skin that Remains

Classical saddle-making started to decline-noticeably after World War II. This was connected with the abandoning of harnessing animals, especially horses and cattle. Furthermore, the demand for this special equipment in equestrian sport was minimal. But things have begun to change in recent years. There has been an increased interest in horse-breeding for the purposes of sports, recreation and tourism, so the products of saddlers and strap-makers are again in demand. Two modern Slovene saddlers are Milan Kokalj from Moravče (Picture 3), and Franc Gladek from Ljubljana, (Picture 4).

3

4

SADDLERS and **STRAP-MAKERS** also used leather to produce their products. The main saddlers' products were pointed collars for horses and cattle, and also saddles, reins, traces and other leather equipment. Today, this handicraft has all but disappeared because there is little need for hors-or cattle-harnessing. Among modern makers of pointed collars, i. e. saddle-makers, **MILAN KOKALJ** from Moravče and **FRANC GLADEK** from Ljubljana must be mentioned. There are some other Slovene saddle-makers, but altogether only a handful.

THE SKIN THAT REMAINS

Records of Slovene **COBBLERS** are even older. We can find records of a cobblers' guild in Škofja Loka from the mid-15th century, while the Turnišče cobblers' guild from Prekmurje was preserved the longest. Tržič was the largest Slovene cobblers' center, where a true shoemaking industry began to develop from individual cobblers' workshops in 1874. Between 1903 and 1906 Peter Kozina started a shoe production plant, which in 1911 grew into the large *Peko* shoe factory.

But despite the development of the shoemaking industry, numerous excellent cobblers' workshops have survived in Slovenia. Amongst others, **ČEVLJARSTVO VODEB** is the best-known Ljubljana cobblers' workshop, where superb footwear is produced. One of the oldest Slovene cobblers' workshops, which is a true museum, is master **LEVOVNIK**'s workshop in Slovenj Gradec - also because the cobbler's equipment has been entirely preserved. The town should consider preserving it as a cobblers' museum once Levovnik stops making shoes; a reminder of a handicraft that helped shape entire communities would therefore be preserved in its original cultural enviroment. This is also one of the ways in which handicrafts can be preserved and carried on. **MARIO HERZOG** from Pesnica near Maribor shapes and produces unique designer shoes, which are veritable artistic masterpieces and a synthesis of handicraft knowledge with classical cobblers' technologies. His custom-made shoes for individual customers combine the best experience from the past and the human needs of the future: the best quality available in this handicraft in Slovenia today.

THE SKIN THAT REMAINS

Today, the old Levovnik cobbler's workshop (Picture 1) in Slovenj Gradec only carries out minor shoe repairs, and it is slowly becoming a part of the historical memory of this town in the Koroška region. It is necessary to emphasize the importance of such old workshops for the future production of footwear, and the need to preserve them in the form of museums. There are several famous workshops in Slovene towns which boast a considerable tradition: one of these is Čevljarstvo Vodeb in Old Ljubljana, with its selection of superbly-crafted footwear (Picture 2). Shoes from the Herzog workshop (Picture 3) are indeed masterpieces and a synthesis of classical expert manufacturing technology. They are made for specific customers, and thus also represent a part of their personality.

243

The Skin that Remains

As in other crafts, a number of exceptionally-gifted craftsmen started working with leather as a hobby or as a continuation of family traditions, which often reach peak creative dimensions. The theater actor **Sebastian Nared** is such a craftsman. Coming from a Ljubljana family of cobblers that established the nationally-recognized *Derby* trademark, Nared now designs unique leather jackets and other items of clothing and accessories, as well as theater costumes. Part of the products they used to make is now included in the production of other leather goods.

Today, many of the young are taking up the design of leather clothes and accessories. To some of them this activity is an additional profession, while others work independently in their own creative workshops. Sebastian Nared from Ljubljana is a superb craftsman of leather goods. He has turned from a hobby craftsman to an original designer who also designs and creates his unique items himself.

THE SKIN THAT REMAINS

In the field of designing leather products and clothes, **VIKTOR BARLIČ** is known for creating leather goods and clothing in the center of Old Ljubljana. The long family tradition of making leather goods is still continued at the **CUNDER** workshop in Židovska ulica in Ljubljana. The **LEROTA** company from Trzin specializes in high-quality designer leather wallets and belts. They also have a salon of leather goods in Ljubljana.

Designing leather goods has a long tradition in Slovenia, and is represented by a number of excellent workshops. Three fine workshops are presented here: Barlič (Picture 1), Cunder (Picture 2), and Lerota (Picture 3).

THE SKIN THAT REMAINS

Part of the production formerly carried out by girdlers and strap-makers evolved into a specialized craft in which unique products or small lines of products are crafted. **THE MAKING OF LEATHER GOODS** is further specialized, since some craftsmen design clothes while others specialize in manufacturing leather handbags, for example. The handbags created by **MARJETA GROŠELJ** from Ljubljana represent superb craftsmanship and are comparable to the products of any internationally-recognized firm.

Leather and animal skins are important materials which modern Slovene craftsmen use to design numerous products, and which challenge them to seek new design ideas. Some of their creative ideas are extremely original, providing a solid base for the future of any handicraft, and not only those using leather, animal pelts or fur as basic materials.

MARJETA GROŠELJ

Leather bags are a special branch or domain of leather goods. The products of Marjeta Grošelj, marked with the letter G (her trademark), represent the peak of this craft. The designer's refined and elegant products represent a contrast to provocative trends in the garish, fast-changing world of fashion, and also make her style recognizable abroad.

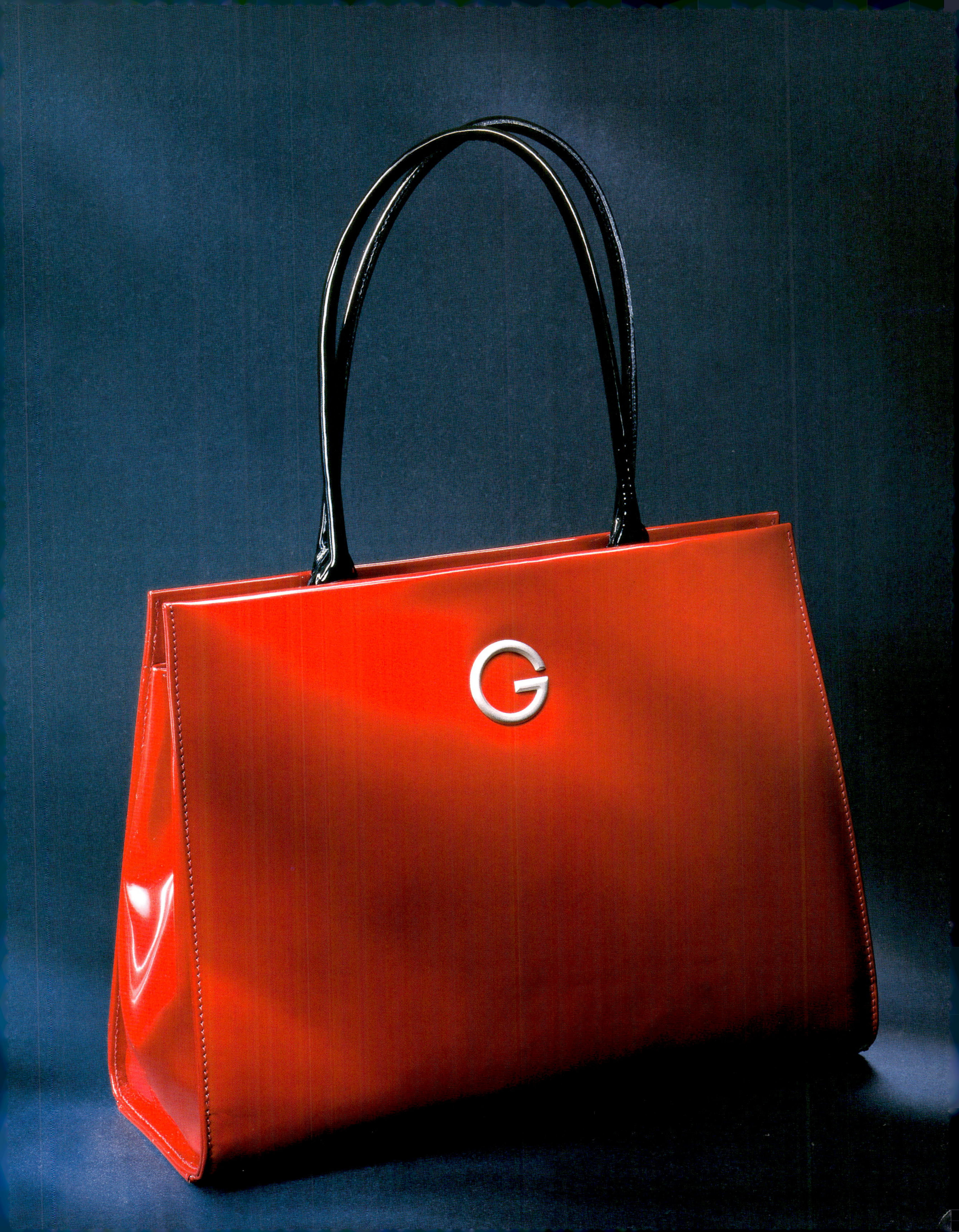

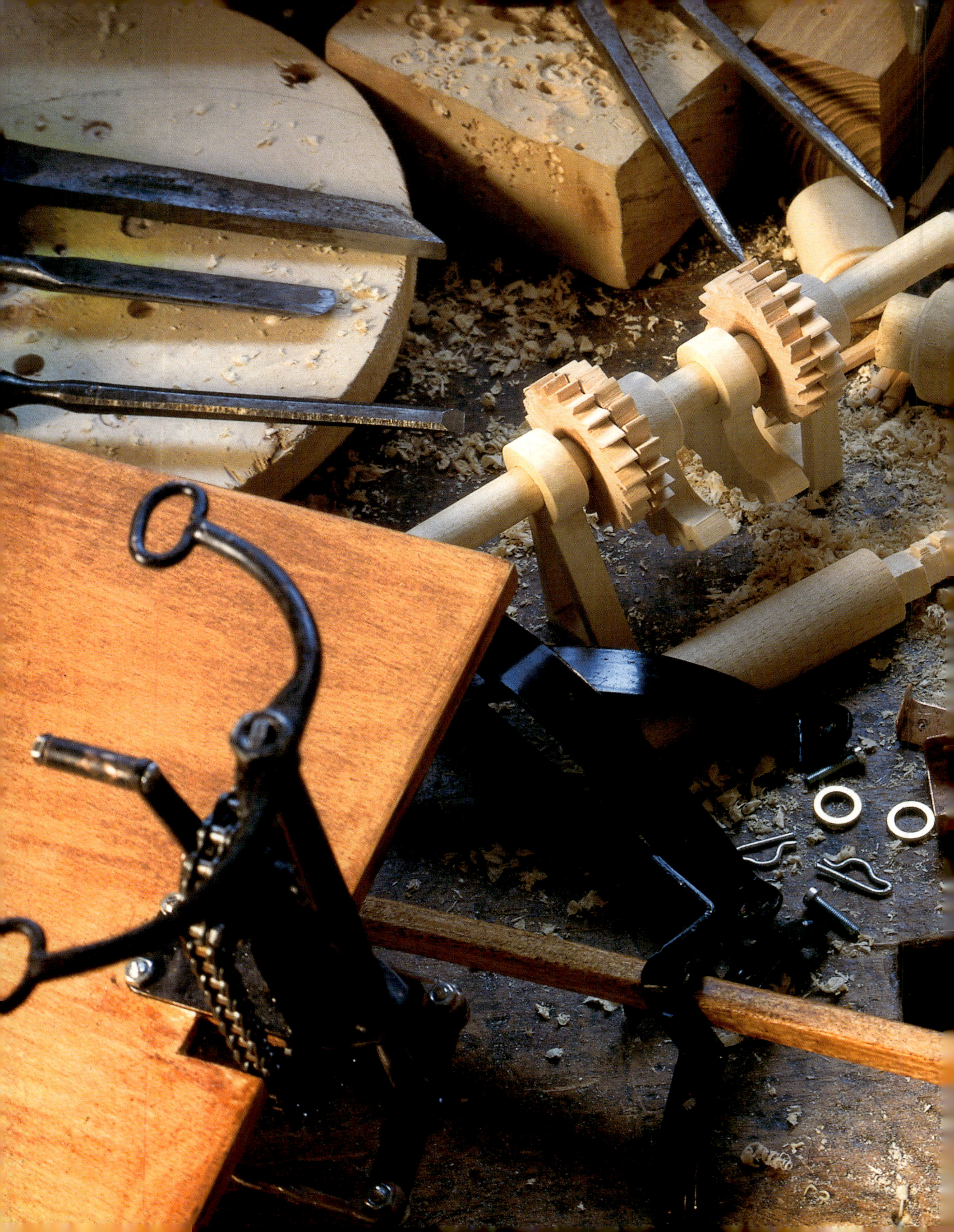

Replicas of the National Heritage

The desire to replicate handcrafted masterpieces from various historical periods is very old. In the beginning, the upper clases commissioned replicas of famous paintings, statues or furniture, which had to resemble the originals in every detail. Especially with the development of tourism from the second half of the 19th century onwards, replicating became more popular, and replicas became accessible to a wider number of potential buyers.

REPLICAS OF THE NATIONAL HERITAGE

Replicating means the repetition of traditional memory, or the replication of an original item from a given historical period. There are two ways craftsmen of replicas can choose: they can either produce a replica of the original as it was when it was first created; or they can make it as it was at the time of its decline, in the period when it was no longer a part of people's daily lives and festive occasions.

Handcrafted replicas, that is to say copies or imitations of certain "originals" kept in Slovene museums or private collections, are presented in this chapter. They are often made from a combination of materials, and could therefore not be described in any of the previous chapters. The same goes for some materials that were not mentioned because they are only used in combination with others, and because of the number of craftsmen working with them.

MAKING REPLICAS is surely one of the more demanding handicrafts, even though one would think that replicating any product is an extremely simple task. It is not easy to produce exact copies of the original, unless the craftsmen choose various technological shortcuts. But replicating a product means making an exact copy of the original, to repeat precisely the craft testimony handed down through historical memory. That can only be achieved by using same materials and techniques as were used to make the original. That cannot be done without constant study of and learning about traditional techniques and materials. Variations, simplifications, additions or reductions in replication are unacceptable. It is often the case that even individuals with no basic art education and talent take up replication. Another commonly noticeable trend is conscious alteration of the original. Some authors simply start inventing new motifs, ornaments or color combinations. These are particularly common in the replication of painted chests or beehive panels. Such replication is frivolous because it reduces replicaton to the production of kitsch. Of course, a market for such products does exist, limited to certain social levels or groups. The replication of some traditional objects has already been described in previous chapters.

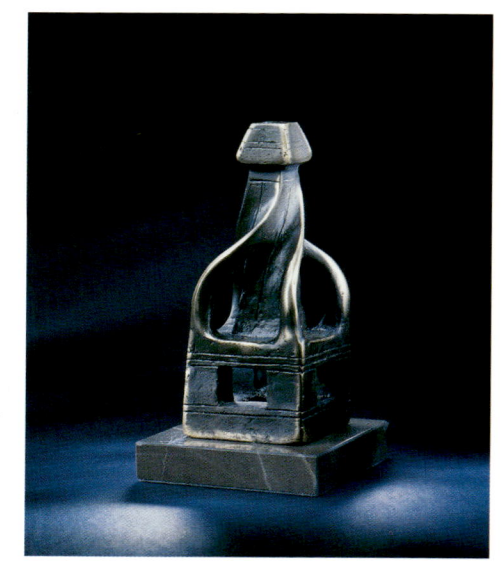

REPLICAS OF THE NATIONAL HERITAGE

The biggest misconception about replica-makers is that they tend to invent their own, new solutions. Replicating is acceptable only for specific objects of the national heritage. Slovenia lags behind in the field of replicating individual objects kept in the nation's museums. Such a state of affairs is often the consequence of completely subjective opinions and dubious expert preferences rather than of a defined strategy which ought to encourage the market orientation of museums and the openness of museums as institutions of a communicative nature.

Replication is extremely well developed in Slovenia today. It started to develop in the 1980s, even though individual attempts occurred some time before. Replication is a growing activity due to the gradual revival of museum exchange, which is common in this sphere of culture in the developed world. The replication of various archaeological finds and objects that were part of daily life in urban and rural areas in the second half of the 19th century is most popular today. Those studying the Slovene national heritage with a narrow-minded approach often wrongly label these objects as ethnological heritage. Replicas from material culture, which represented the lifestyle of the upper classes, is modestly represented today. Thus, there are not many replicas of objects originally used by the privileged Slovene social classes, or replicas of works of art (sculptures, for example), thus making it difficult to trace the development of art through different historical periods. the **ROKUS PUBLISHING HOUSE** from Ljubljana has recently developed the number of replicas from the body of work of the architect Jože Plečnik. The fact that some handicrafts are not represented as well as others can be attributed to expert narrow-mindedness, and we could also say to the expert favoring of certain crafts.

REPLICAS OF THE NATIONAL HERITAGE

The **REPLICATION** of **FOLK ART PAINTING** is the best developed, and is of the highest artistic quality within the replication industry. **ZDENKA** and **JANKO MLAKAR** from Ljubljana specialize in replicating painted farmhouse furniture from the Slovenian Alpine world, and painted beehive panels. Their workshop is the largest of its kind in Slovenia. They also replicate furniture with intarsias, and furniture once found only in the houses of the higher social classes.

ZDENKA AND JANKO MLAKAR

A mastery of replication also includes extensive expertise in various old technologies, painting techniques, the mixing of color coatings, glazing, and also "aging" techniques, or the creation of an artificial patina of time on a painted or differently-treated replica.

Making replicas of objects from the Slovene or any other national heritage has a further big advantage: It makes the objects available to anyone who desires to ennoble his life with messages from historical memory. Through replication, more originals will appear in specialized institutions (museums, for example). Making replicas also hinders international trade in original heritage objects a trade, which impoverishes the basic environment from which they were taken.

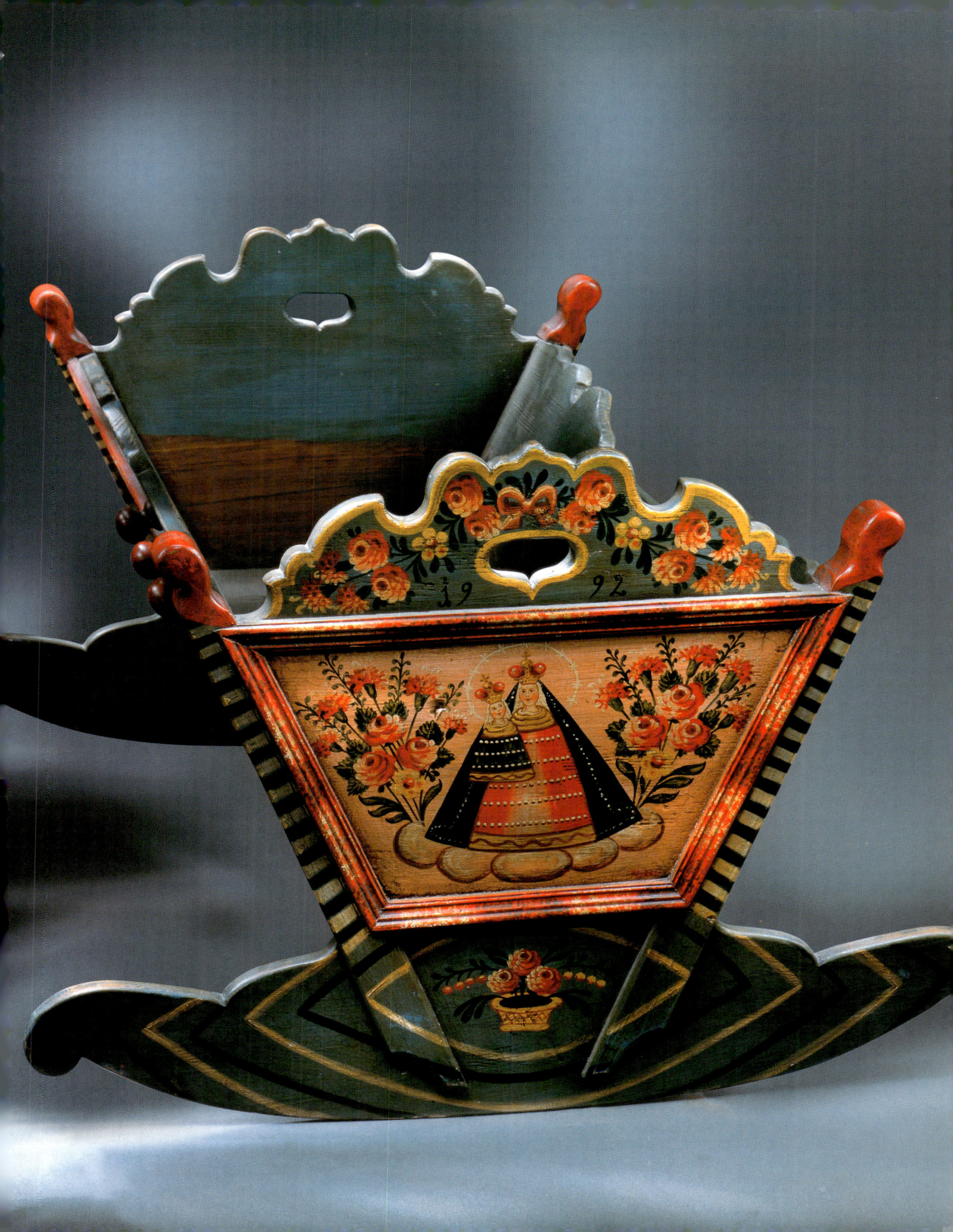
19 92

REPLICAS OF THE NATIONAL HERITAGE

Vlado Purič from Maribor replicates painted chests from north-east Slovenia, especially from Prekmurje. In his workshop he also crafts miniatures of painted chests, which are then turned into boxes. The craftsman naturally respects all the laws of making miniatures which, together with their component parts, have to be made in correct proportions and from original materials.

OTO SVETLIN from Radomlje also replicates painted beehive panels, furniture and various other items from the Slovene national heritage. He uses his replicating expertise to craft objects composed of individual elements, both domestic and foreign in origin. In this respect, his products are not mere replicas but new interpretations of traditional models, for which a market exists. **MITJA PERKO** from Ljubljana makes excellent replicas of **PAINTED WOODEN FARMHOUSE CHESTS** from the second half of the 18th century and the 19th century. Besides making entire chests, Perko also paints figures and floral or geometrical ornaments on individual sides. His replicas are flawless imitations of the originals, and even mimic the current state of preservation of original items. **VLADO PURIČ** from Maribor replicates Prekmurje-style wooden chests. He has also attempted to transfer the traditional ornamentation of painted chests onto modern furniture, which is a challenging task that calls for thorough aesthetic and expert consideration.

Oto Svetlin from Radomlje near Domžale crafted this fine replica of a chest from a prosperous farm in the Gorenjska region. Only perfect copies of objects kept in museums and various private collections are acceptable from an expert standpoint and considered suitable reproductions of the originals, whole life stopped decades or centuries ago.

REPLICAS OF THE NATIONAL HERITAGE

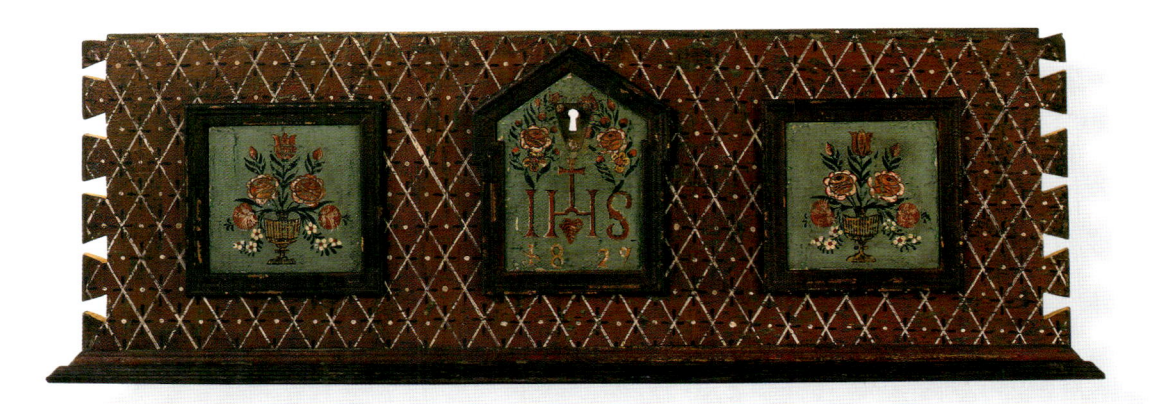

Painted farm chests from the Alpine regions of Slovenia, especially from Gorenjska, are most suitable for replication. The few makers of replicas who craft such products imitate individual originals consistently. The replicated chests have completely modern and functional interiors, adapted to the modern way of life. Replicas of individual parts of the chests - be they individual sides or painted elements in the frames - are also quite common. In this case, the replicas have representative and decorative purposes, or are used in completely new functions (e.g. as wall panels). Mitja Perko from Ljubljana crafted both replicas presented here.

Replicas of the National Heritage

In the 1980s the market was flooded with all sorts of replicated painted **BEEHIVE PANELS**. I used the words "all sorts" to emphasize that they were not really replicas of the originals but, rather, free interpretations and adaptations thereof. Painted beehive panels are not only a part of the Slovene heritage but a craft exclusively unique to Slovenia. Therefore, special attention ought to be paid to replicating them. Their popularity started to decline with the introduction of new bee-keeping techniques. They have been researched and documented sufficiently to ensure that no free experimentation with ornamentation and design is necessary. Freely interpreting and inventing new ornaments would be the same as adapting and changing Rodin's sculptures at the Louvre to suit one's personal taste. The ideal replica of a painted beehive panel ought to resemble the original in every detail. To achieve that, the original technological procedure(s) should be executed as accurately as possible. **DARJA KLEVIŠAR** from Ljubljana is the only modern artisan who comes close to replicating painted beehive panels perfectly. She does not only replicate the composition, color tones and drawings but also imitates the decaying parts, the effects of weather and sunlight on the wood, and even the traces of woodworm. She produces replicas that are just like the originals that we can admire in museums.

Painted beehive panels are also a defunct part of material history, related to an important economic activity – bee-keeping. Painting beehive panels is a uniquely Slovene characteristic. That is why the replication of these masterpieces from the national heritage demands strict adherence to the originals. Adaptations in terms of content, color or other alterations of motifs, or even the introduction of new ones, does not belong to expert replication. Darja Klevišar from Ljubljana makes outstanding replicas of beehive panels.

REPLICAS OF THE NATIONAL HERITAGE

A distinguishing feature of Rateški žoki (Rateče slippers), made by Anica Kopavnik, is their material. To make them, Kopavnik uses leather which is over forty years old. This makes the slippers firm and durable, and also enables us to make contact with basic materials (leather, woollen textiles). In addition to this, the slippers are of a simple, pure design, despite the fact that they were created as a continuance of historical memory.

The traditional accessory for carrying burdens on the head (a pad or roll - svitek) does not serve its original purpose today. But replicating it opens new possibilities of use which are still acceptable. The search for new purposes of "formerly" functional objects can be a very tricky activity which can soon result in trivial uses, banality and kitsch.

MARIJA HUMAR from Banjščice makes replicas of **SVITEK** (a pad or roll). A *svitek* is a round pad made of intertwined cloth strips. Women placed this round, plaited pad of cloth ribbons under the load to be carried on the head, which was predominantly considered a women's chore. Making such life-size or miniature rolls is a popular handicraft today. Of course, the product does not serve its original transportation purpose; however, it has a decorative character. Today, these rolls are used as decorations or pin cushions, for example. In the chapter on woodcrafts, making wooden clogs was also mentioned.

ANICA KOPAVNIK from Rateče in the Gorenjska region makes replicas of **ŽOKI** (traditional slippers). Unlike some other objects, *žoki* are not used in a decorative way but are still seen as functional. They are made of environmentally-friendly materials. Their exterior is made of home-tanned cow leather, while the interior is woollen - so *žoki* resemble socks in a way.

REPLICAS OF THE NATIONAL HERITAGE

JANKO SAMSA

One of the handicrafts for which a detailed knowledge of various materials and their characteristics is essential is the craft of **MAKING MINIATURES,** or miniaturization. This is a very popular craft, with many self-taught artisans. Unfortunately, they often fail to answer the fundamental question as to what objects should or should not be miniaturized. Sometimes, a craftsman makes a miniature farmhouse or a hayrack, and then glues straw onto its roof. On one occasion, a craftsman asked me if he ought to make miniature straw too. His question is a sufficient answer in itself. In terms of their function, miniatures are mostly useless collectors of dust in our homes. However, there are also exceptions to this rule, especially if the miniatures are of educational or representative importance. It would, for example, be impossible to fit life-size replicas of all 19th century types of Slovene farmhouses into a museum. Plans and photographs would be insufficient as well. In such cases, accurately-made miniatures seem appropriate solutions. **JANKO SAMSA** from Žirje near Sežana makes fine miniatures of carts for horse- or ox-teams. The carts are all made to a scale of 1:7 and resemble the originals down to the smallest detail. For example, he produces miniature brake mechanisms and forges wheel rims. A speciality of his miniatures is that he makes all types of Slovene cart and their regional variants, and also shows how they were used. They were intended for transporting wood or hay, or for other types of short-or long-distance transport, known from the rich typology of carts in the Slovene heritage of horse and cart driving, with all regional variants and specialities.

Fine miniature replicas of wagons, with a demonstration of the types of material and the means of transportation, are not only technological masterpieces but also have a didactic value.

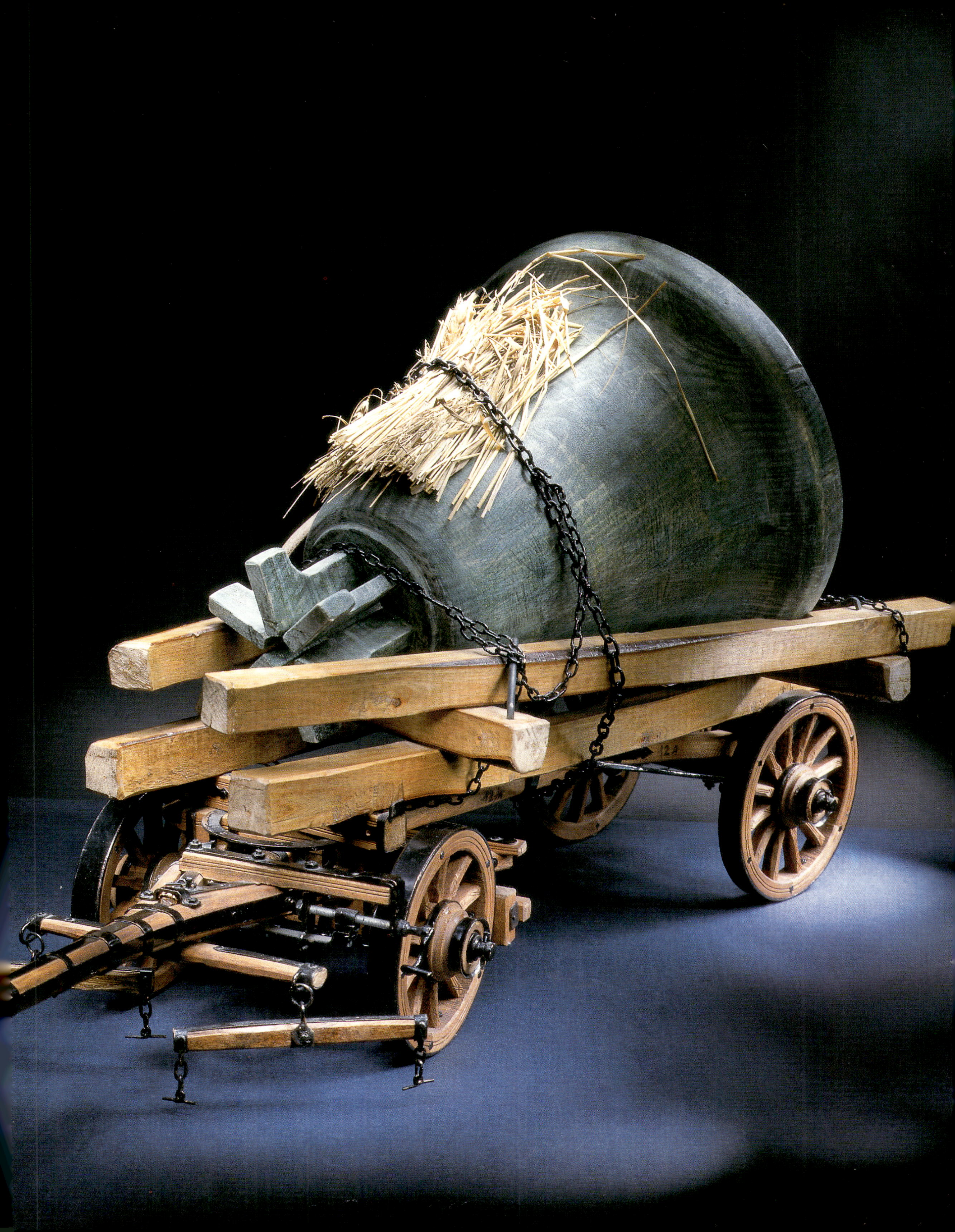

REPLICAS OF THE NATIONAL HERITAGE

Not much attention has been paid to making miniatures in Slovenia, and some attempts have resulted in fairly unsuitable products in aesthetic terms. But today, many museums (abroad as well) are turning to miniatures to present objects or even fragments of lifestyles. Museums frequently use miniatures to render the typology of regional architecture, as well as to demonstrate the use of certain devices, or to show how work and chores were carried out. Dušan Žerjal from Pliskovica crafts miniatures of the Karst world.

REPLICAS OF THE NATIONAL HERITAGE

Figurines of turned wood with painted folk costumes or the traditional dress styles of the Slovene regions are a rare exception in the otherwise modest field of turned-wood figurines. The figurines come in a pair for every Slovene region, and are stylized renditions of graphic representations, preserved from the period of regional diversity, which is also reflected in clothing, i. e. from the second half of the 19th century. The creator of the figurines is Vilina Hauser from Slovenj Gradec.

Dušan Žerjal from Pliskovica in the Karst region makes miniature farmhouse objects (like baskets with shoulder straps) once used daily in the region, and miniature Karst farmhouses. Every year he makes a partly mobile Nativity scene, which he displays at the local church. This is special for two reasons: the figurines are perfectly executed, and they are conceptually adapted to the Karst region. The whole scene of Christ's birth is essentially transferred to the Karst environment. The Nativity scene is a reminder of life in the region, as Žerjal experienced it as a child.

Making figurines or **mascots** dressed in **traditional** or **regional folk costumes**, is a handicraft in which Slovenia still lags behind in comparison to similar products produced in other countries. In the first years after World War II, **Jula Molnar** from Bled cultivated the art of making the Gorenjska folk costume but, unfortunately, her work was not carried on later. Today, the souvenir market is full of completely unacceptable products in terms of technology or content with regard to the rendition of clothing styles. No attempts were made to find at least adequate stylized representations of traditional folk costumes, with the exception of *Janez*, the mascot of the Kompas Agency. However, even *Janez* was never developed beyond mass-produced plastic figurines.

At the 6th Exhibition of Home and Applied Crafts in Slovenj Gradec in 1986, a local artisan named **Vilina Hauser** surprised everyone with a stylized set of mascots turned from wood and painted with selected regional folk costumes. She further developed her original idea in the subsequent years, and has created a wide selection of stylized renditions of traditional folk costumes from all regions of Slovenia. The latter makes her mascots especially valuable because stylization is a very challenging task in which all the distinguishing characteristics of the originals must be preserved.

REPLICAS OF THE NATIONAL HERITAGE

INSTRUMENTS are made from various materials. Only wood is used in the production of stringed instruments, the craft of which has been presented in the chapter on woodcrafts. There are several unique folk instruments in the area of Slovenia which are part of the history of rural music culture. **DARKO KOROŠEC** from Ljubljana specializes in replicating traditional Slovene folk instruments. He makes reed pipes (syrinx) and various wooden rattles such as *drdre* and *žvegle*. **VERA VARDJAN**, from Veliki Nerajec near Dragatuš in the Bela krajina region, makes an instrument called a *gudalo* or *lončeni bajs*, which is characteristic of Bela krajina and Prekmurje. The *gudalo* is an instrument used to give rhythm to music. It is made of an earthen ware pot, with a pork bladder membrane stretched over its top. A reed stick is stuck and sewn into the membrane. Rubbing the reed with one hand, which should always be wet, makes the membrane vibrate and produce a hollow tone.

The zither was an internationally popular stringed instrument. Playing it was highly esteemed in Slovenia, too, as background music to vocals, as well as instrumental music played in inns *(gostilne)*, or other public places. Besides imported zithers, self-taught Slovene craftsmen also made these instruments. **JOŽE HOLCMAN** from Selnica on the river Drava continues the Slovene zither-making heritage. He makes superb instruments which have been received awards several times for their exceptional quality both at home and abroad. When talking of Slovene instruments, we often first think of the accordion which, however, is one of the youngest in origin. This internationally-known instrument appeared in Slovenia in the 19th century, and several technological and sound alterations were subsequently made.

Folklorists and ethnomusicologists have researched the veritable treasury of Slovene folk instruments. It is, therefore, surprising that it was only recently that craftsmen like Darko Korošec from Ljubljana decided to replicate this part of the historical memory connected to national musical culture.

REPLICAS OF THE NATIONAL HERITAGE

The Holcman (Picture 1) zither is a superbly-crafted traditional Slovene instrument, even though it is fairly new in origin. It was supposedly used in Slovenia and in other parts of Central Europe only from the beginning of the 19th century. A true contradiction to the refined zither is the simple but previously very popular instrument called gudalo or lončeni bajs. All that was required was material: an earthen ware pot, a pig's bladder and a stick of Indian millet. But this "usual" instrument of yesteryear has become an object produced by expert craftsman and woman such as Vera Vardjan from Bela krajina (Picture 2).

REPLICAS OF THE NATIONAL HERITAGE

Many modern craftsmen make various types of accordions (e.g. piano or diatonic accordions). **VALENTIN ZUPAN** masters the different handicraft skills which are needed to produce accordions. In his workshop in Menges, he makes some of the world's finest accordions. Even after establishing his name, Zupan continues to make improvements to enhance the sound quality. This is the reason why his instruments are so popular with musicians and audiences. Today, even the external appearance of his accordions has become a sort of distinguishing feature, giving the instrument a unique artistic design.

VALENTIN ZUPAN

Diverse types and varieties of Zupan accordion are top Slovene trademarks in the area of musical instruments. Master craftsman Valentin Zupan still develops new technical improvements and the overall appearance of these instruments.

264

HANDICRAFTS OF SLOVENIA

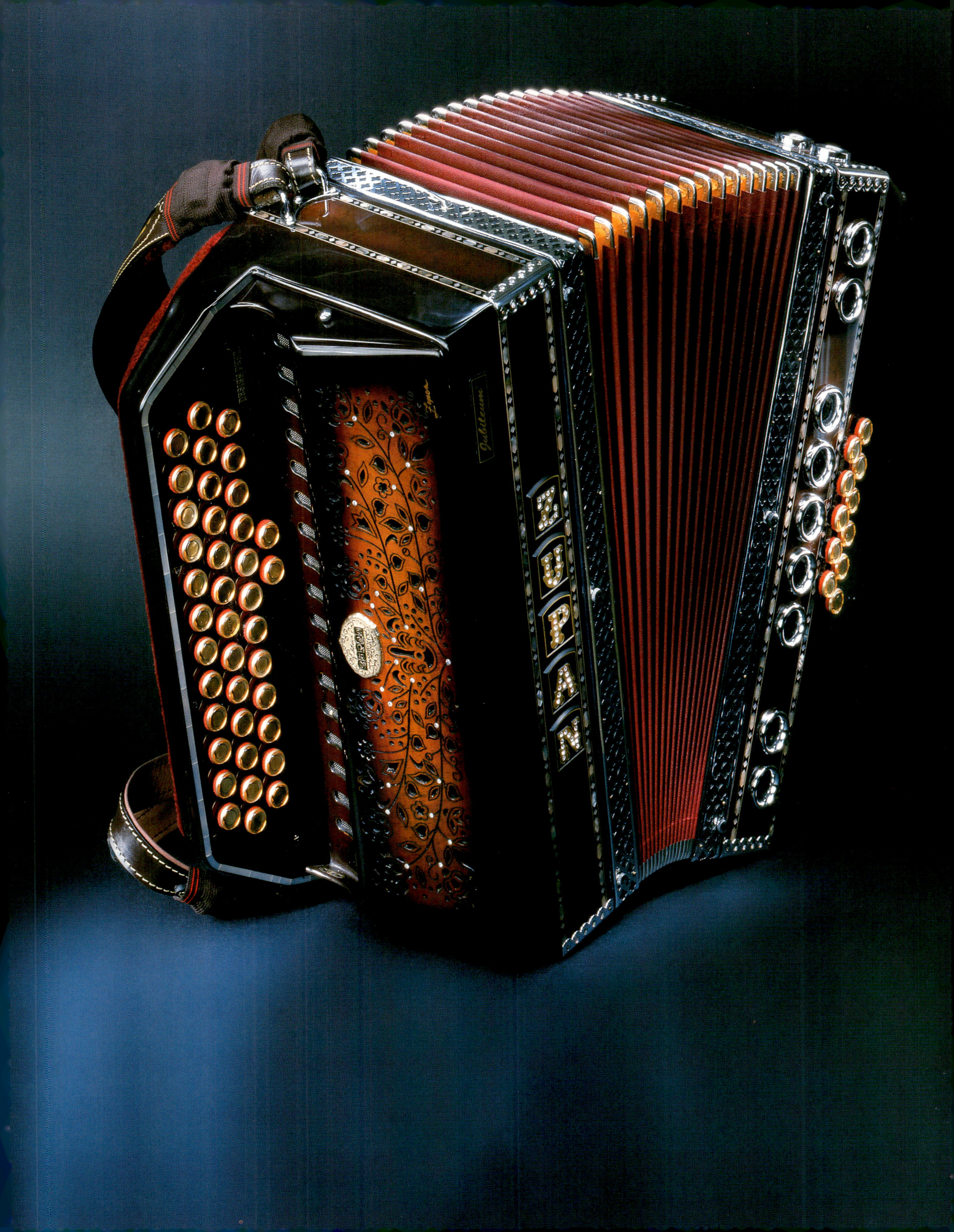
Jubileum
ZUPAN

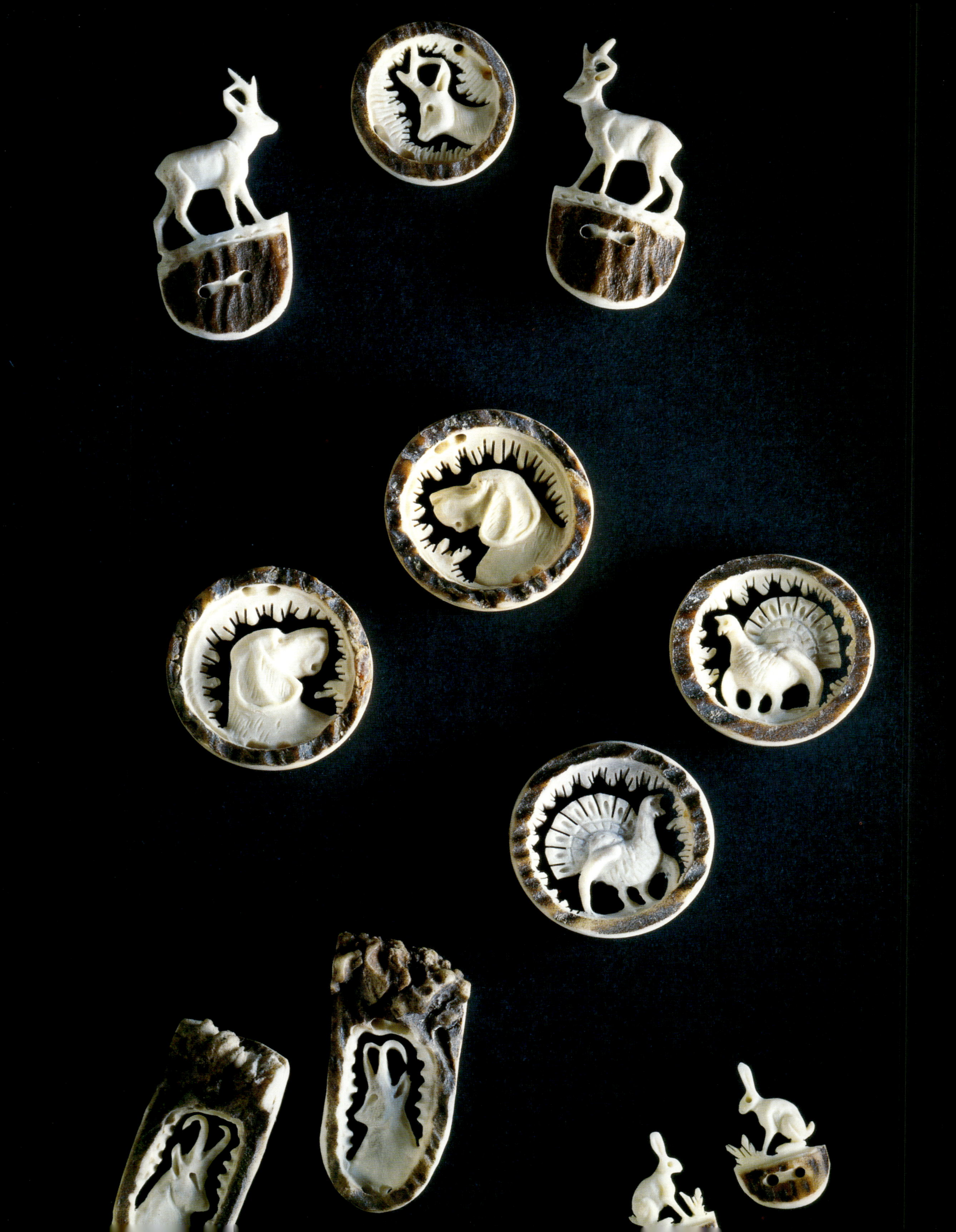

REPLICAS OF THE NATIONAL HERITAGE

Hunters have been nicknamed "the green fraternity". They are a social group with their own special lifestyle, rites, beliefs and moral values. They also differ from others by their uniform. A special handicraft developed in relation to this, namely the **CARVING OF FIGURE-SHAPED OR ORNAMENTED BUTTONS FROM THE HORNS OF WILD ANIMALS**. Every single button, normally depicting wild animals, is a unique item, produced by precise carving in bone or horn. A true master of this trade is **BORIS LESKOVIC** from Ljubljana. After carving, Leskovic hones and polishes the buttons down to their characteristic shine.

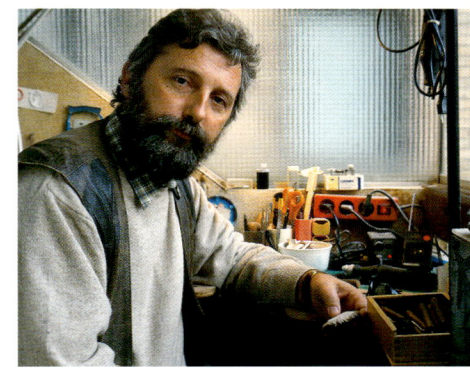

BORIS LESKOVIC

The official hunter's attire is naturally a uniform, so there are several rules as to how the dress and its accessories should appear. Even buttons on the hunter's uniforms - which are of a functional (and/or) decorative character - play a specific part.

267

HANDICRAFTS OF SLOVENIA

REPLICAS OF THE NATIONAL HERITAGE

If buttons are hunters' jewelry, some words need be said about **JEWELRY** in general. As is the case with silk-painting, many people take up making jewelry, but the originality and quality of their work is not very high. On the one hand, there is plenty of jewelry composed of imported, industrially-produced pieces; on the other, there is very little original, designer jewelry. It is interesting that sculptors, painters or designers rarely venture into this domain. Perhaps the exceptional preference for gold and gemstones over jewelry made of other materials is to blame. **ROMI BUKOVEC** from Medvode first exhibited her collection of body jewelry at the 11th Exhibition of Home and Applied arts in 1996. She uses various metals and synthetic resins. She resists the classical ideas of jewelry as regards the parts of the body on which jewelry is usually worn. She sees it as an aid in enhancing the body or individual body parts, and in emphasizing the individuality and personality of the owner. Her jewelry items become character signifiers of the person wearing them, emphasizing his or her communicative characteristics.

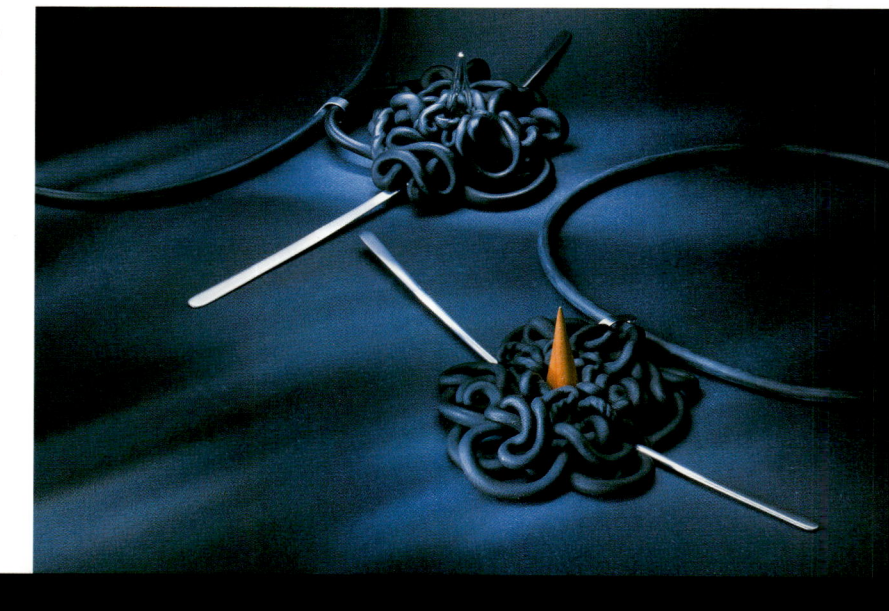

The jewelry crafted by Romi Bukovec surpasses the classical concepts of adorning the body, as do the traditional materials of which it is made. Jewelry for her is not only a decoration or an accessory to enhance those parts of the body which are usually considered suitable for jewelry (head, neck, hands, fingers). Instead, her creations are an association of various materials to accompany the body as a whole. They are directed to the person, the inner self and reactions to contacts with the external world.

268
HANDICRAFTS OF SLOVENIA

REPLICAS OF THE NATIONAL HERITAGE

With the revival and transformation of the heritage of putting on Lent costumes, numerous spontaneous creative elements have become a part of the craftsman's range of modern services. This has also happened in making Lent costumes with the creation of masks, clothes and other paraphernalia. Of all traditional Slovene Lent characters, the crafting of materials for the character of korant *from the Ptuj plain has become most extensive, and is also still developing. This means that we cannot describe this activity as a mere repetition of historical memory but rather as the development of a certain traditional, archetypal character.*

In modern times, the role and significance of handiwork can sometimes bear a negative tag. Some handicrafts took over the creation of various products, used daily or on festive occasions, that were originally made at home, thus changing individual and family creativity into a kind of production of service. Today, we tend to disregard the relaxing, creative side of handiwork which can help us escape from the frantic, alienated world of modern consumer society. Let us stop at the time of Lent, for example. The production of carnival masks and costumes is an excellent creative challenge, and in traditional societies they were made weeks in advance, often in complete secrecy. These traditional costumes are so rich and varied that one could call them "Europe in miniature". However, times are changing, and the traditional Lent figures are only included in parades, serving as a "theater of history", and instead of being reminders of tradition they become evidence of personal material wealth. The best example illustrating the misuse of Lent characters is that of *korant* from The Ptuj plain. Today, the *korant* masks and complete outfits are made in workshops. The craftsmen that make superb *korant* masks and outfits are not to blame for following the laws of supply and demand, nor for taking over a once home-executed handiwork. **Marko Klinc** from Spuhlja near Ptuj makes excellent *korant* costumes. And if this really is the "Korant service", it is carried out exceptionally well. His work is similar to that of workshops where traditional folk costumes are made for folklore dance groups. As these particular workshops are rare, they also serve as museums of the Slovene national dance heritage.

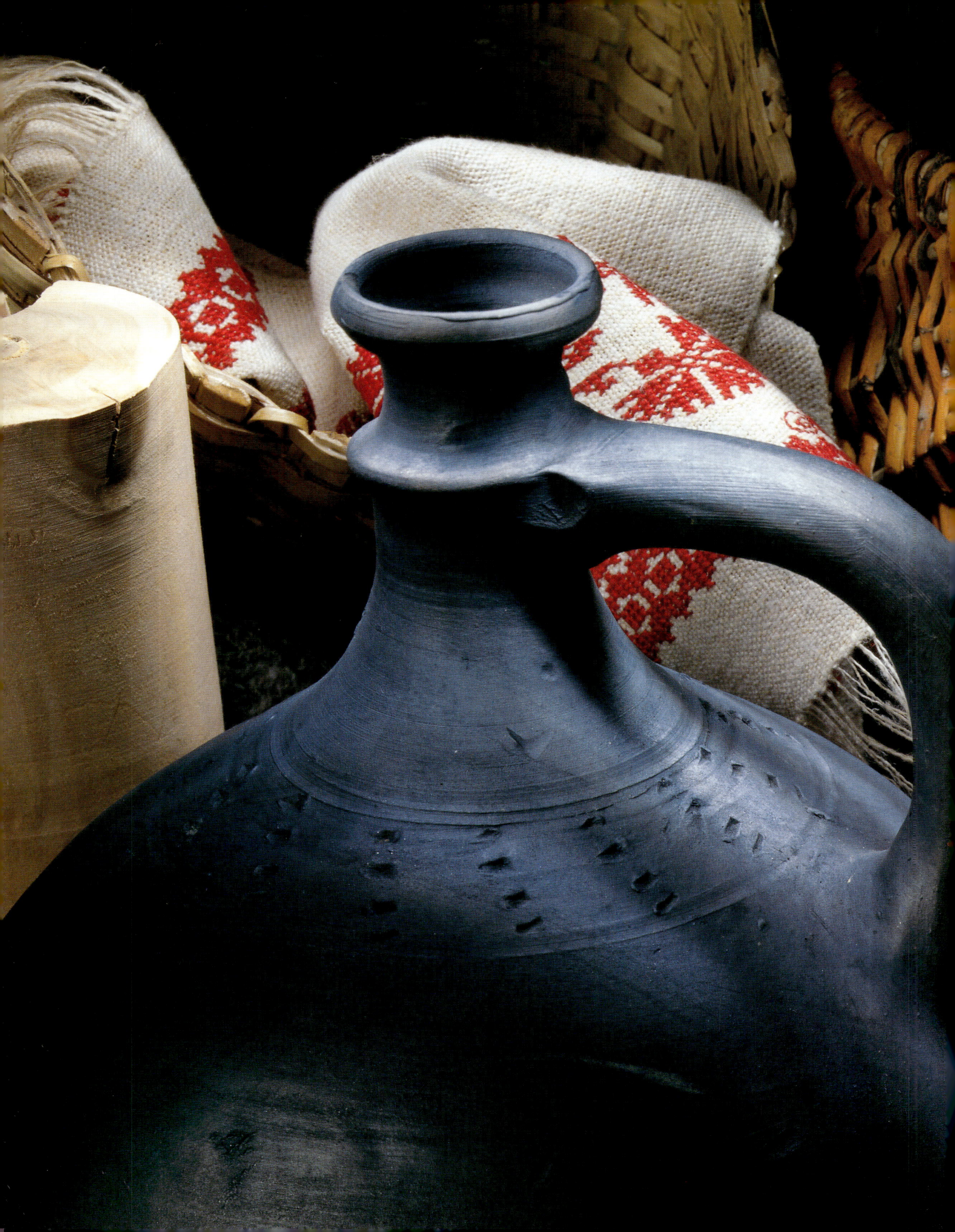

The encounters Continue...

Modern craftsmen are bound by specific sociological, organizational and professional boundaries. While Slovenia lags behind in some aspects related with handicrafts, it can also pride itself on several models and solutions that are important contributions to the international efforts towards the preservation of handicrafts. Handicrafts should preserve cultural diversity, which is essential for the spiritual and general improvements in our daily lives…

The encounters continue

The presentation of materials, craftsmen and their products proves that handicrafts are a **RICH, DIVERSE** and **VITAL FIELD** of **CREATIVITY**. First, there are handicraft disciplines, which are the continuation of older activities from different historical periods, with their own history and development. Other handicrafts are those related to replicating products of historical memory. In some cases, products that have survived to the present day are replicated, while in others the subjects of replicating are products which became obsolete in the 19th century, for example. Furthermore, new handicrafts appear all the time. Here, it is also necessary to differentiate between new handicrafts developed on the foundations of historical craft technologies or products, and handicrafts born out of new lifestyles and global influences. To conclude, handicrafts are not a dying phenomenon that we are trying to revive and preserve artificially, separated from our daily lives, but a part of daily and holiday occasions.

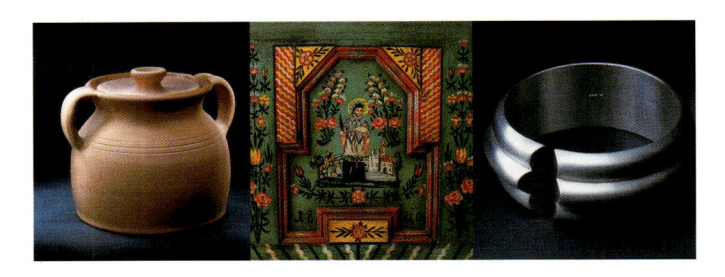

Even though new procedures and technologies are being constantly invented, people increasingly resort to historically tested traditional models to find inspiration. Working in handicrafts is not a nostalgia that is occurring at the end of the 20th century. They offer many economic and employment opportunities to individuals, creative groups, studios and schools. They are a noble response to the complete automatization, electronics and de-personalization that are characteristic of the modern world; and handicrafts wish to re-establish a positive relationship with our natural environment. It has often been said that nature turned against man, but I believe the opposite to be true. Modern man turned against nature, and is now trying again to become a part of nature's vital circle.

An element of personal experience is returned to man through handicrafts. He can attempt to craft an object from any material himself instead of looking for stickers and certificates of quality on mass-produced items.

Today **FORTY-SEVEN DIVERSE HANDICRAFTS** are listed in Slovenia, within which there are some sub-groups regarding craft procedures. Of course, the list is neither permanent nor definite, as is often presupposed by the authorities used to bureaucratic categorizations. Handicrafts change and develop like every vital organism. Some are new; others die out, or develop on the foundation of the former ones.

Of course, only an expert can determine which activities belong within handicrafts and which do not. Even though some craftsmen from nearly all handicrafts represented in Slovenia have been mentioned, **A LIST OF ALL MODERN SLOVENE HANDICRAFTS** follows. It seems useful for international comparison, because the experience in dealing with handicrafts differ from country to country.

According to the official list compiled on September 9, 1997, modern Slovenian handicrafts are as follows:

- Traditional and modern **POTTERY,** in which products are made on the potter's wheel or by other manual craft techniques.
- The crafting of modern unique ceramic objects, made from a range of materials (clay or china, for example) and by different techniques, such as *raku*.
- **WICKERWORK,** as a continuation of the rich weaving heritage, and the creation of new products from rods, straw, wood shavings, corn husks, rushes and other natural materials.
- **STRAW HATS-MAKING,** as a discipline of traditional and modern weaving, including the craft of strapped bags (*cekarji*), handbags and other unique products of modern design.
- Traditional and modern **WEAVING** and **TAPESTRY-MAKING** of unique products using horizontal or vertical traditional weaving looms and other weaving tools.
- **PATCHWORK,** as the composition and sewing of cloth of assorted figures or colors - only select products showing some artistic creativity.

- **KNITTING,** as manually-produced knitwear (traditional woollen socks and gloves, for example), and unique knitted products as a means of artistic expression in wool.
- **CROCHETING,** as the manual production of exclusive, artistically-original tablecloths, curtains and accessories.
- **WOOD-TURNING** and crafts related to the making of traditional and modern *suha roba* products.
- **MEAD-MAKING,** the production of sculptured gingerbreads, and the making of *mali kruhek*, *dražgoški kruhek* and *lect*. The replication of traditional models and the crafting of original products are considered.
- **CANDLE-MAKING,** as the replication of items of the Slovene heritage: the classical manual crafting and decoration of candles of natural materials or the design of new, unique candles.
- **DOUGH-SCULPTING,** for decorative items such as hearts of plaited bread or work with dough-like substances, for example salt dough.
- **SADDLE-MAKING,** as the manual crafting of saddles, pointed collars, reins and riding equipment.
- **CLOY-MAKING**, replicating traditional models from the Slovene national heritage.
- **MANUAL IRONWORK,** to produce replicas of traditional products or unique, original modern items from forged iron. This group also includes replicas of traditional items needed in the preservation of the national architectural heritage.
- **ARTISTIC IRON FOUNDING,** replicating traditional objects (kept in museums) from copper or other metals, or creating modern original jewelry or decorations.
- **TRADITIONAL HEWING,** as the building of hayracks and other buildings (a part of the national architectural heritage), as well as the production of traditional wine presses, wooden elements used in traditional types of mills, various restoration projects, and the replication of other traditional products for which extensive knowledge is essential.
- **CABINETRY,** as the replication and restoration of objects from the national heritage, and the production of unique, modern wood products.
- **WOOD-CARVING,** as an independent handicraft, the production of modern objects of carved wood, or as an activity connected with the restoration of objects of the national heritage, together with gilding and other related techniques.
- **MOSAIC-MAKING,** intarsias, including the crafting of unique wood, straw, stone or metal intarsias replicated from traditional models or original modern intarsias.
- Classic **CASK-MAKING,** as one of the oldest national handicrafts.
- **WHEEL MAKING** - the production of wooden wheels and other equipment used for carts or carriages.
- **BOBBIN LACE-MAKING,** as the manual production of traditional or modern lace using various threads or metal wires.
- **MANUAL EMBROIDERY** of unique pieces, using different embroidering techniques (counting threads, cross-stitch or Richelieu-style embroidery).
- **PIPE-MAKING,** as the manual replication of traditional smoking pipes.
- **DESIGNING MODERN ORIGINAL LEATHER PRODUCTS.**
- Various techniques of **TEXTILE-PAINTING** or **TEXTILE PRODUCTS** (silk scarves, handkerchiefs, ties, items of clothing).
- **SEWING** and tailoring replicas of traditional folk costumes.

THE ENCOUNTERS CONTINUE

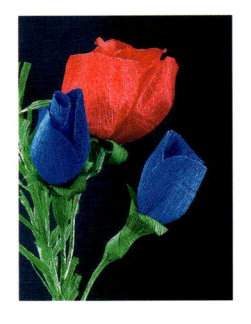

- Classical **PAPER FLOWER-MAKING** (waxed paper flowers included).
- Manual **PRODUCTION** of **COPPER CAULDRONS** for cooking, cheese-making and other special uses.
- **LIME-MAKING,** in classical forest lime kilns to be used for the renovation of buildings which form part of the national architectural heritage.
- **CHARCOAL-COOKING,** in forest piles as a continuation of this traditional home craft.
- **STONE-DRESSING,** as in the making of replicas of traditional objects or of unique modern stone products (gravestones and other graveside accontrements are excluded).
- **ROPE-MAKING** – domestic production of hemp and flaxen ropes.
- **WHIP-MAKING** by manual wood-turning or by plaiting wooden strips.
- **MASCOT-MAKING,** whereby the quality of design and technical execution are considered.
- **MAKING DECORATIVE OBJECTS** from combined materials. The combinations can include gold or other metals, as well as stone of various qualities. Only original, unique products of a high artistic value or limited editions with a precise number of products stated are considered.
- **REPLICATING** the original **WORKS** of **PAINTERS, SCULPTORS, DESIGNERS** or **ARCHITECTS**, using the original crafting techniques and materials, or variations on the latter. Only limited editions of products that have been certified by experts are considered.
- **REPLICATING** items or sets of **ITEMS** of the Slovene **NATIONAL HERITAGE**. Only numerically-limited quantities of products with certificates from institutions of experts are considered.
- **PRODUCTION** of **MODERN, UNIQUE PRODUCTS** or limited editions in which several materials can be combined.
- **GLASS-MAKING** and **BLOWING** in which (certified) replicas of traditional objects are produced. Another activity within the craft is the creation of original modern products
- **MANUAL GLASS-CUTTING** - to decorate glass products, whereby the artistic and aesthetic quality of the product is considered.
- **MAKING UNIQUE STAINED GLASS WINDOWS,** compositions using the **TIFFANY** technique, and compositions created by etching glass.

- **HAND-PAINTING** of various products of the Slovene national heritage (beehive panels or painted glass), or completely original modern artistic experiments (painting glass products). The criteria for this handicraft are very strict and selective.
- **MODERN INTERPRETATIONS OF** objects of the Slovene national heritage, or the design of modern products on the basis of traditional models or concepts.
- **HAND-CRAFTING OF TOYS**, playthings and puppets based on tradition (replicas or interpretations), or on quality modern design. The craftsmen have to obtain the opinion of a special committee, which then awards them the *Dobra igrača* (Quality Toy) mark.
- **MAKING UNIQUE ITEMS** which are interpretations of traditional objects, using modern Slovene or foreign creative approaches.

Today, some burning questions regarding the role and future of handicrafts still remain unanswered. The first is certainly that of **EDUCATION** and training for specific handicraft disciplines and knowledge. In this field, the old model of education for handicrafts, established in the Habsburg Empire, still remains paramount, even though this may sound improbable. Of course, their bureaucratic apparatus considered handicrafts useful and therefore worthy of systematic support at all levels. Individuals and families were encouraged to take up handicrafts, which were further promoted by various courses and specialized schools.

The second problematic area is **DOCUMENTATION**. Detailed data on traditional and modern handicrafts would function as a warehouse of tradition, serving the sole purpose of giving a solid information base from which new, original solutions could be derived. It would also be useful for the improvement of the craftsmen's knowledge of materials and crafting techniques. There are two different fields of the documentation of handicrafts: compilations of data about the works of individual authors, and institutionalized data on handicrafts and artisans in general. Neither of these exist in Slovenia today. The fact that even many basic traditional Slovene handicrafts and crafting procedures are insufficiently documented is most ironic.

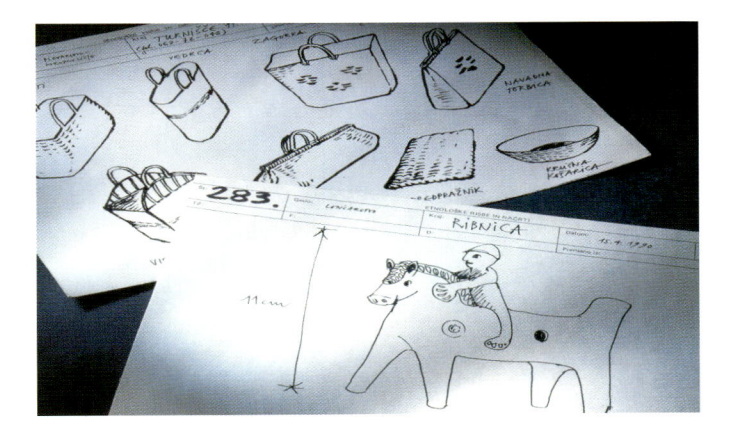

Some details on classical crafting techniques, procedures and (special) tools used still remain unknown. In the circle of experts studying handicrafts, the methods of the imperfect description and repetition of stereotypes are still common.

Modern life often discourages systematic thinking and the wise, gradual accumulation of knowledge. Both of these are slow processes for which modern consumer society has no time. If things are not produced quickly and with immediate profit, they are considered useless.

UNAUTHORIZED COPYING, THEFT OF IDEAS OR PLAGIARISM, rather than the search for original ideas, are the consequences of this constant lack of time. Many authors resort to copying ideas they find in literature. Craftsmen with artistic potential and original ideas need to become more self-confident and better informed about the protection of their intellectual property. If the craftsmen are well informed of all aspects of their trade, the handicraft is likely to be well developed. Sunday afternoon hobby craftsmen, however, usually do not think like this, even though their work occasionally results in original concepts. These ideas can become subject to imitation by more cunning individuals, even if only exhibited at a single local exhibition.

One cannot classify the replication of traditional objects of the cultural heritage as the theft of intellectual property or as the copying of ideas. Replica-making is specific because the traditional models are well known, safely stored in various museums and private collections.

The hardest part of the replication process is obtaining the owner's permission to view and study the original, as well as the documentation pertaining to it. Because the owners or custodians are often reluctant to cooperate, the craftsmen are forced to study partial plans, copies or photographs from other available sources. This is why replicas are imperfect and burdened with various unoriginal additions, such as the invention of new ornaments, additions to motifs, the uniting of various types of ornaments in invented compositions, the transfer of motifs to different types of products, and so forth. To illustrate, such additions of details or motifs occur because the craftsman could not clearly make out the original pattern from a photograph. Furthermore, the craftsmen often lack knowledge of the traditional techniques and special work procedures, such as the artificial aging of paintings or carvings. Replicas of replicas also occur. Because of difficulties in obtaining the original models, some craftsmen use replicas available on the market (which are mostly of poor quality) to create their own. Replicating bad replicas is a step back in creativity.

The chaos related to the protection of intellectual property in the field of modern handicrafts has already caused some negative responses. Individual artisans who make unique items of exceptional quality are not versed in the use of the legal mechanisms available to them for the protection of their inventions. Uninformed as they are, they presuppose that this is a long, expensive and complicated procedure, even though that is not the case. I feel that the mentality of craftsmen ought first to change. Between 1990 and 1998, there were only four craftsmen who sought to protect their ideas according to the established legal procedures. Artisans need to understand the necessity for having their techniques and products documented in detail.

One of the problems of modern Slovene handicrafts is that no strategy for an **INTERDISCIPLINARY APPROACH** in the design of individual items, series, collections or trademarks exists. The unemployment crisis, a relatively small market and vague legislation are to blame for the great individualism in Slovene handicrafts. The motto "every man for himself" is now obvious, even in handicrafts that originally practised the division of labor (e.g. the craft of *suha roba* products).

This extreme individualism is exemplified by the fact that craftsmen strive to control the entire creative process (the concept, test production, regular production, the design and type of packaging, and marketing) rather than the production phases only. Some craftsmen even issue their own certificates testifying to the authenticity and limited number of their products, and equip them with explanatory leaflets.

One of the ways to encourage the interdisciplinary approach to handicrafts, and thus raise the quality and general standard of products, is through the establishment of small creative studios and centers in which experts of various fields work together to improve the design and quality of their products. To say it plainly, we shall have to re-establish the thought of the greatest Slovene poet that "a cobbler should only judge shoes."

This model is ideal for the establishment of smaller family handicraft businesses in which every member of the family is trained and directed to find his role in the creative handicrafts process.

Some original solutions for the preservation and continuation of the national heritage, which exerts an **IMPORTANT INFLUENCE IN CERTAIN FIELDS OF OUR EVERYDAY LIFE,** have already been found in Slovenia, while some aspects related to handicrafts, such as training, must be improved as soon as possible. In the present Slovene school system, the traditional handicrafts are not well represented on the curriculum. Some crafting techniques, like modeling clay, are included in primary school art classes, but they represent only a fragment of the rich national heritage.

The positive fact that the basic handicraft materials are natural, and often available in schoolchildren's immediate environment, should be emphasized in the alienated world of today. By gathering materials, a child can be in direct contact with nature, which is invaluable today. Handicrafts can be included in the education system in two ways. The first way involves the **REGULAR FORMS OF EDUCATION** and **TRAINING** for specific handicrafts; the other entails a **SUPPLEMENTARY EDUCATION** intended mostly for adults. There has been a substantial increase in the second approach, particularly with the organization of bobbin lace-making courses and some other handicrafts, mostly imported to Slovenia from abroad. Some of these are silk-painting, the modeling of salt dough, various synthetic modeling materials and *raku*. Students acquire basic craft skills in these, mostly market-oriented courses. Because of that, one cannot expect the organizers to apply selective mechanisms in the form of tests of the skills and talents of every prospective student. The lack of selectivity hinders craftsmen who acquire their basic knowledge in this manner. Raising false hopes of would-be artisans in such courses is unfair and unprofessional. They often exhibit their first product made in the course, and are disappointed when it does not achieve public and expert acclaim. Therefore, selective methods, whereby the most talented individuals could acquire new skills and knowledge, ought to be set up by the state. More effort needs to be invested in the preservation and continuation of traditional Slovene handicrafts and the crafts descended from them. More space needs to be given to them within the framework of various adult-education programs. First and foremost, new ways of introducing handicrafts to potential artisans need to be found.

To illustrate, Austrian television regularly broadcasts various demonstrations of individual handicrafts. These broadcasts are a form of TV education course. Of course, television cannot demonstrate the social dimension of handicrafts, but it does enable all those interested in particular craft techniques to learn about them, without attending special workshops or craft centers.

Several younger Slovene craftsmen welcome young visitors (especially children) to their workshops, and offer basic training and craft equipment. Some good results have been achieved in the fields of pottery and ceramics by young artisans. One such attempt was Nataša Prestor's cycle of courses of pottery and ceramics for children.

A selection of handicrafts is included in the curriculum of specialized education programs for agricultural occupations in secondary schools of agriculture. This shining exception to the rule has an additional positive trait. The young farmers leave school equipped with a basic knowledge of economy and marketing, both of which are necessary for the preservation of various handicrafts in the rural regions.

Not enough attention is paid to the possibilities of **EMPLOYMENT** in the field of handicrafts. The present situation makes them supplementary sources of income. To change handicrafts into truly profitable activities, a complete strategy of education, development and marketing would have to be proposed. Crafting wooden products and the production of *suha roba* are very popular in the Ribnica valley in Slovenia. Recently, the government attempted to abolish the tax deductions for local producers of *suha roba*. This abolition would mean denying craftsmen the only encouragemant to continue their trade. I remember a meeting on the subject where the Mayor of Ribnica underlined the importance of *suha roba* production for the economic survival of the entire region by saying: "I suggest you should find a suitable solution for the great number of *suha roba*-makers. You must realize that crafting *suha roba* products in the municipality solves a major part of the unemployment problem in Ribnica."

Some experiences from the past indicate that handicrafts are suitable for the employment of groups with special needs. However, only handicrafts best-suited to the skills and needs of such individuals ought to be considered. Some excellent models from the past (wickerwork production by the blind after World War II) and present ought to be considered in the organization of other similar programs. There have been less successful programs, too, organizing the manufacturing of conceptually esthetically and technologically unsuitable products. Therefore, more attention must be paid to the education and training of therapists who work on such projects. The same could be said for handicraft tutorials offered in old people's homes. In addition to some truly outstanding products, a lot of average kitsch is produced there. We neglect the fact that the senior citizens are often the last individuals to master certain craft skills and knowledge. In emotional discussions about the inclusion of the elderly in society, we are overlooking the possibility of including vital individuals in handicrafts education processes. The rich variety and exceptional quality of their products can be observed at numerous annual exhibitions of handcrafted objects in old people's homes.

The **COUNTRYSIDE** is still the cradle of various handicrafts because of the greater connection with nature and the possibilities for craftsmen to grow their own material (flax, wool). The function of handicrafts has changed considerably from the past. Many procedures (or entire handicrafts) have become completely redundant with the appearance of factory-produced objects and various technical improvements. Some of the traditional handicrafts have been lost in this process, while others produce a much narrower range of products compared to the past.

Today, some of the products are used as items of decoration, to the dismay of many craftsmen. A Dolenjska maker of wicker baskets - which were adapted for carrying coal - was invited to produce them as decorative items. He refused to do so because he felt they were unsuitable items for sale in a shop selling interior decorations.

Handicrafts are **SUPPLEMENTARY ACTIVITIES** in the countryside. They offer many possibilities, most of which remain unused. A wide range of quality foods is produced in the Slovene countryside, but there is no suitable, locally-produced packaging available. Thus, on the one hand we face the lack of ideas for creating lines of products, while on the other we ignore possible uses for a certain product. It is lamentable that, for example, ecologically-produced, homegrown fruit is not yet offered to the market in home-produced wicker baskets.

The migration of skilled artisans from the urban areas back to the countryside is an interesting phenomenon, resembling the migration of individuals born and bred in the city to the American countryside. These people are referred to as "gentlemen farmers," in association with the general predominant rural orientation in the United States.

Handicrafts are becoming more popular with the development of **COUNTRYSIDE TOURISM**, or farm holidays. Handcrafted items have an increasing number of buyers who are tourists who, in turn, have an increasing incentive to buy such products. While spending their holiday or spare time on farms, tourists can witness the production of such items, or even test their own skills by crafting some personally. This is one of the elements of active holidays from which people return enriched with new knowledge acquired in more direct contact with nature. Though this, tourists acquire new values, and countryside tourism acquires new, nobler dimensions. Despite strong encouragement, the immense opportunities for the combination of handicrafts with farm holidays still remain mostly unused.

There is also a psychological dimension to this problem, especially in Slovenia. For decades after World War II, rural culture was synonymous with backwardness. The inclusion of various handicrafts in the range of products and activities available to tourists in the countryside can strongly contribute to the preservation and continuation of traditional handicrafts. Young people learn about traditional handicrafts and objects of national heritage through youth **RESEARCH PROJECTS** in various **WORKSHOPS**. The best research projects at the level of primary or secondary school education are presentations of handicrafts by craftsmen from the local cultural environment. Through these, the young learn about the lifestyles of the artisans and their families, and the details of crafting individual products. In this way, a lot of information about handicrafts, their historical development, and type of work is accumulated. Such research projects are an excellent additional educational factor which can motivate the young to craft in one of the disciplines with which they have become familiar through theoretical work. The development of **THE CULTURE OF GIFT-GIVING** in the last fifteen years has been of paramount importance for Slovene handicrafts. The popularization of various business, promotional and state gifts has given a new creative élan to certain handicrafts. Since lace products are often presented to business partners, potential customers or statesmen, lace-making has become very popular in recent years, and the market has expanded. Moreover, new, inventive approaches to the craft have appeared, resulting in truly accomplished original products. Of course, all aspects of gift-giving must be carefully considered.

State or business gifts are used to establish relations, but also to introduce part of the tradition and heritage from which the gift-giver comes. The cultural and spiritual dimension of the gift must always exceed its material value. If this is not the case, the gift can only be described as a bribe.

The importance of promotional, business and state gifts is twofold. First, it is a potential new market in which good craftsmen can prosper. Second, their products enrich business and other relations with new ideas and messages, which in turn enrich the culture of every individual or group (family). Gifts crafted by local artisans are the best representatives of the gift-giver's creativity. Special gifts are only one of the ways by which we recognize the importance of handicrafts. Their role is becoming increasingly important in relation to a general understanding of the **QUALITY OF LIVING,** and life in general. In these times of automated mass production, people seek refuge in traditional hand-made items already tested by time, but also in those modern products whose form and function are based on modern concepts. These products are crafted from elementary, natural materials, and with their role and overall image help shape and accentuate the higher qualities of life and the environment in which we live.

For these reasons the development of handicrafts and conditions for the development of individual crafts ought to be supported and encouraged at all social levels.

The beginnings of organized support to or **STATE CARE** for individual handicrafts can be traced back to the second half of the 18th century, and are connected with education. France was the first European country to establish trade schools in the mid-1700s. Other European countries followed suit later. In Slovenia, some even older isolated examples of support for individual handicrafts can be found. On **OCTOBER 23RD, 1492** Emperor Frederic III issued a patent allowing the free production and trade of *suha roba* in Carniola. Besides woodcrafts, which were most widespread in the regions of Ribnica and Kočevje, the patent also mentions the production and trade of cloth, linen, butter, oil, hazel tree hoops, and spruce wood rims for sieves. The production and trade of all these products were essential for the survival of these regions. The Emperor needed a satisfied populace in this area (they were also his potential soldiers) with their basic means of survival secured.

Organized attention to handicrafts was renewed in the second half of the 18th century and continued well into the 1900s. Various trade schools were established, courses were organized, and individual handicrafts promoted, creating economic opportunities for the local populace. The period after World War II was not particularly supportive of handicrafts, despite the fact that the State Institution for the Marketing of the Products of Arts and Crafts was established in Ljubljana in 1946. This institution later evolved into the trading enterprise *Dom*. Handicrafts were still practised in various enterprises and cooperatives, but with no systematic planning, expert support, documentation or training. Numerous handicrafts there for soon started to decline. Some were carried on only by individual artisans, who had to rely on their own resourcefulness to survive. Their biggest consumer - the state - saw them as services for producing state gifts and national mascots rather than as an area of national economic importance.

Along with the decline in traditional handicrafts, there was the increasing appearance of new ones from abroad. Those artisans who took them up had very little opportunity to expand their knowledge of crafting technologies, design and art. In 1977 Slovene craftsmen established the Board of Home and Applied Crafts and organized the first exhibition of home and applied crafts in Slovenj Gradec, which has since become a tradition. The board continued with their work in the Association of Trades of Slovenia and later in the Chamber of Trades of Slovenia. The Board changed its name to the Section at the Chamber of Trades of Slovenia, within which there are representatives of individual handicrafts; and a special Expert Committee was appointed to judge and evaluate handicraft products. In the beginning, the Committee's marks at exhibitions were helpful in obtaining various tax deductions, which are the most efficient form of state support. With the establishment of this committee, expert attention was finally paid to handicrafts as well. After 1977 individual craftsmen were awarded the title *Mojster* (Master) and their workshops the title *Mojstrska delavnica* (Master's workshop). Products of high quality were awarded signs of quality, which differed for home and applied arts products. There were some gross exaggerations, which became obvious with the indiscriminate awarding of titles and quality signs. The success of individual handicrafts was measured by the number of masters and signs of quality. Despite that deviation, the two titles and the mark were important indicators of quality, and instrumental in obtaining various tax deductions. They were the first incentives for artisans producing items of exceptional quality in the postwar period. They also proved useful in the promotion and development of handicrafts. In 1985 a special settlement was ratified regarding this, but was never implemented in full. Products of Slovene artisans first appeared at international exhibitions in the 1970s and 1980s, successfully promoting the country and its handicrafts.

The first notable results were achieved at the Munich trade fair. In 1992 a new law regulating sales tax was ratified. It granted a tax deduction of five per cent per individual product to good craftsmen. To be eligible for this benefit, every product has to be evaluated by the Expert Committee, and on the basis of this evaluation also obtain the approval of the Ministry of Finance. All approved products must be equipped with a corresponding declaration of origin and quality. The titles and quality marks were abandoned in 1988, even before the introduction of the new legislation. Today, the system of standards for the marking and evaluation of handicraft products is very precise and has been studied by some other countries as well. It encourages handicrafts and helps to distinguish products of exceptional quality from those that are creatively and aesthetically mediocre (including kitsch). It is to be hoped that this efficient, internationally-recognized system will not be destroyed with the excuse that Slovene legistation has to be brought into line with that of the EU.

At the base of it lies the **EVALUATION AND GRADING OF HANDICRAFT PRODUCTS**. This was established in the 1986 research project of the Institute of Regional Economics (IREL). Between 1990 and 1992 it was supplemented in the light of additional results from Slovenia and abroad. Before being implemented in handicrafts, the system was tested on several products at the Institute for the Research and Promotion of Cultural Heritage at the Faculty of Arts at the University of Ljubljana. Because it is impartial, the system is useful for the orientation of craftsmen. But expert opinions are often not respected. Many craftsmen who make products of poor quality tend to disagree with the Expert Committee, arguing that their products must be good since they sell well.

There are two sets of **standards** for the evaluation of handcrafted products. The set for home arts comprises eleven standards, and the set for applied arts comprises twelve. The standards for the evaluation of home arts are presented first. **The Standard of Quality** is there to evaluate the general quality of the products. In evaluating replicas of the national heritage, the original and the replica are compared. The Committee also evaluates the quality of colors, binding elements and coatings. **The Standard of Technological Procedure** or **Production** considers classical manual production, and also the use of modern tools and appliances. Extra attention is paid to the originality of material and to how economic the crafting process is. A special **Standard of Material** is used to consider locally-available materials. In evaluating products crafted using one of the techniques from abroad, all innovations are considered. With some product groups (toys, for example) the Committee pays special attention to their didactic and educational value. The use of new, substitute materials for the traditional ones (e.g. plastic prongs on wooden *suha roba* rakes) is also considered here. The **standard of (cultural) heritage** is one of the most important standards, and can gain a substantial number of positive points. The Committee awards more points to products that help preserve the dying handicrafts or even revive those that are already extinct. The wholesome or overall image of the product is judged by **the Standard** of **Wholesomeness**.

The Standard of Applicability determines the functionality of a product. **The Standard of Educational content** judges the educational value of a product and promotes those crafts important for the young, in order to develop a sense of identity, continuity and creativity. The possibilities for the inclusion of handicrafts into school curricula are also considered. **The Standard of Economic Value** considers the marketing of a given product which, however, mostly rests in the hands of the craftsman himself. **The Standard of Marketing** is there to determine whether or not the product is ready for the market (equipped with certificates, declarations and hallmarks). **The Standard of Place or Region** helps to determine the importance of the craft or product to the regional or local environment. The last is **The Standard of Number**, which is most important with regard to replicas. It complies with the international standards of ninety-nine items in one series of products. It requires that every item be equipped with a hallmark and additional information.

The standards for applied arts vary from those enumerated above. Different standards are applied to products of applied arts because they are mostly unique or produced in limited numbers. **The Standard of Quality** helps determine the degree of creative originality. The committee often comes across poorly-copied products of other artisans or copies derived from foreign sources. This standard demands regular study of the development of individual crafts.

THE STANDARD OF TECHNOLOGICAL PROCESS considers the wide variety of technologies and work procedures used in the creative process. Objects of applied arts are also replicated, and **THE STANDARD OF DESIGN HERITAGE** is used to determine their quality. The same standard is also applied to evaluate modern, original products. Materials, shape and esthetic quality are considered. The latter is evaluated separately by **THE STANDARD OF AESTHETIC, ARTISTIC OR ORIGINAL DESIGN QUALITIES**. The Committee applies it very strictly, particularly to evaluate popular handicrafts (knitting, textile-painting, silk, tiffany) alongside mass-produced items. **THE STANDARD OF MATERIAL** considers all materials presently available. Special attention is paid to the detection of materials that are environmentally-unfriendly or potentially harmful to health. **THE STANDARD OF HERITAGE** is important in comparing the replica to the original. The overall image of a product is judged by **THE STANDARD OF WHOLESOMENESS**. It is often the case that products (even though of exceptional quality) lack hallmarks or declarations. The **STANDARD OF APPLICABILITY** helps determine the functionality of a product. **THE STANDARD OF EDUCATIONAL CONTENT** is also important, while **STANDARDS OF ECONOMIC VALUE MARKETING** are not regarded essential in this set. The twelfth standard is the **STANDARD OF NUMBER**, which also determines the maximum number of products within one series. Compliance with the standards of wholesomeness and number is tested by market inspectors, while the product is in shops, and not by the Expert Committee. The same holds true for checking the necessary marks on the products.

The wide selection of handicraft products (from replicas to hand-crafted modern products) requires that experts from various areas constitute the Committee. External, university educated specialists join the Committee of four members in the evaluation of specific products. Upon completing the evaluation, the Committee issues a statement. If the product has been recognized as good, the Ministry of Finance can allow a five-per cent tax deduction for a two-year period. All products marked by the Committee as positive must be exhibited at the biannual Exhibitions of Home and Applied crafts in Slovenj Gradec and Ljubljana.

The system of marking and evaluation, which is connected with the possibility of tax deduction, is the biggest achievement for handicrafts since World War II. In addition to this, another form of state support though symbolic, must be mentioned. With the introduction of the new system of education in crafts in general, i. e. with the introduction of masters' certificates (*Mojstrsko spričevalo*), the Chamber of Trades of Slovenia opened the question of a special diploma or certificate for craftsmen in home and applied arts. The former titles of *Mojster* and *Mojstrska delavnica*, which were last awarded at the 1988 Exhibition of Home and Applied Arts in Slovenj Gradec, had become insufficient, and was abolished in 1990. The two titles are, in fact, too similar to those obtained through "regular" education, regulated by education legislation. The Chamber of Trades of Slovenia therefore introduced a special honorary certificate and diploma called *Zlata vitica* (the Golden Vine) in 1998.

This is awarded biannually to individual craftsmen who have contributed significantly to the preservation of their craft and who have created an exceptional body of work. certificate is exclusive because the law allows it to be awarded to only four craftsmen, every two years, which prevents it from losing value. The name of each winner is also entered in a special "golden book" at the Chamber of Trades of Slovenia.

Exhibitions of various types also contribute to the preservation and development of handicrafts. Their tradition reaches back into the 19th century. Their main purpose then was to promote handicrafts and encourage customers to buy the exhibited products. Today, there are specialized fairs for this, such as **Tendence** in Frankfurt or the **International Gift Show** in New York.

Products of handicrafts can also be seen at the annual international trade fair in Celje, which is one of the largest of its kind in Europe. Their role, however, is reduced to that of decoration and demonstration only. **Hiša obrti** (the House of Trades) at the Celje fair is important because various demonstrations of Slovene handicrafts take place there. The biannual exhibition of Home and Applied Crafts has been organized in Slovenj Gradec since 1977. The first biannual exhibitions were predominantly market-oriented. In terms of the number of participants, the quality of the products, the style of exhibiting and the effects aimed for, we should consider them, for the most part, as fairs of the highest quality. After 1990 the representative character of the exhibitions started to turn in another direction. They started exhibiting products for which the craftsmen received the above-mentioned tax deduction. With this, the exhibitions showed the true state of affairs in handicrafts, and the progress as well as the stagnation of individual trades. The skillful and visually-attractive presentation has given way to a gallery-type presentation of all positively-marked products in the past two years. The event is set to be an expert exhibition, but also serves to educate craftsmen and raise their self esteem, which should, in the long run, make them more independent of tradesmen, agents and sellers of their products. From the 1980s, more regional, thematic, solo and group exhibitions were organized in addition to those in Ljubljana and Slovenj Gradec. Since 1997 the Chamber of Trades of Slovenia has organized numerous theme and solo exhibitions throughout the country. All these efforts underline the importance of handicrafts and their role in modern society.

Numerous questions remain unanswered regarding the relationship between the **state** and **handicrafts**. Many of them are connected with the fact that the opinions of politicians and bureaucrats are often diametrically opposed to expert opinions. Making unique jewelry of gold, other precious metals and gemstones are not considered handicrafts, simply because they do not comply with the standards relating to material. This is a good example of their backward thinking. There are no suitable education programs for individual handicrafts, despite a number of attempts and studies. The conditions in some handicrafts (the weaving of wicker products) are downright frightening. Some educational programs (at secondary schools of woodcrafts in Škofja Loka and Nova Gorica, for example) include a few handicraft elements. In comparison to the past, however, these attempts all boil down to nothing. In the Habsburg Empire, or later in the Kingdom of Yugoslavia, there was a well-organized educational system for handicrafts, on top of which there was the central State School for Handicrafts in Ljubljana. The system was supported by suitable textbooks and manuals which even today attract our attention if we come across them in some dusty attic. Today, there are only two textbooks in the entire sphere of handicrafts, namely *Klekljanje 1 and 2* (for bobbin lace-making), and a publication for silk-painting, which is officially not a textbook.

The state often justifies its irrational actions connected with the preservation and development of handicrafts by appealing to the norms and regulations of the EU. **Adapting national legislation** to that of the EU must not be the basic argument for the destruction of all the positive changes that handicrafts have seen. Quite the opposite. Handicrafts are essential for the preservation of cultural, creative, national and regional diversity within the (united) Europe of the future. A quick look back into history tells us that a Europe like that once existed. In it, handicrafts and handcrafted products were the media through which international contacts were created, and experience and new findings transmitted.

THE ENCOUNTERS CONTINUE

In 1988 the Institute for Research and Promotion of the National Heritage, and countries from the Alps-Adria working Community, launched a project for a unified trademark for handicraft products. The project was presented at the 1990 Community convention in Zagreb. It was well received because it established unified criteria for products in all the countries of the Alps-Adria community. The project included the proposal to make a joint tourist guide, a map with important handicraft centers, workshops, schools, exhibitions and fairs, and an annual award for the best achievements in the field of handicrafts. If this program had ever been implemented, craftsmen would have benefited from it most. It is ironic that in the computerized era of rapid communication, nobody in Slovenia or abroad knows exactly who the craftsmen are, where they live or what they produce. Slovenia, as a country, is neither a member of any of the international networks, nor of the World Crafts Council, whose European headquarters are in Frankfurt.

The Unesco decade of the promotion of handicrafts worldwide was also important for the preservation and development of modern Slovene handicrafts. In the course of this project, monographs on the national heritage of arts and crafts in Slovene, English and German were published (by Domus Publishing, Ljubljana, 1993), but other possibilities remained House unused.

The Unesco decade was also important for the preservation and development of modern Slovene handicrafts. In the course of this project, monographs on the national heritage of arts and crafts in Slovene, English and German were published (by Domus Publishing House, Ljubljana, 1993) were published, but other possibilities remained unused.

Many European countries support handicrafts organized in small businesses because they see these as important elements of their national economies. They also grant their craftsmen many benefits that are ignored or even unheard of in Slovenia. There are five directions in which modern European handicrafts develop and, consequently, five groups of craftsman. **Hobby craftsmen** belong to the first group, while **exceptionally talented individuals** who have exceeded the hobby production through education and hard work belong to the second group. Craftsmen who have established their own and **art design studios** and specialize in various types of products represent the third group. **Classical workshops** that also market and sell their products are in the fourth group, while the last group comprises **SMALL BUSINESSES** operated by **ART DIRECTORS**. European experts emphasize the importance of these five groups in dealing with the problem of unemployment. There is another dimension to handicrafts. The craftsmen control all creative phases of their product, unlike factory workers who are just links in a chain of endless conveyer belts. Artisans enjoy their work and earn their living from it.

Some European countries pride themselves on their rich experience in the preservation of old and the development of new handicrafts. Great Britain, with the British Crafts Council, is one of them. Holland and some Scandinavian countries are equally effective. German handicrafts, especially those from Bavaria, have been presented in events parallel to the Munich Craft Fair.

The central Swiss institution for the development of handicrafts and the marketing of products is the renowned Heimatwerk. In Mediterranean countries the development and preservation of handicrafts still lie in the hands of small, traditional family businesses. Handicrafts are generally given more state help in the north of Europe.

Because of various experiences in the field of education, European countries wish to retain their education systems and do not strive for international unification. Within the EU, many new projects have been initiated in the hope that handicrafts will be preserved for the future. One aspect of this care is a suggestion of the 23rd EU commission for the European grand prix for modern handicrafts.

This has been a brief presentation of efforts to preserve the heritage of trades and to develop modern handicrafts an Europe. It needs to be emphasized that this is very important work, for it will help shape the future of this part of the world. The work of craftsmen should not be devalued or automatically placed on an equal footing with other economic activities. Handicrafts demand special care and attention, and are special because of their vitality and dynamics. In Slovenia, new craftsmen are constantly appearing, bringing with them new concepts and ideas to help better the quality of our lives. All of this is proof that the heritage of handicrafts is a vital base to which modern craftsmen resort in order to find original solutions for the production of new masterpieces. In the words of the poet Octavio Paz:

If we wish to be truly modern
We must always keep up with tradition!

From Words to People

Boža Grafenauer

Polona Pogačnik

Nataša Rogelja

Špela Pogorelec

With the vast diversity of itineraries and trips available around Slovenia, this is the first guidebook to present the national heritage of Slovenia which is the subject of ethnological research. The itineraries suggested here offer you the possibility of learning more about Slovene handicrafts and their original environment. Through this, one can also learn about the rescued and the developing cultural heritage, and the discovery of many modern Slovene craftsmen. One can become familiar with the distinguishing features of crafts, architectural image and the way of life in certain regions only by travelling through them. Five one-day trips across Slovenia are presented here. You will learn more about the Slovenes, their daily life and festive occasions, their culinary delicacies and other regional characteristics through visiting workshops open to visitors, amateur collections, smaller regional museums, and natural points of interest. You will discover a large number of special characteristics one can find in this part of the world. It has to be emphasized that not all the workshops are included in the tours presented in this book. Many craftsmen do not have appropriate facilities for accommodating larger groups. This book should thus also serve as an encouragement to craftsmen to promote Slovene handicrafts in the future. Head towards new adventures with this book, and good luck!

A trip to Bela krajina along the Krka basin

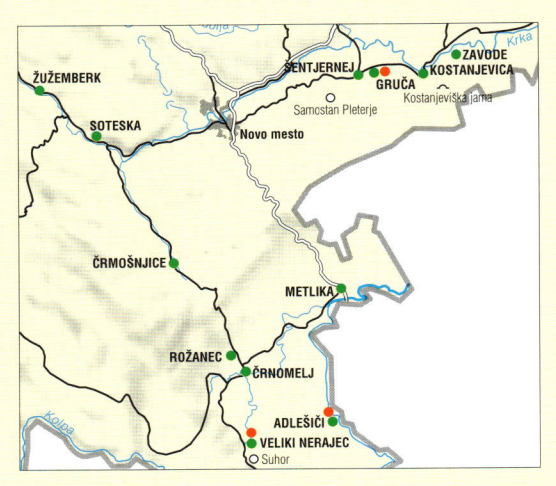

Crafts presented:
• *Weaving of linen* • *Making* pisanice, *the Bela krajina style Easter eggs* • *Making folk instruments* • *Pottery*

The hilly area of Gorjanci is situated in the south east of Slovenia. Its northern face is turned to the flatland part of Dolenjska and the Krka river, while its southern part faces Bela krajina, which lies between Kočevje and the Kolpa river. Start your journey at the very source of the Krka river. Proceeding down the Ljubljana - Novo mesto road, turn at Ivančna Gorica and head into the Krka basin towards Žužemberk. You will notice numerous remains of water-powered grain mills and saw mills, reminders of the two most important economic activities of the past specific to these parts. Millers and sawyers started to disappear after World War II, and their mills were left in ruins. In the settlement of Soteska you will notice the impressive ruins of the once-mighty Soteški grad (Soteska Castle). The ruined Baroque building was built for Jurij Sigismiund Gallenberg around 1760. The ruins of Stara Soteska Castle, scattered nearby, are even older.

In the previous century, the Auersperg court brewery was situated in the castle. Despite the fact that growing hops is normally associated with the valley of Savinjska and its surroundings, brewing beer was well developed in other Slovene regions as well. The wild variety of hops was grown for brewing beer and as a means to pay tax to the landlord.

You will come to Črnomelj, past Črmošnjice and across Gorjanci. You can admire the Bela krajina landscape at Brezovica. The origin of the name Bela krajina (white marshes) remains unclear. We can speculate that the area was named after the traditional white regional folk costumes, sewn from white linen cloth, or perhaps because of the white bark of the numerous birches that grow there.

The Roman Mithraeum

A few kilometers before Črnomelj, the road turns into the village of Rožanec. It is situated on the stony edge of a Karst field in the vicinity of the Semič - Črnomelj railway line. Having parked in the village, follow the curved, marked footpath to one of the most interesting archaeological remains in Slovenia – the Roman temple to the god Mithras. The temple, formerly a subterranean cave into which the ceiling had collapsed, resembles a natural colosseum. In it stands a pagan altar from the 3rd century dedicated to one of the Persian gods of war, Mithras. The image of Mithras slaughtering a bull is carved on one of the cave walls.

The locals call the temple, featured in many stories and legends, Judovje *(the Jewish place). A legendary story tells that the local pagan people, afraid of the Roman invaders, melted all their gold, cast a golden calf from it, and buried it in the forests adjacent to Rožanec. In addition to the temple near Rožanec, other Mithraic temples can be found in other parts of the country as well. Most of them date back to the 3rd century BC. The Christian kings attempted to exterminate paganism by eradicating the temples; nevertheless, some of them survived. The fact that churches dedicated to St. George were usually built in the immediate proximity of the Mithraic temples seems most compelling. In ecclesiastical iconography, St. George is depicted with a slaughtered dragon, symbolizing the victory of light over darkness, and Christianity over paganism.*

Črnomelj is one of the regional centers of Bela krajina., situated between the rivers Lahinja and Dobličica. It was already inhabited in the Early Iron Age, but several Roman finds have also been unearthed. The most common remains from Roman times are the gravestones, some of which were used in the building of the mills, called *Mestni mlin* or *Flekov mlin*.

There are many stories about the Flekov mlin, *which was named after its last owner. The mill was supposedly situated on the river Lahinja even before the Castle of Črnomelj was built, and occupied by a wealthy and stingy miller. One day, a fairy, dressed as an elderly woman, came to his mill to ask for some white flour for her ailing son. The mean spirited miller gave her black flour instead, claiming it was as white as snow. Enraged by his deceit, the fairy returned to the mill, poured the flour back into the spindle, and cursed the miller. From then on, only black flour was produced in the mill, and the miller was nicknamed* Črnomelj *(miller of black flour).*

Bela krajina, and especially Črnomelj, are famous for the celebration of spring called **Jurjevanje**. *Jurjevo (23rd April) celebrations are a Christian version of much older pagan festivities celebrating the arrival of spring. The main event of Jurjevanje is the visit of Zeleni Jurij, who is clad in fresh birch branches and the ritual tree called* **maj**. *At the beginning of this century, Jurjevanje was also developed in other parts of Slovenia. Today's celebrations are organized on a much smaller scale. Processions of children or young men going door to door to gather presents, as well as the making of bonfires, were typical for traditional Jurjevanje.*

Weaving and coloring eggs in Adlešiči

After a twelve-kilometer drive from Črnomelj, near the Lahinja river the road brings you to Adlešiči, near the border river of Kolpa. Aside from Pobrežje Castle and the adjacent hilly wine country, the place is also a renowned former center of linen-weavers and makers of colored Easter eggs. Originally from Asia, flax was used by the Egyptians, the Phoenicians, the ancients Greeks and Romans, as well as by the Germanic and Slavic tribes. In use for 6,000 years, this plant was also used to make linen in the area of present-day Slovenia. Today, weaving has almost died out, but a native, **Marica Cvitkovič**, still produces it. At her home you can learn about all the stages of linen production: sowing, harvesting, threshing, thread-making and whitening, and eventually the weaving of it into linenware. Her husband, **Alojz Cvitkovič**, has written several historical accounts of Bela krajina and Adlešiči. He will gladly tell you a story or two if you decide to visit. Larger groups should call 068/70-219 to announce their arrival in advance. You will be most warmly welcomed and given a tour of the workshop, products, Bela krajina-style Easter eggs, and a small family museum.

Marica Cvitkovič has been making linen goods since she was a child. Even as a little shepherdess, she regularly took her crocheting things to the pasture. She still recollects her self-imposed daily crocheting schedule: "I never returned home before finishing seven rows in the morning and eleven rows in the afternoon. The cows ate well whenever I took them to pasture."

Veliki Nerajec:
A visit to Vera Vardjan and the regional park

From Adlešiči you can continue through Vinica towards Dragatuš, and stop at Veliki Nerajec, which lies in the center of Bela krajina. The Lahinja Regional Park is also situated there. In her small gallery, **Vera Vardjan** makes and exhibits folk instruments called *gudalo*. A *gudalo* is made of an earthenware pot with a pork bladder membrane stretched over its top and a stick of Indian millet stuck and sewn in its center. The instrument is used to add rhythm to music. Vardjan also exhibits typical Bela krajina products crafted by other craftsmen. The two-hundred-year-old farmhouse with its museum of arts and crafts, and the Lahinja Regional Park, are also worth visiting. During summer, you can visited the park on foot or from a wagon, while in wintertime you will be taken to the source of the Lahinja river in a sleigh made in 1907. The area around it, called Lahinjski Lugi, is a protected natural reserve and a true botanical treasury. You can also enjoy pony rides organized by the local Krnica Tourist Society. All visitors must announce their arrival in advance (Tel. 068/57-428 or 068/57-609).

The admission fee for the museum and the Regional Park will also buy you a free sample of *ajdova potica* (buckwheat *potica*), a local culinary delicacy. Don't leave Bela krajina without tasting other culinary specialties such as suckling lamb, sheep or pig, buckwheat bread, *belokranjska povitica* (Bela krajina roll cake), and excellent regional wines, among which *metliška črnina* is the most famous. Enjoy a good meal in one of these fine *gostilnas* (inns):

- Gostišče Župančičev Hram – Štefanič, 8343 Dragatuš, (Tel.: 068/57-347)
- Kmečki Turizem Zdravko Bahor, Dragovanja vas 15, 88343 Dragatuš, (Tel.:068/57-455)
- Gostilna Peter Badovinac, Jugorje 5, 8331 Suhor, (Tel.: 068/50-133)
- Gostilna Roman Kapušin, Krasinec 55, 8332 gradac (Tel.: 068/69-154)

Continue towards Novo mesto via Metlika, where the **Bela krajina Museum** is situated. It houses collections of coats of arms from the Metlika and Črnomelj regions, archeological finds, and objects associated with wine-making, livestock-rearing and agriculture, as well as items of folk art typical of Bela krajina. The latter include Easter eggs, a life-size replica of a *črna kuhinja* (a chimney-less smoke kitchen), and objects used in working flax and hemp.

No fairer place than Šentjernej, no fairer bird than the rooster

The local wine road (*vinska cesta*) starts on the outskirts of Novo mesto with the first *gorice* (wine-growing hills), where *cviček* is produced, and takes you via Šentjernej to Kostanjevica na Krki. The town of Šentjernej owes its name to St. Jernej. It is famous for its symbol (the rooster), and exceptionally-developed horse breeding. On St. Jernej's Day (24th August), the local populace organizes rooster races. A statuette of a rooster is found on virtually every house in the area. The rooster-shaped *majolika* is a must in every wine-hut.

The local tradition of horse-breeding is one hundred and ten years old. A former forester in the forests of Podgorica, and the inventor of the first ship propeller Josip Ressel (1793-1857), first introduced horse-breeding to the region. Breeders annually organize several top harness-racing tournaments. All those interested in riding or simply admiring horses will find what they are looking for at the Andrej Hosta horses-breeding farm in Sela near Šentjernej 6, 8310 Šentjernej (Tel. 068/81-043).

St. Stephen is the patron saint of horses, so 26th December or štefanovo (St. Stephen's Day) is the town's biggest holiday. From the town racetrack, a procession containing one hundred or more horses heads to Stara vas to be blessed by the parish priest against accidents and disease.

The famous Pleterje Monastery (Kartuzija Pleterje, Drča 1, 8310 Šentjernej, Tel.: 068/81-225) is located three kilometers outside Šentjernej. The oldest preserved parts of the charterhouse, built by the French order of Carthusians, is the Gothic Holy Trinity Church, the only part of the monastery complex open to the general public. The farmhouse in front of the charterhouse has been renovated in the traditional Dolenjska architectural style.

In the direction of Kostanjevica, stop in the village of Gruča to visit a master potter, **Jože Pungerčar**, in his workshop (Gruča 2, Šentjernej, Tel.: 068/81-246). The hospitable owner will show you around in about an hour. Phone him in advance to announce your arrival.

In and around Kostanjevica na Krki

On your way back from Gruča, turn right onto the wine road before Kostanjevica Castle. If you are a keen botanist, turn right before the signpost for the village of Grič and head for the Kuhar farm (Zaboršt 4, Tel. 068/87-141). The owner will show you *Kuharjev gaber*, which is the thickest beech tree in Slovenia with its 4.4m circumference.

The white beech tree (Carpinus betulus) *grows next to a water spring, formerly used as a well. The place was featured in the novel by Josip Jurčič, Kloštrski Žolnir. The local inn, Gostilna Pri Žolnirju, owes its name to the same novel. The folk tale of a pretty maiden called Ana, the illegitimate daughter of a Pleterje monk, is still widely known among the local people. Ana was in love with a monk from Pleterje Monastery, and the Kuhar beech tree was the place for their secret meetings. Angered by news of this affair, her father attacked her lover, and in the ensuing fight both men were killed. Ana died of a broken heart shortly afterwards. It is said that in the blackest of nights, her ghost, clad in a white lace robe, still mourns her loss under the old beech tree. Have a little too much of the excellent* cviček *in the Žolnir vineyard cottage, and you stand a fair chance of meeting her!*

After this short diversion turn back to Slovenia's smallest town – Kostanjevica. Surrounded by the Krka river on all four sides, Kostanjevica is a river island. It was given the town charter in the 13th century. The former Cistercian Monastery at Kostanjevica Castle houses a fine art gallery of works by Slovenian painters: the brothers France (1895-1960) and Tone Kralj (1900-1975), and the impressionist Božidar Jakac (1899-1989). Wooden sculptures created by international sculptors during the former annual workshops (1961-1988) called *Forma Viva* are exhibited in the castle grounds (Grajska cesta 45, 8311 Kostanjevica na Krki, Tel. 0608/87-008, 87-333).

Šelmarji are typical of Kostanjevica. They are a group of men that symbolically drive out winter at Lent. Today, the Kostanjevica carnival is an organized tourist event. Father Selme, with his masked entourage of fools nicknamed Perforcenhauza, *heads the carnival procession. The word* Perforcenhauza *is derived from the German phrase "Parforce-Hatz" - a hunt. The Carnival was given this name to mock the well-to-do locals, who were the only ones able to afford such a luxurious pastime.*

Don't leave the area before exploring Kostanjevica Cave, full of stalagmites and stalactites, created by tectonic activity and subterranean waters over many millennia. The cave is famous for the largest bat colony in Slovenia. The cave is accessible on foot (by a well-marked path), or by bus. Between mid-April and October, tours of the cave are only organized on weekends and holidays from 10 am to 6 pm, with daily tours at the same hours from July to August. If you travel with a larger group, call the local Speleologists' Society (Tel.: 0608/87-088) to arrange a tour, regardless of the time of year. The guided tour around the cave, which has a constant temperature of 12 degrees Centigrade, lasts for about forty minutes.

The wine cellars of Dolenjska

At the end of your trip you can relax and recuperate in the *Žolnirjeva zidanica* in Zavode, where you will be invited to sample the increasingly popular local wine – *cviček*. Nibbling on buckwheat bread and homemade *klobase* (sausages), you will admire the spectacular view of the Krka plain, Krakovski gozd, the Gorjanci hills and even the Kamnik Alps. Fanika Sevšek from Gostilna Žolnir in Kostanjevica (Tel.: 0608/87-133) will feed the hungriest of customers by preparing one of the local culinary delicacies, such as homemade *sirovi štruklji* (cheese dumplings).

According to an anecdote, men from Dolenjska never part from their alarm clocks, which warn them when it is time to roll over in bed to prevent cviček *from making a hole in their stomach. The ruby red* cviček *is one of the most original Slovene wines, containing slightly more acid and less alcohol than other wines. Vine-growing in the region started in the 15th century, and Janez Vajkard Valvasor in his* **Glory of the Duchy of Carniola** *reports that* cviček *was even popular at the Habsburg Court in Vienna. During the time of the Illyrian Provinces (1809-1813) and afterwards, the quality of* cviček *declined and the ethanol content in it increased. In recent decades, however, the quality of* cviček *has improved immensely.*

THE LACE ROUTE

CRAFTS PRESENTED:
- *Lace-making* • *Ceramics* • *Perforating egg shells*
- *Decorating eggs with appliqués*

The Idrija region is not the distant, dull, inaccessible place it is often portrayed as. In fact, quite the contrary. As we have discovered in gathering material about Slovene national heritage for this book, the trip along the lace route was one of the most interesting trips presented. We hope you will discover the same upon visiting these parts. Besides lace-making there are other crafts in this region, but because lace-making dominates this part of Slovenia the Lace Route seemed the most appropriate title.

PLANINSKO POLJE – A STOPPING PLACE FOR CART DRIVERS

Head towards the Adriatic Sea from Ljubljana and a view of the Planinsko polje (the Planina plain) will open on your left only a couple of kilometers outside of Logatec. The whole area is full of Slovene natural and cultural heritage. The town of Planina boasts many exceptionally large houses with richly adorned portals and the Planinsko polje lake, the second largest intermittent lake in the country. Planinsko polje is a Karst field of porous limestone, periodically flooded by the Unica river. The remains of numerous *gostilnas* and stops for cart drivers testify to the once lively economic activity of the town. You can stop for coffee at Gostišče Demšar, a house which is over three hundred years old and which welcomed many cart drivers in the past. After announcing your arrival in advance (Tel.: 067/565-013), the inn-keeper will tell you more about the local history, and show you his collection of former farming and driving equipment used in the area. The nearby Castle Hasberk, first mentioned in historical records in 1295, and the 15th century Ravbar Tower with the adjacent Planina Cave are worth seeing, too. The rock wall entrance is one of the most attractive cave entrances in Slovenia.

Due to the strong mercantile influence, the traffic on the route from Vienna to the Adriatic Sea increased drastically at the beginning of the 18th century. Trieste and Rijeka were declared free ports in 1719. In the period of the Illryan Provinces (1809-1813), the road system was modernized. Roads were widened to allow two carts or carriages to meet. Planina near Rakek was an important stop (stacjon) for cart and carriage drivers. It was a merchant's as well as a smuggler's center. The smugglers of the time were called kontrabantarji. *At the peak of cart and carriage transportation there were 30 inns offering food and board to traveling merchants in Planina. Cart and carriage transportation started to decline after the building of the Vienna-Trieste railway line in 1857. However, it remained a smuggler's center long afterwards. Kontrabantarstvo (smuggling) was especially widespread between the two world wars. Horses, tobacco, salt, coffee and other goods that were in demand were smuggled nightly over the Italian border to-the then Yugoslavia. To silence the noise of the horses' shoes,* kontrabantarji *wrapped horse hoofs in sackcloth. Elderly people still remember many local verses on smuggling.*

"To Gorica I drove, the wheat I drove, I bought me some coffee to give to my lassie."

You will find more information on driving with horse and cart, as well as trade routes in these parts, in the book **ALONG THE MAST ROAD** *by Miroslav Pahor and Ilonka Hajnal. The book describes the transport of spruce trees to these parts, where masts were built from them. The central event to mark the driving tradition of the area is* **FURMANSKI PRAZNIK***, held in Postojna on every second Sunday in July.*

On your way from Planina back to Logatec, turn left at the cemetery and head for Laza. This small, idyllic village at the other side of the Planinsko polje boasts an original range of tourist delights. Potter Nataša Prestor lives in the local farmhouse with her family. She makes witty and caricatured ceramic figures depicting various characters, figurines of folk-tale heroes, and figurines clad in local folk costumes. She also revives motifs found on beehive panels in clay. She welcomes visitors in her workshop, and also organizes the village museum for children. The Laze Sports and Cultural Society organize trips to Planina and the Skedena Caves, a study tour through the Planinsko polje guided by a biologist, paddling, and ice-skating. For more information on these activities call 061/744-803. The village also has an outstanding bakery in which delicious bread is baked daily.

Idrija, a town of lace-making and mining

From Laze, return to the main road to Logatec and turn towards Idrija in Kalce. Idrija was once also a smaller regional center to which transport by horse and cart was redirected after 1857. Besides lace-making, Idrija is distinguished by an exceptional technical and scientific culture, and a rich legacy of mercury mining.

A colony of German and later Czech miners has strongly influenced Idrija. The technique of making bobbin lace was brought to Idrija by the miners' wives from the Czech and German lands. The oldest records of this skilled art date from the 17th century, when it was essential for the survival of the miners' families. Lace-making was a useful and entertaining pastime in the long winter evenings. The lace-making instruments are fairly simple. All you need is bula *(a bun), onto which is printed or drawn pattern on paper* papirc *is pinned. The bun is then placed into a* jerbas, *a basket specially adapted for lace-making. The first local independent lace-making school was established in 1876. The school has continued to train numerous (mostly women) lace-makers since then. It has elevated lace-making from a form of handicraft and folk art into a highly aesthetic creative process.*

You can see lace-making training at the **Lace-Making School**, organized by the Jurij Vega secondary school. Since 1993, a three-year professional training program for lace-makers has been organized, upon completion of which the pupils are awarded the title *Čipkarica, Čipkar* (Trained Lace-Maker). The school is located at Prelovčeva 2 in the town center. If you would like to visit it, announce your arrival in advance (Tel.: 065/71-713). You will see the school's showroom and learn all about the lace-making procedure. If you are lucky, you will even catch a glimpse of the students at work. The school has published a high-quality textbook on lace-making. You can admire and buy lace or lace-making equipment at the following fine shops and galleries in the town center: Studio Koder, Mestni trg 16, 5280 Idrija (Tel.: 065/71-359); Studio Čipka, Mestni trg 17, 5280 Idrija (Tel.: 065/71-584): Pri črnem orlu, Mestni trg 2, 5280 Idrija (Tel.: 065/71-636); Trgovina Vanda, Trg sv. Ahacija 7, 5280 Idrija (Tel.: 065/71-444); Trgovina Danica, Mestni trg 17, 5280 Idrija (Tel.: 065/71-029); Vezenine Munh, Kosovelova 17a, 5280 Idrija (Tel.: 065/741-202).

Strolling through Idrija you will notice the prominent face of Gewerkenegg Castle, perched on top of the hill, which has dominated the town horizon since 1533. Until World War II, Gewerkenegg housed the mine administration offices. The castle was the starting-point for countless mercury loads for destinations worldwide. In 1953 Gewerkenegg became the municipal museum. It has been entirely renovated since then. In 1995 an exhibition entitled *500 years of the Mercury Mine and Town of Idrija* opened there. The museum also houses an ethnographical collection, a collection of bobbin lace, and a presentation of miners' lives. Do not leave the museum without stopping to admire the impressive lace tablecloth, which was custom-made for Jovanka Broz (Tito's wife) in the 1970s.

For a number of centuries, miners were summoned to work by pounding on a hollowed piece of wood. The procedure is called kljukanje na šino. *The sound was heard through the entire town, waking up everyone but the inhabitants of a particular neighbourhood, which has been called* Zaspana grapa *(Sleepy Hollow) ever since.*

The museum's exceptional quality was recognized in 1997, when it won the Luigi Micheletti Prize for Best Technical Museum in Europe. Do not miss an opportunity to see it. It is open daily between 9 am and 6 pm all year round, while other viewing times can be arranged for larger groups. All additional information is available on: 065/71-135.

While you can learn about miners' lives by viewing the exhibition's miniatures, sketches and photographs, you literally walk into the past upon entering **Antonijev rov** (Anthony mine shaft). *Antonijev rov*, dug in the 1500s, is the oldest part of the mercury mine and has been adapted for visitors. First you will be shown a video describing the history of the mine and the town. Then you will be guided into the shaft down to the renovated chapel, dedicated to St. Barbara, patron saint of miners, and St. Ahac. There are two tours daily: at 10 am and at 4 pm during the week, and 10 am, 3 pm and 4 pm at the weekends and on public holidays. Group visits should be announced in advance on: 067/71-142.

The most widespread legend about how mercury was first discovered in Idrija is the one about an anonymous local tub-maker. While he was soaking a dried tub, the mercury ore accumulated inside it. The year was 1490. This event is said to have taken place at the foot of the Kobalove Planine, where the Church of the Holy Trinity stands today.

Take a walk along the trail called *pot ob rakah* (water canals for the mine) to *Divje jezero* (Wild Lake). This wonderful tiny lake is the central point of interest of the Krajinski park Zgornja Idrijca (Zgornja Idrijca Regional Park). The water for the lake comes from an underground Karst spring and from the hillside around it. The reflection of the impressively high stone wall in the water, creating the illusion of infinity, has given wings to the imagination of the local people, who believed the lake was bottomless. The flora surrounding the lake includes endemic and relict plant species such as *kranjski jeglič* (*Primula carneolica*), and *dlakavi sleč* (*Rhododendron hirsutum*) which has attracted botanists for centuries. Janez A. Scopoli (1723-1788), Balthasar Hacquet (1793-1815), and even the king of Saxony, Fredric August II, are among the most prominent visitors to *Divje jezero*. Today, the dark green waters attract many divers and speleologists.

Before leaving Idrija, try some of the local cuisine. You can taste delicious *žlikrofi* (pasta, stuffed with a mixture of chives, potatoes, bacon and herbs), as well as other local delicacies at these fine restaurants:

• Gostišče Barbara, Arkova 43 (just above Antonijev rov), 5280 Idrija Tel.: 065/71-142

• Pivnica Kos, Tomšičeva 4, 5280 Idrija Tel.: 065/712-315.

Spodnja Idrija

Located 4 kilometers from the bigger and world-famous Idrija, there is Spodnja Idrija. This small town at the confluence of the rivers Idrijca and Kanomeljca has kept its Slovene national character. It lies in hilly surroundings, very suitable for afternoon hiking trips, such as Cerkovski vrh, Vojskarska planota and Ledinska planota.

Beware! If you head for any of these trips, beware of the prophet Šembilija, who, according to folk tales, still travels the hills and vales in this part of Slovenia. If you want to learn more about her, read the works of Dr. Jože Felc, a native of Spodnja Idrija.

Two places really worth visiting are **The Church of Mary on the rock** (Pri Mariji na Skalci), erected in 1136, and the renovated **Kenda Mansion**. You can admire frescoes by Jože Mrak on the church ceiling from the organ loft to the presbytery. Mrak was also the architect and constructor of the mighty *klavže* (barriers) on the rivers Belca and Idrijca. In the past, Spodnja Idrijca was the religious center of the neighboring parishes. That is why the town has been nicknamed *Fara* (the Parish) and the populace *Prfarci* (the parishioners).

A local legend about the building of this church tells the story of a count from Tolmin who regularly went hunting in the forests around the Idrijca river. On one such occasion he climbed Skalca in pursuit of game. He was very surprised to find an image of the Virgin Mary there, and took it with him to Tolmin Castle, from whence the image mysteriously disappeared at night. His inner voice told him to return to Skalca, and he found it there. He took it back home with him, but it returned to Skalca again. He built a chapel on the spot where he first saw her, and placed the image in it. The news of the chapel spread rapidly and pilgrims from near and far started turning up soon after.

The 500-year-old Kenda Mansion is the former mighty Kenda farm estate. Today it caters mostly to business tourists of the highest rank. They prepare dishes according to tested, old local recipes. To round off the excellent food, select Slovene wines are served with it. Phone them in advance (065/176-490) and they will prepare excellent *žlikrofi* for you.

The old and mighty Kenda farm has always dominated Spodnja Idrija. It was built as a farm mansion. Its inhabitants did not depend on farming only. They also possessed a sawmill, a grain mill and workshops for craftsmen. The thresher was powered by a large water wheel. Janez Kenda, the master of the mansion at the beginning of this century and the town mayor, supported local societies (especially the firemen), and worked for the cultural progress of the town.

To Žiri across the divide between the Adriatic and the Black sea

From Spodnja Idrija, a twisting road will take you uphill to Ledinsko razpotje. Take the first left exit to go to the village of Ledine. You will taste home-cooked delicacies such as *žlikrofi*, buckwheat groats, and nut or hazelnut dumplings at the Jureč family farm (Ledine 19). At Easter, you will be served *aleluja* (a fast dish made from turnip peel and potatoes). The Jureč family also organizes farming demonstrations, called *zemlja-pšenica-kruh* (soil-wheat-bread), from which you will learn all there is to know about working the soil, growing wheat and preparing bread. A collection of traditional farming tools and machines is kept in their barn. The Jureč farm is open to visitors at weekends. For visits from Monday to Friday, call in advance (065/79-069).

Descend to Žiri, another lace-making center, from Razpotje. Žiri boasted its own lace-making school at the beginning of the 20th century, and there were over 2000 women lace-makers in the wider Žiri region.
The local lace-making and lace-trading business A. Primožič, located at Jobstova 29 (Tel.: 064/692-532) was established in 1888. Anton Primožič greatly contributed to the popularity of Slovenian bobbin lace in Europe and the United States. The lace you can buy at their workshop, open to visitors, is one of the finest in Slovenia. Today, the lace-makers combine their original and inventive ideas with tradition to make wonderful lace.

Perforated easter eggs from Vrhnika

From Žiri, it is possible to return to Ljubljana by several roads. If you would like to stop by at Franc Grom's home in Vrhnika, you take the road via Logatec, along the avenue of linden trees planted at the time of Napoleon's Illyrian Provinces. This road is more suitable in winter time. The far more scenic route to Stara Vrhnika is via the villages of Smrečje and Podlipa. This route is much shorter, but check the road conditions before heading down it.
Franc Grom lives at Stara Vrhnika 92a. You can admire emptied eggshells, which he has perforated and decorated with lace patterns, images of blossoms, grapes, and animals since 1993.

You will not realize the amount of precision and effort invested in decorating individual eggshells, until Grom tells you the number of holes per piece…

Roaming through Gorenjska

Crafts presented:
- *Making wooden objects* • *Making pipes in Gorjuše*
- *Making wooden rimmed boxes*

An hour's drive takes us from Ljubljana to the cobblers' center of Tržič. In the past there was a cobbler's workshop in nearly every house there. The strong cobblers' guild had chosen St. Crispin as their patron saint. His image adorned the walls of every cobbler's workshop.

Cobblers' town

A cobbler came
From foreign lands,
He brought his lasts,
And started sewing shoes.

The waters of Tržiška Bistrica and Mošenik, the deposits of iron ore, and the extensive forests were the base on which ironworks, leather tanning and other crafts developed, making Tržič a borough with special rights as early as 1492. Only historic remains testify to the existence of these crafts today.

Ages ago, a monstrous dragon came over the Alps and stormed through Carniola as well. It was so mighty and powerful that every mountain upon which he trod collapsed. The former borough of Tržič was situated at the south end of the Košuta Plain. When storming across the Karavanken, the dragon also stepped on Košuta. The rocks from it crushed the old borough and its inhabitants were forced to move to the new Tržič.

Today, the traces of the former craftsmen's activities can be seen in the old town center, where you can also visit the birthplace of the poet and wheelwright Vojteh Kurnik (1826-1886). His house is at Kurnikova pot 2, 4290, Tržič. If you would like to visit it, contact Zvonko Pretnar (Zavod za kulturno izobraževanje – *Enota Tržiški muzej*), Muzejska ulica 11, 4290, Tržič, Tel.: 064/564-172. The same building also houses a permanent museum collection and a gallery.

Tržič is never a boring town. In February you may take part in the Lent carnival, and the traction of the plank. You may **FLOAT BOATS** called **GREGORČKI** down the river in March (on St. Gregory's Day), attend the exhibition of minerals and fossils in May, or attend the Cobblers' Sunday in September.

Regardless of the season, **JERNEJ KOSMAČ** and his son **MATEJ**, who make hand-made replicas of wooden objects, always welcome visitors to their workshop at: Pod Šijo 7, Bistrica pri Tržiču, 4290, Tržič. Their most attractive products are the shepherd's pocket sundials, the cobblers' lamp with glass balls, and the lace-makers' lamp. To visit them, announce your arrival in advance on 064/516-787.

Three kilometers from Tržič you can enjoy a walk along the Tržiška Bistrica valley. The scenic Dovžan geology nature trail is distinguished by its luxurious vegetation, various Paleozoic rocks, and an untamed river.

On your way back to Ljubljana you can stop at Begunje. The town is famous for the Elan factory, where skis and other sports equipment are made. The pioneers of popular folk music - the brothers Slavko and Vilko Avsenik - are natives of Begunje. They have been developing a new variety of popular folk music since the 1950s. The Avsenik family also owns an inn and a restaurant in Begunje, as well as a gallery in which you can learn about their musical achievements. You can find them at Begunje 21, 4275 Begunje, Tel.: 064/733-402.

As you drive from Tržič towards Lesce, you will pass Radovljica, an old town with town rights dating back to the 15th century. The rectangular town square is rimmed with one-storey 16th and 17th century town houses. Situated at the end of the square is the Baroque mansion in which the Apiculture Museum and a memorial room to the prominent local Enlightenment historian, ethnologist and playwright Anton Tomaž Linhart (1756-1795) have been set up for the public.

The Apiculture Museum represents the rich and original tradition of Slovene beekeeping and painted beehive panels, which play an important part in Slovene folk art. Six hundred of them are kept at the museum, and the oldest dates back to 1758. Beehive panels are unique to Slovenia.

Lesce became an industrial town after the Gorenjska railway was built in 1870. Here is the well-known sports airport of Alpski letalski center (Begunjska cesta 10, Lesce, Tel.: 064/715-188), while the popular Šobec bathing-place and camp site (Šobčeva cesta 25, Lesce 4248, Tel.: 064/718-006) is situated on the shore of the Sava river. One of the most attractive golf courses in Slovenia is also situated nearby. You can obtain more information about it at Golf zveza Slovenije (the Golf Association of Slovenia, Cesta svobode 13, 4260, Bled, Tel.: 064/700-777). From Lesce, the road takes us to Bled, which is well worth a short stop.

The charms of Bled and its surroundings

In times long gone, the beautiful Lake Bled did not exist. Fertile fields, rich pastures and meadows were all one could see in its present location. There was a prosperous village in the middle of them, but its inhabitants were known to be harsh and ruthless people. They even disliked the Christian faith.
Not all Bled people, however, reveled in prosperity. A small boy called Janezek was an orphan who supported himself as a shepherd to the rich farmers. One day, he noticed that there was one sheep missing from his flock. He didn't dare return home because he knew he would be punished. So he started looking for the stray sheep and in his search he climbed the hill, the top of which still peaks out of the lake as an island. He had a vision of the Virgin Mary, and told her about the cruelty of the Bled people. She was so angered by what she heard that she decided to destroy the beautiful Bled village. A horrible storm came upon the Bled valley, and flooded it shortly afterwards. Only the peak of the small hill remained above water level. The locals claim that the church to the Virgin Mary on the island had been built to commemorate this occasion.

Lake Bled was created by glaciers, and is one of the most popular holiday resorts in Slovenia. You can admire the vista of the rock with the medieval castle on top, the lake with the island and church in the middle of it, participate in one of the many organized sports activities yourself, or simply enjoy the beauties of nature. The health resort tourism for which Bled is famous was introduced to these parts by the Swiss doctor Arnold Rikli.

The poet France Prešeren (1800-1849) wrote the following lines about Bled: "Carniola has no fairer place than this wondrous Heaven's face."

Pilgrims regularly visited Bled island in the 9th and 10th centuries. The present Church of Mary's Ascension was built in the 12th and 13th centuries, while the foundations of the 9th century pre-Romanic chapel are still visible today.
Once in Bled, do not forget to taste the delicious Bled cream slices called *kremšnite*. The best are made in the pastry shop of Hotel Park, Cesta svobode 15, 4260 Bled, tel.: 064/79-30, and in the Šmon pastry shop, Grajska 3, 4260, Bled, tel.: 064/741-616.

After a short drive from Bled towards the Pokljuka plateau you can find the village of Gorjuše. Situated at a height of 940 meters, Gorjuše is said to be the biggest Slovene village, since it takes you about an hour on foot from the first to the last house in it. The village is famous for its handmade pipes.

The Gorjuše pipes were being made as early as the 18th century. They were of various sizes and shapes, adorned with a variety of ornaments, which distinguished them from other pipes. Čedra *was the most famous of all. Valentin Vodnik (1758-1819), an Enlightenment poet and journalist, first made them famous. He mentioned Gorjuše in his 1795 travel book* A Description of the Country of Carniola *(Popisovanje Kranjske dežele). While working in the neighbouring Koprivnik, Vodnik lived at the Gorjuše hunting lodge of the Enlgihtenment supporter Baron Žiga Zois, the patron of the Slovene literati. In 1901 pipes were made in 14 houses out of the total of 62 in the village. Pipes were made while working at pasture in the summer, and in the long winter evenings. They were sold throughout Slovenia, and also exported to England and the United States. At the beginning of this century, they annually sold between 3,000 and 3,500 pipes. After World War I, cigarettes came into fashion, causing the decline of pipe-making.*

Master craftsman **Alojz Lotrič** still continues to make pipes at his house in Spodnje Gorjuše 274264 Bohinjska Bistrica. If you would like to visit him, announce your arrival in advance on 064/721-306.

Ivan Jeklar who makes rimmed boxes, also lives in Gorjuše. After announcing your arrival in advance (Tel.: 064/721-356), you will find him at his home at Spodnje Gorjuše 3.

From the edges of the Pokljuka plateau, descend eleven kilometers to Bohinjska Bistrica.

Bohinj, or a walk through the landscape in which the rain breeds

Because of the abundant rainfall all year round, the locals jocularly say that Bohinj is the place where rain breeds.

The name Bohinj was given to two valleys (the lower and the upper), the Bohinj lake basin, and Nomenj. It is a true pearl of the Julian Alps, situated fully on the area of *Triglavski narodni park* (Triglav National Park). Bohinjska Bistrica, situated at the edge of the basin, is the biggest settlement in the area. It prides itself on the renovated castle of the famous Slovene baronet Žiga Zois. The 16th century iron-works were taken over by the Zois family in the mid 18th century, and the last blast furnace in Bohinj was closed in 1901.

Bohinj Lake (3.3 square kilometers in length and with a depth of 44.5 meters at its deepest end) is the largest glacial lake in Slovenia. In Ribčev Laz on Bohinj lake in Slovenia, a monument to Luka Korošec, Štefan Rožič, Matej Kos and Lovro Wilomitzer was erected. These four men were the first people who officially climbed Mount Triglav (2864m), the highest Slovene mountain, in 1778. The nearby 15th century church of St. John, with its simple Gothic architecture and frescoes, is an important cultural and historical monument.

The village of Koprivnik is situated in the vicinity of Bohinjska Bela in the direction of Pokljuka. Valentin Vodnik was once a parish priest here. At Gostilna Korošec in Koprivnik, Koprivnik 8, 4264 Bohinjska Bistrica (tel.: 064/721-047), you will be served the famous trout just as they prepared it for Vodnik.

There are plenty of destinations for shorter trips in the vicinity of Bohinj. Depending on the season, and your general physical fitness, you can choose:
• A hike along the Bohinj lake to the nearly eighty-meter-high Savica waterfall, described in the famous Prešeren poem *Krst pri Savici* (The Baptism at Savica). Savica is the natural outlet of waters collected in the subterranean depositories of the Triglav Lakes.

I will head to high Savica
To drink at the cool poem's source;
To the master poets' health,
May I enjoy this sip.

(Valentin Vodnik)

• A trip to the village of Stara Fužina, where you can admire the Alpine building style or stop at the Dairy Farming Museum (*Planšarski muzej*, Stara Fužina 181, 4265 Bohinjsko jezero), set up in a former cheese dairy. The museum houses a collection of original dairy-farming equipment, while the documentary material narrates the stories of dairy farmers, cheese dairies and cheese-making in the mountains, as well as its transport to the valley, typical dairy farming buildings, and mountain settlements. For more information call Lidija Mlakar (tel.: 064/723-095).
• A trip to the village of Studor, with its famous hayracks called *studorski stogi*, one of the most typical groups of double-linked hayracks.
• A visit to the Oplen house, where you will learn about the local culture of living indoors. It is still possible to make a fire in the old, open fireplace in the kitchen. The house was turned into a museum, and also offers special programmes for its young visitors. You will find it at Studor 16, 4267 Srednja vas v Bohinju. Call the caretaker Gregor Resman (Tel.: 064/723-522).

You can return to Ljubljana by the same road you came, or decide to make your way across the Soriška planina, a well-known ski resort with several ski slopes. The road takes you through the village of Sorica (821 meters above sea level), the birthplace of one of the most famous Slovene impressionist painters, Ivan Grohar (1867-1911). You can learn more about his life, time and career there.

On your way home, stop for dinner in one of these fine *inns*: Gostilna pri Planincu, Grajska 8, 4260 Bled (Tel.: 064/741-613) Gostišče Mayer, Železniška cesta 7, 4260 Bled (Tel.: 064/741-058); Gostilna Lectar, Linhartov trg 2, 4240 Radovljica (Tel.: 064/715-642); Gostilna Kunstelj, Gorenjska cesta 9, 4240 Radovljica (Tel.: 064/715-178). Alternatively, stop at Brezje, the most popular place for worshippers of the Virgin Mary, and have dinner at Gostišče Zvon, Brezje 7, 44243 Brezje (Tel.: 064/738-862).

THE RICH HERITAGE OF CRAFTS IN THE SURROUNDING AREAS OF LJUBLJANA

CRAFTS PRESENTED:
- *Accordian-making* • *Candle-making* • *Pottery*

Past Ljubljana, the road takes us to the town of Trzin. The name is derived from the word *trzni* (meadows of inferior quality), indicating the fact that the town is situated on marshlands. During the French occupation in the 19th century, the nearby forests provided shelter for gangs of robbers called *rokovnjači*. Because they stole from the French, *rokovnjači* were supported by the Austrian authorities. But they were not mere romantic heroes. They were vindictive, and if someone betrayed them, he was robbed or even murdered and his house burnt down.

The daring Trzin robbers Dimež and Pepelnak were feared throughout Carniola. After returning drunk to the Narobe brick-kiln one January night, they suffocated with smoke after making fire in the stove...

Domžale developed into a thriving economic center after World War II. Crafts and businesses have a rich and long tradition in these parts. Making straw hats and bags started in the 18th century but has nearly died out today. The so-called *kranjski cekar* (a narrow two-handled bag of plaited straw braids), produced locally, has become a necessary accessory of women's formal attire and folk costumes in the Gorenjska region.

Today, Domžale is famous for the biggest Slovene tennis tournament and the summer festival of chamber music at the Baroque church in nearby Groblje. Past the village of Vir we get to Dob, where we find the signpost for Jamarski dom, situated at the outskirts of the village of Gorjuša.

THE ŽELEZNA JAMA CAVE, THE COLLECTION OF STRAW PRODUCTS AND KRUMPERK CASTLE

The Jamarski Dom building houses the Hohennwart speleological collection of rocks and fossils found in the Domžale region. Through the collection of straw hats, one can trace the development of this craft from its beginnings to the present day.

Several Karst caves are located in the vicinity of Jamarski dom. A visit to the Železna Jama cave, where we can admire the splendor of stalagmites and stalactites, takes about an hour. The name of another cave, Babje jame (Hags' Caves) is a remnant of the times of Turkish raids in these parts. During the raids, women and children sought refuge in it. Visitors to Železna jama and to the Jamarski dom collections are only admitted if arrangements are made in advance. You will find them at Gorjuša, 1233 Dob, Tel.: 061/721-577 or 061/721-878.

Krumperk Castle, first mentioned in historical documents in 1338 when Hercules of Krumperk was the residing lord, is situated within walking distance of Jamarski dom. The castle is the birthplace of Ana Marija Ravbar, mother of the first Slovene historian, chronicler and ethnologist Janez Vajkard Valvasor (1641-1963). The castle is on private property and closed to tourist excursions. Like many other Slovene castles, it is in grave need of renovation. The adjacent horse-stable recreates some of the castle's former atmosphere. It houses the horse rearing facilities of the Biotechnical Faculty in Ljubljana. Riding can be arranged on: 061/721-576.

One of the Krumperk's masters, Adam Ravbar, a 16th century defender against the Turks, has been awarded the status of a national hero, and appears in folk tales and songs:

Quickly let us seek protection,
To Master Ravbar send we letters,
He's a man, an army he commands,
In the front lines with his men he stands.

A white paper was written,
And to Krumperk sent,
Where the mighty Ravbar lives,
Not a beaten swindler.

A Domžale tavern, where a very tasty beer is brewed, has also been named after him. Following the signposts, return to the village of Dob, and proceed towards Radomlje and Mengeš.

The exhibition and production of accordions by the Zupan family in Mengeš

Mengeš thrived in the 19th century because of its favourable location. It prided itself on its eighty-three workshops and twenty-five inns. The writer Janez Trdina were born here. Trdina (1830-1905), who wrote *Bajke in Povesti o Gorjancih* (*The Tales of Gorjanci*), spent the second half of his most interesting life as a teacher and a bohemian in Novo mesto. His first published volume, *Narodne pripovedke iz Bistriske doline* (*Folk Tales from the Bistrica valley*), was based on the folk tales and myths of the creation of Mengeš and other settlements in the vicinity. He had intended to compile an ethnographical description of the people from the Dolenjska region, but failed. His notes have been published in **Podobe davnih prednikov** (*Images of Our Ancients*). This is an excerpt from it:

Folk tales explain the creation of Mengeš thus: the story begins more than a millenium ago, in the times of constant clashes between the Christianized locals and the pagan newcomers - the Slavs. Many men were slaughtered in the severe fighting, but the pagan elder Mengo was one of the few lucky survivors. Together with his sons and friends, he had a settlement built on a local hill, and simply enslaved its previous occupants - two Christian hermits. They endured their hardships with so much faith that they convinced one of Mengo's servants to convert and escape soon afterwards.
Mengo himself became convinced of their goodness when the three fugitives saved his life and cured him after he was attacked by boars. In penitence for having sinned against the Christians, he had a house built and welcomed any newcomer in it. Many of them have stayed forever, and the town that developed was named after Mengo.

Mengeš is also an important popular folk-music center. A fair is organized annually to attract more visitors. In the Zupan workshop at Rašiška 7, 1243 Mengeš, **Valentin Zupan** makes accordions. He made his first accordion when he was sixteen years old. He learned his craft as an apprentice at the local *Melodija* factory. In the past, accordions were made exclusively by watchmakers. The inventive Zupan continuously finds ways to improve his accordions, and has even patented several of his inventions. You will be shown a few of his oldest accordions and explained any particulars of their production that might interest you. Considered among the best in the world, these fine instruments are also manufactured under the Zupan trademark in Italy. Visitors should announce their arrival in advance on: 061/737-139.

Outside of Mengeš, in the direction of Kamnik and on the right side of the Kamniška Bistrica river, lies Homski hrib, an isolated hill (394m) locally called *Homc*, overgrown with fir trees. A small church, dedicated to the Virgin Mary and to which pilgrimages were made, was built on it. In the period of the Turkish raids, the church was protected by a mighty stone wall. In the 18th century, the Gothic church was rebuilt in the Baroque style.

The treasures of Veronika's town

Kamnik is one of the oldest towns in Slovenia. It was the most influential Slovene town in the 12th century, but its prime importance was later taken away by Ljubljana. Throughout the 19th and at the beginning of the 20th century, it was even renowned as a health resort. The old town center is distinguished by its narrow streets with medieval and Baroque facades, and a Romanesque chapel - Mali grad (Little Castle) - which is one of the oldest Romanesque monuments in Slovenia. The ruins of Stari grad (Old Castle) also testify to the former grandeur of the town.

A legend has it that the two castles standing side by side were just as big as the hill they occupied. In a horrendous storm, the lightning tore the clouds and split the hill in half. The two adjoining castles were separated forever.

Stari grad is situated much higher than Mali grad, on the opposite side of the Kamniška Bistrica river, and an inn was opened here. Visitors to Stari grad can also admire the vista of the surroundings from it. The mythical treasure of Veronika supposedly lies hidden in the two-storey crypt and behind the portal of Mali grad.

The oldest story of Veronika reports that she was a beautiful, wealthy and extremely mean countess. The townspeople had asked her for some gold to finance the building of a new church. Veronika furiously replied she would sooner become a snake than pay the smallest dime for a stupid building like that - and she really did turn into a monster that was half-woman, half-snake. She is believed to guard her vast treasure in the underground cellars even today. She will be saved by a fortunate coincidence in a thousand or more years.

Veronika's figure is also featured on the Kamnik coat-of-arms. Chandlers, leather-tanners and *majolika* makers have lived and worked in Kamnik for centuries. The Stele workshop in the Lectarjeva domačija (the Lectar house) boasts a three-hundred-year-long tradition in making candles. Master Janko Stele (1899-1976) was one of the select craftsmen who regularly collaborated with Jože Plečnik (1872-1957), the greatest Slovene architect. You can also find replicas of Plečnik's candles adorned with ornaments found on *škofjeloški kruhki* (the Škofja Loka gingerbreads) in the Stele workshop on Glavni trg 16, 1240 Kamnik, Tel.: 061/832-339.

Stranje Parish Church, the interior of which was decorated by Jože Plečnik, is also well worth visiting. You can take interesting walks in the vicinity of Kamnik.

You can find refreshments at the Veronika café, Japljeva 2, 1240 Kamnik, Tel.: 061/813-143.
Take one of these two short walks in the vicinity of Kamnik.

The source of the river Kamniška Bistrica and the Arboretum Volčji potok

Take one of these two routes to the town of Kamniška Bistrica. One will take you there via Smodnišnica (the old powder magazine), and the other via Mekinje, past the local convent. You will reach the source of the river Kamniška Bistrica after a 12-kilometer drive through the scenic countryide.

The famous Arboretum Volčji Potok is Slovenia's largest. It was designed by its former owners in the previous century and is planted with Slovene and exotic trees. Today, the arboretum houses over 4,000 plants from all over the world on its seventy-nine hectares. Small and larger sculptures by sculptor Janez Boljka can be admired in the small pavilion in the park grounds. If you would like to see them, call 061/812-844, or 061/812-345 to arrange a visit. Golf afficionados will also feel satisfied at Volčji Potok (Arboretum Volčji Potok 3,1235 Radomlje), since the park prides itself on one of the most beautiful golf courses in the country.

The pottery heritage of Komenda

Komenda was one of the largest Slovene pottery centers before World War II. The local potters organized a Potters' Cooperative as early as in 1929. Until the 1960s, Komenda was the place where potters from all over Slovenia came to obtain the masters' certificate of their trade. Today, Franc Kremžar continues the local potters' tradition. You can see and buy his products at his elegant workshop. You will find him at Gmajnica 65, 1218 Komenda, Tel.: 061/842-035.

Also in Komenda, you can stop by the monument to the victims of World War I, designed by Jože Plečnik, on which this significant phrase is appended: Let us pray for common sense!
Komenda is also famous for the highly intelligent former parish priest Peter Pavel Glavar (1721-1784), who taught his parishioners to be good farmers. He also wrote the first expert treatise on the improvement of beekeeping in the world.

On the way to Ljubljana, the road takes you through Vodice and past Smlednik. Make a stop for coffee at Zbiljsko jezero (Lake Zbilje), or at Goričane Castle (Muzej neevropskih kultur, Goričane 38, 1215 Medvode), which houses a museum collection on non-European cultures.

Lake Zbilje is man-made. It was created in 1952, when the river Sava still propelled the first turbine of the Medvode hydroelectric plant. The lake is only about a couple of hundred meters in width at its widest part, but measures about seven kilometers in length. It is a safe haven for a variety of birds, as well as for aquatic and forest animals.

In Goričane on the right bank of the Sora river, one finds the former Diocesan Palace in which the Museum of Non-European Cultures was opened in 1963. All visits must be arranged in advance (Tel.: 061/611-506), because the museum is currently being renovated.

The town of Medvode is situated at the confluence of the rivers Sora and Sava. In the first years after the building of the railway line, it was a popular excursion spot for many inhabitants of Ljubljana. It is also a good starting-point for various hiking trips to the hillsides around Škofja Loka and Polhov Gradec. To round off a lovely day, refresh yourself at Gostilna Mihovec in Zgornje Pirniče 54, 1215 Medvode, Tel.: 061/621-180

Looking towards Ljubljana from Medvode, you will notice the 669-meter-high, isolated hill of Šmarna gora. Numerous pilgrims encouraged the building of the church, dedicated to Mary mother of God, in 1430, in the mid-17th century, and in 1711. Today, Šmarna gora is a popular excursion point for the people of Ljubljana.

The locals testify that hollow thundering can sometimes be heard from the center of Šmarna gora. They say that the noise is the snoring of the giant Hrust, who will wake when the river Sava changes its course. It was he who made Šmarna gora by slinging rocks across the river in a day-long fit of rage. At the end of the day, he is said to have crawled into the center of the mountain he had made.

With the storks to the Prekmurje craftsmen

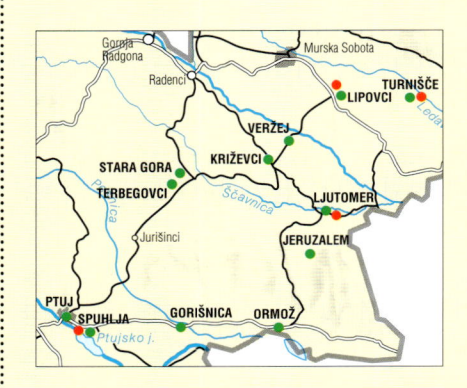

Crafts presented:
- *Pottery* • *Weaving corn husks* • *Weaving straw*
- *Making Korant masks*

To Ptuj

The first stop on this trip is the oldest Slovene town, Ptuj. It was already inhabited in the Late Stone Age, and developed into a township called Poetovio in the times of Ancient Rome. The whole town is protected as national architectural heritage because of its rich culture and history. Many locals have come across shards of Roman earthenware when digging in their gardens. Such discoveries are normally kept as family secrets, because the townspeople fear extensive archeological excavations (which could possibly cover as much as a half of Ptuj) on their property.

Ptuj is also one of the larger European Mithraic centers, because as many as five temples dedicated to the Persian god of light and war - Mithra - were found in the town and its surroundings. Upon entering the town, you will notice the steep slopes of Grajski grič, with the mighty Ptuj Castle on top of it. The castle began to grow in the 10th century, and underwent some major alterations in the 16th century. From 1946 onwards, the castle has housed the permanent collections of the **Ptuj regional museum** (Pokrajinski muzej Ptuj, Muzejski trg 1, Tel.: 061/771-618). You can admire an impressive collection of chamber and band musical

At the end of the 19th century, there were around 410 potters in Slovenia. Their number has decreased significantly today; there are only about twenty of them left. Even today, people believe that St. Florian will protect them against fire. People prayed to him when there was a fire, and potters saw him as the protector who prevented the post in the kilns from burning. Florian died a martyr's death in 304 because he refused to deny his Christian faith despite ridicule and torture. He was drowned in the river Aniža with a millstone round his neck, and water became one of his attributes.

DOWN THE WINE ROAD TO JERUZALEM

A few kilometers from Ljutomer towards Ormož, turn to the wine road in the direction of Železne dveri and Jeruzalem. You can see vineyards and orchards all around from where you can hear the noise of rattlers, the "merry musicians of Slovenske Gorice" as they are called in these parts. The rattlers are a particular feature in Slovenia and the fans on those from Haloze differ from those found in Prlekija.

On the hill where the village of Jeruzalem is situated today, the Knights Templar built a tower in the 13th century. They erected a statue of the Grieving Mary, which they brought from the Holy City of Jerusalem. The village was named after that statue, and pilgrims from near and far visited it.

You will find the inn - Gostišče Jeruzalem - Brenholc (Tel.: 062/714-504) in Fischerjeva graščina (the Fischer mansion), right next to the 17th century church of the Grieving Mary. Stop there to have a glass of excellent wine.

Descend past Ormož and towards Ptuj by the road, which offers one of the most beautiful views of Prlekija. Before returning to Ptuj, stop at a place called **GORIŠNICA**. This is the place where the 300-year-old Dominikova domačija (Dominik farmstead) is situated. It is the only typical thatched Pannonian farmhouse, plastered with mud in this area. It is renovated and open for tourists. Its caretaker, Stanko Arnejčič from Gorišnica 37 (Tel.: 062/708-220), will introduce you to the history of the farmhouse. You will learn about the use of millstones, spindles and other traditional implements.

Let us leave the world of grain mills, vineyards, storks and hospitable people, and return to Ljubljana.

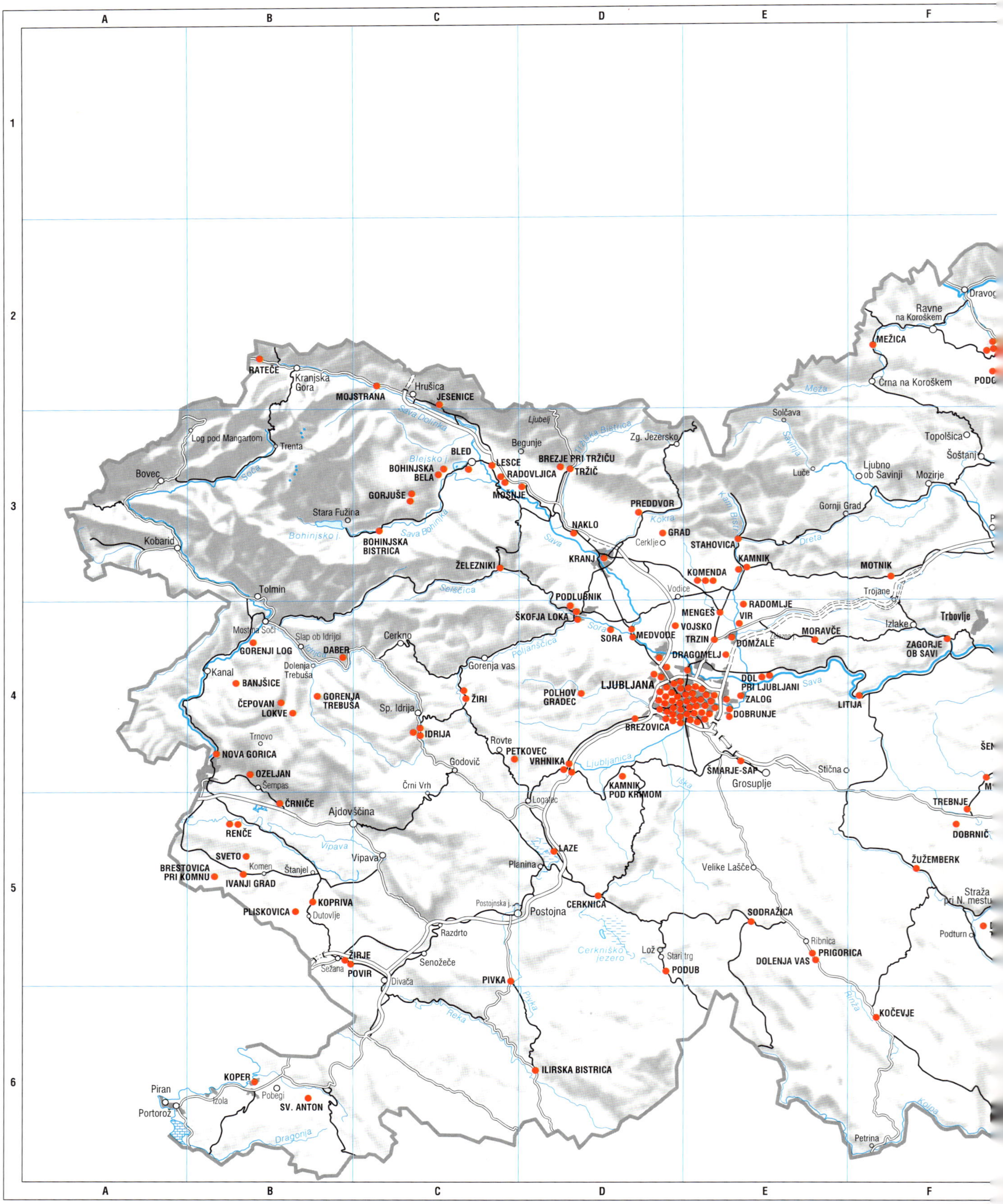
A
B
C
D
E
F
1
2
3
4
5
6
RATEČE
Kranjska Gora
MOJSTRANA
Hrušica
JESENICE
Log pod Mangartom
Trenta
Bovec
BLED
BOHINJSKA BELA
LESCE
RADOVLJICA
MOŠNJE
Begunje
Ljubelj
BREZJE PRI TRŽIČU
TRŽIČ
Zg. Jezersko
GORJUŠE
Stara Fužina
BOHINJSKA BISTRICA
Kobarid
PREDDVOR
NAKLO
GRAD
Cerklje
STAHOVICA
KRANJ
ŽELEZNIKI
KOMENDA
KAMNIK
Tolmin
PODLUBNIK
ŠKOFJA LOKA
SORA
MEDVODE
Vodice
MENGEŠ
VOJSKO
TRZIN
RADOMLJE
VIR
DOMŽALE
DRAGOMELJ
Mostna Soči
GORENJI LOG
Slap ob Idrijci
DABER
Cerkno
Dolenja Trebuša
Kanal
BANJŠICE
ČEPOVAN
LOKVE
GORENJA TREBUŠA
Sp. Idrija
Gorenja vas
ŽIRI
POLHOV GRADEC
LJUBLJANA
DOL PRI LJUBLJANI
ZALOG
DOBRUNJE
BREZOVICA
Trnovo
NOVA GORICA
IDRIJA
Rovte
PETKOVEC
VRHNIKA
Godovič
OZELJAN
Šempas
ČRNIČE
Črni Vrh
Ajdovščina
Logatec
KAMNIK POD KRIMOM
ŠMARJE-SAP
Grosuplje
Stična
RENČE
SVETO
BRESTOVICA PRI KOMNU
Komen
Štanjel
IVANJI GRAD
Vipava
LAZE
Planina
Velike Lašče
PLISKOVICA
KOPRIVA
Dutovlje
Postojnska j.
Postojna
CERKNICA
SODRAŽICA
Razdrto
Ribnica
Lož
Stari trg
PRIGORICA
DOLENJA VAS
PODUB
Cerkniško jezero
Sežana
ŽIRJE
POVIR
Senožeče
Divača
PIVKA
KOČEVJE
ILIRSKA BISTRICA
Piran
Portorož
Izola
KOPER
Pobegi
SV. ANTON
Dravograd
Ravne na Koroškem
MEŽICA
Črna na Koroškem
Solčava
Topolšica
Šoštanj
Luče
Ljubno ob Savinji
Mozirje
Gornji Grad
MOTNIK
Trojane
Izlake
Trbovlje
MORAVČE
ZAGORJE OB SAVI
LITIJA
TREBNJE
DOBRNIČ
ŽUŽEMBERK
Straža pri N. mestu
Podturn
Petrina
Soča
Sava Dolinka
Sava Bohinjka
Bohinjsko j.
Blejsko j.
Sava
Kokra
Selščica
Poljanščica
Idrijca
Ljubljanica
Vipava
Reka
Pivka
Dragonja
Rinža
Kolpa
Savinja
Dreta
Meža
Kam. Bistrica

THE PLACES WHERE CRAFTSMEN WORK.

Index

Acacia 23, 24
Accordion 264, 265, 299, 300
Acer campestre 28
Air vent 118
Airport (sports) 296
Alder tree 22
Alleluia; a fast time dish of turnip and potato peels 295
Angewandte Kunst 11
Apiculture 160
Apiculture Museum 296
Applied art 11
Arboretum 301
Archer 45
Art pedigree 252
Artesano 11
Artigianato 11
Artisanat 11
Artistic iron foundry 273
Artistic ironwork 194, 195, 198-201, 273
Ash tree 25, 61
Astol 46
Barn 295
Baroque 41, 42
Basket (jerbas) 60, 62, 76
Basket (korba, škundra) 58, 60, 62, 67
Basket (korpa) 70
Basket (koš) 70, 75
Basket (košara) 57, 60, 62, 70, 72-77, 304
Basket for hay 57, 58
Basket for leaves (listni koš) 57, 58
Basket for storing grain and fruit (bedenj) 84
Basket; for carrying food to church to be blessed (žognjeki, žognjiči) 72
Basket; for carrying on the back (šbrinca) 62
Basket; for raising bread (pehar, štručnica) 84, 85
Basket; narrow, two handled straw basket (cekar) 66, 76, 96-99
Basket; one handled (košara) 62, 76
Basket; oval, two handled, characteristic of southeastern Slovenia (cajna) 67
Basket; small, one handled (košek) 62
Basket; strapped, for carrying on the back 62, 75
Basket; two handled (koš) 58, 75
Basket; two handled (košara, škundra) 62
Basket; wicker, two handled (camboh) 62
Bat 291
Bathing site 296
Bee keeping 160, 301
Beech tree 22, 56, 61, 291
Beehive (kočnica) 84
Beehive panel 160, 250, 252, 256, 296
Bela krajina Easter eggs 136, 172-175, 289
Bela krajina roll cake (povitica) 290
Bela krajina wine 290
Bellows 238
Billy goat 290
Birch 56, 58, 288
Birch broom 59
Black Prekmurje earthenware 117-119
Black stone 182
Blacksmiths' center 194
Boats (gregorški) 296
Bobbin lace of wire 154
Bobbin lace-making 146-156, 273
Body jewelry 268
Bosman (wedding bread) 168
Bow 45

Bowl rack 34
Bowl, turned 22
Bowl; for cracking nuts and hazelnuts 22
Bowl; of wood shavings 78, 79
Box 27, 96, 269, 297
Boxes with rimmed lids 30, 31
Braided bread (pletenica) 169
Brdovita (type of wood) 56
Bread 81, 168, 169, 293
Bread basket 84
Broom 58, 59
Buckwheat bread 290, 291
Buckwheat groats 295
Buckwheat roll 290
Bundle of fresh greenery (butara, potica, prajtelj, beganca) 78
Burdening 289
Business gift 278, 279
Butter mold 21
Candle 165-167, 300
Candle-making 160, 165, 273, 299, 300
Cardboard 235
Cardboard production 235
Carpet 96
Cart 258, 259
Carthusian monastery 290
Carthusian monastery in Žiče 68
Carver of gun butts 202
Carvers (self-taught) 40, 42
Carving 34
Carving hunters' buttons 266, 267
Carving wood 40, 43, 273
Cask making 23, 51, 273
Castle 288, 290, 299
Cave 291
Cello 48
Céltis australis 27
Ceramics 102-133
Chair 46
Chandelier, straw (lujster) 92
Chapel 294
Cheese dairy 298
Cheese dumplings 291
Cheese knife 195
Chest 44, 250-252, 254, 255
Chestnut 56
Chimney-less smoke kitchen 298
Christening bread (botrina) 168
Christening candle 165
Christening flat cake 168
Clay 102-133, 303
Clay bowl 108, 111
Clay musical instrument (bajs) 262
Clay statuettes 107, 108
Clematis 56
Clog making 273
Clogs 28
Clothing of corn husks 96
Coat of arms 290
Cobbler 242, 243
Cobbler's workshop 242, 243
Cobblers' lamp 34, 296
Cobblers' Sunday 296
Coffee 292
Competition bow 45
Confirmation candle 165
Cooking 294

Cooper 51
Corn 94 101
Corn husks 94-101, 303
Corrugated cardboard 235
Coucher 230
Couching 230
Countryside 277
Countryside tourism 278
Cover 96
Cradle 253
Craft 11
Craftsman 290
Cream slice 297
Crescents 160, 161
Crocheting 273, 289
Crucifix 34
Culture of gift; giving 278
Cutting glassware 274
Cviček (red wine from Dolenjska) 290
Dairy 298
Dairy Farming Museum 298
Dairyman 298
Dairyman's clogs 28
Decorative candles 166, 167
Decorative ceramic figurines 124, 125
Decorative straw lampshade (doužjek, doužnjek, do(v)žnjek) 92, 93, 304
Decorative straw products 92
Design 10
Designing glassware 206-219
Designing jewelry 204, 205
Designing leather goods 273
Designing products of ceramics 272
Design-led-craft 11
Diatonic type of accordion 264, 265
Dirjenca (wedding bread) 168
Dogwood 20
Doll 261
Domžalski cekar (Domžale narrow, two handled bag) 90, 91
Donation box 34
Doormat 96, 97
Dormouse goulash 27
Dormouse hunter 27
Dormouse hunting (polahrija) 27
Dormouse stew 27
Dormouse trap (škrinca, škrlup, toplarca, samojstra, poušna) 27
Double-linked hayrack 298
Dough 168, 169
Dove; wooden image of the Holy Ghost 37, 38
Dražgoše bread 160-163
Dress making 273
Dried goods (suha roba) 18
Dried goods heritage 273
Drill; for manual drilling (črvar) 196
Drivers' holiday (furmanski praznik) 292
Drivers' station (furmanski štacjon) 292
Driving (furmanstvo) 25, 27, 293
Dutch basket (holandarca) 77
Easter egg (pirh, pisanica, remenica, remenka) 172, 175, 179
Education 274, 276, 279, 283
Egg 172-179
Egg shell 295
Egg-shaped cask 23
Electrically powered grain mill 302

Index

Elm tree 22, 61
Embroidering 141, 142, 273
Embroidery 141, 142
Employment 277
Engraving 202
Engraving glass 208, 218
Etched glass 208, 222, 223
European Grand Prix for Modern Handicrafts 284
Evaluation and marking 280
Exhibiting products 283
Exhibition of Lent masks 302
Farmhouse 290
Felt 28
Festival of chamber music 299
Fiddle making 48-51
Fiddler 48-51
Flax 290
Flint 182
Floating mill 303
Flour 302
Folk art 40, 252
Folk costume 299
Folk instruments 262, 263, 290
Folk music 269, 300
Folk ornaments 44
Folk songs 299
Folk tales 299
Folklore 300
Forest glasswork (glažuta) 209-211
Forma Viva 291
Formgebung 11
Fossils 296
Fruit basket 57
Fur 240
Furriery 240
Geological nature trail 296
Gestaltung 11
Gilding 40, 43, 273
Glass 206-225, 305
Glass blower 212
Glass blowing 274
Glass cutting 208, 218
Glass dust 214
Glass jewelry 219
Glass maker 206-219
Glassmaking 206, 219, 274
Glassmaking school 208, 212, 213
Glassworks 207-219
Glinčan (*stone from the Ljubljana region*) 182
Goat 290
Golden altar 40
Golden Vine (diploma) 282
Goldsmiths 202, 204
Golf 296, 301
Gorjuše pipes (fajfe) 32, 297
Gourd 22
Grain measuring cup 84
Green tuff 182
Grey sandstone 182, 191
Grinder 289
Grindstone 182, 184
Gudalo (*traditional folk instrument*) 289
Gun making 202
Hamper basket 62, 63
Hand made paper 228-231
Hand painting objects 274
Handicraft discipline 272

Handicraft heritage 299
Handicrafts 11, 295
Handicrafts and Europe 283
Handwerk 11
Harvest time 92, 289
Hayrack 298
Hazel 20, 56, 61
Hazel osier 72
Hazelnut dumplings 295
Heather 56, 58
Heimatwerk 11
Helix 46
Hemp 290
Henry Ford European Conservation Award 68
Hewing 50, 272
Holy Ghost (wooden dove) 37, 38
Home and applied arts 11
Home crafts 11, 290
Home made dried goods 273
Home wooden goods 18
Honey 158-165
Honey dough (lect) 160, 164, 165
Honey dough heart (lectovo srce) 164, 165
Horse breeding 290
Horse equipment 241
Horse races 290, 304
Horse with the whistling bottom 107, 108
Hosier 145
Hosiery 145
Hotaveljčan (*Hotavlje stone*) 182
Hunters' buttons 266, 267
Hunters' uniform 266, 267
Hut 295
Ice skating 293
Idrija lace 146, 148-153
Indian millet 58
Indian millet broom 58, 59
Inn (gostilna) 290, 292, 294, 296, 298, 301, 303
Inn keeper 292
Instrument 262, 302
Interpretations of objects of national heritage 274
Ironwork 194-201, 296
Jewelry 268
Joiners' center 46
Joinery 46, 273
Kadunja (*vessel, used in home bread preparation*) 18
Karst hole 299
Karst stone 188
Karst stonemason 182, 186-189
Kemping wool 289
Klavže (*water barriers*) 294
Kneaded thing 128
Knitters 144, 145, 273
Knitting 144, 145, 273
Knitwear 145
Kočevje stone 182
Komenda pottery 112, 113
Kontrabant (*smuggling*) 292
Korant 269, 302
Korant mask 269
Kranjski cekar 90, 91, 299
Krosne (*weaving loom*) 136
Kunsthandwerk 11
Kurent 302
Kurentovanje (*Lent festivities*) 302
Laboratory glass 208
Labore (*type of stone*) 182

Lace 295
Lace maker 293
Lace makers' lamp 296
Lace making 146-156, 293, 295
Lace making course 148
Lace Making Day 149
Lace Making Festival 149
Lace-making School 148, 149, 293, 295
Ladies' handbag 96
Ladle 18
Larch tree 28, 31
Leather (leder) 236-247, 273
Leather clothes 244
Leather goods 244, 247
Leather production 238, 296, 300
Legend 294, 300
Lent carnival 296
Lent masks 269
Light stone (lahki kamen) 190
Limestone 182, 190
Linden tree 295
Linen 136, 288, 289
Lipica stone 188
Ljubljana Palm Sunday bundle 78
Loški kruhek (*Škofja Loka little bread*) 39, 122, 301
Majolika 104, 105, 108, 111, 290, 300
Making bags 246-247
Making belts 203
Making charcoal 274
Making decorative objects 274
Making intarsias 273
Making knives 196, 197
Making Korant masks 302
Making mascots 274
Making miniatures 258-261
Making modern unique products or small series of products 274
Making paper flowers 274
Making shoes 242, 243, 296
Making tapestries 272
Making toothpicks 20
Making toys, play things and puppets 274
Making unique products 274
Making vitrages (colored windows) 274
Making wooden rimmed boxes 296, 297
Male Lent character (Škoromat) 233
Mali kruhek (*small bread*) 39, 122
Maple 28
Mascots 261
Masks 269
Mast 292
Mauterle (*a vessel for bread preparation*) 18
Mead 165
Mead making 160, 164, 165, 273
Mengeški cekar (*the Menges two handled straw bag*) 90, 91
Metliška črnina 290
Mill 288, 289, 294, 302, 305
Millers 288
Mine 293
Mineral 296
Miniature wicker products 70, 71
Mining 293
Mithraeum 289, 302
Modern handicrafts 272
Monachus albiventer (*morska medvedjica*) 188
Monks (menihi) 169

Index

Mortar 183
Music stand 40
Musical instrument 48-51
Nail making 194, 196
National Weavers' School 55
Nativity scene 34, 41
Nežke (*a vessel for bread preparation*) 18
Nut dumplings 295
Oil mill 302
Ornamentation of pipes 32
Osier 56, 57
Otirač (*linen towel*) 136
Oven 114
Packaging 235
Painted windows 208, 220, 221
Painted wooden chest 44, 250-252, 254, 255
Painting glass 208, 224, 225
Painting glassware 222
Painting textiles 273
Palm Sunday bundles 54, 78, 79
Pannery 274
Pannonian farmhouse 305
Paper 226-235
Paper bouquet 232-234
Paper flower 323-234
Paper garland 232-234
Paper mill 226-234
Park 301
Patchwork 157, 272
Patron saint of horses 290
Patron saint of potters 305
Pen (*for adorning Easter eggs*) 172, 173
Period furniture 46, 47
Pilgrims 294, 297
Pipe (*for smoking*) fajfa, čedra 32
Pipe making 273, 296
Plagiarism 275
Plank 296
Planks (*roofing material*) 24
Pocket sundial 34, 269
Podirjenca (*wedding bread*) 168
Podpeč stone 182
Polter, poltr (*oval, two handled wicker basket*) 58, 67
Pony 290
Poplar 28
Porcelain doll 124
Potato basket 57
Potica (*rolled walnut cake*) 169
Potica mold 112
Potters 293, 304
Potters' wheel 304
Pottery 102-133, 272, 299, 301, 302, 304
Pottery guild of Filovci 118
Prekmurje potters' kiln 117
Prekmurje-style painted chest 251, 254
Prekmurje-style pottery 166-119
Prekmurska remenica, remenka
(*Prekmurje Easter egg*) 172
Primula carneolica (*Kranjski jeglič*) 294
Procka (*basket with one handle for picking fruit*) 74
Pub 300
Pumpkin oil 302
Pütra 117
Quality of living 279
Quarrying stone 182
Quick sliver 293, 294
Rain 297

Rateče slippers (Rateški žoki) 257
Rattler 305
Recruiting bouquets 232, 233
Recruiting wagons 233
Reeds 56
Regional Park 290
Replicas 33, 47, 129, 184, 209-211, 222-225, 248-269, 262, 263, 274
Replicas of designers' creations 274
Replicas of objects of national heritage 34, 47
Research 278
Restoration 46
Ribnica style pottery 106-108
Riding 290
Ritaša (*basket with two bulges*) 67, 77
River Sava conglomerate 182
Roast dormouse 27
Rococo 41
Rods 18, 54
Rokovnjač (*robber*) 299
Roll, pad 257
Rooster, symbol of the town of Šentjernej 108, 109, 290
Rope making 274
Rowing 293
Saddle maker 241
Saddle-making 241, 273
Salt 292
Salt box 123
Saw 294
Sawing 288
School of Applied Arts Famul Stuart 127
School of Wood Industry and Craft 55
Sewing 273
Shaping dough 273
Sheep pelts 238
Shingles (*wooden*) šiklni, šintlni 24
Shingles from the Gorenjska and Koroška regions 24
Ship 292
Shoemakers' lamp 34
Shop gallery 304
Sift (*earthen, for drying cottage cheese*) 114
Skiing resort 298
Skin 236-239
Skinning 96
Skis 296
Slippers 96, 98
Society of Potters and Ceramists 120
Soča River stone 188
Sowing 289
Sowing basket 84-87
Speleologist 293
Spoon 32
Spoon holder 34
Sports bow 45
Spruce, spruce wood , 31, 56, 72
Standards of evaluation 280
State-care 279
Stonemasonry 180-191, 274
Stork 305
Stove 114
Stove making 114
Strap-maker 241
Strap-making 241
Straw 80-93, 292, 303
Straw bag (*narrow, two handled*) cekar 90, 91
Straw braid 90

Stringed instrument 48, 262
Studorski stogi (*the Studor hayracks*) 298
Suckling pig 290
Sunflower oil 302
Supplementary activity 277
Tally 34
Tanners' guild 238
Tannery 238
Tanning bark, tan. 238
Tanning liquids 238
Tapestry 96
Tennis 299
Terrasglia (*a technique of working with clay*) 121
Thatching 82
Threshing 289
Tiffany 221, 274
Tkaničenje (*a special embroidering technique*) 143
Tobacco 292, 297
Tourism 278
Towel 136
Town house 296
Trailer camping spot 297
Transparent glazing 106
Travertine 190
Trout 298
Tržič cobblers 34
Veneers 44
Vineyard 305
Vineyard cottage 291
Viola 48
Violin 48
Vitrage 208, 220, 221
Vrhniški pirhi (*Vrhnika Easter eggs*) 176-179, 295
Vrtanek (*wedding bread*) 168
Vrtanj (*wedding bread*) 168
Wall spice containers 123
Water well 186, 188
Wax 165-167, 172, 173
Waxed flower 233
Weaver 52 79
Weavers 67, 289
Weavers' club 65, 66, 74
Weavers' company 55
Weavers' course 55, 66
Weavers' society 74, 89
Weaving 272
Weaving corn husks 302
Weaving loom 136
Weaving straw products 302, 303
Weaving, unique products 138-140
Wedding bouquets 232
Wedding bread (bosman, dirjenca, podirjanca, vrtanek, vrtanj) 168
Wedding candles 165
Wedding flat cakes 168
Wedding spoons 32
Wheat 292
Wheat ear 92
Wheel (*cart*) 25
Wheel making 25
Whetting stone 182
Whetting stones (osli) 191
Whip 26, 27
Whip making (škarabac) 27, 274
Whitened rod 56, 57
Whitening linen thread 289
Wicker furniture 71

Index

Wicker umbrella stand 62
Wicker weaving 52-79, 84-93, 272
Willow 55, 56
Willow growing 55
Windmill 302
Wine 305
Wine flask Štefan 213
Wine pitchers 104, 105, 111, 114, 115, 117-119
Wine road 305
Wood 51
Wood intarsias 44
Wood turning 22
Wooden chain 32
Wooden dove (Holy Ghost) 37, 38
Wooden mold for honey dough 39
Woolen gloves 145
Woolen socks 145
Woven straw chandelier 92-93
Wreathed bottles (korpflaše) *60, 61, 68-70, 74*
Yoke 241
Youth research workshop 278
Žiri lace 146, 147
žlikrofi (*pasta stuffed with chives, bacon, potatoes and herbs*) 294
Žolnir 291

CRAFTSMANSHIP AND MASTER CRAFTSMEN

BLACKSMITHS
Miha Krištof 198, 199, H2
Vlado Zupančič 194, 200, 201, F2

BOW MAKER
Franc Oblak 45, C3

CARVERS AND GILDERS
Erik Curk 40, 42, C3
Jože Lapuh 40, 41, D4-E4
Miha Legan 42, 43, F5
Franjo Srnel 41, 42, D3

CARVER OF HUNTERS' BUTTONS
Boris Leskovic 266, 267, D4-E4

CARVER OF GUN BUTTS
Robert Flerin 202, E3

CERAMISTS AND POTTERS
Ljubo Blagotinšek 126, 128, D3
Božena Blanuša 127, 128, D4-E4
Mojca Božič 127, 128, B6
Stane Božič 127, 128, B6
Hedvika-Vika Čipak 124, 125, D4-E4
Silva Dravšnik 124, G3
Alenka Gololičič 128, 129, B4
Majda Gregorič-Trost 128, 132, D4-E4
Ljubica Kočica 128, 154, 218, H3
Workshop for Pottery and Ceramics Magušar 128, D4-E4
Urban Magušar 128, 131, D4-E4
Matjaž Matko 128, G5
Jana Mihelj 128, 131, B6
Anica Mihorko 128, 129, D4-E4
Majk Mulaček 128, 131, B6
Lorna Novak 127, 128, H2
Marjeta Pikelj 122, D4-E4
Barbara Plevnik 120, D4-E4
Nataša Prestor 120, 121, 293, D5
Sašo Rus 123, 128, G3
Mojca Smerdu 128, 133, D4-E4
Tanja Smole-Cvelbar 120, 130, D4-E4
Snežana Sotlar 120, 130, D4-E4
Brigita Vogrinec 123, 128, H2
Danica Žbontar 126, 128, D4-E4

CHANDLERS
Apiculture Božnar 165, 167, D4
Carmelites 166, D4
Bogdan Kogovšek 166, 167, D4-E4
Sonja Kogovšek 166, 167, D4-E4
Rafael Samec 166, 167, D4
Candles Stele 166, 300, E3

CLOG MAKERS
Martin Koprivnik 28, G3
Dejan Ogrin 28, 29, C3
Jože Žlaus 28, G3

COBBLERS
Mario Herzog 242, 243, H2
Vladimir Vodeb 242, 243, D4-E4
Jože Levovnik 242, 243, F2

COOPERS
Jožef Lozej 23, 24, B5
Franc Marin 23, J2

DESIGNERS
Matjaž Deu 104
Barbara Dovečar 219, B4
Marjeta Grošelj 246, 247, D4-E4
Miša Jelnikar 204, 205, D4-E4
Ljubica Kočica 128, 154, 218, H3
Oskar Kogoj 45, 50, 186, 212, 213
Jure Miklavc 195
Peter Ogrin 213, D4-E4
Tanja Pak 154, 214 – 217, D4-E4
Janez Suhadolc 46, D4-E4
Stane Turšič 166, 167
Stanislava Vauda 100, 101, I3

DESIGNERS OF LEATHER GOODS, LEATHER CLOTHES, BAGS
Viktor Barlič 245, D4-E4
Anton Cunder 245, D4-E4
Marjeta Grošelj 246, 247, D4-E4
Božena Lerota 245, E4
Sebastian Nared 244, D4-E4

DESIGNER OF SPECIAL BREADS
Marjanca Dobnikar 168, 169, D4-E4

FIDDLE MAKER
Vilim Demšar 48 – 51, D4-E4

FURRIER
Milena Eber Štimac 240, D4-E4

GLASS ETCHER
Aleš Lombergar 222, 223, D4-E4

GLASS-MAKERS, GLASSBLOWERS, GLASS CUTTERS
Stjepan Bukvič 212, H3
Vlado Češnjaj 212, H3
Barbara Dovečar 219, B4
Ljubica Kočica 218, 128, 154, H3
Glassworks Luminos 213, H3
Leopold Miklavžič 212, H3
Tanja Pak 214 - 217, 154, D4-E4
Franc Sajko 209, H3
Mitja Sajko 209, H3
Glassmaking School 212, 213, H3
Branko Zagorščak 212, H3
Ciril Zobec 209, 210, 211, H3

GOLDSMITHS AND JEWELRY DESIGNERS
Miša Jelnikar 204, 205, D4-E4
Tine Šrot 204, D4-E4

GUN ENGRAVERS
Cveto Frelih 202, D3

GUN MAKER
Milan Šteh 202, D4

HONEY AND MEAD SELLER, CHANDLER
Hrabroslav Perger 164, 165, F2

KNIFE MAKERS
Stane Miklavc 195, D4
Jože Rijavec 196, 197, B4

KNITTERS
Mojca Kavčič 144, 145, D4-E4
Marija Pezdirnik 144, 145, C2
Helena Pratnekar 144, 145, F2

LACE-MAKERS
Kornelija Brecl 149, H2
Andraž Debeljak 154, 155, E3
Breda Jamar 149, 152, C3
Mira Kejžar 149 - 151, D4
Studio Koder 149, 152, 153, 293, C4
Lace-making School 148, 149, 293, C4
Lapajne company 146, 149, 293, C4
Primožič company 146 - 149, 295, C4
Saša Pušnar 154, 156, D4-E4
Vanda Lapajne 152, 293, C4
Marija Vončina 149, 152, B4

MAKER OF CARDBOARD PACKAGING
Dušan Pavšič 235, H2

MAKERS OF DECORATIVE METAL OBJECTS
Joško Pezdirc 203, D4-E4
Alojz Pirnat 203, D4-E4
Janez Žmuc 203, D4-E4

MAKER OF DORMOUSE TRAPS
Bojan Štefančič 27, D5

MAKERS OF DRAŽGOŠE BREADS
Ana Selan 162, 163, D4-E4
Cirila Šmid 160, 161, C3
Frančiška Zalaznik 162, D4

MAKERS OF DRIED GOODS *suha roba*
Alojz Cej 20, 21, B4
Matija Kobola 18, 19, F6
Anton Marolt 21, E5

MAKERS OF EASTER EGGS
Mihaela Gregorčič 173, 174, G6
Franc Grom 176 - 179, 295, D4
Milena Starešinič 172, 174, 175, G6

MAKERS OF INSTRUMENTS
Jože Holcman 262, 263, H2
Darko Korošec 262, D4-E4
Vera Vardjan 262, 263, 290, G6
Valentin Zupan 264, 265, 300, E4

MAKER OF INTARSIAS
Stanislav Šalamon 44, H2

MAKERS OF MINIATURES
Janko Samsa 258, 259, B5
Dušan Žerjal 260, 261, B5

MAKER OF PUPPETS AND MASCOTS
Vilina Hauser 261, F2

Makers of replicas of wooden objects
Monika Klemenčič 36, 37, C4
Jernej Kosmač 34, 35, 296, D3
Matej Kosmač 34, 35, 296, D3
Andrej Ozebek 38, D3
Robert Perko 36, 37, C4
Petra Plestenjak - Podlogar 39, D4
Bogomir Samec 37, F4

Makers of Palm Sunday bundles
Mrvar family 78, 79, E4

Makers of paper flowers
Agneza Bezjak 232, J2
Marta Kušnik 233, 234, H2
The women of Laško 233, G4
The women of the Pivka 233, C5
Andreja Stankovič 233, G5

Replica makers (replicating furniture, beehive panels etc)
Marija Humar 257, B4
Darja Klevišar 256, D4-E4
Marko Klinc 269, 303, I3
Anica Kopavnik 257, B2
Janko Mlakar 252, 253, D4-E4
Zdenka Mlakar 252, 253, D4-E4
Mitja Perko 254, 255, D4-E4
Vlado Purič 254, I2
Oto Svetlin 254, E4

Makers of vitrage glass
Tomaž Perko 220, 221, D5
Stojan Višnar 220, 221, C3

Maker of wooden boxes with rimmed lids
Ivan Jeklar 30, 31, 297, C3

Maker of wooden shingles for roofing
Bojan Koželj 24, E3

Maker of wooden spoons on a chain
Janez Golob 32, F4

Needlepoint embroiderers
Anamarija Dijak 141, 142, C2
Jožica Grobelnik 141, 142, G3
Marija Lapanja 141 – 143, B4
Miroslava Ritonija 141, 143, G6
Rozalija Strojan 141, 142, D4

Painters of glass
Irena Jurjevič 224, 225, D4-E4
Ivan Jurjevič 224, 225, D4

Paper maker (maker of hand-crafted paper)
Jože Valant 228-231, D4-E4

Patchwork artist
Margareta Vovk-Čalič 157, D3

Pipe maker
Alojz Lotrič 32, 33, 297, C3

Potters
Bojc family 105, 106, 108, G5
Alojz Bojnec 116 – 118, J2
Franc Buser 114, 115, G3
Štefan Gomboc 118, 119, J2
Franc Kremžar 105, 112, 113, 301, E3
Jože Kržan 110, 111, G5
Komenda Pottery Company 109, E3
Nosan family 106, 107, E5
Jože Pungerčar 108, 109, 291, G5
Franc Zelko 118, J1
Branko Žuman 114, 304, J2
Sašo Žuman 114, 304, J2

Saddlers and strap makers
Franc Gladek 241, D4-E4
Milan Kokalj 241, E4

Stonemasons
Marjan Antolinc 190, 191, H3
Zvonko Čehovin 183, 188, B4
Jože Gavez 188, 189, B5
Pavel Gulič 186, 187, B5
Jože Leva 190, 191, H3
Mužina Stonemasonry 186, B5
Tavčar Stonemasonry 186, B5
Boris Udovč 184, 185, D3
Dušan Volk 188, B5

Stove maker
Marko Avguštin 114, E3

Tanners and leather makers
Janez Grad 238, 240, F3
Janez Grčar 238, 239, E4

Thatcher
Franc Barbič 82, 83, H5

Toothpick makers – 20

Weavers of linen
Neda Bevk 140, D4-E4
Marica Cvitkovič 136, 137, 289, G6
Vesna Hrovat 140, G5
Zvezdana Kržič 138, 139, D4-E4
Majda Mrzelj 138, 139, D4
Jernej Ručigaj 138, C3
Marjeta Sieberer 138, 139, D4-E4

Weavers of products from corn husks
Terezija Bence 96, 97, K2
Marija Rajtar 96, 98, 99, 304, K2
Stanislava Vauda 100, 101, J3

Weavers of straw products
Franc Jeriha 84, 85, D4-E4
Jožef Mišica 84, 89, G6
Matilda Prosenc 90, E4
Brigita Smodiš 92, 93, 304, J2
Jani Smodiš 92, 93, 304, J2
Veronika Starin 90, 91, E4
Frančiška Vrbinc 84, 86, 87, E4
Anton Zakrajšek 88, 89, F4
Bernarda Žižek 93, J2
Ivan Žižek 93, J2

Wheelmaker
Franc Brenčič 25, C4

Whip makers
Marjan Semolič 26, 27, B5
Alojz Sever 27, G6

Wicker weavers
Jože Duh 70, 71, J2
Marjan Golmajer 62, 63, C3
Anton Gorenec 74, 75, F5
Janez Hočevar 74, 76, G5
Jože Javšnik 56, 57, G3
Branko Jazbec 61, B5
Tončka Jemec 66, E4
Alojz Jerman 58, 59, E4
Štefan Kalšek 68, H3
Ivan Kašnik 72, F2
Ana Marija Klančičar 74, F5
Jožica Končar 58, 59, E4
Zvonko Kostevc 68, 69, H4
Franc Koželj 58, 74, F5
Ignac Kustec 72, 73, G2
Alojz Možina 60, 61, D6
Jože Omerzu 72, 73, G2
Milan Petek 70, J2
Janko Zabavnik 70, 71, J2
Alojz Zaviršek 66, 67, E4
Janez Zupan 69, 74, F4
Matija Zupan 62, 64, 65, D3

Wood turners
Božo Fornezzi 22, 23, G2
Janez Golob 22, D4-E4
Borut Karnar 22, 23, F2

Communities and their craftsmen

Ajdovščina
Stonemasonry Mužina, Črniče *186, B5*

Beltinci
Brigita Smodiš, Lipovci *92, 93, 304, J2*
Jani Smodiš, Lipovci *92, 93, 304, J2*
Bernarda Žižek, Lipovci *93, J2*
Ivan Žižek, Lipovci *93, J2*

Bled
Erik Curk, Bled *40, 42, C3*
Breda Jamar, Bohinjska Bela *149, 152, C3*
Jernej Ručigaj, Bohinjska Bela *138, C3*

Bohinj
Ivan Jeklar, Gorjuše *30, 31, 297, C3*
Alojz Lotrič, Gorjuše *32, 33, 297, C3*
Dejan Ogrin, Bohinjska Bistrica *28, 29, C3*

Brezovica pri Ljubljani
Milan Šteh, Kamnik pod Krimom *202, D4*

Celje
Jože Javšnik, Celje *56, 57, G3*

Cerklje
Ljubo Blagotinšek, Cerklje *126, 128, D3*

Črnomelj
Marica Cvitkovič, Adlešiči *136, 137, 289, G6*
Jožef Mišica, Črnomelj *84, 89, G6*
Miroslava Ritonija, Črnomelj *141, 143, G6*
Vera Vardjan, Veliki Nerajec *262, 263, 290, G6*

Dobrova-Polhov Gradec
Apiculture Božnar, Polhov Gradec *165, 167, D4*

Dol pri Ljubljani
Tončka Jemec, Dol pri Ljubljani *66, E4*
Alojz Jerman, Dol pri Ljubljani *58, 59, E4*

Dolenjske Toplice
Ana Marija Klančičar, Dol. Toplice *74, F5*

Domžale
Janez Grčar, Dragomelj *238, 339, E4*
Marjeta Grošelj, Domžale *246, 247, E4*
Matilda Prosenc, Vir *90, E4*
Veronika Starin, Domžale *90, 91, E4*
Oto Svetlin, Radomlje *254, E4*

Duplek
Vlado Purič, Žikarce *254, I2*

Grosuplje
Alojz Zaviršek, Šmarje–Sap *66, 67, E4*

Idrija
Studio Koder, Idrija *149, 152, 153, 293, C4*
Lace–making School, Idrija *148, 149, 293, C4*
Lapajne Company, Idrija *146, 149, 293, C4*
Vanda Lapajne, Idrija *152, 293, C4*

Ilirska Bistrica
Alojz Mužina, Ilirska Bistrica *60, 61, D6*

Jesenice
Anamarija Dijak, Jesenice *141, 142, C2*

Kamnik
Andraž Debeljak, Kamnik *154, 155, E3*
Robert Flerin, Kamnik *202, E3*
Janez Grad, Motnik *238, 240, F3*
Bojan Koželj, Stahovica *24, E3*
Candles Stele, Kamnik *166, 300, E3*

Kočevje
Matija Kobola, Kočevje *18,19, F6*

Komen
Branko Jazbec, Sveto *61, B5*
Jožef Lozej, Ivanji Grad *23, 24, B5*
Marjan Semolič, Brestovica pri Komnu *26, 27, B5*

Komenda
Marko Avguštin, Komenda *114, E3*
Franc Kremžar, Komenda *105, 112,113, 301, E3*
Komenda pottery Company, Komenda *109, E3*

Koper
Mojca Božič, Sv. Anton *127, 128, B6*
Stane Božič, Sv. Anton *127, 128, B6*
Jana Mihelj, Koper *128, 131, B6*
Majk Mulaček, Koper *128, 131, B6*

Kranj
Margareta Volk-Čalič, Kranj *157, D3*

Kranjska Gora
Anica Kopavnik, Rateče *257, B2*
Marija Pezdirnik, Mojstrana *144, 145, C2*

Križevci
Jože Duh, Križevci *70, 71, J2*
Franc Marin, Boreci *23, J2*

Krško
Franc Barbič, Podbočje *82, 83, H5*
Jože Kršan, Raka *110, 111, G5*

Lendava
Terezija Bence, Genterovci *96, 97, K2*

Litija
Bogomir Samec, Litija *37, F4*

Ljubljana
Viktor Barlič, Ljubljana *245, D4–E4*
Neda Bevk, Ljubljana *140, D4–E4*
Božena Blanuša, Ljubljana *127, 128, D4–E4*
Anton Cunder, Ljubljana *245, D4–E4*
Hedvika-Vika Čipak, Ljubljana *124, 125, D4–E4*
Vilim Demšar, Ljubljana *48–51, D4–E4*
Matjaž Deu, Ljubljana *104, D4–E4*
Marjanca Dobnikar, Ljubljana *168, 169, D4–E4*
Milena Eber-Štimac, Ljubljana *240, D4–E4*
Franc Gladek, Ljubljana *241, D4–E4*
Janez Golob, Ljubljana *22, D4–E4*
Majda Gregorič-Trost, Ljubljana *128, 132, D4–E4*
Franc Jeriha, Ljubljana *84, 85, D4–E4*
Irena Jurjevič, Ljubljana *224, 225, D4–E4*
Ivan Jurjevič, Ljubljana *224, 225, D4–E4*
Mojca Kavčič, Ljubljana *144, 145, D4–E4*
Darja Klevišar, Ljubljana *256, D4–E4*
Bogdan Kogovšek, Ljubljana *166, 167, D4–E4*
Sonja Kogovšek, Ljubljana *166, 167, D4–E4*
Jožica Končar, Zalog *58, 59, E4*
Darko Korošec, Ljubljana *262, D4–E4*
Zvezdana Kržič, Ljubljana *138, 139, D4–E4*
Jože Lapuh, Ljubljana *40, 41, D4–E4*
Boris Leskovic, Ljubljana *266, 267, D4–E4*
Aleš Lombergar, Ljubljana *222, 223, D4–E4*
Magušar Workshop for pottery and ceramics, Ljubljana *128, D4–E4*
Urban Magušar, Ljubljana *128, 131, D4–E4*
Anica Mihorko, Ljubljana *128, 129, D4–E4*
Janko Mlakar, Ljubljana *252, 253, D4–E4*
Zdenka Mlakar, Ljubljana *252, 253, D4–E4*
Mrvar family, Dobrunje *78, 79, E4*
Sebastian Nared, Ljubljana *244, D4–E4*
Peter Ogrin, Ljubljana *213, D4–E4*
Tanja Pak, Ljubljana *154, 214–217, D4–E4*
Mitja Perko, Ljubljana *254, 255, D4–E4*
Jožko Pezdirc, Ljubljana *203, D4–E4*
Marjeta Pikelj, Ljubljana *122, D4–E4*
Alojz Pirnat, Ljubljana *203, D4–E4*
Barbara Plevnik, Ljubljana *120, D4–E4*
Saša Pušnar, Ljubljana *154, 156, D4–E4*
Rafael Samec, Ljubljana *166, 167, D4–E4*
Ana Selan, Ljubljana *162, 163, D4–E4*
Marjeta Sieberer, Ljubljana *138, 139, D4–E4*
Mojca Smerdu, Ljubljana *128, 133, D4–E4*
Tanja Smole-Cvelbar, Ljubljana *120, 130, D4–E4*
Snežana Sotlar, Ljubljana *120, 130, D4–E4*
Famul Stuart Shool of Applied Arts, Ljubljana *127, D4–E4*
Janez Suhadolc, Ljubljana *46, D4–F4*
Tine Šrot, Ljubljana *204, D4–E4*
Stane Turšič, Ljubljana *166, 167, D4–E4*
Jože Valant, Ljubljana *228, 229, 230, 231, D4–E4*
Vladimir Vodeb, Ljubljana *242, 243, D4–E4*
Frančiška Vrbinc, Dobrunje *84, 86, 87, E4*
Rokus Publishing House, Ljubljana *251, D4–E4*
Jože Zupan, Ljubljana *46, 47, D4–E4*
Danica Žbontar, Ljubljana *126, 128, D4–E4*
Janez Žmuc, Ljubljana *203, D4–E4*

Ljutomer
Agneza Bezjak, Ljutomer *232, J2*
Milan Petek, Bučkovci *71, J2*
Branko Žuman, Ljutomer *114, 304, J2*
Sašo Žuman, Ljutomer *114, 304, J2*

Logatec
Franc Brenčič, Petkovec *25, C4*
Nataša Prestor, Laze *120, 121, 293, D5*

Loška dolina
Bojan Štefančič, Pudob *27, D5*

Lovrenc na Pohorju
Božo Fornezzi, Lovrenc na Pohorju *22, 23, G2*
Ignac Kustec, Lovrenc na Pohorju *72, 73, G2*
Marta Kušnik, Fala *233, 234, H2*
Jože Omerzu, Lovrenc na Pohorju *72, 73, G2*

Maribor
Kornelija Brecl, Maribor *149, H2*
Miha Krištof, Maribor *198, 199, H2*
Lorna Novak, Limbuš *127, 128, H2*
Dušan Pavšič, Maribor *235, H2*
Stanislav Šalamon, Maribor *44, H2*
Brigita Vogrinec, Maribor *123, 128, H2*

Communities and their craftsmen

MEDVODE
Romi Bukovec, Medvode *268, D4*
Carmelites, Sora *166, D4*
Rozalija Strojan, Medvode *141, 142, D4*

MENGEŠ
Valentin Zupan, Mengeš *264, 265, 300, E4*

METLIKA
Mihaela Gregorčič, Metlika *173, 174, G6*
Milena Starešinič, Suhor *172, 174, 175, G6*

MEŽICA
Helena Pratnekar, Mežica *144, 145, F2*

MIREN - KOSTANJEVICA
Oskar Kogoj, Miren *45, 50, 186, 212, 213*
Jože Gavez, Renče *188, 189, B5*
Dušan Volk, Renče *188, B5*

MORAVČE
Milan Kokalj, Moravče *241, E4*

MORAVSKE TOPLICE
Alojz Bojnec, Filovci *116–118, J2*
Štefan Gomboc, Tešanovci *118, 119, J2*

NAKLO
Boris Udovč, Naklo *184, 185, D3*

NOVA GORICA
Alojz Cej, Lokve *20, 21, B4*
Zvonko Čehovin, Ozeljan *183, 188, B4*
Barbara Dovečar, Nova Gorica *219, B4*
Marija Humar, Banjšice *257, B4*
Jože Rijavec, Čepovan *196, 197, B4*

NOVO MESTO
Vesna Hrovat, Novo mesto *140, G5*
Matjaž Matko, Novo mesto *128, G5*
Andreja Stanković, Novo mesto *233, G5*

ORMOŽ
Janko Zabavnik, Gomila pri Kogu *70, 71, J2*

PESNICA
Mario Hercog, Pesnica *242, 243, H2*

PREDDVOR
Matija Zupan, Preddvor *62, 64, 65, D3*

PTUJ
Marko Klinc, Spuhlja *269, 303, I3*
Stanislava Vauda, Ptuj *100, 101, J3*

PUCONCI
Franc Zelko, Pečarovci *118, J1*

RADOVLJICA
Marjan Golmajer, Radovljica *62, 63, C3*
Franc Oblak, Radovljica *45, C3*
Andrej Ozebek, Mošnje *38, D3*

RIBNICA
Bojc family, Dolenja vas *105, 106, 108, E5*
Nosan family, Prigorica *106, 107, E5*

ROGAŠKA SLATINA
Stjepan Bukvić, Rogaška Slatina *212, H3*
Vlado Češnjaj, Rogaška Slatina *212, H3*
Ljubica Kočica, Rogaška Slatina *128, 154, 218, H3*
Leopold Miklavžič, Rogaška Slatina *212, H3*
Franc Sajko, Rogaška Slatina *209, H3*
Mitja Sajko, Rogaška Slatina *209*
Glassmaking School, Rogaška Slatina *212, 213, H3*
Branko Zagorščak, Rogaška Slatina *212, H3*
Ciril Zobec, Rogaška Slatina *209–211, H3*

ROGATEC
Marjan Antolinc, Rogatec *190, 191, H3*

SELNICA OB DRAVI
Jože Holcman, Selnica ob Dravi *262, 263, H2*

SEMIČ
Alojz Sever, Semič *27, G6*

SEŽANA
Pavel Gulič, Kopriva *186, 187, B5*
Janko Samsa, Žirje *258, 259, B5*
Stonemasonry Tavčar, Povir *186, B5*
Dušan Žerjal, Pliskovica *260, 261, B5*

SLOVENJ GRADEC
Silva Dravšnik, Mislinja *124, G3*
Vilina Hauser, Slovenj Gradec *261, F2*
Borut Karnar, Podgorje *22, 23, F2*
Ivan Kašnik, Slovenj Gradec *72, F2*
Jože Levovnik, Slovenj Gradec *242, 243, F2*
Hraboslav Perger, Slovenj Gradec *164, 165, F2*
Vlado Zupančič, Slovenj Gradec *194, 200, 201, F2*

SLOVENSKA BISTRICA
Jože Leva, Koritno *190, 191, H3*
Glassworks Luminos, Slovenska Bistrica *213, H3*

SLOVENSKE KONJICE
Štefan Kalšek, Žiče *68, H3*

SODRAŽICA
Anton Marolt, Sodražica *21, E5*

ŠENTJERNEJ
Jože Pungerčar, Gruča *108, 109, 291, G5*

ŠENTJUR PRI CELJU
Zvonko Kostevc, Planina pri Sevnici *68, 69, H4*

ŠKOCJAN
Janez Hočevar, Škocjan *74, 76, G5*

ŠKOFJA LOKA
Mira Kejžar, Škofja Loka *149–151, D4*
Jure Miklavc, Podlubnik *195*
Stane Miklavc, Podlubnik *195, D4*
Petra Plestenjak-Podlogar, Škofja Loka *39, D4*

ŠTORE
Franc Buser, Prožinska vas *114, 115, G3*

TOLMIN
Alenka Gololičič, Gorenji Log *128, 129, B4*
Marija Lapanja, Daber *141–143, B4*
Marija Vončina, Gorenja Trebuša *149, 152, B4*

TREBNJE
Anton Gorenec, Trebnje *74, 75, F5*
Franc Koželj, Dobrnič *58, 74, F5*
Anton Zakrajšek, Mirna *88, 89, F4*
Janez Zupan, Šentrupert *69, 74, F4*

TRZIN
Miša Jelnikar, Trzin *204, 205, E4*
Božena Lerota, Trzin *245, E4*

TRŽIČ
Cveto Frelih, Brezje *202, D3*
Jernej Kosmač, Tržič *34, 35, 296, D3*
Matej Kosmač, Tržič *34, 35, 296, D3*

TURNIŠČE
Marija Rajtar, Turnišče *96, 98, 99, 304, K2*

VELENJE
Jožica Grobelnik, Velenje *141, 142, G3*

VODICE
Franjo Srnel, Vojsko *41, 42, D3*

VOJNIK
Jože Žlaus, Globoče *28, G3*

VRHNIKA
Franc Grom, Vrhnika *176–179, 295, D4*
Majda Mrzelj, Vrhnika *138, 139, D4*
Frančiška Zalaznik, Vrhnika *162, D4*

ZAGORJE OB SAVI
Janez Golob, Zagorje ob Savi - *32, F4*

ZREČE
Martin Koprivnik, Zreče *28, G3*

ŽALEC
Sašo Rus, Petrovče *123, 128, G3*

ŽELEZNIKI
Cirila Šmid, Železniki *160, 161, C3*

ŽIRI
Monika Klemenčič, Žiri *36, 37, C4*
Robert Perko, Žiri *36, 37, C4*
Primožič Company, Žiri *146–149, 295, C4*

ŽIROVNICA
Stojan Višnar, Lesce *220, 221, C3*

ŽUŽEMBERK
Miha Legan, Žužemberk *42, 43, F5*

Sponsored by:

•

GENERAL SPONSOR

Ministry of Small Business and Tourism of the Republic of Slovenia

SPONSORS

TUS Prevent d. d.

City of Ljubljana

Europapier d. d.

Anars d. o. o.

Kompas Holidays d.d.

Municipality of Vrhnika

Government Public Relations and Media Office

Scientific Institute of the Faculty of Arts

•

HTTP://WWW.MOJSTROVINE.COM

ROKUS

Rokus Publishing House Ltd.
Studenec 2a, Grad Fužine, 1260 Ljubljana
Phone: 061 140 97 99, Fax: 061 140 02 77
http://www.rokus.com, e-mail: rokus@rokus.com

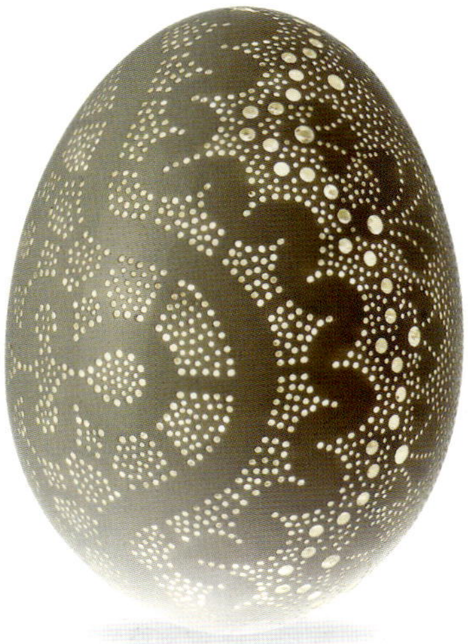